"Written with insight and forthrightness, THE GOLDEN BOYS will answer almost every question you might have had about the Dream Team. . . . At the heart of Stauth's book are twelve different stories of men who loved the game of basketball with a passion. . . ."

—*Staten Island (NY) Advance*

PROFILES FROM AN OLYMPIC PANTHEON: THE FINAL CUT

MAGIC JOHNSON: He had lived a dream . . . only to reach the rudest of awakenings. He'd thought he was immortal until a virus proved he wasn't. He had succumbed to so many temptations before; now, in Barcelona, he faced the most powerful of all: the possibility of a triumphal return to the NBA.

MICHAEL JORDAN: The reluctant Olympian, he was tired of being a god, and did everything he could to prove he was only human. But he was always ready to play, on the basketball court or in the Monte Carlo casinos.

LARRY BIRD: He refused to be merchandised as the Great White Has-Been, but for Larry the summer of gold would turn into a season of excruciating pain—both physically and emotionally. His life was basketball . . . and that life was fast slipping away. Barcelona was to be his last hurrah.

CHARLES BARKLEY: When he was good he was great . . . when he was bad he was even better. When the press went looking for an ugly American, Charles was happy to oblige. He proved he's the man with the biggest mouth—and the biggest heart—in basketball.

CHRIS MULLIN: A spot on the Olympic team required superior skill, supreme confidence, and a fierce competitive will. But no one had overcome greater odds than Chris Mullin: a long and bitter battle against his own personal demons.

SCOTTIE PIPPEN: In high school, he barely made the varsity team. Not a single college offered him a scholarship. Even in Chicago, with his immense talent emerging, the media questioned his mental toughness. But in Barcelona, all doubts were buried. Born in poverty, Pippen had come a long way to prove he was solid gold.

PATRICK EWING: He played in New York, the toughest town of all, had gone to war with management, the writers, the fans . . . had gone to war with himself, the scowl on his face like a battle scar. But what the public didn't see was his surprising sense of humor. And he found on the Olympic team an unexpected kindred spirit.

DAVID ROBINSON: He was born with a crippling defect: too much brain. Not only that, he was a devout Christian. Basketball seemed to come in a poor third . . . until he began to put it all together. David had intelligence, he had religion, and finally, he had the killer instinct.

JOHN STOCKTON: Widely considered to have the best basketball mind in the world, he looked like a choirboy, played like a demon. He believed in fundamentals: play hard, play rough, play to win . . . and it would take more than a cracked bone in his leg to keep him out of the Olympics.

KARL MALONE: As gentle as a teddy bear off the court, as ferocious as a grizzly on. Ask Isiah Thomas. When he drove the lane—into Karl's lair—bad blood turned to real blood, and Isiah came away from the encounter with forty stitches in his head. In Karl Malone, USA basketball had found its enforcer.

CLYDE DREXLER: Blessed with extraordinary gifts as a basketball player . . . cursed to live in the same universe as Michael Jordan. The two things Drexler wanted most—respect and an NBA championship—eluded him. But finally he received an invitation to join the Golden Boys, even if it did come at the last minute.

CHRISTIAN LAETTNER: Used to being a superhero at Duke University, he wasn't happy about being overshadowed by his Olympic teammates. He may not have enjoyed equal time on the playing floor, but he did generate more than his fair share of controversy.

COACH CHUCK DALY: The "Prince of Pessimism," his election as head coach made recent presidential elections seem tame by comparison. He loved to coach, hated to lose, and he reached deep into his bag of coaching tricks to insure that his superstars stayed focused on the gold.

Most Pocket Books are available at special quantity discounts for bulk purchases for sales promotions, premiums or fund raising. Special books or book excerpts can also be created to fit specific needs.

For details write the office of the Vice President of Special Markets, Pocket Books, 1230 Avenue of the Americas, New York, New York 10020.

THE GOLDEN BOYS

CAMERON STAUTH

POCKET BOOKS

New York   London   Toronto   Sydney   Tokyo   Singapore

The sale of this book without its cover is unauthorized. If you purchased
this book without a cover, you should be aware that it was reported to
the publisher as "unsold and destroyed." Neither the author nor the
publisher has received payment for the sale of this "stripped book."

POCKET BOOKS, a division of Simon & Schuster Inc.
1230 Avenue of the Americas, New York, NY 10020

Copyright © 1992, 1993 by Cameron Stauth
Photo of Magic Johnson © 1992 by Brian Drake/SportsChrome
East/West
Photo of medal ceremony by Richard Mackson/Sports Illustrated

All rights reserved, including the right to reproduce
this book or portions thereof in any form whatsoever.
For information address Pocket Books, 1230 Avenue
of the Americas, New York, NY 10020

ISBN: 0-671-76050-5

First Pocket Books paperback printing November 1993

10 9 8 7 6 5 4 3 2 1

POCKET and colophon are registered trademarks of
Simon & Schuster Inc.

Jacket design by Matt Galemmo

Printed in the U.S.A.

for Shari

Acknowledgments

There's just one person without whom this book would not have been written: Lorraine Stauth, my mother. It was her idea.

It was a great idea—one that seems obvious now but wasn't so obvious about two years ago, when she first came up with it, ahead of anyone else in the publishing industry.

Before she hit upon this idea, though, she'd come up with about five hundred other book ideas for me over the past twenty years. Some of them were good and some were excellent but all of them had gotten shot down—either by me, my agent, or various publishers.

It takes special qualities to keep coming up with ideas in the face of that kind of unremitting rejection. It requires creativity, tenacity, optimism, and—mostly, I think—a mother's love. It's a gift I won't forget.

The other person who made a unique and irreplaceable contribution to the book was my wife Shari. Our first baby was born about six months into this year-and-a-half-long project, and Shari did everything for our son while I ran all over the world trying to keep up with this story.

Also of pivotal importance in the creation of this book was Pocket Books senior editor Paul McCarthy. I've worked with about a hundred magazine and book editors—some very talented—but none of them match Paul. His abilities, energy, and demeanor are extraordinary and are reflected in every page of this book.

Another Simon and Schuster executive who was crucially helpful was Jack Romanos.

Acknowledgments

My agent, Richard Pine (of Arthur Pine Associates of New York) was also an important member of the creative team and offered his usual strong support, both personal and professional. Thanks also to Artie Pine, for his encouragement and interest since 1975.

I'd also like to thank Jeanne Withrow, particularly for checking the wrong box on a Federal Express package in July of 1992. It was the first mistake she'd made in the four years we've been working together, and it was a big relief to know she isn't absolutely perfect. Jeanne worked on this book through migraines, root canals, children's illnesses, and my moods—always cheerfully and with the highest professionalism.

Jim Patton made greater contributions to this book than anyone will ever know—because I intend to take full credit for most of what he did. The same goes for Shawn Levy. Both of these guys are excellent writers who'll probably be working on their own books by the time this book is published, and I was lucky to catch them at a moment when they had time to help.

I also got a great deal of help from a group of excellent researchers, including Paul Morgan, Bob Wolfe, Bill Stewart, Pat Bryan, and Nissa Shaw. Paul Morgan was especially resourceful.

In addition, I was impressed by the professionalism and kindness of the NBA's public relations director. My homeboys, John Lashway and John Christensen of the Trail Blazers, were especially cordial and deserved their recognition in 1991 as the NBA's best. I don't know how Chicago's Tim Hallam stays so sane in the epicenter of the Jordan Show, but he does. Thanks also to Julie Marvel, Kim Turner, John Mertz, John Cirillo, Joyce Szymanski, Zack Hill, Matt Sperisen, Bob Price, Jeff Twiss, and Tom James. Thanks, too, to the NBA's chief of publicity, Brian McIntyre.

In every city, I met and usually interviewed a number of beat writers, basketball writers, columnists, and broadcasters. There were too many to name—which says a great deal about the willingness of one journalist to help another. But

Acknowledgments

those who helped know I value their input and their friendships.

Also of great help in this project, which was often a logistical nightmare, was Cheryl Williams of All Star Travel in Portland. She made all my travel arrangements and was the first agent I've ever met who saved me significant money.

Of course, I couldn't have written the book without the cooperation of the players, and also their families, coaches, associates, agents, and friends. I was especially impressed by many of the parents of the players. Many of them are exceptional people; learning about them made it easier to understand why their sons are exceptional. Thanks also to the members of the Selection Committee.

Thanks also to the people who helped me most during my work in Europe: Jorge Hodaly Sanbar, Marcos Beltra Brotons (of the Olympic public relations department), and Lawrence Fishberg.

An important acknowledgment is due to Faith Evander and Gabriel Stauth for what they've meant to me this year and for reminding me that there are more important things than books.

Since I gave first billing in this acknowledgment to my mom, I'd like to give final billing to my dad, Vernon Stauth. He didn't have too much to do with this particular project, but he had everything to do with making me the kind of person who could manage to finish it. Like virtually all of the parents of the Olympians, he worked extremely hard all of his life, with no real recognition. In doing so, he showed me what became one of the themes of this book: It's not the spotlight that makes the hero.

Contents

1 Overkill   1

2 Magic in Paris   10

3 The Greatest Story Never Told   26

4 The List   45

5 Immortality   65

6 Chris Mullin's Courageous Battle
    Against White Man's Disease   77

7 Mike Jordan Is a Dork   97

8 Scottie Sees It Differently   124

9 Magic's Field Trip to the
    Real World   140

10 Charles Barkley in Hell   164

11 Tyrannosaurus Pat   182

12 Getting David's Mind Right   199

Contents

13 Stockton & Malone   219

14 Clyde Is Second Best   244

15 The Great Gringo Hope: Larry Bird at the
Tournament of the Americas   273

16 Beige Like Me: Christian and the
Big Boys in Portland   298

17 Bad Fear in Paradise   321

18 The Ugly American   340

19 Fresh Meat   356

20 Team Nike   367

Epilogue: The 1993 Season   389

Bibliography   407

A Way Out

From dead rims and pot-holed courts,
behind chain link, held
to hard ground
as in bondage.
This gravity defied,
sprung in manumission.
Centuries of hang-time,
climbing the air in grace
for all those who fell before
soaring toward a promised place.

Sphere claimed—a stretch and howl.
Trunk and elbows contoured like a sax
the way Yardbird held his wail
then passed like notes inside the paint
low post quick pick and cut
could be Miles these riffs
double pump then a slam. These bodies
as instruments in sync one organism answering
as if another verdict just came down.

—Norm Levine

Our Pledge to Consumers

To better serve the sports literature consumer, strict quality control by a panel of cliché monitors has resulted in the elimination of the following words and phrases from this text:

awesome
no-brainer
The Dream Team; Team Dream
much-maligned
hapless
flat-out
oft-injured
step up (to the next level) (a notch)
wake-up call
play our game
diminutive (meaning: *short*)
on a roll
The Mailman, Air Jordan, Clyde the Glide, Sir Charles, et al.
big-time
play physical
vocal leader
come up big
110 percent
stay mentally tough
play within ourselves

Our Pledge to Consumers

went off for (meaning: *scored*)
reached inside myself
dug down deep for something extra
play one game at a time
we're not looking past anyone
lit up (meaning: *scored*)
players middle names (Christopher Paul Mullin, et al.)
money player
he came to play
prime-time player
good work ethic (meaning: *work ethic*)
carried us on his back
cheap shot
class individual
unheralded
run and gun
struggling (meaning: *playing badly*)
buzzer-beater
slam-dunk
change of scenery
garbage time
pumped
fat lady sings

THE GOLDEN BOYS

1
Overkill

The Gringo from Hell • Michael Jordan
Rubs It In • Laettner the Lap Dog •
Magic's Temptation • Patrick Ewing Risks Death •
The Greatest Game of H-O-R-S-E in History •
Heaven Is a Playground •
Sweet Charles • Mean Larry •
Kicking the Ass of the Nightmare Team

Preserve your memories. They're all that's left to you.
—Paul Simon

"Can't repeat the past?" he cried incredulously. "Why
of course you can!"
—F. Scott Fitzgerald
Jay Gatsby, in *The Great Gatsby*

The true object of all human life is play.
—G. K. Chesterton

Why make the rubble bounce?
—Winston Churchill, discussing nuclear overkill

• **The Tournament of the Americas, July 1992**

Charles Barkley grabbed his balls and pretzeled into a
cringe. "Oh, no!" he shrieked. "Not Oscar *Schmidt!* Please,
help me, y'all! I'm scared to damn *death.*"

I'd just asked him a simple question, along the lines of:
Are you looking forward to playing Schmidt, the great

Brazilian? But Barkley didn't want to *hear* about Oscar Schmidt, or any other Third-World punk with fantasies about going one-on-one with the baddest son of a bitch in basketball.

Charles was, at this point in the pre-Olympic competition, sick to death of whipping every butt in the Western Hemisphere. Everywhere he went, either reporters were whining about "overkill"—saying the U.S. was *wrong* and *mean* to play so well—or they were trying to concoct some glimmer of dramatic jeopardy. Such as: Oscar Schmidt's going to throw a *real* scare into the Americans.

"Wait a sec!" said Barkley, coming out of his crouch. "When you say Oscar, do you mean that little knucklehead that dicks around in *The Odd Couple?* With Felix?"

"No."

"Oh, you mean the *basketball* player! Well, if I was *that* Oscar, I wouldn't wanna come nowhere *near* these guys," Barkley said, nodding at the few members of the U.S. team who'd bothered to show up early for shooting practice. "If he does, it means he's been sniffin' too much coffee down there, with Juan Valdez."

Christian Laettner, who'd been shooting with Barkley, bleated a little half-laugh and fired a quizzical glance at Barkley, like: Can you really *say* stuff like that in the pros? Actually, it cost Barkley (by his own estimate) about $2 million a year in endorsement money to be so loose and honest. The Olympics were generating about $30 million in new endorsements for the twelve players—but Barkley would get only a relatively small share of that.

Laettner edged away. "You want a quote on Oscar, right?" said Barkley.

"Sure."

"Okay." Barkley held up his forefinger, like an orator. "Fuck Oscar."

Barkley smiled sweetly and went back to his shooting.

At the other end of the floor, Larry Bird was gunning jumpers in a hypnotic rhythm. He grabbed every ball with his hand straight up and his fingers spread, planted his right foot with his toes pointed at the basket, flexed his knees, stared at the rim, hopped upward, released the ball, and snapped his wrist in follow-through as the ball ripped the net. Each shot was exactly the same: plant-flex-hop-follow-rip. Plant-flex-hop-follow-rip.

Bird was virtually crippled. The nerves in his legs felt like red-hot wire. His career was slipping away—while he lay in front of the bench—and it was making him crazy with anger and hurt. But his shot was as smooth and beautiful as a waltz. His eyes were caught in a thousand-yard stare.

Nobody bothered Bird when he was shooting like this. He had a down-home mean streak in him and could make you want to vanish from the face of the earth with one cold look.

Plant-flex-hop-follow-rip. Plant-flex-hop-*splack*. Bird whipped around—to see who was going to *die*.

Patrick Ewing was in Bird's face. "'Scuse me," growled Ewing.

"Damn, Patrick." Bird glared up at him—the icy hillbilly.

Bird picked up the ball, faced the basket. Plant-flex-hop-*splack!*

"'Scuse me." Ewing again—grinning. A smile looked out of place on Ewing's dour face. Bird tried to glare but ended up grinning back at Ewing.

Over the last two weeks, Bird and Ewing had become buddies. They were an odd combination. So were Barkley and Laettner, who'd become pals. But that's what the Olympics was all about: Bringing together disparate people —even enemies—to fight a common foe.

On the surface, it seemed as if the U.S. team had no common foe—just a set of pathetic patsies to whip and humiliate. But that was just the surface.

In fact, the players on the U.S. team were all engaged in very real battles—ones of great consequence and drama. Their battles, though, were no longer just on the basketball floor. They had all transcended basketball. Their real wars were their struggles to grasp the things all people want: love, respect, money, power, health. They had been grappling for these things all year. And they would pursue them for years to come.

Much more than most people, these men were very close

to having everything life could offer. This was their blessing. And their curse. Theirs was a world of limitless opportunity —and limitless temptation.

Basketball had vaulted these men into a strange and exciting world. But basketball—at this point in their lives— was an escape from their most difficult conflicts. Basketball returned them to the children within them. That was why they loved it.

Barkley sauntered off the floor, with Laettner in tow. Barkley was the only Olympian who'd befriended Laettner, the token college player on the team. Laettner was deferential to Barkley, and to all the other Olympians. It was a strange role for him. At Duke, he'd been the golden boy— the gifted tyrant. But now, for the first time, he was face-to-face with *real* arrogance.

As Barkley stepped into the hallway leading to the dressing rooms, one of the Brazilian players bounded up to him. "Char-lee!" he said, sticking out his hand.

Barkley looked at the number on the guy's uniform. "Are you the clown that said Brazil was the Nightmare Team?" asked Barkley, as the guy pumped his hand.

"Habla español?" said the player.

Barkley shook his head. "Do you know what 'We're gonna whip your butt' means?" said Barkley. He smiled gently: the Gringo from Hell.

"No hablo inglés."

"Well, good luck." He sounded as if he really meant it. Barkley was tart and mouthy, but he was probably the most compassionate player on the U.S. team.

Magic and Michael walked past, on their way to the floor. Jordan had the hint of a Wilt-style mustache and goatee. He said the goatee symbolized vacation. A year earlier, no one could have guessed that the Olympics would be a vacation. But the world had changed. The two other primary basketball powers—the Soviet Union and Yugoslavia—had ceased to exist. It had been a tumultuous year, both in world politics and in the lives of the American players.

When Magic and Michael got to the floor, Magic started tossing in his "junior skyhook," the move he'd learned from

Kareem that looks easy—until you try to do it. Magic ran the baseline left to right, leaped off his left foot, and feathered in the ball with his right hand. "Nobody can do that," Magic said, grinning at Michael. His face glowed.

"Let's *see*," said Jordan. He swept across the lane, leaped, lofted it. *Swish*.

"Lu-u-u-ck," said Magic. "Do it again."

He did it again. When the ball fell out of the net, it made a soft-echo pop on the floor of the empty stadium.

"Okay, smart aleck," said Magic, "do this." He walked a few steps away from the hoop, palmed the ball, and hooked it under his leg toward the basket. It rattled in. The Magic smile.

Drexler and Pippen were shooting on the other side of the floor. They started watching. Jordan made the under-the-leg shot. "My turn," Jordan said. He walked to the sidelines and stood out of bounds. Eyed the hoop. Pushed it up. *Swish*.

"That's a Mike Smrek shot!" boomed Magic, invoking the name of a notably bad shooter.

"M.J.!" Pippen yelled, signaling for the ball.

"Let Magic make that one first," Jordan said, his little mustache wrinkling into a smile.

Magic shot; missed. "Okay, here's the deal," said Magic. "You gotta keep callin' the shot 'til you miss, and you can't shoot the same shot twice." He looked at Pippen. "You wanna play?"

"Sure!"

"You in?" Magic asked Clyde. Drexler beamed and nodded. Drexler knew how good he was, but he wasn't sure everyone else knew.

"Okay, I'll start," said Magic.

"Uh-uh!" cried Jordan. "You just *missed*."

"Good!" said Magic. "Ever-buddy agrees." Magic stepped back to take his shot. Nobody bitched. He was, after all, Magic. He'd been the king of the playground since he was ten years old. Besides, he had even greater authority now. He was fighting the most serious battle of all of them. He might well lose that battle. But the *way* he was fighting—

smiling, acting . . . like Magic—was majestic, and it had elevated him even further.

Magic looked at the basket—but tossed the ball to Pippen.

Pippen dribbled twice, paused. He planted his feet, crouched, faced the basket, and tossed the ball between his legs—into the hoop. Then Magic made it. Everybody else missed. Pippen's ball again. He stood at the top of the key, held the ball over his head with both hands, and hurled it at the floor. It bounced up and in.

"Ohhh!" said Jordan. "I've seen him do that."

"Then *you* oughta be able to do it," said Magic. Off to the side, Chris Mullin stood watching, a ball tucked under his arm.

With a jerk of his head, Magic signaled Mullin to join the game.

Jordan tried Pippen's bounce shot. Made it. Magic poked his fist into the air. "Nice!" Then it was his turn, though, and he missed. So did Drexler and Mullin.

"I got one that's not in *anybody's* repertoire," said Magic. He took the ball just past the free throw line and dribbled in for what looked like a lay-up. But he sailed under the glass, then shot from behind the backboard. The ball floated high into the air, hit the front of the rim, and plunked in. The other players roared. Jordan doubled over, holding his belly. Magic's face looked like it was going to explode with happiness.

"I've got one," Clyde said softly. Clyde looked beatific, as if being included in this game meant more to him than any All-Star Game he'd ever played.

"Let's see it," said Jordan.

Clyde walked to the top of the key, angled off to one side, paused, then knifed toward the hoop. He leaped into the air, reaching a height that usually only Jordan hit, but moving forward with even more horizontal force than Jordan. It was his famous glide. As he neared the basket, he pushed the ball toward the hoop. Pulled it back. Glided more. Jerked it toward the hoop again. Smashed it down.

"Ohhh, shit," said Mullin, turning away.

"Oh, no, you don't!" shouted Magic, tossing a ball to Mullin. "You're up." Mullin did a pale, awkward imitation of it. What could he do? He had white man's disease: he couldn't jump. But Magic, Pippen, and Jordan made it.

There wasn't a sound in the stadium except for the cries of the players. It was still virtually empty. Over the past year, as I'd traveled from city to city to spend time with each Olympian, this was what so many of them had talked about as their idea of heaven: an empty gym, with just a few of the best players on earth. No fans. No money. No pressure. No broadcasters. No score. Just . . . a game.

So much is made of a player's work ethic. But more important than that is his play ethic. Excellence doesn't come from drudgery. It comes from love.

Magic grabbed the ball and walked to the free throw line. He faced away from the basket, squared his shoulders, and flipped the ball backward, over his head. *Rip!*

None of these shots had been perfected during college or pro practices, nor certainly during games. They were playground shots. They were the shots of children—not powerful multimillionaires.

"Still my ball," said Magic, after most of the guys had missed his backward shot. He stood on his left foot and lifted his right leg high into the air, like a drunken stork. Then he canted his head at a bizarre angle and fired up the shot. *Rip!*

Nobody else made it. Magic looked ecstatic. The past week had been like a narcotic to him, filling him with the irresistible temptation to come out of retirement. To do so might shorten his life. But for him, basketball *was* life.

Mullin grabbed the ball and hit from outside the three-point line. The other players all made his shot. But then—to get around the rule of not shooting the same shot twice—he just moved a few feet to the side and shot again. Perfect. But they all made it. He moved again—perfect. This time, they didn't all make it.

"Bor—r-r-ring!" Jordan moaned.

"How 'bout this, then?" Mullin said, marching back to the half-court line. He sized up the basket and heaved the ball. The shot took a hard rattle around the rim and went down. "Still bored?" said Mullin.

"I am," said Magic. He walked to half-court and swished it. But nobody else made it.

"Watch," said Clyde. He pitched the ball from straight in front of the hoop, well behind the three-point line. It hit the glass and banked in. Only great shooters know how hard that shot is.

"Jeeeze!" Magic yelped. "That's a Mike Brown shot," he yelled, referring to the clumsy Utah shooter.

Magic glanced at the courtside seats. They were beginning to fill with spectators, all of them slack-jawed at stumbling upon the greatest game of H-O-R-S-E in basketball history.

There would probably never again be a playground game quite like this, because it was unlikely that so extraordinary a team would ever again be assembled. This week NBA Commissioner David Stern had said the next Olympic team would probably be about half college and half pro. Stern hated all the bitching about "overkill." He was in the midst of an unprecedented expansion of the NBA to the rest of the world, and the last thing he needed was for his boys to look like vicious bullies. Besides, it had become clear this week that a U.S. team with only a few pros could kick ass against any team on the globe.

So this was a once-in-a-lifetime event.

"You want to see a *real* three-pointer?" Jordan said to Clyde. "Observe." Jordan grabbed the ball with his left hand on top and pushed up a left-hander. It rattled in.

"Owww!" said Magic.

"Nuthin' personal, guys!" said Jordan, strutting around in a little one-man parade. "I don't *mean* to rub it in."

Magic lined up his left-handed three. It clanged off. Again, Magic looked at the spectators out of the corner of his eye. They seemed to make him uneasy. This was a part of him that wasn't meant for the public. It was too precious for that.

"Let's wrap it up, guys," he said. "You talkin' about threes? I'll show you a three." He stood just behind the line. Studied the basket. Closed his eyes. Squeezed them tight to show: Look, no cheating. With one soft, liquid motion, he arced it toward the rim. *Swish!*

"Whoa!" Magic exulted. "I still got it."

The others tried, but none came close. Simple reason. It's impossible.

"I won!" Magic crowed.

"Who *says?*" Jordan said.

"I made the *last* one. And I made the *most.* You're just gonna have to live with it."

Clyde and Michael laughed and gave each other a high-five.

Magic started to walk off the floor. His face seemed to be bathed in light.

As he got to the sidelines, a spectator—a big whisker-stubbled guy, some kind of ex-jock—held up a baby in Magic's face. Magic looked at the guy—the baby was practically drooling on Magic.

"I just wanted him to see you," the big guy said sheepishly.

Magic paused for a second. "I got a little one of my own now," he said. He touched the baby's cheek softly with his index finger. The finger seemed to cover half the baby's face.

"I just wanted him to see you," the guy repeated. "You know, to tell his grandkids."

"Oh, he'll be seein' me."

"Good. Great." What could the guy say? I hope you make it?

"I'll be around," said Magic. He was gone before the big, whiskery guy could reply.

The guy turned his son around and looked into his eyes. "That was Magic," he said softly. "I hope you can *really* see him some day." It looked as if there were tears in his eyes.

2
Magic in Paris

Ronald McDonald in Hell • Love and Money •
The Gauntlet of Temptation • David Stern's Worst
Nightmare • The Warrior's Ethic •
Magic and Cookie • Kinky Sex and Big Lies •
The New World Disorder

The time you won your town the race
We chaired you through the market-place,
Man and boy stood cheering by,
And home we brought you shoulder-high.

Today, the road all runners come,
Shoulder-high we bring you home,
And set you at your threshold down,
Townsman of a stiller town.
>   "To an Athlete Dying Young,"
>   —A. E. Houseman, 1896

I like Paris. They don't talk so much of money,
but more of sex.
>   —Vera Stravinski, 1969

If we're gonna live together, we've gotta play together.
>   —Spike Lee, Nike commercial, 1992

● **Paris, October, 1991**

"Ma-jeek! Ma-jeek! Ma-jeek!" Magic Johnson practically

floated with joy. What a golden moment! My God! It was like being one of the Beatles!

Magic stood beneath the Eiffel Tower as the Paris breeze caressed his face. At his side were his Laker teammates, all glowing with the happiness of youth and wealth and strength. Surrounding them was a huge, affectionate crowd. Ecstasy! It was like a dream.

Then Magic—who'd risen to greatness by learning to share glory—pointed at Laker Vlade Divac. "What about your homeboy?" he yelled. France—where the Lakers had come for the McDonald's Open—wasn't exactly Vlade's home. But the throng shouted his name anyway.

It had been eleven years since Vlade had left his humble Yugoslavian home, at age twelve, to live in a government basketball camp. He'd survived there only through the support of buddies like Drazen Petrovic, Toni Kukoc, and especially Velimir Perasovic, his roommate. They had been like brothers.

As children, they'd talked endlessly of only two things: playing in the NBA, and beating the U.S. team in the Olympics. Now their dreams were turning real. They were all NBA-caliber players, and they had a good shot at the gold medal—if only politics stayed out of the way. They'd already won a silver medal in the last Olympics and had won the European championship four months ago. They would be hard to beat at Barcelona. If they got to Barcelona.

Right now, there was fighting in Yugoslavia between Serbs and Croats. Vlade was Serbian. Petrovic and Perasovic were Croats.

Vlade could see how the Croats could hate the Serbians, who'd dominated the brutal communist dictatorship for the last forty-five years. But many Croats had sided with the Nazis fifty years ago. There were scars on both sides.

Vlade, however, had hoped his band of brothers could unite and set an example for all Croats and Serbs. Their unity might help stop bloodshed. Maybe, when order returned to the world, they could all play for Yugoslavia's Split team, the most famous pro team in Europe. By then, Split might be in the NBA.

The NBA was, after all, muscling into the European market. That's what the McDonald's Open was all about. The Open, the only international tournament for pro teams, was the NBA's first step into Europe. It was just a matter of time until European teams would join the NBA. And, already, NBA players were flooding into European leagues. Standing here, listening to the fans scream, made Vlade want to play in Europe. Magic, too. Even Terry Teagle was thinking about it. Teagle was *huge* here, thanks to satellite TV. The Lakers were more popular in France than the best French teams.

Last night, like a conquering hero, Teagle had gone out on the town. Had to—no cable TV in the International Hotel. And it had been testosterone heaven. All night long: French women, American women, Scandinavian women, all trooping over to his table at the Hard Rock Cafe, hoping to get lucky. It was like an Elvis movie. Teagle had passed on all the women, though. He wasn't a notable Laker hound— short for *pussyhound*.

It was *hard* to be a standout hound on the Lakers. The Hollywood environment, and Magic's presence, made the Lakers hound heaven. Some of the guys on the team put great energy into building their hound stats. Or at least into lying about them. There were a number of categories. For example: Most girls, single night. Most girls, single bed. Most ethnic groups. Wildest freak. Most sex in public with a celebrity (Magic seemed to have that one hands down, thanks to his rumored series of liaisons in cars and theaters with a newscaster).

Some players also prided themselves on their manipulation skills, considering it preferable, for example, to get the girl to pay for the hotel room herself. Or to manipulate the girl into some form of kinky sex with an outrageous line. One of the recent Lakers—a big fan favorite—had talked a particular girl into solely anal sex, on the grounds that the two of them had, in a past life, been Greek lovers. Plus, he always got her to pay for the room.

There was also another avenue of sex for a Laker hound, one in which he was as much used as user: liaisons with the world's most desirable women. These women weren't available at the back door of the Forum but expected an actual date. Uniformly gorgeous, they also dated movie and rock stars, studio executives, and wealthy businessmen. They weren't out for sex; they were out for marriage.

Often, Magic and two close buddies would bring one of these classy women on a road trip. They'd get the woman a room or discreetly lodge her in their own. Then, if Magic's girlfriend, Cookie, or one of his buddies' wives called, they'd cover for each other.

Of course, Cookie, who was quite bright, was not easy to fool. It was widely believed that Magic's infidelity had caused her to stay in Michigan throughout most of their romance, which had begun in college. But Cookie also knew she was the love of Magic's life—next to basketball. She couldn't bring herself to cut him loose.

Their relationship had changed a few months ago, however, when she'd gotten pregnant. She'd wanted the whole enchilada or nothing. And she'd gotten it. Big ring. Big wedding. Big reception. Magic had even managed to get Michael and Isiah in the same room. Now, during the Open, Magic and Cookie were honeymooning in Paris. It was idyllic—as if life had just started. He'd given her his playoff check—about $20,000—to blow in the Paris boutiques. And she was doing a hell of a job of it.

Before the Lakers had gone to the Eiffel Tower—for a team picture—Magic had been talking about Cookie. He'd said, "We've had a chance to go back to our, like, college days. We've had nice long walks at night and sat in cafés talkin' to two or three in the morning—things people don't let you do at home, 'cause of, like, autographs. This has been *nice*."

Not so nice last night, though. Magic and Cookie had gone for a walk, and for the first time they'd gotten ambushed by paparazzi. The hell of it was, it had happened in front of a McDonald's, and for Magic, McDonald's was *poison*—because he'd just signed a deal with Kentucky Fried Chicken. If a picture of him in front of McDonald's got back to the States, it would be his ass. The KFC corporate types took that kind of thing very seriously, and these days Magic took the corporate types seriously. Because he had a dream.

He wanted to own a sports franchise. "I want to be in the one hundred million dollar to two hundred million dollar range," he'd said recently, "because that's basically what you have to have for a franchise." He knew he couldn't make that kind of money from playing. "The money I make from the Lakers," he said, "is—how can I say it—small. It's just small." It was, in fact, $2.4 million. But he made about $9 million annually from corporate deals.

So the corporate deals were absolutely vital. They were the only way he'd ever achieve the highest level of fortune in the NBA: immortality.

There were four levels of fortune in pro basketball. The first was toy level—available to any guy who stayed in the league for at least a few years. At about $150,000 a year, a player could afford a nice set of toys. Most chose the same toys: a house for Mom, and a hot car and designer wardrobe for themselves. The small remainder was pissed away with ease.

If you could hang on for five or six years, you graduated to security level. You could build a nest egg of maybe half a million, from which you could pull about $50,000 a year for life. Reach stardom, though—$1 million to $2 million a year for eight or ten years—and you hit the power level. That kind of money bought managers, ghostwriters, beer distributorships, friends in media and business, and all the alimony you wanted.

But the last level was the cruncher.

The last level, immortality, came only to select superstars. Its source was never salary, but always corporate money—endorsements and investments. You needed to make $5 million to $10 million a year for five-plus years. That level made you into an institution. Products would bear your name and likeness. Scholarships would carry your name. A street would be named for you near the stadium. Your biography would be in libraries. You'd be known worldwide by just your last name: Nicklaus. Ali. Jordan.

Jordan! That's who'd inspired Magic's quest to reach immortality level. Magic had once been happy to make his money, have his flings, and win his championships. Then along came Michael. Jordan had blazed the trail as the world's first black commercial icon, at a time when Magic's people had been telling him that black men couldn't effectively market to white America.

Jordan's agent, David Falk, cut deals that made Jordan about $20 million per year. Falk had set Michael up in the Jordan Foundation and had made several deals in which Jordan got a fat percentage of all product sales—such as sales of Air Jordan shoes, which made Michael about $8 million a year. Jordan, easily an institution, could die at any moment and remain immortal.

Seeing Jordan's success, Magic had realized what a true . . . pauper . . . he was. Jordan was beating him in a major stat. So Magic had gone out and gotten new people, primarily Pacific Rim taipan Michael Ovitz.

Ovitz, a Laker courtsider and the most powerful man in the entertainment industry, helped agent Lon Rosen put together a serious plan, founded on deals with Kentucky Fried Chicken, Gatorade, and Pepsi. Magic's high income was not publicized, to keep from alienating fans, who still believed Magic should be a home-team warrior, playing for glory. Of course, to a Hollywood mogul, that was ridiculous, since even a second-tier entertainment act, like Siegfried & Roy, made about $15 million a year (without anyone bitching about it).

With Ovitz's help, Magic had finally begun moving toward immortality. That's why it had been so horrifying to be photographed in front of a McDonald's. The whole point of being here was to build worldwide marketability. The McDonald's Open was an excellent opportunity to stroke the European market, and the Olympics would be even better. Magic had said, "The Olympics are going to put a whole new light on things in the business world for NBA stars. Michael and myself are really going to be able to cash in on it."

As a rookie, Magic hadn't conceived of worldwide earning

ability. He had signed at toy level. But the money had been fine. He'd have played for nothing. Both he and Bird played basketball out of love for the game—no matter how much money they made. But by revitalizing and glamorizing the league, Magic and Larry had forever changed the NBA's structure of rewards. And temptations.

After the Eiffel Tower, the Lakers went to practice. Easy practice. Even though the season was only about a month away, half the Lakers were fat and sloppy—by NBA standards. Magic, surprisingly, seemed to be the worst of the lot. He was wheezing, rheumy, and puffy, and his eyes looked yellow. Coach Mike Dunleavy got pissed off. "Come on," he yelled, "shake this place!"

As they were finishing their workout, Vlade's old roommate, Velimir Perasovic, walked onto the court for the Yugoslavian Split practice. Vlade's face lit up. He bounded over to Perasovic. Stuck out his hand.

Perasovic walked by without a glance. Vlade looked stunned. He didn't know that for over a month Perasovic had been diving into bomb shelters ten times a day. He just knew his best friend had turned on him. Now, when they met in Barcelona, it would be as enemies.

One of the Laker peons showed up with lunch. Fat bags of Big Mac's.

Magic eyed the reporters and photographers. "Damn." He sighed. He signaled for his sack to be taken to the locker room. He trudged in there to eat, alone.

• Love and Death

Insanity! Kids—everywhere. They were crawling like bugs across the counters and standing on the yellow tables inside a McDonald's where the Lakers were promoting the Open. A photographer was trying to get a team picture, but Magic kept dematerializing, trying to stay the hell away from Ronald McDonald. Outside, thousands of people were blocking traffic and setting off a tremendous racket: "Ma-jeek! Ma-jeek! Ma-jeek!" Rain poured and wind shrieked. Nobody had an umbrella—no room to spread them. The Lakers, a little edgy, kept glancing at their ex-cop body-guards, but the NBA officials looked ecstatic. They had big plans for Europe. That was why they'd wanted the pros in the Olympics.

The only player who seemed comfortable in the mob was Magic—who had the least reason to be. Kids were hanging off him, shoving mementos into his face, creating a clot of flesh so dense it was hard to breathe. Magic seemed to be almost gulping for air, and he looked awful: baggy eyes in a face bloated with exhaustion. But the smile! Always the electric smile.

Then the Lakers slipped through the kitchen to a stream-lined silver bus and roared off with a press bus in tow.

Minutes later, they pulled up in front of a square little building in the suburb of Villejuif. The mob! The rhythmic chant: "Ma-jeek! Ma-jeek!" Hundreds of the kids sur-rounded the bus—black, Algerian, white. They were all decked out in wild American-style baggies and baseball caps and doing the woo-woo-woo and Arsenio fist-churn. The team refused to leave the bus until the ex-cops had cleared a path. They made a run for it. The rain whipped sideways, darkening their purple and gold warm-ups. The Lakers hustled inside. The door closed behind them. Silence.

Suddenly they were staring at the saddest collection of little kids: bald boys and girls, children in wheelchairs, kids who were chalky white, children with heartbroken eyes. New Laker Elden Campbell felt horrible; he tried to smile—couldn't. Ronald McDonald stood there looking helpless. He'd been fine with the healthy kids at the restaurant, but this was, like, Ronald McDonald in hell.

A guy in a white doctor's jacket muttered, "It's show-time." Very cynically.

Then Magic stepped out of the clump of players and scooped up a little girl with a Laker cap over her bald head. "Hey, sweetheart!" The Magic smile. "How you doin'?" The little girl, maybe six or seven, looked at her parents for reassurance. *"C'ést* Magique," said her father, who was staying at this Ronald McDonald House while his daughter was being treated for cancer at the adjacent hospital.

The little girl touched Magic's face. *"Magique le héros,"* she said.

"She's saying, you're the hero," said her father.

"You tell her she's the hero," Johnson said, pulling a Laker T-shirt out of his gym bag. He gave her the shirt, and the rest of the kids came to life and started to swarm. James Worthy picked up a little boy and hugged him tightly. A. C. Green showed a little kid how to high-five. The players showered the kids with caps, T-shirts, and assorted NBA trinkets, but most of the players looked pretty uncomfortable. Not Magic. He'd had lots of practice dealing with people who were suffering. Before almost every game, the Laker PR staff would wheel in people, often children, whose dying wish was to meet Magic. Many of the NBA stars blew off the wheelies, as they called them, but not Magic.

Ronald McDonald migrated over to Magic. An NBA official grabbed him by the elbow and pulled him away. "I under*stand,"* said Ronald, trying to free his elbow.

About forty minutes later, Magic was touching the hair of a little girl when one of the NBA officials said, "Gotta get back to the bus." They opened the door to a wall of sound: "Ma-jeek! Ma-jeek!" The rain was lashing straight into their eyes. As they streamed onto the bus, a wail came from the crowd. The plan had been for the Lakers to put on a brief basketball show on the small court beside the Ronald McDonald House. But in this downpour? Screw the kids.

Magic was the last one on the bus. Clearly beat to hell, he was wheezing and wiping his nose with his cuff. He looked out at the crowd. All the little kids with plastered hair. He grabbed a basketball. "It's showtime," he said quietly. Alone, he walked onto the court and started splashing down fancy dribbles. He popped up a jumper—*swish, splash.* He splashed after his own rebound; nobody on the bus moved. *Swish-splash!* Then he ran to the end of the court, took off for the basket, and sunk it. The crowd roared.

He grabbed the ball. For no more than a second, he looked

completely at peace. There seemed to be no corporate promotions in his mind, no sick kids, no exhausted body. Just the pure feeling of holding a basketball, knowing he could bring it to life. Just the feeling of being in love with a game. He was little Earvin back in Lansing, out playing in the rain.

Then he walked off the court. With achy slowness. Soaking wet, coughing. In the building, the little girl he'd held pressed her face against a window. He caught sight of her. He pointed at her, the way players do after an assist.

She pointed back.

The Magic smile.

• Women & Money

Stunned silence. Then a roar. "Ma-jeek! Ma-jeek!" Magic had just dribbled left behind his back, then right behind his back, then he'd flipped the ball backward over his head to a streaking Vlade Divac, who scored. The fans at the McDonald's Open had been cheering for the French team, Limoges, but after the pass they chanted Magic's name. He waved at them, and they screamed like fans at a rock concert.

Magic had transformed the NBA with this kind of passing. Before him, the NBA game had dulled into a selfish pattern of dunk-jumper-dunk. But he and Bird had brought back passing.

Magic ended the rout of Limoges with 19 assists, a new record. Afterward, he percolated with excitement about the future. "This year," he said, "we want to *run*. We learned a lot from the Chicago series. We're stronger now."

The European journalists seemed excited to be around him. But, to some of them, there appeared to be something wrong with him. He looked sick.

A couple of hours later, the Laker team bus pulled up in front of the International Hotel. The Lakers piled out and marched single file through an entrance that was cordoned off with a thick nylon rope. Fans—many of them women (luscious women)—pressed against the ropes. The Lakers had an entire floor of the hotel to themselves, and it was tightly guarded. So this was one of the only chances that women had to meet them.

Many of the women were less than discreet about their desire for an intimate interlude with one—or more—of the players and leaned forward with scraps of paper bearing their phone numbers. They were practically shivering with availability.

Thus, the path to the hotel was more than just a protected, exclusive corridor. It was also a gauntlet of temptation.

There were gauntlets of temptation outside almost every NBA stadium and outside many hotels where teams stayed. Not long ago, Magic could have worked a gauntlet like this for twenty minutes, making all kinds of contacts. He was genuinely gregarious and warm, and it wasn't just women who were charmed by him—it was everyone from businessmen to journalists to children.

Last night, he'd worked a room at a sponsors party—money men and their wives—like a man running for office. For him, that kind of work was now more lucrative than basketball, and no less pleasing to his ego.

But coming through now, he only smiled and waved. No flirting, no schmoozing, no networking—no autographs.

• War Is Hell

David Stern, sitting next to Olympic czar Juan Samaranch, looked sick to his stomach. Disaster! Championship game—and the Lakers were *blowing* it. They'd led Badalona of Spain by 19, but near the end of the game the life seemed to have drained out of Magic, and the Lakers had pissed away the lead.

A few minutes ago, Stern had been casually chatting into a cellular phone. But now he put down the phone. Stared grimly at the court.

Magic was at the top of the key. He paused. Then took a huge step and was suddenly in the air, with all the Spanish players still rooted to the ground. He flipped up an easy underhand lay-up.

The Badalona coach erupted from his chair. "Take a *charge!*" he screamed at his players.

Badalona streaked downcourt and started clawing at the Laker defenders. The Lakers looked frantic. They'd expected an exhibition game. But now they were covered with scratches and laminated with sweat. Their chests were heaving.

Magic got the ball again. Went downcourt. He raced across the free throw line and leaped into the air. His massive right arm hooked over his head, sailing a perfect pass to A. C. Green under the basket. Green exploded up for the dunk. *Splack!* A Badalona player crashed the ball back to the floor. Badalona ball. Two-point game.

Stern's eyes widened. It was a *war* out there.

But that was no coincidence at all. Sports had always been a war. It had been designed that way.

Every culture throughout history had derived its sports primarily from war. In fact, the first recorded sports, around 2000 B.C., had centered on chariot racing, wrestling, boxing, sword fighting, archery, and javelin throwing. Practical stuff. To train soldiers to fight.

Some of the ancient battles had been "single combat" affairs: our best guy against yours, one-on-one, winner-take-all—like David and Goliath. These symbolic battles had saved on men and munitions. But more often, sports had been used to train whole armies to fight.

One of the countries most excited by sports—and by war—was Assyria, the ancient empire that later became Syria. By 1288 B.C., the Assyrians were talented enough to fight one of the great battles of history—2,500 chariots fighting to the death in the sands of Egypt. The Assyrians won the battle. But they lost the war when their generals gave them a day off for rape, pillage, and wine. That phenomenon was a historical constant among elite athlete-warriors: with power came privileges, often ruinous.

In fact, Greece's Olympic Games, begun around 776 B.C.,

had declined after hundreds of years because of the indulgence of its athletes. The Olympics, begun as a contest for ordinary soldiers, had been taken over by professionals who expected big prizes. Even the Greek word for *athlete* was derived from *athlon,* meaning: *prize.* By about 336 B.C., when Alexander the Great took over, he was said by Plutarch to be "averse to the whole race of athletes." He preferred soldiers with fewer skills and fewer demands.

Even so, athletics remained a major part of virtually every culture. It satisfied the primal need to fight and conquer, even if only symbolically. Sports events became bloodless warfare, a way for locales to compete without destroying each other. As such, these events were taken quite seriously. The captain of the losing team of an ancient Mayan ball game, for example, was beheaded.

In many cultures, sports grew to be more than just practice for war. Often, a sport was refined to a psychic battle for perfection. The Polynesians separated their finest competitive canoeists from the rest and taught them the beauty of struggle. These special athletes, whom they called "the children of the gods," approached their sport as a quest for the impossible dream of perfection. As they paddled into the open sea, the children of the gods would chant, "The horizon lifting in front of us; the horizon coming closer; the horizon of doubt; the horizon with strange power; the horizon never reached."

The children of the gods learned to subordinate their own selfish pursuits to a simple love of athletic competition, regardless of its outcome.

Even in societies where the military model of sports predominated, many athletes learned to put the team's goals ahead of their own. They served as soldiers in their city's or school's battles. This selfless warrior's ethic was common in sports—even in professional sports. It was common for centuries. Until about 1970.

Then, the do-your-own-thing politics of the era combined with a huge increase in sports money—all from television —to doom the concept of home-team spirit among most athletes. Selfishness—which had always been a temptation for athletes—quickly became epidemic.

Most fans, however, still believed in home-team spirit and resented athletes for getting rich off their home's symbolic wars. But fans didn't matter. They could be manipulated by the media.

But there remained a few athletes—very few—who rose above all that. For these few, who embraced the warrior's ethic, the game stayed free of selfishness and vanity. For them, the game was an art, a spiritual experience. This mind-set freed them to reach even greater heights of excellence. They could achieve extraordinary mental feats of concentration and confidence.

But with this greater excellence came greater temptation. And often destruction.

. . . Forty seconds left in the Badalona game—Badalona had the ball and a chance to tie. A beefy Badalona guard dribbled restlessly at the free throw line. Lunged toward the hoop.

Magic jumped over to cut him off. But a muscle-thick Badalona forward jammed his forearm into Magic's chest and belly. Magic went, *"Whooof!"* and the guard whipped by him. The guard leaped up toward the basket.

David Stern's face tightened.

Losing this tournament had to be Stern's worst nightmare. It would puncture the NBA's mythological invulnerability.

That would be bad for business and bad for David Stern. He'd just signed a $3-million-per-year contract with the NBA, with a $10 million signing bonus. He was already recognized as the most powerful man in global sports and had almost unimaginable opportunities ahead.

In the post–Cold War world, sports might reach a historic level of importance. Satellite TV and the fall of communism were expanding audiences geometrically. With the nuclear threat metastasizing to the Third World and superpower trade wars looming, nations needed a harmless vent for their competitive urges. Sports were the perfect outlet.

Someone like Stern could emerge from the new world disorder as one of the world's most powerful men. Not by holding some compromised and ephemeral public office. But by presiding over a multinational sports-entertainment-media conglomerate. Capitalism was now certain to rule the world. And Stern could help rule capitalism. Of course, that was contingent upon a number of factors. Starting with: not blowing this damn game.

The Badalona guard, as he got to the basket, tossed the ball to his right, into the hands of a clumsy backup center. The center had an easy six-foot shot. He heaved it up. *Clang!* No good. A dozen hands groped for it. The ball slid free and hit James Worthy's foot. It caromed out of bounds.

Referee Ed Rush—the NBA half of the officiating team— blasted his whistle and pointed downcourt. Laker ball. The crowd howled. The European team had been screwed, and everyone in the stadium knew it. The game ended. Worthy suppressed a smile. After the game, one of the Laker players gave his assessment of the MVP voting: "Five votes for Magic, three for Worthy, and two for Ed Rush."

David Stern stood, stretched, and beamed, betraying not a trace of irony. A win was a win. At midcourt, the Yugoslavian team—all Croatians—unfurled a banner: "Stop the war in Croatia."

Magic, with another 17 assists, got MVP. But he still felt horrible. Muscles on fire. Exhausted. He pulled his jacket over his wet shoulders and went to meet the reporters. "I always thought, even *before* I came here," he said, "that the Olympics were going to be tough. It's not gonna be a cakewalk."

But he was being kind. Or maybe just paranoid. Only two teams could have beaten America. One was the Soviet team, which, over the last month, had ceased to exist. The other was the Yugoslavian team, which was quickly falling apart.

Now there was only one team left that could destroy the Americans. And that would be the Americans themselves.

Magic looked relieved. "I'm happy to get *out*," he said. "We want to get home to get our rest." He seemed to lose his train of thought. ". . . To get our rest," he repeated. To no one in particular, he murmured, "I don't feel strong. I don't feel like me."

The fans, some still in their seats, were chanting his name—as if he would come back for an encore. Not to *do* anything, just to . . . be Magic.

But he didn't feel like Magic. He felt like hell. He thought it was going to be a long season. It would, as always, be a war. It would be a war for a championship that could be won. And it would, as always, be a war for perfection—a war that could never be won: "the horizon never reached."

But as he pulled off his Laker uniform, he had no idea that the hardest war of his life—a war against death—was just beginning.

3

The Greatest
Story Never Told

**Backstabbing and Betrayal • Money Grubbing •
Whining for Dollars • Quick-and-Dirty Chuck
Daly • The Two Faces of Isiah • Magic's Shuttle
Diplomacy • The Strange Dream of Michael Jordan**

Like great statesmen, we encourage those who betray
their friends.

—John Gay, 1715

Jordan was going to blow them off. People monitoring the
situation said Michael had already sent a back-channel
brush-off to the Olympic Selection Committee. Jordan
didn't *need* the Olympics. He was *already* God. But there
was an interesting footnote.

Part of the reason for his snub, it was said, was because
Isiah would be on the team.

A crack in the door! Thank God.

Getting Jordan was crucial. Not for winning. Hell, with
the Soviets and Yugoslavs decimated, our scrubs could kick
worldwide ass. But Jordan was crucial for *marketing*.

The real job of the committee was to create a team of
mythic proportions: the golden boys. Because only a team of
epic grandeur could fulfill the committee's actual—but
unstated—mandate: the global marketing of the NBA.
Bringing a mythic team to Barcelona would cement the
league's expansion into foreign media, merchandising, and

appearances, and pave the way for European teams to join the NBA.

It was an opportunity no other American sport had. Baseball was too slow, and football was too complicated; there was no foreign interest in either. But basketball was simple, beautiful, and paced to an electronic-era nervous system. Worldwide fiscal conquest was in the *bag.* If only Mike would quit acting like a putz.

Stern, as well as Jordan's own money men, was reportedly squeezing him. To no avail. Jordan's primary power broker, agent David Falk, was saying, "Michael is worried that we may be overreacting to the world catching up to us in basketball. He feels that by having so many NBA stars, it's like trying to solve a small conflict with nuclear warheads." In other words: Screw off.

As the selection deadline neared, Jordan went to L.A. for Magic's United Negro College Fund all-star game. Jordan could say no to the league, but he couldn't say no to Magic. Magic (who'd just given up $100,000 to fit Terry Teagle under the salary cap) called Michael up to the podium. "I'm going to *pay* him to play in the Olympics," Magic announced. "If I can give Terry one hundred thousand dollars, I know I can give Michael two or three million."

Jordan stepped up and whispered into Magic's ear.

"He said five million!" Magic crowed, "All right!" Magic, a master politician, didn't push it. He knew Jordan was sick of being shoved around.

But after things quieted down, Jordan didn't budge from his position.

Later that week, Jordan put together a card game with his old Bulls teammate Jack Haley and Indiana's Reggie Miller, who'd played with Haley at UCLA. Jordan and Miller were supposedly bitter rivals, but that was just sportswriter bullshit. While they played cards, Jordan told Miller he hoped Reggie made the Olympic team, because of the way they complemented each other: Miller, the pure-shooting zone-buster, could crack defenses for Jordan to penetrate. Did that mean Jordan would play? No, said Jordan, not *necessarily.* But it sounded like Jordan was working on it.

The next time the media pounced on Jordan, he revealed the "real reason" he wouldn't play. He needed the summer "for golf." Because: "It relaxes me." Nobody bought it.

But nobody knew what he was thinking or knew about the backstage maneuvers that were creating the U.S. team. So a couple of sportswriters started calling the selection process "the greatest story never told." And left it at that.

• Warriors and Fat-ass Bureaucrats

In fact, the U.S. Olympic basketball team was born of backstabbing, fear, politicking, greed, manipulation—and pure love.

The fear had begun the instant the selection process started. At that time, more than two years before the Olympics, the Soviets and Yugos had fearsome teams. At the same time, the Americans were enduring humiliating butt-whippings in international competition: second in the 1987 Pan Am Games, second in the 1988 Olympics, second in the 1989 Goodwill Games, and third in the 1990 World Championships. Of course, America's best players hadn't been in the 1988 Olympics—but David Robinson, Danny Manning, Charles Smith, and Hersey Hawkins had been.

And there was another reason for fear. The U.S. team and everyone who'd built it would be playing by Mayan Rules: win or die. If they blew the gold, heads would fall. A loss would deflate NBA mythology, crippling global marketing. Stern would be *pissed*.

There was fear even within the committee. The amateurs seemed scared to death of the pros. American Olympic basketball was being run by a group called USA Basketball, which looked to me like just a pooped-out clique of fat-ass jock-bureaucrats and professional amateurs. USA Basketball used the classic survival mechanism of nonprofit agencies: they whined for a living. They begged for donations on the grounds that they were keeping American basketball pure. And if they got enough money from a company, they'd let it call itself an Official Sponsor. They had a good thing going.

USA Basketball had fought to keep the pros out. Only two countries voted against letting pros play: Russia and America. The Soviets' motivation: They thought they could win the Olympics and still control their pro players. They were, after all, a police state. USA Basketball's motivation: Supposedly, a love of the amateur ethic. But, it looked like USA Basketball was simply more afraid of David Stern than the Russians. They seemed very uneasy that the men from the NBA—capitalists! from the private sector!—were suddenly taking such an interest in their affairs. When the pros came in, USA Basketball lost about seventy-five percent of its traditional funding. Their deal with Converse vanished because the pro players had their own sneaker deals. Also, they could no longer play lucrative exhibition games against NBA players.

Even though this conflict was partly a clash of ideologies, it got personal in a hurry. For example, Duke coach Mike Krzyzewski had been odds-on favorite to coach the 1992 Olympic team, because he'd paid his dues in dinky USA Basketball amateur events. But when the pros came in, Krzyzewski was out on his ass. The best he could hope for was an assistant's job. Also, players like Christian Laettner and Jimmy Jackson lost out. They'd done grunt work in low-profile USA Basketball tournaments, and in the old days they'd have been paid off with an Olympic berth. But now they'd have to claw their way onto the team. The biggest losers, though, were the USA Basketball executives themselves. That included executive director Bill Wall, who'd been there since about the Pleistocene Era. It was Wall who'd embarrassed America internationally by pulling the 1991 Pan Am team out of the athletes' village in Havana. He'd chartered a $10,000 flight and lodged the team in $200-a-night rooms in Miami. Then he'd defended his actions by saying, "If we're spoiled and arrogant, so be it." Shortly after the pros invaded his organization, Wall announced his retirement.

Almost as soon as it was formed, the Olympic Selection Committee broke into two uneasy camps: pro and amateur. But the amateur members thought they had an ace in the hole, something that would return their power: no pro player in his right mind, they thought, would play for free.

Former college coach Al McGuire had the classic line on that issue: "No player who is in the NBA will represent the U.S.A. in the Olympics in our lifetime." Most of the amateur-related committee members agreed. These members included Krzyzewski, Seton Hall coach P. J. Carlesimo, Southern Cal coach George Raveling, and Kentucky athletic director C. M. Newton. But the idea seemed ridiculous to the NBA men: general managers Jack McCloskey (Detroit), Wayne Embry (Cleveland), Bob Bass (San Antonio), Donnie Walsh (Indiana), Jan Volk (Boston), and Billy Cunningham (Miami), and NBA vice president Rod Thorn, former player Quinn Buckner, and NBA Players Association executive director Charles Grantham.

Walsh and a couple of the other pro guys tried to explain. The Olympic-level players, Walsh thought, were different from even other good NBA players. They didn't play for money, or power, or even glory. They had the warrior's ethic. Walsh's view was: "When you get to the highest level—the level of a Magic, or a Jordan, or a Bird—you're combining the physical, mental, and spiritual all in one package. They have the ability to get so inside a game, so into a moment, that they're working in a different realm of time and space than the rest of us." In other words, they'd play. Out of love.

Walsh, an erudite attorney, didn't have his head in the clouds. He'd been a player and a coach, and he knew well the arrogance and selfishness that riddled the NBA. The players would put up with no money. But they wouldn't put up with bullshit. Such as: tryouts and practices.

It was time for a quick, quiet survey of The Boys, the first of many. Walsh was exactly right. The players were interested. But they wouldn't put up with bullshit. Kevin McHale, on tryouts: "Why would you want to have thirty players come in and beat each other up? Would you take the last ten that were standing?" Charles Barkley: "I'm too *good* to try out."

Nor did Barkley want much practice. Even patriotic David Robinson put his foot down on giving up the whole summer. Players Association vice president Rolando Blackman told Charlie Grantham to forget about a lengthy schedule. Summer, Blackman reminded Grantham, was money time. It was the time to make commercials, run basketball camps, do deals, polish the image.

If you cut into that, you cut into a player's chance of rising to power level or immortality level.

Plus, there was the injury-and-fatigue factor. Boston's Jan Volk thought it would be nuts to "put them through a six-week regimen to qualify, and then practice them to death." That could kill an old man like, oh, let's just say Larry Bird. The other GMs agreed. Their own players would be on the team, and they were paid to win NBA championships, not gold medals.

There was only one way to do it: quick & dirty.

Which led directly to the next problem, which was just as divisive. Who was the world's greatest quick & dirty coach?

• Politics

The college committee members had an immediate answer: a *college* coach. College coaches were *teachers*. They could quickly teach twelve players one system.

Which made the pro members want to puke. They were sick of hearing what great teachers the college coaches were. If so, how did so many stupid players make it to the NBA? They argued that a Don Nelson or Larry Brown could teach circles around any college coach—present company excluded, of course. With Krzyzewski, Carlesimo, and Raveling sitting right there, the discussions had to be devoid of personal attack, or promotion. Krzyzewski couldn't very well come right out and scream, *It's my turn.* And that set the tone for the entire process. The members wouldn't promote their own players. Conducting themselves like statesmen kept the peace. It took three sessions, spread over several months, to pick a coach. Over that same time, they kept sounding out pro players. One by one, the best players said that they'd be interested if the bullshit could be minimized. As these opinions filtered in, the notion of having a college coach petered out. No way would NBA stars let a college coach scream at them or give a rah-rah speech. Even before Charles Barkley had been in the NBA, he hadn't let 1984 Olympic coach Bobby Knight scream at him. Back then, it had cost Barkley a spot on the team. Now Barkley would probably just kill a little punk like Knight. It would be embarrassing all around.

So the committee established criteria for the coach, to eliminate candidates and kill the idea of a college coach. The coach, they decreed, had to have at least eight years of head coaching experience, with at least three in the NBA. And he had to have been active within the past three years. Initially, they'd wanted an active coach, but that had ruled out Pat Riley, who'd resigned from the Lakers. So they'd stuck in the "within-three-years" clause, and unofficially called it the Riley Rule.

But there was a consensus that an active coach should be favored. It gave the coach more clout. It also worked against older coaches, like Jack Ramsay. Ramsay was a basketball genius and an expert on the international game, from giving European clinics. But the players would want somebody young enough to relate to. And they'd want a "players' coach." A player's coach was basically just a coach who was willing to eat shit to keep his job. Thus, active older coaches like Dick Motta, Bill Fitch, K. C. Jones, and Dick Harter were low on the list. They were sick of kowtowing to twenty-five-year-old egomaniacs. And there were certain to be egomaniacs. Quinn Buckner believed, "You can't even *play* in this league without a big ego."

But they didn't want somebody *too* contemporary, like Rick Adelman, Phil Jackson, or Stu Jackson. If the guy hadn't been in the league long enough to have trashed his larynx from screaming, he was too young. And too soft.

The Greatest Story Never Told

Mostly, they wanted a star, another mythic hero. The short list boiled down to: Riley, Don Nelson, Chuck Daly, Larry Brown, Lenny Wilkens, and Cotton Fitzsimmons.

Riley had three great attributes: his winning percentage (.733), his four championships, and his neurosis. Nobody touched his winning percentage, and nobody else was quite as obsessed. Riley was tough as hell. For this situation, though, he might be too tough, too obsessed. There would be no slackers on this team, and he might look for one, just to stay in shape. But he'd be plenty quick. And he was definitely a golden boy.

Like Riley, Wilkens and Fitzsimmons were also long shots. Lenny was on his way to the most coaching wins in NBA history; by 1990 he was only five decent seasons short of Red Auerbach's record. He'd won a championship and was a "players' coach." Rod Thorn thought, "Very few people have anything negative to say about him." Ironically, Lenny's lack of bile worked against him. It made him the natural choice for assistant coach.

They had decided to have one NBA assistant coach and two collegiate assistants. The purported reason for two college coaches was because they'd know the zone defenses that international rules allowed. But the real reason was just to shut the amateurs up.

The two collegiate assistants would be the committee's own Krzyzewski and Carlesimo. It looked like sleazy backroom politics. But Coach K. was brilliant and obsessed, and P.J. actually had some charm—not that common among college coaches, who tended to be one-dimensional dictators. When their selections were announced, there wasn't a peep from anybody.

Cotton Fitzsimmons was also a strong candidate for an assistant's job. He'd started coaching in 1958, with nine years of junior college at $5,500 per year. He'd rebuilt Phoenix out of a dung-heap of drug abuse and had won two Coach of the Year awards. He was considerate and well-liked. But he wasn't box office like Riley, and he'd never won a championship.

The long shots disappeared. Riley was too obsessed,

Lenny was too nice, and Cotton didn't have the glamour. It got down to Nelson, Brown, and Daly.

Nellie: the coach's coach. Shrewdest in the game. Only coach in the NBA who could regularly advance in the playoffs with dogmeat teams. By the end of the 1990 season, Nelson had won 620 games, seven division titles in Milwaukee, and two Coach of the Year awards. Plus, he was working his butt off for the job. He'd spent the last two summers scouting European teams, had gone to the Goodwill Games, and was adamant about wanting to "represent the country." Patriotism was a big thing with Nelson, and that didn't hurt.

But Nelson loved complex systems, not quick-&-dirty, seat-of-the-pants stuff. Also, some of the guys on the committee thought he was trying *too* hard. Did he have a hidden agenda?

Larry Brown was pissed off that Nellie was lobbying so hard. "I don't think you need to campaign for the job," Brown said. "I think the job should go to the most qualified coach. And, to be honest, I know more about the international game than anybody." Subtle way of saying he'd paid his USA Basketball dues. Brown had played on the 1964 Olympic team, was an assistant coach in 1980, and had put in time on some of the low-voltage amateur events.

In seven college seasons Brown had made three trips to the Final Four, and in eight NBA years he'd won four division titles. Brown was a *master* technician, though, and no aficionado of the quick fix. But, he had a clean-cut "teacher's" image, was a winner, was articulate, and knew how to dodge egos. Strong candidate.

But so was Chuck. Daly was, in many ways, the deepest of the coaches. He had some perspective. He was as neurotic as every other coach about the necessity of winning *every . . . single . . . game*. He was a worrier. But he didn't deep fry his own belly in stomach acid. After a loss, he'd be snotty to reporters, but that was about the extent of it. He was too smart a players' coach to pick a fight with his stars.

Even his obsession with clothes was tongue-in-cheek. Daly knew that no matter how many Italian suits he bought, he'd never make a *GQ* cover, like Riley. Didn't have the face. He'd been handsome as a youngster, but if thirty years of coaching didn't fold and mutilate your face, nothing would. Still, Chuck played the pretty-boy game and made fun of himself for doing it. His subordination of ego was his primary asset. He'd said that, "A coach basically has a three-day contract written in ice, while a player may have a ten-year contract for twenty million. That makes the player CEO of his own corporation. You wouldn't scream at the CEO of a corporation, would you?"

Daly refused to campaign for the Olympic job, even though he needed it. He was on the verge of divorce from Detroit and bringing back a gold medal would position him perfectly for another coaching or media job. One source close to Daly commented, "Chuck wins Barcelona, he's automatically Bob Costas's new boy, at eight hundred grand."

Daly already made over half million a year, but unlike many other coaches, he'd never played in the NBA, so he didn't have that hard kernel of arrogance at the core of his personality. He'd started coaching at $3,500 a year, and that served as a psychic anchor.

Daly also understood superstars, having put in ten years with one of the game's most complex characters, Isiah Thomas. Daly believed, "While players are tycoons, they're also children worrying about scoring a basket. They're really no different than the children I coached at Punxsutawney High School thirty years ago. They all want to hear the crowd cheer. What you have to do is ignore the fact that they're wealthy men in a serious business and address them as kids playing a game. Because that's the aspect of their personality that's going to win games. And, ironically, make them rich."

Daly was a players' coach, but he was no wimpy little ass-kisser. Regardless of what he said about not screaming at players, he had the larynx of a chain-smoking bullfrog. He'd won two championships with a team of prima donnas and maniacs.

Almost unanimously, the committee thought Daly was the best possible candidate to manage its zoo of egos.

Of critical importance, he was the best quick-&-dirty coach available. A student of individual players, he already knew every star intimately. And he wouldn't waste time playing mind games. His two championships spoke volumes about his ability to quickly adapt to new situations. You never won a ring with "Plan A." Nor did Daly strive to be a great teacher. Guys like Donnie Walsh thought that was good. Walsh's attitude was, "Just give them their game and let them get going with it."

Time to vote. They talked about having a weighted system—three points for first place, two for second, etc. But abandoned it. Daly was going to win in a walk, so why complicate things?

Daly won. In a walk. Lenny won assistant coach. C. M. Newton, chairman of the committee, called them both. Daly was surprised—or at least said he was. Lenny wasn't surprised and didn't pretend to be. Actually, he was pretty casual. It was toward the end of the '91 season—a rotten year for Cleveland—and Lenny's concern was survival, not glory.

Over a year of haggling had taken place. And not a single player had been selected. At the beginning, all the committee members had been thrilled about building the greatest team in sports history. Now some were disenchanted.

They asked Daly to make a list of the players he liked.

Daly came to the next meeting. With his list.

• The All-Ego Team

He looked worried. But Daly always looked worried—he called himself the Prince of Pessimism. He started his presentation by reciting his concerns.

Number one: time. They'd have exactly one week to practice before their qualifying tournament. So they'd need smart players and enthusiastic players. Two: injuries. The

The Greatest Story Never Told

Olympics would come at the end of another lethal NBA season, and some of the selected players would be crippled. The remaining players would have to fill their roles. In Barcelona injuries would be an even bigger problem. If somebody got hurt there, they couldn't replace him. Therefore, they'd need maximum flexibility—players who could cover different positions. They'd also need multidimensional players who could shoot, pass, rebound, and defend. Three: leadership. This would undoubtedly be an All-Ego team, so they'd need at least one or two cops. Like Magic and Larry. Four: teamwork. This was no time to choose an All-Flash team, or an All-Media team or an All-Marketing team. They needed players who would complement each other. They needed unselfish people who would give up the ball, play defense, and box out. Five: long-range shooters. The three-point line would be three feet closer, and they had to take advantage of it. They hadn't had great shooters in '88, and that was part of the reason they'd lost. Six: a mobile center. Because of the emphasis on three-pointers, they'd need someone who could go outside and get back in quickly.

Then he revealed his list. It was broken down by position, four to six players deep. It was only of NBA players—he'd let the committee decide which college players to choose. If any.

Daly never released his list to the media, and he wouldn't give it to me, either. But committee members remembered it, and—to the best of their recollection—here it is:

The Official Unauthorized Version of
Chuck's Wish List

Center	Point Guard	Shooting Guard
1. David Robinson	1. Magic Johnson	1. Michael Jordan
2. Pat Ewing	2. Isiah Thomas	2. Joe Dumars
3. Brad Daugherty	3. John Stockton	3. Clyde Drexler
4. Robert Parish	4. Kevin Johnson	4. Reggie Miller
5. Bill Laimbeer	5. Tim Hardaway	
	6. Terry Porter	

The Golden Boys

Small Forward	Power Forward
1. Scottie Pippen	1. Karl Malone
2. Chris Mullin	2. Dennis Rodman
3. Larry Bird	3. Charles Barkley
4. Dominique Wilkins	4. Buck Williams
5. Bernard King	5. James Worthy
	6. Kevin McHale

The only real surprises were how highly Daly rated his own players—Rodman, Dumars, and Thomas. But Daly loved those guys—even Isiah, who could be an incredible pain in the ass, but was a true warrior.

Daly also had a short list of seven players he considered most vital. Again, the source of this list was not Daly himself, but committee members.

The Official Unauthorized Version of
Chuck's Short List

1. Michael Jordan
2. Magic Johnson
3. David Robinson
4. Patrick Ewing
5. Scottie Pippen
6. Karl Malone
7. Chris Mullin

The only surprise on the short list was Scottie Pippen. He hadn't even made the All-Star team in '91, and his only superstar performance had been in the Eastern Finals. But that had been against the Pistons. Apparently, he'd burned himself into Daly's brain.

A few members were surprised Bird wasn't on the short list. But Bird swore he didn't want to play, and Daly was taking him at his word.

Nobody was surprised by the player at the top of the list. Jordan was God. Of course, from a *competitive standpoint*, it didn't matter if he played. If he stiffed them, they'd decided to just go with Clyde Drexler. Clyde could do most of what Jordan did and was a better rebounder and passer. But Clyde wasn't box office. He was less flashy, came from the puny Portland media market, and had never become a Wheaties box.

So everybody was still drooling over Jordan. And Jordan was still playing hard to get.

• Michael, Magic, and Isiah

Michael Jordan was twisting in the wind. What to do? What to do?

On the one hand, there was love. Jordan probably loved playing more than anyone else in basketball. Because he got more out of it. Not the rewards—those were very secondary. What he got was an experience, a feeling, that was out of this world. In almost every important game, he would drift into the "zone of altered consciousness" and experience a supernatural feeling of power and joy. It was like a strange dream, a religious experience. The ordinary realm of perception would slip away, and he'd find himself wandering in a transcendent world of slow motion, altered shapes and sizes, warped time, and absolute quiet. When he'd jump, he'd feel freed from earth—flying, floating.

All those special effects of him in ads weren't as farfetched as they looked—that was *really how it felt.*

Other players sometimes felt that way, but some never did. Even an excellent player, like Jordan's teammate John Paxson, almost never drifted into the zone of altered consciousness.

For Jordan, this feeling was fed by the excellence of his teammates. As the Bulls had grown into one of the great teams in basketball history, the frequency of the feeling had increased.

How often would he get this feeling if he were on the greatest team on earth? Very often. He knew that. And it was a powerful lure.

Besides that feeling, there would also be the feeling of love for his Olympic teammates. There was a sense of brotherhood among the great players. Part of it was narcissism. But part of it came from sharing a very unique experience: we few, we happy few, we band of brothers. By the early summer of 1991, Jordan knew that "Magic and all those guys" were going to play. And he knew that Magic and Chuck were talking about making the Games as much a party as possible—playing softball together, golfing, going to the discos. It would be the kind of party Michael wouldn't want to miss.

And let's not forget money. *Michael loved money.* He even got a kick out of toy-level money. He was building an immense mansion on the North Shore of Chicago, and he had a fleet of hot cars. And that was nothing compared to his immortality-level money. Jordan felt quite comfortable as an institution. He gave away tons of money through the Jordan Foundation—his own philanthropic organization—and he enjoyed every dollar of it.

It was hard to estimate what he could make from the Olympics. Even by his standards, Barcelona would be an orgy of self-promotion. The Olympics would have an audience of 2.5 billion viewers: *half the earth.* Half the earth bought a lot of T-shirts. What was easier to figure, though, was what he'd lose if he blew it off. He'd lose the cozy, was-it-good-for-you-too feeling he now enjoyed with his sponsors. All of his immortality-level money (about $20 million annually) came from sponsors. He couldn't afford to piss them off. Two of his biggies, Gatorade and Nike, were also USA Basketball sponsors, and—more important—NBC Olympic advertisers. One close observer of the committee's courtship of Jordan noted, "Gatorade doesn't want to buy TV time during the Olympics and have their main guy sitting home. They want Mike there in the limelight." This observer thought Gatorade might have slipped Jordan some extra money to show up: "Gatorade's feeling would be, 'We know you want to take the summer off, but here's an extra hundred grand. Just show up and smile.'" Others close to the scene, though, doubted that any money changed hands. They thought there was already enough money on the table to motivate Jordan.

There was also a widespread belief that the league was tightening the screws on Jordan. They had too much to lose.

But the pressure had to be carefully applied. For years, Jordan had tried to accommodate all the money men, and he was sick of it. Jordan, discussing the pressure, said, "I still have a mind of my own."

There were also good reasons *not* to go. Michael, unlike Magic, had already won a gold medal (in 1984). There was also the torture factor. Jordan got whipped and beaten more than virtually anyone else in the league. Part of it was the way he played—flying & skying, crashing & burning. When you play above the rim, you land with a force-factor six times your body weight. But most of the torture came from thugs trying to maim him. If you were the guy who knocked Mike out of a crucial game, one way or another you'd see money. It was a fact of life, and it burned Jordan's ass. He was supposed to be this valuable commodity to the league, but every night they let some stiff beat the shit out of him. Mayhem was, after all, very telegenic—great for ratings. So after every season, he needed a couple of months to recuperate. He did *not* need some vicious, Third-World monster pulling his thumb off in hopes of creating the big fluke.

Plus, there was golf. Jordan really did love it. He got a sense of peace from it, and peace was getting hard to find.

Plus. There was Isiah. It looked as if Isiah was going to play. He was one of the primary people the committee had been quietly conversing with. Jordan had been saying, all along, that Isiah had nothing to do with him not wanting to play. But nobody else was saying that—not even Jordan's samurai, David Falk. During the summer of '91, when Jordan was at the height of his indecision, Falk was saying, "Anyone who knows the NBA knows the relationship between Michael and Isiah is frosty at best. The Olympic team will be in close quarters for thirty-seven days." Jordan and Thomas had been feuding since Michael's rookie year, and no truce was in sight.

It was beginning to look as if the only person who could mediate the dispute—and get Jordan on the team with Isiah—was Magic.

Magic had been close to Isiah ever since he'd advised
Isiah to drop out of college early, as Magic had. They'd
become confidants and finally best friends. For a long time,
they'd gotten together every summer for an epic, extended
guys-night-out.

But Magic had become close to Michael only very recently. Early on, Michael had disliked Magic just because Magic
was Isiah's buddy. But Magic had gone to Michael and
basically said: How can two guys as cool as us be enemies?

Now Magic seemed tighter with Michael than he was with
Isiah. Over the past couple of years, when the Lakers and
Pistons had been in the Finals, the Magic-Isiah friendship
had chilled. Magic had said, "The style Detroit plays had an
effect on our relationship. You have to hate Detroit to beat
Detroit. And to hate Detroit, you've got to hate Isiah."
Magic had tried to leave the hate on the court, but it hadn't
been easy.

It had isolated Isiah to lose his closeness to Magic. For
years, Isiah had been unpopular with many of the players,
coaches, and writers, even though he was maybe the best
small player in history. While Magic and Bird had saved the
league by bringing back the pass, Isiah had shown that a
small man could dominate. Before Isiah, the league had
been dominated by hulks, whom the fans had a hard time
identifying with. In changing that, Isiah had put money into
everyone's pockets. But he was still disliked.

For one thing, he played rough—some would say dirty.
He poked, scratched, elbowed, kneed. Even though he was
small by league standards, he was still 6–1 and 182—big
enough to hurt anyone. In fairness, though, the mean stuff
was just to win, not for fun. Zeke would much prefer to beat
you with a shot or pass—partly because he always got the
worst of rough stuff. In late '91, opponents tore apart his
hand so badly that it was questionable if he'd ever be the
same (which would make it easier to justify leaving him off
the team). But he'd borne the injury with remarkable
stoicism, even when the Bulls had banged at the hand in the
'91 playoffs.

What really pissed off people, though, was his apparent

duplicity. On the surface, he was Sweet Zeke: thousand-dollar suit, million-dollar smile. But there was a ghetto-boy ruthlessness to him. He'd manipulated Adrian Dantley off the team, and over the summer of 1991 he was said to be trying to engineer the trade of Dennis Rodman. Though he'd long denied it, he'd apparently led a freeze-out of Jordan in Jordan's first All-Star Game, denying him the ball on offense. Furthermore, he had insulted Larry Bird by agreeing with Rodman that Bird was "just another good player" who owed his fame to being white. In '91 he'd directed the infamous Piston walk-off at the end of the Bulls series; before the game had even ended, he'd moped to the locker room—past Jordan—without offering congratulations.

One Detroit source said, "He's a phony. A fuckin' phony. He's a backstabber, and he's only looking out for Isiah. It's not that he does stuff that no other guys in the league do—like cheat around and gamble a little—it's just that he's not honest with his image. I think that a lot of people around the league see through him, and they just say, why doesn't this guy come clean?"

Another close observer of Isiah noted, "He's pissed off a lot of people. The Dantley episode, the Bird episode, the walk-off. Every couple of years he does this stuff. My contention is: enough. If this is the way you want to behave, fine. But don't expect anybody to give a shit if you get left off the Olympic team."

Isiah had become pretty defensive about his image. He'd said, "There's always been the sense of, 'There's something about this guy—I don't like him; I don't trust him.' There's always been the sense that I'm up to something. But if I was up to something, wouldn't I be through with it by now?"

Time for any possible backdoor diplomacy was running out. It was midsummer, and the selection process had to be final by early fall. No action, by Magic or anyone else, had brought a reconciliation between Michael and Isiah.

Jordan appeared to be forcing a choice. The choice was ostensibly solely up to the Selection Committee. But, as one

NBA coach close to the situation said, "Magic is the most powerful guy in the league. If Magic wanted Isiah on the team, it would have been a done deal."

Magic did not step forward and campaign for Isiah. And the impasse suddenly ended.

Michael was leaning toward playing.

4

The List

The Great White Has-Been •
• The Most Hated Man in Basketball •
Good Charles and Bad Charles • Tyrannosaurus
Pat and the Valley of Death •
The Sweet Sixteen, the Elite Eight, and the Two
Pissed-Off Prima Donnas •
Isiah's Whine and Cheese Party

"For undemocratic reasons and for motives not of State,
They arrive at their conclusions—largely inarticulate.
Being void of self-expression, they confide their views to
  none;
But sometimes, in a smoking room, one learns why things
  were done."

—Rudyard Kipling

Big news from Dave Gavitt. Bird might play. That changed everything.

Gavitt, the Celtics vice president, had been urging Bird to play. The pushing had begun to pay off.

When the NBA had invaded USA Basketball, Gavitt had been made president of USA Basketball. Smart move by the amateurs. Gavitt could help them bring the NBA legends to Barcelona. Most notably: Larry Bird.

Bird was perfect for international marketing: the quintessential mythic representative. There were two archetypes in American basketball: the inner-city black leaper, and the rural white shooter. Bird was pure essence of rural white shooter. He not only was supremely talented but had the Huck Finn personality that typified (at least in the minds of New York media types) Middle America. He was just the thing to wrap in red, white, and blue and ship abroad.

Only trouble was, Bird knew all that. He may have been Huck Finn, but he wasn't stupid. He knew their interest in his passion-broken body had more to do with marketing than playing. And Larry was a warrior—not a spokesmodel. He'd passed up most immortality-level business opportunities, preferring to scrape by on three or four million a year in player money. The idea of being packaged in Barcelona as the Great White Has-Been had pissed him off.

And that didn't reflect very well on the clout of the NBA. They were supposed to be able to deliver the big names.

USA Basketball wanted the names to be as big as possible. For practical reasons. USA Basketball got a cut of merchandising. And merchandising could be worth a fortune. Selling trinkets would beat hell out of whining for a living in the boardrooms of big corporations. In 1992 the NBA's retail merchandising would hit about $1 billion. But merchandising wouldn't amount to much if they ended up with people like Alton Lister and Tony Campbell on their T-shirts. USA Basketball was a nonprofit agency, with most of its money going back into amateur basketball. Still, it was better to be a rich nonprofit agency than a poor one.

Ever since the Selection Committee had been formed, Bird had resisted its overtures. Gavitt and Red Auerbach had bent Bird's ear, but Bird kept saying that he didn't want to take a spot away from a younger guy. He meant, of course, a *better* guy. Since '89, when he'd begun spending most of his leisure time in major surgery, he'd declined. His back was always on fire, and his legs were shot. He couldn't beat anybody off the dribble, so he wasn't getting to the foul line. Knowing he couldn't drive, defenders crowded him, bringing his shooting percentage to a career low. Bird, like the other Olympic candidates, had always played with abandon, and it had destroyed his body.

There'd been some hesitation on the committee about even inviting him to play. One person close to the situation noted, "Bird's not anywhere near what he used to be. It's purely a marketing thing."

But what if Bird got healthy? Donnie Walsh's Pacers had been killed by Bird in the '91 playoffs, and Walsh thought Bird would be perfect for the Olympics. He was a multidimensional player with the shooting skills they needed. Other members agreed.

Rod Thorn brought up Bird's leadership. Other than Magic, Bird would be the only player that everyone else would listen to. Also, Bird brought an incredible mind to the game. His mental abilities were often described as coming from perfect "court vision" and "anticipation." It was said that he could "see the future"—see plays before they happened. Bird had described it as breaking free of the sense of time and seeing things in slow motion. It was something only a few players had, and it was of incredible value in critical moments. If some team did threaten to pull off the big fluke, Bird's psychic acuity might make the crucial difference.

Even so, unless Bird was close to full strength, he'd be a liability. And no one wanted that. To hell with marketing; if the team lost, they'd all look like idiots.

But they had an ace in the hole: Bird's pride. Unlike a lot of players, if Bird wasn't at full strength, he'd bow out.

The proposition to him was reworked. Now it stressed flexibility. It would be a no-obligation deal. If he changed his mind at the end of the '92 season, nobody would squeeze him. Gavitt assured Bird that they wanted him strictly for his ability and nothing else. If Bird didn't believe him, Gavitt said, he could pick up the phone and call anybody on the committee. Bird was much more receptive. Now if he went, it would be as a player, not a product.

So they penciled in Larry. But that changed everything.

• Whom to Leave Off?

It changed everything because the choice of virtually every player depended on the choice of every other player.

Especially when you got toward the bottom of the list. There were only three guys who'd make it regardless of who else made it. Jordan. Magic. And Healthy Larry. After that, things got murky. Chuck's short list was a valuable guide, but there was no consensus, at this stage, that his short list would help make the best possible team.

The smart thing, they decided, would be to whittle Chuck's wish list of twenty-five players to sixteen. After that, they would choose the elite eight players—the core of the team. Then they'd give each a call and put it to him point-blank: Are you in or out? Based on who said yes, they'd pick the rest.

During a series of conference calls and meetings, they waded into the list. Although the working assumption was that Bird, Magic, and Michael were already on the team, the committee members knew Magic was the only one they could count on. But thank God for that.

Magic was the cornerstone. Not just because he could play all five positions. His physical skills were secondary. The most important thing he offered was validation. His enthusiasm made the team cool in the eyes of the players. If Magic had just laughed off the Games, it would have been a disaster. Athletes, accustomed to being the white-hot center of the in-crowd, were very sensitive about popularity and exclusivity.

But Magic had come through. A lot of it was apparently just to grab more immortality-level money, but so what?

Of course, it would be redundant, from a leadership standpoint, to have both Magic and Larry on the team. But not very. As Rod Thorn pointed out, "Larry's a leader by what he does; Magic's more talkative." Thorn also thought, though, that ego might not be a problem. He argued that when the elite players were surrounded by their equals, they'd be generous.

And Magic was more than just a diplomat. He was also a point guard who could play center. That was extremely important, because there weren't many gifted centers around.

The List

There were only three. Ewing, Robinson, and Daugherty. Parish was great, but too old. And Laimbeer was . . . Laimbeer: the most hated man in basketball.

Daugherty was a long shot. Daugherty was the best-passing big man in the game; one year he'd had 333 assists, which was about 100 more than Ewing in Ewing's best year. And Daugherty could shoot; he had an 18.5 career average, with a .521 field-goal percentage. But he'd never entirely lived down his early reputation for being soft, and modern centers had to be able to drink blood.

Not that David Robinson did. But Robinson was very special. David played point center almost the same way Pippen played point forward. He was the game's only top-ten performer in five major stats (points, accuracy, rebounds, steals, blocks). He was the fastest man on his team and by far the fastest center in the league. He could also play power forward, and this versatility made him their first choice.

From a marketing standpoint, Robinson was exceptional. In the eyes of the major ad agencies, he was the future of basketball. When Jordan retired, Robinson would still be around with his genius-level IQ, his charm, and all those teeth. He was a money machine. Not to mention patriotic. Robinson would be about the only player on the team who actually gave a damn about playing for his country. For most of the rest of the guys, America meant one thing: free enterprise. But Robinson knew that America was more than just capitalism.

Most valuable of all, Robinson was adaptable enough to play alongside a classic, "true" center. And there was no truer center than Patrick Ewing.

Except maybe Shaquille O'Neal. O'Neal, who could have been the number-one draft pick after his freshman year, was elixir of monster-in-the-middle. But nobody on the committee was ready to hand him the spot. Still too early. Bizarre things happened to kids when they got a whiff of security-level money. Some became lazy, some became insufferable, some became uncoachable, and some—like Len Bias—

became dead. And Shaquille would *enter* the league at immortality-level money: about $5 million in salary, plus a million or two in sneaker money.

It was much safer to bank on Ewing, a proven example of a dying breed: the dominating center. As defenses had become more adept at denying shots from right under the basket, dominating centers had become dinosaurs. Centers could still control the game defensively, as Robinson did, but the days of offensive machines like Chamberlain and Jabbar were history. Nonetheless, Tyrannosaurus Pat lumbered on, transforming the lane into a valley of death. He wasn't the mobile defender Daly wanted, he wasn't a world-class rebounder, and he was personality-free. But he could rip your tongue out and laugh about it, and that made up for a lot.

There was talk about getting a third center, in addition to Robinson and Ewing, but having Magic obviated that need. O'Neal was also an ace in the hole. If Robinson or Ewing got injured during the season, they could pick up O'Neal in the spring without disrupting their balance of big and small men.

So they left Robinson, Ewing, and Daugherty on their Sweet Sixteen list—with big stars next to the names of Robinson and Ewing.

Choosing big men had been relatively easy. Give the assist to God: He hadn't made many of them. But as the positions decreased in size, the difficulty of choosing increased. The smaller you got, the more great players there were.

They moved to power forward. The choices: Malone, Barkley, Dennis Rodman, Buck Williams, James Worthy, Kevin McHale. Technically, Barkley was a small forward, but he played "bigger" than he was.

The two standouts were Malone and Barkley. Malone was a relatively easy pick, for two primary reasons: he excelled at his own position and was versatile enough to play others. He was fast enough to play in a front line consisting of him, Ewing, and Robinson, and strong enough to play center, if necessary. He also brought a wonderful fear-factor to every game. If some Third-World stud tried to globalize his reputation by dismembering Michael Jordan, Malone could come in and terminate him with extreme prejudice.

Off-court, though, Malone would be a goodwill ambassador for the Big Three: U.S.A., NBA, and NBC. He was preternaturally photogenic and was known as "good with the press." That meant he sometimes made eye contact with reporters.

Barkley was a much tougher choice. Not because of skills. Some of the committee considered him the game's greatest "impact player," ahead of even Jordan. Barkley's problem was what the committee referred to publicly as the "citizenship factor"—and privately (among certain GM circles) as the "asshole factor." Charles often was, no doubt about it, an asshole.

Not on every occasion, mind you. Barkley regularly made the NBA reporters' All-Interview Team. That team was theoretically based on quotability but in fact reflected how a player treated the press. Bill Laimbeer, for example, was very quotable but was such a world-class ball-breaker that he never came close to the team. Barkley made the team for one reason: there was a Good Charles at least as often as there was a Bad Charles. Quinn Buckner argued that Barkley had matured, that Good Charles now predominated.

But what if Bad Charles got poked in the eye by a Syrian and *ate him on television?* Would Qaddafi retaliate? Would David Stern have to go into hiding, like Salman Rushdie?

The committee put Barkley on the back burner and checked out his competition.

Rodman: Daly was pushing for him. Harder, it seemed to some, than he was pushing for Isiah. The committee loved Rodman's defense—he could be the designated stopper. Thorn pointed out, "Put him on a Toni Kukoc, and he'll take him out of the game."

But Bob Bass thought that Pippen could play defense just as well as Rodman and could score too. They couldn't afford role players. There was also some doubt about Rodman's personality. He had, after all, touched off a minor race war when he'd said Bird was considered great because he was white. But Bird's own GM, Jan Volk, wasn't even remotely concerned about Rodman's personality. Just his shot.

Buck Williams was almost as good a defender as Rodman, almost as good a rebounder, was a much better scorer, and had the heart of a lion. But Olympic material? Not anymore. Same went for Worthy and McHale. Also for Sam Perkins and Tom Chambers, who hadn't made Daly's list. These players were stars, possible Hall of Famers. But not 1992 Olympians. After all, only ten players would be anointed this fall, and there were twenty-four players in every All-Star Game. Some great players—some Hall of Famers—were going to get left off. And they were going to be pissed. Some of the committee members, as the choices began to narrow, began to feel uneasy. Virtually all the GMs on the committee had candidates on their own teams.

Rodman, Malone, and Barkley made the cut onto the Sweet Sixteen list. Buck Williams and James Worthy didn't but were still candidates. Roy Tarpley was a strong candidate. But only if they could figure out how to graft a grown-up head onto his body.

Small forward. An even tougher set of decisions. If Bird played, that would leave only one spot. Candidates: Pippen, Mullin, Dominique Wilkins, Bernard King. And you could play Rodman and Barkley at small forward.

Did you go with a slasher, like Dominique, or a shooter, like Mullin? If Bird played, Mullin might be unnecessary. The nicest thing people said about Mullin was that he was the modern Larry Bird. Did that make him expendable—or irresistible?

Like Bird, Mullin was a master of the psychic art of basketball. Rod Thorn thought Mullin had elevated powers of perception: he could see patterns in spatial relationships that most people simply could not. Mullin could gauge variations in speed like a computer and had a remarkable ability to concentrate. Plus, he was largely free of neurosis. And he was a warrior.

Mullin's greatest skill was shooting. At this point, he was a better shooter than Bird. He had better legs, and shooting started with the legs. Mullin had incredible reflexes, mostly because of his mental abilities—like Bird, he "saw the future" and often got a head start. He was a slow runner, though, probably incompatible with a fast-breaking Robinson-Jordan-Malone-Magic unit. But with a half-court unit, like Ewing-Barkley-Stockton-Jordan, he would be deadly.

But did you take Mullin ahead of *Pippen?* Pippen was a better defender, penetrator, rebounder, and runner than Mullin. He wasn't as good a shooter as Mullin but was possibly a better scorer. That would never be known, though, as long as Pippen was on Jordan's team. Walsh loved Pippen's flexibility and thought Pippen could play big forward and small forward, as well as both guard positions. With Pippen's speed and size, Bob Bass thought, he'd be invaluable against classic European-style basketball. The European game was, in Bass's opinion, "very simple: penetrate and pitch. You penetrate in, draw the defense, and pitch it back out for a three." Bass believed that no team could defeat the U.S. inside, but that some team might upset the U.S. by executing a great penetrate-and-pitch game. So Bass wanted to see inside defenders who had the speed to get back out and stop the three. Like Pippen.

Not like Dominique. The committee loved Dominique's scoring but hated his defense. His whole game seemed aimed at making highlight film. His coach, Bob Weiss, had just offered the definitive statement on Dominique's Atlanta team and, by inference, on Dominique himself. Weiss had said, "We're going to be exciting. Of course, so was the *Titanic.*"

Dominique had expanded his game in the '91 season. He'd outrebounded Pippen and Mullin. But he hadn't touched them in assists, steals, or defense. He had the muscles and nervous system of a great defender—hair-trigger reflexes, lateral quickness, and leaping ability. But he didn't have the heart for it. And nobody was going to get onto this team unless his heart ruled his game. The GMs were sick of paying millions of dollars to men who held back. It was understandable that a player would ration his energy and not risk his career diving for loose balls. It was only human. But it was not Olympian.

Bernard King had the heart of an Olympian. Just not the body. His lateral movement had been totaled by knee surgery. Offensively, he was still a freak of nature—28.4 average at age thirty-four. But that wasn't enough to put him on the team.

Only Pippen, Mullin, and Bird made the cut onto the Sweet Sixteen list.

The committee hadn't even gotten to the guards, and the field was crowded as hell. Say they took Magic, Michael, and Larry. That's three. Add Ewing and Robinson. That's five. Add Malone. Add Pippen and Mullin. That's eight. Add Barkley. That's nine. One spot was left. And there was still Stockton, Drexler, Isiah, Joe Dumars, Kevin Johnson, Tim Hardaway, Reggie Miller, and Terry Porter to consider. They would need at *least* one more guard. Maybe two.

Subtract Barkley. Because of the asshole factor. That brought it back to eight.

Subtract Mullin. Assume Bird will cover Mullin's loss. That's seven.

Or leave Mullin—assuming Bird might get hurt during the Games—and subtract Malone. Then, in place of Malone, get Robinson to play big forward alongside Ewing. And pray neither gets injured.

But they had to consider the guards individually first, to see which would fit with the bigger players.

Shooting guard. Jordan was a lock—*if* he played. If he didn't, they'd give it to Drexler. Statistically, you lost very little with Drexler. Compare their '91 stats: Rebounds, 546 (Clyde) to 492 (Michael); Assists, 493 to 453; Steals, 144 to 223; Blocks, 60 to 83; three-point accuracy, .319 to .312. There was a drop-off in flashiness, but if flash was what they'd wanted, they'd have chosen Dominique. Also, Drexler wasn't playing mind games with them, like Jordan was. If they chose him, he would play.

But Jordan was indicating he probably *would* play. So what now? Keep Clyde off because he was too similar to

Jordan? Was having too many Michael Jordan types *really a problem?*

Drexler was certainly versatile. He could fill in at the point and at small forward. He could run, or he could play half-court. And imagine having Drexler and Jordan together in the backcourt. An opposing coach would swallow his fist and go mad.

But Drexler wasn't the outside shooter that Joe Dumars was. Nor could he play point as well as Dumars. Nor could he defend like Dumars. Because of these skills, Dumars might be a much more complementary player to Jordan. Even if Jordan didn't play, maybe they should go with Pippen, Malone, Barkley, and Robinson for penetration and get Dumars, Bird, and Mullin for perimeter shooting.

Dumars would keep his ego in check and set an example. Dumars and Pippen, who'd always been overshadowed by Isiah and Michael, could show the prima donnas how to act. Dumars had a great rep among GMs. Better than Drexler's. A few years ago, Don Nelson had savagely bad-mouthed Drexler, saying he was selfish and wouldn't practice. The tirade had apparently been meant to help Nelson's old buddy Mike Schuler, with whom Drexler had clashed when Schuler had coached Portland. But the put-down had stuck, long after the politics behind it had been forgotten.

Another possibility was to bring in Reggie Miller, who was an incredible outside shooter, and let Clyde take Mullin's place. Donnie Walsh, who'd drafted Miller, thought Reggie was the best perimeter shooter in the league. He argued that for a shooter like Miller, the short international-rules three-pointer would "be a given." But he didn't argue too hard because none of the GMs were hyping their own guys.

They discovered that there was really no way to reach a decision about the shooting guards, though, without looking at them in relation to the point guards.

Magic would be getting most of the minutes at point, barring a disaster. So it would be possible to take Dumars, call him your other point guard, and go with bigger guys, like Drexler, Mullin, and Rodman. Possible, but stupid.

Reason number one: disasters happen. Number two: the whole emphasis of the game had shifted toward guards. If anything, some of the committee members argued, they should go with three point guards, just to be safe. There were some hot ones. Isiah. Kevin Johnson. Hardaway. Porter. Stockton. Even Mark Price, if his leg healed.

With all the egos, it would be vital to have a respected floor general playing at all times.

The obvious choice was Isiah. He was a brilliant tactician, third highest in assists in NBA history. He was a great scorer, averaging just under 20. Tough as a Spartan. He had unearthly mental abilities—and was an elite clutch player. And he was box office.

On the other hand. Michael.

To his credit, Jordan wasn't allowing any of his white-collar bodyguards to publicly campaign against Isiah.

And, to the credit of the committee, the Isiah-Michael rift was never invoked as a legitimate reason to torpedo Isiah.

On the other hand. The rift existed, and anybody who tried to pretend it was inconsequential was either naive or a USA Basketball public relations hack.

Jordan did not like Isiah—never had, never would—and everybody trying to lure Jordan to the Olympics knew that.

Besides, there were legitimate reasons to leave Isiah off. The primary reason: Jordan wasn't the only person who disliked Isiah. Far from it.

A number of superstars disliked him. Not always for the most noble reasons. For years, Isiah had been president of the Players Association, and during his tenure, he'd worked hard for the rank-and-file players, whose gains had often come at the expense of the superstars. Isiah, for example, had strengthened the NBA pension plan, helping the medio-cre players, but costing the superstars millions.

Some of the committee also thought Isiah was too selfish, that he'd be looking to score on a team full of scorers. Piston GM Jack McCloskey didn't think that, but he didn't push his view. He didn't want anyone to think he was promoting his own players. Anyway, despite the rift with Jordan, McCloskey assumed he wouldn't have to push too hard for

Isiah. Thomas had been named to nine consecutive All-Star teams. He had been the MVP of two All-Star games. The MVP of one finals. He'd won two NBA championships. One NCAA championship. That put him six All-Star games, three MVPs, and three championships ahead of his closest rival, John Stockton.

But Stockton had a lot of support. Walsh thought Stockton was the best assist man in the league and also thought Stockton had the patience to sit on the bench while Magic played. But when Stockton did come in, there would be no doubt about who was running the team—Stockton was the only man in history with four 1,000-assist seasons. He was respected. But he was respected as a playmaker, not a scorer—so there wouldn't be any fear of him.

Also, Stockton could shoot the perimeter jumper—which could not be said of Kevin Johnson. K.J. was the fastest and was an excellent scorer. But he was not a pure shooter. Terry Porter was probably the best pure shooter and easily the best three-point shooter. He was also an excellent clutch player: Fourth Quarter Porter. But Porter was not the playmaker that Stockton was, didn't have K.J.'s speed, and didn't have Isiah's fame.

Most unfamous of all—and possibly best of all—was Tim Hardaway. Hardaway had been in a grand total of one All-Star Game in his two-year career. But he was the guard all the GMs wished they had. He was fast as light, a great scorer, a finesse passer, and an ice-hearted competitor. At the University of Texas at El Paso, he'd mastered a crossover dribble—the UTEP two-step—that Magic was in awe of. But there was no way in hell he'd make this team. Didn't have the fame.

So Hardaway got left off the Sweet Sixteen list. Isiah made it. Stockton made it. K.J. made it.

The list was set.

**The Official Unauthorized Selection Committee's
Sweet Sixteen List**

1. David Robinson (center)
2. Pat Ewing (center)

3. Karl Malone (power forward)
4. Charles Barkley (power forward, small forward)
5. Dennis Rodman (power forward, small forward)
6. Larry Bird (small forward)
7. Scottie Pippen (small forward)
8. Chris Mullin (small forward, big guard)
9. Michael Jordan (big guard)
10. Clyde Drexler (big guard)
11. Joe Dumars (big guard)
12. Reggie Miller (big guard)
13. Magic Johnson (point guard)
14. Kevin Johnson (point guard)
15. Isiah Thomas (point guard)
16. John Stockton (point guard)

• Yes or No

Time was flying. The summer was more than half over, and the committee had only cut its candidate list from twenty-five to sixteen. Even that had been a bitch. Now it was time to narrow it to an Elite Eight list and get those eight players on the phone.

But the process of narrowing the list to sixteen had clarified things. As they were preparing to vote on the Elite Eight they realized it wasn't really necessary. There was already virtual consensus.

So they scrapped the vote and went to a simple yea-or-nay system. First, they ruled on the three easy choices: Bird, Magic, and Michael. Unanimous approval. Then the two centers, Ewing and Robinson. Unanimous approval. Then Malone, Barkley, and—the name that had grown in renown during the discussions—Pippen. Malone and Pippen were approved. Not Charles. Asshole factor.

So they covered that ground again. Yes, Charles had abused a fan—but for Christ's sake, it was not a *human being*. It was that obnoxious fan and gifted sadist who had forced the NBA to rewrite its rules to protect players from fans. Also, Charles had spit on a girl. But that had been an *accident*—he'd meant to spit on *someone else*. He'd said losing made him feel like beating his wife. But it was a joke.

They voted again. Charles was in.

They authorized Rod Thorn to make the calls.

When Thorn called, Michael Jordan wanted to know two things. Who was the coach? And what was the time frame? Thorn told Jordan he'd be done by August 9th—almost a month ahead of Jordan's 1984 Olympic schedule.

"Good," Jordan said. "That'll make it easier." He told Thorn he'd call him back within twenty-four hours. Jordan didn't ask who else would be on the team. If he already knew, he offered no hint of his knowledge.

Thorn called Pippen. Pippen, who was hanging around the house with his brother, Carl, was thrilled. He said yes immediately.

Barkley wanted details on the time frame. But he sounded very positive about it.

Thorn began to relax. He'd thought that the pros would play. But he hadn't been sure. So he'd made mental notes on selling points. He was going to point out what a tremendous business opportunity the global exposure would be. And how satisfying it would be to play with the other elite players. And how they would be making history. But the pitch wasn't necessary.

Thorn called the rest of them. Each said yes.

Jordan called back. Yes.

Thorn was elated.

The Official Unauthorized Selection Committee's Elite Eight

1. Michael Jordan
2. Magic Johnson
3. Larry Bird
4. David Robinson

5. Patrick Ewing
6. Scottie Pippen
7. Karl Malone
8. Charles Barkley

Two more spots were now open. Then, in the spring, the last two positions would be filled.

The leading candidates were Isiah, Clyde, Mullin, and Stockton. Rodman was a possibility. So was Dumars. The only other variable candidate was Reggie Miller. Daugherty had an outside chance.

But they didn't really need Daugherty anymore because both Ewing and Robinson had signed on. Same went for Rodman. They had Pippen, who provided most of what Rodman offered at small forward, and they had Malone and Barkley as big forwards.

Reggie Miller was head-to-head against Mullin. It was Isiah vs. Stockton vs. Dumars. And Clyde was . . . out.

It didn't matter that Clyde was the finest athlete still available or the most explosive scorer. He was simply too much like Jordan—and they *finally* had Jordan. If Clyde had possessed a great perimeter shot, like Mullin or Miller, they'd have taken him. Clyde had improved his outside shooting, but he still couldn't touch Mullin or Miller. So he was out.

They decided, though, that Clyde was the leading candidate for one of the two spots they'd fill in the spring. But he'd have to earn it. If he didn't have a great year, they wouldn't take him.

Mullin or Miller? Not such a hard choice, when it finally came down to just the two of them. Miller was maybe a better shooter, maybe not. He had better range, was a significantly better three-point shooter, and was probably the NBA's best free-throw shooter. But Mullin had a more complete game. Owing to his fitness, which was now legendary, he was a blur of action, tipping rebounds, boxing out, making steals, filling the lanes.

They voted again. Mullin won.

That was bad news for Joe Dumars. Dumars had some of

the same traits as Mullin, particularly the completeness of his game. With Mullin on the team, their need for Dumars decreased. They needed more of a pure point guard.

The last decision in a long, difficult process: Isiah or Stockton?

They had already discussed to death their relative merits. And, of course, each of the committee members was all too aware of the Isiah-Michael rift. Michael was already on the team now, but would it be smart to alienate him at this point? Would he feel double-crossed? Would he change his mind?

McCloskey, who'd tried not to push too hard for his own players, argued for Isiah.

But it wasn't going to happen. They took one last vote. Isiah was out.

Thorn called Mullin. He started telling Mullin about the time scheduling, but Mullin wasn't even listening. Mullin cut him off. "Count me in," he said. But even after Thorn hung up, Mullin felt unsure about his status. Thorn had told him not to discuss it with anyone—Mullin was afraid that meant his selection wasn't certain.

Thorn got Stockton on the phone. While Thorn was talking, Stockton put his hand over the receiver and mouthed the word "Olympics" to his wife, Nada. Stockton told Thorn he couldn't answer until he'd talked it over with his wife and two little boys. Fifteen minutes later Stockton called back. He was in.

The team was set. For now.

**The Unauthorized Official
Selection Committee's
Top Ten List**

1. Michael Jordan
2. Magic Johnson
3. Larry Bird
4. David Robinson
5. Pat Ewing
6. Scottie Pippen

7. Karl Malone
8. Charles Barkley
9. Chris Mullin
10. John Stockton

• Isiah's Lament

Klieg lights bounced off the white buttons on Charles Barkley's shirt, making tiny stars that ricocheted around the soundstage. "We oughta make this a whine and cheese party," Barkley said. "Isiah can bring the whine. Hey! Know what I think? Fuck Isiah!" The reporters laughed. Isiah was a joke now. When he'd found out he wasn't on the team, he'd made the mistake of saying how he really felt. In sports, that simply wasn't done.

To hype this show—NBC's September 21st unveiling of the team—Bob Costas had vowed to get to the bottom of the Michael-Isiah controversy. Of course, that was just broadcaster bullshit. There was no way Jordan was going to break down on-camera and start babbling about how he'd tunneled Isiah. But the show had needed hype. The network's original plan had been to build unbearable tension about who'd make the team. But *Newsday*'s Jan Hubbard, basketball's best investigative reporter, had figured out the Top Ten list. Which had totally pissed off NBC. Dick Ebersol, head of NBC Sports, had called up Hubbard and freaked out. NBC had paid $401 million just for Olympic broadcast rights and would spend tens of millions more covering the Games. The network needed Barcelona to be as big as possible. This show could have helped promote it. And it could have been a ratings blockbuster in its own right. If only Hubbard hadn't screwed it up by being a reporter.

Even after Hubbard revealed the team, NBC had begged the players not to say anything. Their silence could preserve at least a little interest in the show. Jordan had taken NBC very seriously. It was a matter of professional courtesy, from one institution to another. At immortality level, you had to operate like that.

But his professional courtesy had bitten him in the ass. When he'd refused to admit that he was on the team, reporters had assumed he wasn't. They'd further assumed it was all because of Isiah. So, despite every effort to conduct his affairs quietly and diplomatically, he was now on the hot seat.

Costas hit Jordan—via remote—with the Isiah question. Jordan replied, "If I had anything to do with the selection, my brother and sister would be going to Barcelona. My relationship with Isiah Thomas had nothing to do with who was on this team. That was blown way out of proportion." Costas looked satisfied.

But Isiah wasn't. When Cliff Brown of *The New York Times* had called him, Isiah had said, "I don't know if Michael's feelings toward me had anything to do with this. Do I believe it? I don't *want* to. I'm disappointed and I'm hurt. I've gone over every incident in the last ten years of my career to try to understand why this happened. I don't understand what the criteria was. No other player has come into the NBA and done what I've done with this franchise." Isiah said he was feeling "an emotion that I've never really felt before."

Isiah had taped a segment for this show. But it hadn't been venomous. So the producers had canned it. Bad video.

After Isiah had gotten left off the team, Piston GM McCloskey had resigned from the Selection Committee. He'd written a resignation letter saying that not having Thomas on the team was "ridiculous, because we are penalizing perhaps the greatest small man ever to play the game." McCloskey had written, "Because of my inability to convince a majority of the committee on the subject, I feel I can no longer contribute."

Bill Laimbeer, infuriated by Isiah's situation, had threatened a court injunction against the selection process. He'd tried to get the Players Association to pay for it. They'd refused, and he'd dropped it. It was exactly what Isiah needed: support from the biggest jerk in basketball.

Chuck Daly had been less inflamed by the issue. "As a Piston," he'd told a reporter, "I'd like to see Isiah Thomas,

Joe Dumars, and Dennis Rodman on the team. But I don't think that's going to be the case."

This was supposed to be Daly's big moment. But he was preoccupied. It was being widely reported that he'd helped sell out Isiah by not pushing for him. And Chuck still needed Isiah.

Isiah wasn't the only player who was angry. Dominique Wilkins had exploded when he'd gotten the news. "It was a total slap in the face for me not to be picked," he'd told a writer in Atlanta. "Nothing against Pippen, but I should have been on that team. They said I shot too much. They said I didn't pass enough. But I *did* something about that. I incorporated everything in one year."

The lights went dead. The show was over. Without the lights, the Seacaucus, New Jersey, studio looked painfully drab. The NBC executives seemed to be disappointed. Last summer, they'd had high hopes for this show. But it had been a dud. No suspense. As the players walked upstairs to meet with the print media, the NBC guys began bumming rides from each other, anxious to get back through the Lincoln Tunnel to their idea of civilization. One of them murmured, "At least Michael came through." Meaning, he'd kept his mouth shut about being on the team.

The sense of anticlimax carried over upstairs. Only Pippen, Mullin, Barkley, and Ewing had attended the show, and none of them said anything worth quoting. It was mostly just rah-rah Uncle Sam stuff that didn't even interest the people who were saying it. The only good laugh came when Dave Gavitt said he hadn't pressured Bird to play.

The next day, Magic issued a press release. It said, "I am very disappointed that Isiah Thomas was not selected to represent Team USA in Barcelona. Isiah is truly one of the most exciting players in the game today." It was a ringing endorsement. Total support.

And right on time: two months late.

But Michael Jordan was on the team. The golden boys were together—all on one team.

Anyway, there would be time for Magic to patch up his friendship with Isiah. All the time in the world.

5

Immortality

Clyde's Lament • Charles's Ultimatum •
Patrick to City: Drop Dead • The Toll of the
Sexual Carnival • Best Friends •
Welcome to Hell • "Are You Scared?"

> Real are the dreams of gods,
> And smoothly pass their pleasures
> In a long immortal dream.
> —John Keats

> The saddest thing in life
> Is that the best thing in it should be courage.
> —Robert Frost, 1947

> It ain't over when it's over.
> —Bob Rich
> Dewar's Profile, 1992

Michael Jordan was ripping through the big-money suburb
of Deerfield, Illinois, in one of his hot cars after practice.
Jordan loved to drive. Loved to speed too. Needless to say,
he got pulled over once in a while. Chicago cops could be
nasty about black guys in expensive cars, especially in the
slums around Chicago Stadium (Isiah's old neighborhood).
In that area, some of the police precincts had long employed
a program of systematic torture of prisoners, including

near-suffocation with plastic bags, and electric shock to the ears and genitals. Amnesty International and a panel of police investigators had traced the torture back at least twenty years. It was no threat to Michael, though. It was part of an America Jordan didn't have to deal with. Jordan didn't even get traffic tickets. When the cops saw who it was, they'd drool all over themselves. If he gave them a couple of Bulls tickets, they'd purr like cats. It was good to be the king.

And good to live on the North Shore too. It was beautiful this time of year. The basketball season was just a few days old, and the maples around the mansions were already turning the colors of sunset. Jordan was vastly relieved the season had begun. The games would give the media something to talk about other than what an asshole he was.

First, they'd blamed Isiah's Olympic exclusion on him. Said he was into a vindictive power trip. Now he was touchy as hell about the subject. He'd just hosted *Saturday Night Live,* and that had been the one topic he wouldn't let them write jokes about. Then, after that lost news value, Jordan blew off a White House invitation, and the press freaked out again—as if George Bush wasn't just another manipulator angling for a photo-op. A *Sun-Times* guy had called it "the most disturbing, irresponsible, irrational thing Jordan has ever done in public life." During the furor, Horace Grant, Scottie's buddy, had chimed in about how it just showed what a prima donna Jordan was. Didn't matter that Bird had done exactly the same thing a few years ago, saying that the President knew where to find him. Jordan was Instant Asshole, and he couldn't figure out why. What did people *want?*

Thank God they'd bought his story about needing time with his family. If they'd found out he'd been at a Hilton Head golf orgy—where he'd "loaned" $57,000 to a golfing pal who was a convicted drug dealer—they'd have had a *major* tantrum.

Jordan was confused, unhappy. At immortality level, where image was everything, this was the worst kind of problem you could have.

The car phone rang. It was Lon Rosen, Magic's agent. Magic had an urgent message.

As soon as Jordan got Magic on the phone, Magic blurted out the news. Jordan's car swerved hard to the right. It almost went off the shoulder.

Life sucked.

Clyde was pissed. He'd tried to bury his pain about not making the Olympic team, but he couldn't. He was standing around the locker room after one of Portland's first games, talking to a couple of friends and a couple of reporters.

"How can they say it's the best possible team without me and Isiah on it?" Drexler said, his face alternately hot-eyed angry and sad as a hurt kid's. "It's *political*. That's why Isiah didn't make it."

Clyde's teammate Buck Williams agreed. He thought politics had killed Clyde's chances. Don Nelson's trashing of Clyde had done him in. "That's the only reason for him being left off the team," Williams said.

Clyde was, as usual, quiet and careful. But, by Clyde's standards, he was pretty bent out of shape. "Nobody likes Isiah," Clyde said softly. "But he should *definitely* have made it. I'll be the first one to say that he's an assho—" Drexler stopped, glanced at the reporters. ". . . That he's objectionable sometimes, but he's a nine-time All-Star. And he has the two *rings*."

"But Clyde," said one of the reporters, "you've never won a championship. Why should you use that as a yardstick?"

Drexler allowed the rebuke. He had only a small-market level of arrogance; he was used to being treated like God, but only a few times a day.

"Why should *Pippen* be on it?" Clyde countered. "I do everything better than Pippen. Rebound, pass, shoot. Pippen just had a couple of good months at the end of the season. I'd take *McHale* over Pippen. Or Worthy. And Mullin? They pick him as a *guard?* He hasn't been a guard in five years."

"He's a good outside shooter."

"I'm a good outside shooter."

Clyde began rating the point guards, in order: Magic, Isiah, K.J., Stockton, Hardaway. "You know," said Clyde, "I might even take Isiah as number one."

The whole group, almost simultaneously, said, "Bullshit!"

"Okay, Magic's number one," said Clyde. "But after Magic, it's Isiah, hands-down. Who else can do what he can do? He scores points, he does whatever it takes."

"Know who I like?" said one of the reporters. "Hardaway. At this point, he's better than Isiah."

"Are you kidding me, man?" said Clyde. He turned to one of his buddies. "Who'd you take?"

"Hardaway. For the crossover dribble."

"That *is* a monster move," said Clyde, "but I like K.J. after Isiah. Stockton, I put fourth."

"You know why I heard you didn't get picked, Clyde?" said one of the reporters. "'Cause you're too much like Jordan. They didn't want guys who were too much alike."

"Ewing and Robinson? They're not alike?" said Clyde.

The reporter shrugged. "It was you or Jordan."

"Me or Jordan. Me *or* Jordan? Why *or?* Why not both?" Clyde was deflating. "They should have let the players choose," he said. "That's the only way to keep politics out. But you know why they didn't let the guys choose? They didn't want to lose control. That's why I don't even want to think about it. It's just one more thing I can't control."

Drexler looked miserable—as if he had the worst kind of problem a person could have.

Charles Barkley was also disconsolate. He'd marched into 76er owner Harold Katz's office ranting and raving. He'd accused Katz of being a fool for letting go of Bruise Brother Rick Mahorn, while keeping weak, little girly-man Charles Shackleford. He'd bitched about Johnny Dawkins being rushed back from knee surgery. He'd even charged Katz with racism, saying Katz had kept Dave Hoppen on the team just because Hoppen was white. Barkley wanted *changes,* and he wanted them now. Or he wanted out—fast as possible. He felt out of control in Philly, and control was vital to the superstars. Being able to control themselves and others was what set them apart.

But the shrewd Katz, who'd built the Nutri-System empire, just listened and nodded. Barkley felt helpless. What in hell did you have to *do* to get traded around here? Beat somebody up?

Pat Ewing had the same problem—he'd spent half the summer trying to get traded. He wanted more money. He was only taking in $3.1 million and wasn't making much from endorsements because of his mortician's personality. The Knicks had talked to Golden State about trading him for Mullin, but it hadn't happened. Instead, Golden State had traded Mitch Richmond to Sacramento for the bigger Billy Owens. Terrible fate for Richmond. When he'd arrived in Sacramento, Spud Webb had told Richmond, "Welcome to hell."

So now Ewing was stuck in New York, with half the city pissed off at him. He'd violated the warrior's ethic, and New Yorkers were slow to forgive.

It was an ugly way to start the Olympic year. Barkley and Ewing were supposed to look like heroes: America's team. Instead, they looked like assholes.

But nobody in the league looked worse than Roy Tarpley, who had the talent, but not the mind or heart, to be an Olympian. Tarpley—body by Fisher, mind by Fisher-Price—had traded $8.45 million for the chance to get loaded. He'd blown the league's strict drug policy and was out for life. Now he'd be lucky to land a thousand a month in the Continental Basketball Association. Tarpley's teammates were furious because many of them would probably get shipped out in a rebuilding effort. Rolando Blackman had said, "Nobody is safe now."

Even Chuck Daly wasn't safe. He'd been afraid his prima donnas would blame him for not making the Olympic team. He was right. Now they were yammering, "Chuck's preoccupied with Barcelona." What transparent bullshit! If Daly was preoccupied with anything, it was employment. The franchise had already brought in his heir apparent—Ron

Rothstein, who'd been given $100,000 to do an announcing job that Dick Harter had done the prior year for $800 per game. Now everywhere Daly went, there was Rothstein, looking over his shoulder.

The season had barely begun, and there were shattered psyches all around the league. Life sucked.

Jordan regained control of his car. Steadied himself. He told himself it was a joke. For just a moment, he believed it was.

But it wasn't. Magic had the human immunodeficiency virus.

Jordan didn't know what to say. He was very quiet. He asked Magic what he should do.

"Live on," said Magic. "I'm going to be as positive as I can. I want you to be as positive as you can."

Jordan told Magic he loved him.

• How Do You Tell Your Wife?

It had started with Magic's quest for immortality-level money. Magic was only making $2.4 million in salary for the 1991–1992 season, and that was . . . embarrassing. It undercut his ability to be taken seriously by corporate America. Two-five was the kind of money a Wayman Tisdale or Pervis Ellison made. It was less than anybody else on the Olympic team, other than Stockton and Malone, who played somewhere out in the badlands. With Sam Perkins making $3.2, Magic wasn't even top dog on his own team.

So Magic and Lon Rosen had gone to owner Jerry Buss and GM Jerry West and raised a stink. Dr. Buss, to elude salary-cap restrictions, had agreed to fork over a quick $3 million, no-interest "loan." To safeguard the loan, Magic would take out an extra insurance policy, which required a physical.

Magic was in Utah for a preseason game when the results from the physical came back.

Laker team doctor Michael Melman called. "I need to see you in my office," he said. "Today."

Magic flew back to L.A. and drove to Melman's office with Lon Rosen. Magic wasn't worried. Mostly just curious. The flu symptoms he'd had in France were gone. He and Rosen talked about what the problem might be. High blood pressure, maybe. Magic's dad had high blood pressure.

As soon as they got to the doctor's office, Melman told Magic to sit down. Melman said, "Earvin, I have your test results. You're HIV-positive. You have the AIDS virus." Magic felt nauseous, short of breath. Melman quickly told Magic he didn't have AIDS. Magic, numb, was thinking about his wife, Cookie, and the baby she was carrying. And he was thinking that his life was over. But he said, "Tests can be wrong. Can't they?"

Melman told him they would run more tests. He told him Cookie should be tested immediately.

Magic went straight home to tell his wife. To get it over with. But she'd thought he was still in Utah and had gone out with friends. She didn't get home until late. When she arrived, he told her directly and explicitly. He told her she needed to be tested. She was stunned and hurt. He told her he would understand if she left him, and wouldn't try to stop her if she wanted a divorce. She slapped him; she told him he was crazy.

Over the next twelve days, he underwent a definitive battery of tests, and Cookie was tested. Her test was negative, which indicated the baby was also negative. She hadn't developed antibodies to the virus. But there was still a chance the virus was in her bloodstream.

On November 6, twelve days after the initial diagnosis, Melman and another doctor, David Ho, came to Magic's house. With Cookie sitting beside him, Magic listened as they confirmed the diagnosis. They told him he should give up pro basketball, because of its stress on his immune system.

"Okay," Magic said, "that's it. I'll deal with it."

Thus far, the only people he'd discussed it with—other

than Buss and West, who'd heard it from Dr. Melman—
were his parents. Now he had to call his friends.

The first person he thought of was Isiah Thomas. The chill
that had settled into their relationship was instantly forgotten. Magic needed a friend.

Thomas was taping a show about children with AIDS
when Lon Rosen called. Rosen told Isiah to stand by for a
conference call with Magic and mutual friend Mark
Aguirre. Magic conveyed his news. Isiah was horrified. He
didn't want to believe it. Any possible anger he might have
felt over the Olympics was instantly forgotten. He offered
support. But what could he do?

Over the next twelve hours, Magic called Larry Bird,
Arsenio Hall, Pat Riley, and Michael Jordan. He also called
Laker coach Mike Dunleavy and scheduled a team meeting
for early the following afternoon. The news began to circu-
late around the NBA, slowly at first, then with geometric
swiftness.

The initial reaction was fear. For a simple reason. "A lot
of the guys," said a close acquaintance of one of the first
people Magic called, "had been screwing the same women."

The sexual carnival that engulfed the players was of
startling dimensions. It was made up of several types of
women and more than a few men—though the homosexuality was generally well hidden.

Not all the women who were involved with players were
promiscuous. Many were simply young women who were,
quite naturally, attracted to the children of the gods. Some
of these women were misled and manipulated, while others
were less naive about the possibilities of long-lasting romance.

Some ended up marrying players, and a large number of
the marriages were stable and happy. The atmosphere of
hypersexuality surrounding the league often obscured the
fact that the majority of players didn't screw around. The
extraordinary men in the NBA often attracted extraordinary women, who were valued and respected.

But there were also hundreds of groupies, or "freaks,"

available to players. Because these women were so visible, and in such wide circulation, it often seemed as if there were more than there really were. Also available were fringe-level actresses, models, and entertainers. These women often hoped to marry a player—or at least have one's baby. Many believed, falsely, that having a player's baby was a path to financial security. Mark Aguirre, Isiah Thomas, and Dominique Wilkins—among many other players—had been unsuccessfully sued for paternity. Magic had an out-of-wedlock child, ten-year-old Andre Mitchell, (the son of Melissa Mitchell of Lansing, Michigan), whom he acknowledged and embraced.

Some NBA players—particularly the very attractive ones and the superstars—also dated women who were exceptionally beautiful and charming, and successful in their own careers.

Magic, it appeared, was involved with all of these types of women. His sexual appetite was voracious, often involving several women in one evening. He had a condo near the Forum. Party central. After a game, he'd often go there with women. It was reported that he would indicate to a factotum at the Forum that he wanted "a deuce" (two women), or "a rainbow" (three women of different races). These women were supposedly selected from the group waiting outside the players' entrance. It was estimated that he had sex with as many as five hundred women per year.

"Earvin was a notorious womanizer," said Pam McGee, of the U.S. women's basketball team. "He had one-night stands with freaks all across America for the past twelve years." Magic sometimes seemed to regard women as just another measure of his status, remarking, "I was the one most NBA players looked up to when it came to women. I lived the kind of social life that most guys in the league wanted to lead."

Circumspect about picking up women in public, Magic preferred to have someone else contract them, or he telephoned them from a voluminous book of names and numbers. On many occasions, though, he did meet women in restaurants and nightclubs, and at social events.

Parties at his Bel Air home also offered a venue for casual sex. These parties, often attended by teammates, other players, and Hollywood celebrities, usually featured large numbers of beautiful women. At one of these parties, six of the women present reportedly had sex with Magic. At another, he and ten buddies disappeared with twenty women.

He seemed unconcerned about sexually transmitted diseases. He reportedly thought he was safe if the women he was with had not slept with gay men or used intravenous drugs. He had said that he did not generally use condoms.

But when Magic had gotten married in September, he'd told friends he was no longer interested in promiscuity.

His interests had matured. At thirty-two, his concerns were his wife, the baby that was on the way, engineering a graceful end to his playing career, and amassing the immortality-level fortune that would enable him to buy a basketball franchise.

But by then, of course, it was too late.

• Telling the World

"Get out the way! Get out the way!" A pudgy security guard cleared a path for Magic as they made their way through a spillover crowd of reporters. The guard's face was fierce, and he had tears in his eyes. The security and maintenance people at the Forum loved Magic. He knew their names. He knew their wives' names. None of the other players did.

Magic stepped up to a podium. His eyes were still red from the team meeting. He'd begun the meeting with his trademark smile. Byron Scott had thought Magic looked just like the joyous warrior Scott had seen almost every day of the past nine years. But Magic had quickly told them he had HIV, and every one of them had begun to cry. That made Magic cry. It was the first time he'd lost control since he'd found out.

Magic, in a dark suit and flashy silk tie, stepped up to the microphone. At the table with him were Cookie, Kareem, West, Buss, David Stern, player Larry Drew, and Dr. Melman.

"First of all," he said, "lemme say good afternoon, good late afternoon." He paused. "Because of, um, the HIV virus that I have obtained, I will have to retire from the Lakers. Today. I just want to make clear, first of all, that I do not have the AIDS disease. I know a lot of you wanna know that. My wife is fine, so no problem with her. I plan to go on livin' for a long time, buggin' you guys like I always have. I hope to be with the Lakers and the league, and hopefully David'll have me around." He glanced at Stern.

"I guess now I get to enjoy some of the other sides of living, that because of the season . . ." He didn't finish his thought. "I'm gonna miss playin'. But I'm gonna become a spokesman for the virus. Because I want young people to realize they can practice safe sex. Sometimes you're a little naive and think it could never happen to you. But I'm gonna deal with it, and my life will go on. I'll be here. I'm gonna be a happy man. I'll miss the battles and the wars, but life goes on."

He was finished. Somebody shouted, "How do you deal with mortality?"

"I always wanted to live a normal life," Magic said. "Life will change. Hopefully, I'll still own a team. I'm gonna miss comin' in at five o'clock and seein' the security people and the ushers. Then I get to see most of you about six o'clock. I'll miss that. But most of all I'll miss the camaraderie of the guys, bein' one of the fellas."

"What about the Olympic team?"

No response.

"Are you scared?"

"No. It's another challenge. It's like your back is against the wall. I'll come out swingin'. If I'm down, it might be over. I've never been like that.

"Now, I'm gonna go and let you talk to the doctors. I've appreciated *all* of you"—he swept his hand to encompass the whole room. "We go way back. Now, you may be interviewin' me in Dr. Buss's office. Soon as he moves out, I may move in.

"I'm gonna *beat* it. I'm gonna have fun. So thank you again. And I'll see you soon."

He began to leave. First one person stood, then everyone was standing, and then the reporters began to applaud.

Reporters never applaud.

The next evening, Donnie Walsh of the Olympic selection committee was in Portland. He'd just watched Clyde kill his Pacers. Walsh didn't know what the committee would do about Magic. "The eventuality is that you have to replace him," said Walsh. "There are very strict guidelines as to who goes to the Olympics."

A major problem was replacing Magic's versatility. "Because he can play two or three positions, we'll probably have to use two players to replace him. Obviously, a point guard will be one of the players. It may be Isiah." The other player, Walsh said, would probably be a shooting guard or small forward. The obvious candidate was Drexler. Even if Magic somehow managed to stay on the team, they couldn't assume he'd play much.

In the Portland locker room, Drexler was still shiny with sweat. The reporters around him weren't interested in the game. They were interested in Magic.

One of the reporters asked Clyde, "Is this something that's going to happen to other ballplayers in the next couple of years?"

"We don't know," he said. He was even more quiet than usual. "It could happen to anybody at any time. That's what Magic said in his press conference." Clyde's face was grim, his eyes darting and distracted.

"I think you have to . . . I think I really, uh, I think it really helped us. And . . . I'm sorry. What was the question?"

Clyde Drexler had probably just made the Olympic team. Now he could be an immortal.

6

Chris Mullin's Courageous Battle Against White Man's Disease

Dying Young • The Most Famous Alcoholic
in Sports • Pride & Passion • Mork & Mindy •
Chris Mullin Pukes on His Shoes •
Donn Nelson and the Evil Empire •
Mr. Hardaway's Neighborhood

Until you can get into the present, you can't control it. If you ever make that breakthrough, you'll know it. It'll be like you had a player piano, and it's playing a mile a minute, with all the keys sinking in front of you in fantastic chords. You never heard the song before, but you are so far into the moment, your hands start going along with it exactly. Then you start controlling the piano.

—Tom Wolfe
The Electric Kool-Aid Acid Test, 1968

How many a father have I seen,
A sober man among his boys,
whose youth was full of foolish noise.
—Alfred, Lord Tennyson, 1880

"Mullin's in his comfort zone! Dribbles to the top of the key. Checks the shot clock. Goes to his left! Fakes. Goes right. Four on the clock. Shoots! High arching rainbow.

It's . . . off. It's *off!* Doesn't hit *shit!* Mullin can't believe it. Tolbert rebounds. Mullin's *still* shakin' his head."

"Do my play-by-play," said Tom Tolbert.

"Do your own," said Mullin.

But Tolbert was too busy to narrate. He'd beaten Mullin at one-on-one twice the day before yesterday, and now Mullin was out for blood. He hated to lose. Even to Bobcat Tolbert. Tolbert rushed in, pulled up, shot.

"It's off! Mullin, big rebound. Brutal! He backs. He backs. Tough shot! Shiiiit!" Mullin's exclamation started as a falsetto and ended deep in his belly. His gym-bleached face, the color of skim milk, was caught between a grin and a snarl.

Mullin grabbed the ball, froze for a second, and then whipped by Tolbert before Tolbert could move. Tolbert lost. Again. But Tolbert didn't feel bad. He thought Mullin was superhuman. In fact, he had a mythic reference for Mullin. Mullin was Mork from the old *Mork and Mindy* show, where Mork has a special watch that makes everybody else move in slow motion, while Mork moves at regular speed. How else could you explain Mullin?

"Every night," Tolbert says, "I'll watch how slow he goes, *but nobody ever blocks his shot.* He'll be going through, like, mud and molasses, and he'll lay it up and everybody will be just *standing* there. And I'm thinking to myself, 'If *I* did that, I'd get my shot thrown back to half-court, and somebody would step on my face while they ran back to dunk it.'"

Part of Mullin's secret—his Mork power—was an almost surreal psychic ability to anticipate. It was the same rare mental faculty that the also "slow" Larry Bird had, and it was part of the reason Bird and Mullin were often compared. But the other part of Mullin's secret was just plain fitness. His quick first step began with a thousand-mile journey on the StairMaster.

Mullin had only one weakness: a severe case of white man's disease. He was slow, mechanical, and unable to leap. Theoretically, it was racist to say that the black man's body—in general—was better suited to basketball than the white man's. That was supposed to imply that white players worked, while black players were just lucky—as if anybody could luck his way into the NBA. However, according to many anthropologists, including Dr. Edward Hunt, Jr., there are subtle but distinct physical differences in black bodies that make them superior for certain activities, including sprinting and jumping. In general, says Dr. Hunt, blacks have more tendon and less muscle fiber than whites, as well as less subcutaneous fat. Also, he says, blacks tend to have a variation in the structures of their heels that gives them increased leverage for jumping. In addition, Hunt and others claim there are differences between whites and blacks in the proportionate lengths of arms and legs, the density of bones, and the size of hips.

Black people, in general, tend to be more lithe and graceful. To pretend otherwise is as smart as saying Orientals aren't generally short. There are ten million exceptions, but it's still true. Larry Bird has said, "I consider basketball a black man's game. I just try to fit in." Bird was absolutely right, and not remotely racist.

Bird, though—and Mullin, too—had compensated for white man's disease with thousands of miles on the StairMaster. And that was where Mullin was headed now. After half an hour of that, he'd do some weight work—power cleans and explosive squats, aimed at increasing his feeble jumping ability. Then to the Exercycle. Then hot tub. Cold tub. Hot tub. Cold tub. Shower. He didn't want to overdo it. He'd already put in a full practice, and he had a game tonight. But he was addicted.

"We've already determined," Mullin says, "that I'm an addictive personality."

Right now, the compulsive exercising was helping him deal with Magic's illness. The whole league, including Mullin, was still in shock, even though it had been a couple of weeks since the announcement.

The announcement had hit the players harder than anyone could have anticipated. But it was easy to understand. All the players, to some extent, felt invulnerable and immortal. For good reason—their bodies were perfect and pulsing with life, and they were powerful, adored, and wealthy. They were children of the gods, golden boys. But Magic's illness had shattered the myth of their immortality. Magic would die, and so would they.

That same chilling recognition was sweeping the globe. Magic's announcement had had a worldwide impact. For almost a week, it had dominated international news. It was even being widely equated with the JFK assassination. On the surface, it seemed an absurd equation. But the two men had shared one important trait: they were the embodiment of mythic immortality because of their youth, glamour, and heroism.

When both had proven vulnerable, it had mocked the myth of immortality. And reminded people everywhere of their own impending deaths.

When Mullin had first heard about Magic, in an elevator in Milwaukee, he hadn't really believed it. He'd kept thinking Magic was just injured, that he'd blown out a knee or something. The idea of Magic having the AIDS virus was incomprehensible. Then, after he'd realized Magic did have HIV, he'd wondered what it would be like to play against him. He couldn't accept that Magic was out of the NBA forever.

These days, Mullin would sometimes be driving his car, or getting ready for practice, and he'd think of Magic. When that happened, he'd just breathe out a soft "Damn!" and try to think of something else. It killed him to think about Magic. It made him think about his dad.

• The Slow White Zen Master

That night Chris Mullin was the first person on the floor, as usual. The Oakland Coliseum was cold and empty. A few minutes later, Sarunas Marciulionis walked out of the locker room with Warrior assistant coach Donn Nelson (head coach Don Nelson's son) and started shooting with Mullin.

Donn Nelson took a seat in the stands and watched them.

Nelson had a special relationship with Marciulionis—so special that Donny had been made a coach of Marciulionis's Lithuanian Olympic team. It was now official and irrevocable—the Soviet Union was dead and would not send a team to Barcelona. Instead, the former republics, including Lithuania, would send their own teams, and Russia would send a "Unified Team." Marciulionis was thrilled. He hated the Soviets. In 1988 the Soviets had promised to let Sarunas and the other players go pro if they won the Seoul Olympics. But when they had won—holding off the hyperemotional Yugoslavians—the government had reneged. Then Gorbachev had tried to give Marciulionis to Ted Turner's Atlanta Hawks, to pay back Turner for financing the Goodwill Games. But Sarunas, who had become friends with Donny in 1985—when Nelson was touring Europe with Athletes in Action—had resisted. He'd wanted to play for Golden State—specifically, for Donny's father.

Sarunas had become a Nellie fan at the 1987 McDonald's Open, which had been played in Milwaukee. Nellie had just been politicked out of his Milwaukee coaching job, and at the Open the management had stuck him up in the cheap seats. But the fans had spotted him and given him a standing ovation, and it had made a big impression on Sarunas.

Besides, Donny was the only American who'd been willing to risk being Sarunas's friend back then. Donny had come to Lithuania and been spied on and harassed by the KGB. Donny had been there the night Sarunas had shown an underground videotape of the uprising in Soviet Georgia. It had been horrific. The Soviet army's black berets had slaughtered people in the streets with sharpened spades— they'd chopped them in the necks, hitting some so hard it had cut their heads off. Just watching the videotape had been a dangerous crime.

To pressure Sarunas, the KGB had threatened to send his entire family to Siberia, and the secret police had a full-time spy following him. And even that was pale compared to an athlete's life before glasnost. Back then, even the biggest stars, like gymnast Olga Korbut, had been virtual prisoners, barred from travel. Nadia Comaneci had been oppressed so unmercifully by the Romanian government that she'd tried to kill herself by drinking bleach. Some athletes had been forced into medical experiments, receiving steroids twice as powerful as those taken by Canadian sprinter Ben Johnson. Kids as young as fourteen had been given neural hormones to change their brain biochemistries.

But Donny had stuck with Sarunas. Nelson and Soviet chess master Gary Kasparov had orchestrated the media blitz that had finally forced the Soviets to let their player go.

Over the past few months, as the Soviet Union had resisted dissolution, the Soviet black berets had invaded Lithuania. Sarunas, now making $1.2 million, had spent most of his fortune building a basketball complex in Lithuania, and the Soviets had seized it. In one day, Sarunas had lost everything. But then the Soviet Union had died, and Sarunas had told Nelson, "Donny, I feel like Jesus Christ—raised from the dead." So now Marciulionis was looking forward to kicking some "Unified Team" ass, side-by-side with Donny, his comrade-in-arms. Donny was thrilled about it. His dad may have gotten aced out by Chuck Daly, but at least there'd be one Nelson at the Games.

Warrior conditioning coach Mark Grabow, a former pro soccer player who supervised Mullin's fitness program, joined Nelson in the stands. Mullin and Marciulionis were still the only players on the floor, even though the game against Utah was only two hours away. Grabow wasn't surprised that Mullin and Marciulionis were out there alone. They shared the trait of passion. Grabow believed that, "What separates great people is passion. Walter Payton has it, and so do Magic Johnson, Jimmy Connors, and Chris Mullin."

Grabow watched Mullin with palpable pleasure. "Chris *loves* to play basketball," said Grabow. "If he was making three million dollars a year or three thousand, it wouldn't make any difference. The day he retires, he'll be in the backyard playing hoops with his brothers."

Grabow considered Mullin an artist. "The basketball floor is his canvas," he said. "And like other artists, like painters or piano players, he perceives things in a unique way. To guys like Chris, Wayne Gretzky, or Joe Montana, things seem to move a little slower. They see things a little earlier. It's something you can't quantify. There are just certain people who can feel without being touched."

"That's right," said Nelson. "I see him go into a certain mental zone and he just *locks in*. You can see it when he steps up to the free throw line. Doesn't matter what's going on around him—it's just him and the basket. Guys like Magic, Michael, Larry, and Chris, they've got this upper-echelon level of thought that they kick into. They *thrive* on it. They develop a *taste* for it. You're born with that."

"But it doesn't mean anything without drive," said Grabow. "You'll find people who are very talented but not motivated. Chris had to *learn* motivation. He learned it from his . . ."

"From his dad," said Nelson, finishing the thought.

• The Oakland Warriors

Don Nelson's face was white and red and purple at the same time as he paced the sidelines during the Utah game. He'd plowed his hand through his straw hair so many times that it looked like knives stuck into his head. "Aren't you *watching* him?" Nelson yelled at referee Jake O'Donnell. Karl Malone had just crashed his elbow into Mullin's chest for about the third time.

"I'm watching the ball," O'Donnell shouted. "I can't watch the ball *and* watch him."

But Mullin looked as if he hadn't even noticed the elbows. His eyes were caught in a half-trance, and he shuffled rhythmically while Hardaway dribbled and waited. Stockton put his hand on Hardaway's hip; Hardaway shoved it off, waited, dribbled between his legs. Mullin darted toward the basket. But Mark Eaton and Malone stepped together: a 546-pound wall of meat and bone. Mullin bounced off it. He looked stunned. Walked to the perimeter. Glanced at

Hardaway. Caught the line-drive pass his eyes had asked for. Stepped behind the three-point line, looked down, shot. Perfect.

Mullin had added the three-pointer to his repertoire in 1990, improving his percentage that year from .230 to .372. The prior year, he'd increased his shot blocking by almost fifty percent. The year before that, he'd increased his rebounding from 205 to 483. Opposing teams constantly adjusted to each player's strengths, and those who didn't modify their games every summer never became superstars. But adding something took gut-wrenching labor. Players like Mullin and Bird worked as hard in the summer as they did during the season. But that wasn't a problem for Mullin. His father had taught him to work.

All night long, Mullin was in perpetual motion, working for shots, screening, blocking out, tipping rebounds, making steals. Like the other Olympians, whose versatility had put them on the team, Mullin did a little of everything. But unlike most of them, Mullin's skill didn't stem from his body's grace. It existed in spite of his body. And that was fine with the Oakland fans, because it made him easier to identify with. Mullin was a working-class hero—the perfect image for industrial Oakland. In Oakland, even the front-row seats were occupied by real people—instead of the usual corporate drones out schmoozing on their companies' season tickets. And these folks were crazy about Mullin. The cheap seats, though, were filled with Hardaway fans. The kids up there lived in the surrounding district of warehouses and crack houses, and they knew Timmy had come from a similar mean-punk, mean-cop neighborhood in Chicago. Mullin and Hardaway brought pride to poor ugly Oakland, one of only two teams in the NBA so ashamed of its hometown that it had adopted its state's name (the other was the New Jersey Nets).

End of the game. Two-point game. Crucial game too. Golden State was starting a long home stand and had a chance to take a big lead in the standings. Mullin was at the three-point line. Hardaway charged toward the hoop. Flipped the ball backward to Mullin. Mullin felt an absolute

lack of emotion. He had no fear of missing it and anticipated no joy from making it. Whatever happened wouldn't
change his self-image even slightly. He felt alone in the gym,
untroubled, unobserved—totally into the moment. The
shot went up. In. Mullin's face stayed frozen.

"Be a fah-thuh to ya chiiild!" A Warrior's girlfriend had
just gotten pregnant, and now the player was playing the rap
song "Be a Father to Your Child" over and over as the locker
room began to clear of reporters looking for postgame
quotes. The player had already spoken to Mullin about the
situation, and Mullin's advice had been simple: get married.
Marriage was on Mullin's mind. Ten days ago, he'd married
his college sweetheart, Liz Connolly.

Mullin and Hardaway lingered after the other players had
left. Hardaway had his left leg in a big orange Gatorade
barrel filled with ice water. Mullin had both his legs in one.

A reporter from one of the smaller Bay Area papers was
taking Mullin to task for missing two of his seven free
throws. It was the only flaw in an otherwise superb game: 34
points, 10 rebounds, 6 assists, and 2 steals in forty-four
minutes.

"Why isn't Chris Mullin shooting free throws like Chris
Mullin did in CYO?"

"Sheese!" Mullin remembered his stats from church
league, but had no idea anyone else did. "That was when?—
1980? I shot about eighty-five percent, and I'm at eighty
percent so far this year. I guess the answer is, I haven't been
fouled all summer."

Guy wouldn't drop it. "In the third quarter you missed
two free throws—did that kind of epitomize what's going
on?"

"I look at the positive," said Mullin. "I look at the nice
three-pointer. If I looked at the misses"—Mullin smiled—
"I'd be a miserable fuck, like you."

Mullin's smile was warm and genuine. The writer basked
in it. He didn't even seem to notice he'd been called a
miserable fuck.

* * *

Mullin let me come into the training room to talk about the Olympics. That was a big deal. Writers aren't allowed in NBA training rooms. When writers approached Bill Laimbeer on even the training table in the locker room—a writers-allowed zone—he'd make them take a baby-step backward, to stay out of his "training space." About half the players in the league hated writers. And vice versa.

Mullin, neck-deep in an oversize redwood hot tub, recalled the '84 Olympics. *"Lot* more pressure," he said. "A whole summer of pressure. At the tryouts, they cut from seventy, to fifty, to thirty, to twelve. I was sure that would be my only chance to make the Olympics.

"Compared to that, this was easy. Either they picked you or they didn't. I couldn't control it, so I didn't even think about it. I thought I had a chance, but I thought about thirty other people had a chance. But I wouldn't-a been bitter if they hadn't chose me."

"Do you care if you start?"

"Nah."

"But you're so competitive. I'd think you'd wanna be MVP."

"That's the great thing about the Olympics—there's no MVP. No All-Tournament Team, no nothing. You win gold or you don't. So you're gonna see great players playing roles."

"I doubt it. Can you see Charles or Michael playing a role?"

"Oh, absolutely. That's why they're great. In 'eighty-four Michael was our best player, but he did everything just like everybody else. In 'eighty-four you'd have thought we'd been playing together for four years. That's the neat part, seeing guys put down everything for one common goal."

"Do you feel more pressure now that it looks like Magic is off the team?"

He shook his head. Water flipped sideways. "There's too many good players. If *all twelve* of us got hurt, twelve more guys could step in and do just as good. Anyway, I'm not sure Magic won't play. I hear he might."

"Hear from who?"

"Well, from Magic. He's talkin' to people about it. And when Magic talks, people listen." He popped out of the hot tub and jumped into a tub of ice water. "Ahhh!" He started to shiver while sweat still dripped off his face.

"So what's this mean to you—making the Olympics? More money? An ego thrill?"

"Oh, that's easy, man. It's the *payoff.*"

"Payoff for what?"

He looked at me like I'd been on Mars the last few years. "For *stayin' sober,* man." He was, after all, the most famous alcoholic in sports.

For Chris Mullin, becoming a drunk hadn't been easy. There were too many other things to do. And too many people who loved him. Especially his dad. Chris Mullin's father had always accepted him. There were no hoops to jump through, no pressure. Rod Mullin just wanted his five kids to have fun and to stay close to the family. Other than that, no demands.

Chris, the third oldest, was good at sports, and sports became a big part of his life as a little kid. But Rod Mullin didn't push him to excel. Instead, he stressed the fellowship of sports.

"He taught us that sports brought out a sense of family," says Mullin. "He showed us how sports could teach unselfishness. He never worried about himself. He lived to take care of others. He was one of twelve kids, and you get used to being caring and considerate in a situation like that."

Mullin, whose dad had a solid job as a customs inspector at JFK Airport, grew up in a middle-class, family-oriented section of Brooklyn. "We always had people staying at our house. If they came over and it got past a certain hour, my dad made sure they stayed. Made sure they ate. His friends, our friends, anybody. It was open house."

Mullin's dad did insist that he learn the value of work. "Things were not supposed to be easy," says Mullin. "Not that everything had to be the hard way, but most of the things you get, you have to bust your butt for."

To some extent, the drive to bust butt was innate in

Mullin, even as a child. In that regard, he was like every one of the other boys who would one day make the 1992 Olympic basketball team. Guys like Magic, Michael, Charles, and Karl had vastly different childhood experiences, but despite that, they all shared two important traits: aggressiveness and abundant energy. One explanation for this is biochemistry—specifically, brain biochemistry. All these guys, it would appear, had a wealth of the brain chemicals that support aggressiveness and energy: adrenaline, testosterone, thyroxin.

I used to write about medicine, and one of the doctors I wrote about liked to say, "Endocrinology is destiny." Meaning: You are what you secrete. Some people, he said, inherit endocrine systems that pump out the hormones that promote aggressive, energetic behavior. But other people, with weaker systems, were born to be sheep.

But there was at least as much "nurture" as "nature" in Mullin's drive. One pivotal role model for him was his mother, who was extremely active and strong-willed.

"We were maniacs as little kids," says Mullin. "Five kids, all in grammar school at the same time, all coming home for lunch. She nearly killed herself raising us."

Even though Mullin wasn't pushed by his parents, he had an overpowering desire to achieve. "It all started in grammar school," says his mother, Eileen Mullin. "Chris had to do well at something or he wasn't interested. All of a sudden, we noticed he was missing in the evenings. He'd be at the school gym until nine or ten at night. One day a coach came home and told us Chris should play basketball and referred us to Lou Carneseca, the St. John's coach."

Carneseca recalls, "When I first saw him, in grammar school, I said, 'I want you to play for *me*.' He was only six-foot tall, and he was playing in the backcourt. That's where he got all the skills for that position. You knew he was going to be good. You didn't have to be a genius. The big thing is that he was able to do for others. The good ones do for themselves, and the great ones do for others." Mullin, Carneseca says, was always more concerned about his teammates than himself.

At age ten, Mullin won the Elks National Free Throw Contest, hitting 23 of 25 to beat Steve Alford. Mullin didn't take it seriously. "It was really more like *The Honeymooners* Raccoon Club event," he says.

At twelve, he gave up swimming and baseball to concentrate on basketball, because basketball was more fun. "If I didn't like basketball," says Mullin, "I wouldn't do it—God's honest truth. If you push a kid to do it, he's not going to like it."

At the St. Thomas Aquinas grammar school, Mullin and his buddies would sneak into the gym. "We'd hide a guy behind the door," remembers childhood pal Mike O'Reilly, "and when everyone was gone, he'd open the door and we'd pile back in." Once, during a blizzard, they spent the entire weekend in the gym, sleeping in the coach's office and eating in the training room.

The practice paid off. By the time he was in high school—first at Power Memorial (Kareem's school), and then at Xaverian—he was recognized as one of the best young players in the city. And there were good players— Vern Fleming, Ed Pinckney, Sidney Green, Olden Polynice, Kenny Smith, Bill Wennington. But a lot of people thought he was just too . . . white. "They always talked about how I couldn't move, couldn't jump. It was an obstacle. To me, the whole thing was eliminating weaknesses in your game. In high school, I was just a good shooter. I realized if I could shoot *and* handle the ball, then I could drive. If I could drive, I might get fouled. But then I had to learn free throws." After his team won the New York State Championship, and after he dominated the highly competitive Catholic Youth Organization league, recruiters were crawling all over him.

He decided to go to the commuter campus of St. John's. Partly because of Carneseca. Mostly to stay close to the family.

Mullin loved the family atmosphere at St. John's. His girlfriend, soccer star Liz Connolly, kept stats for the basketball team, and after every game there'd be a party at the Mullin house with a taped replay, lots of neighborhood buddies, lots of beer. Beer was a big part of the Brooklyn Irish Catholic social scene. "You drank at weddings, and you drank at funerals," says Mullin. "You drank 'cause you were happy, or 'cause you were sad. If it was a groom, you toasted him. If somebody died, you said, 'Well, he woulda been here,' and toasted the shit outta him."

Mullin became a minor New York celebrity. "We could get into any club in New York," says Connolly. "People would see him in line and roll out the red carpet."

The comparisons to Bird began. They were both warriors, team players, and excellent passers. They'd both learned to compensate for white man's disease. And they both had the extraordinary perceptual abilities that the sportswriters called court vision. Both players could see things that other players simply couldn't.

Mullin's team—which included Mark Jackson, Walter Berry, Ron Rowan, Shelton Jones, and Bill Wennington—reached number-one ranking in the polls and went to the Final Four.

Flying home from the win that put them in the Final Four, Mullin sat with sports journalist Mike Lupica. Lupica ordered two beers. Mullin told the flight attendant, "Why not bring us two each, so's you don't have to keep coming back." By the time they'd touched down, Lupica never wanted to see another beer. But not Mullin.

Mullin realized during his sophomore year that he could go pro. The guys he'd been playing against were making the NBA, and he'd been kicking their butts. Up until then, playing had been for pride and passion—he'd been a starving artist. But: "I realized I could make a living out of it."

After his junior year, when he'd been a first-team All-American, he was named to the Olympic team. Lou Carneseca recalls, "The night before the final cuts for the Olympic team, I remembered I'd forgotten to wish Mul luck. It was about ten at night, and I said, 'I bet you he's in the gym.' I went up to the gym, the lights are on, and who in the hell do you think is in the gym? I felt so good about that—because you could see he was concerned with making the team."

When Mullin arrived home from the Olympics—where he'd won gold and averaged 12 points—he was greeted by a block party of five hundred people.

Draft day, 1985. Seventh pick, Golden State Warriors: Chris Mullin. A stunned look hit his face. He'd have to leave home. "The distance surprised us," says Rod Mullin, "and caused that look on Chris's face."

Liz Connolly: "He was going far away. Six hours from home, by air. The day he left he was so quiet and solemn." Mullin promised to call his father after every game.

Welcome to hell. The Golden State Warriors were a foul, kinky mix of yard-dogs and slugs: druggie Chris Washburn, George Karl in his early Krazy George incarnation, selfish Sleepy Floyd, and Joe Barry Carroll (in his permanent Joe Barely Cares incarnation). It was the quintessential twelve-players, twelve-cabs team.

When he first arrived, Mullin went to the gym for shooting practice, and one of the players told him, "Don't do that. It makes us look bad." Then he had a bad shooting night and the coaches told him to stop working out so much. "Some of the players," Mullin recalls, "would stub a finger and stop playing." Floyd would rarely pass him the ball, and when Mullin passed off, he'd never see the ball again. Karl wanted him to do just one thing—shoot from the perimeter. Mullin's reaction was, "Maybe this *is* just a job. Maybe it's *like* this. Oh, my God."

Mullin began to lose interest in practicing. He gained thirty pounds and his body fat ballooned to sixteen percent. NBA veteran Kermit Washington came to visit and remembers the floor of Mullin's bedroom was littered with candy bar wrappers.

When Mullin would call Liz, he'd sound miserable. "Chris didn't know anyone," she says, "and he was trying to meet people by partying all the time. He was hiding behind the drinking."

Mullin averaged 14 points his first year and was labeled an

immediate has-been: a great college player who was too sick with white man's disease to succeed in the NBA. He called his dad after every game, but the news wasn't always good.

One low point was when the car he was driving hit a bicyclist, who was awarded $3.9 million in damages.

Another was working out with Grabow and getting so sick he puked all over his shoes.

Then Don Nelson came to Golden State. Nelson, like other coaches, talked about having a family atmosphere on the team. Difference was, Nelson meant it. And he didn't want any drunks in the family. So, early in the 1987 season, Nelson confronted Mullin. Mullin denied he had a problem. So Nellie said, "Then quit for a month. It shouldn't be too hard." A few days later, Nellie heard that Mullin was drinking again. On December 10, Mullin missed a practice and Nelson suspended him for a game.

Nelson told Mullin he should take off the rest of the season, or however long it took to whip the problem. Nelson stressed the personal toll it was taking, not the professional toll. "If Coach were thinking selfishly," says Donny Nelson, "he would have said, 'Let's ride it out until the end of the season.' What he did really cost us. It was the darkest day of the franchise."

"Chris called me and said he was going in," says Liz Connolly. "He thought I was going to be really upset, that I would leave him for this. I said, 'No, this is going to be the best Christmas.' He was so upset, crying. He said, 'I don't know.'"

Mullin's parents traveled with him to a hospital in L.A. Mullin's father was relieved. "My dad told me after it was all over that he felt something was wrong," says Mullin. "But he knew eight million people could say things, and it wouldn't help—because I was the only one who could help myself. He always gave us room to make our own mistakes and learn from them."

Rod Mullin: "How do you tell an All-American that he can't drink? I just had to keep the channels open and make sure he knew I was interested." Besides, Rod Mullin had been an alcoholic himself when he'd been younger. What could he say?

"The day I went into rehab I felt like I failed, and I felt so small," says Mullin. "I went in there thinking, 'I'm a professional basketball player. I don't need this shit.'" But the effort was supported by everyone: mother, father, girlfriend, coach—and even his agent, Bill Pollak, who was more interested in Mullin than his commission.

"The program helped calm me down," says Mullin. "I was holding everything in. I was able to let out my feelings. I could *need* help. People there helped me open up."

Mullin's mother says, "His father taught him that if you work hard, things work out in the end. So ever since Chris was in high school, he was always on the go. He was never doing anything for himself; he was always striving to satisfy everybody else. But when he went into that program, it was the first time he did something for himself."

When Mullin got out of rehab a month later, he was scared as hell. They'd told him he could never drink again, and he didn't know if he could handle that. He needed an outlet. So he called fitness coach Mark Grabow, and said, "I need you now, man." They met in the Cal Berkeley gym.

It was late at night, but Mullin worked out for two hours. At the end, Grabow asked him to shoot ten free throws. Mullin hadn't touched a ball in a month, but he made all ten. Grabow told him, "Just shoot until you miss." Mullin made ninety-one straight. At that point, Grabow knew that Mullin—his mind now unclouded by alcohol—would be able to do extraordinary things.

"It was just he and I for three straight weeks," says Grabow. "Solitary figures in the gym. No one bothered us." Mullin was ready to rejoin the team. "It was like an unveiling—all of a sudden, here's this new body."

It was the beginning of the best of times. The legendary workouts began. Six to seven hours a day. Suicide drills. Long-distance running. Thousands of sit-ups. Shooting for hours with a weight vest on. Pumping iron. Balance work. Shooting 360 jumpers per half hour, and making ninety percent of them. Shooting 100 three-pointers with the weight vest on, and making eighty percent. Shooting free throws with the vest, and making up to 190 in a row. Mullin's body fat shrunk from sixteen percent to six percent, and the thirty pounds vaporized.

Meanwhile, Nellie canned people like Sleepy Floyd and Joe B. Carroll. In the seven weeks of Mullin's absence, six new players arrived—tough, generous players. The Warriors were fast, fun to watch, and built around Mullin.

The relationship with Liz deepened. She became convinced he'd stay sober and moved to the Bay Area.

Mullin became close to the new players and incorporated some of them into his extended family. Several of the players bought houses in the same Alameda neighborhood. "I lived about three houses down from him," recalls Tom Tolbert, "and I was over there eating lunch one day and talking to his dad about how I couldn't get one of my lights to work. And his dad's, like, 'lemme take a look at it.' And, sure enough, he comes over with this little box and fixed it up. It seemed like that was something Chris got from his dad, helping other people."

Mullin's scoring hit about 25 per game. Perennial All-Star. Twenty-five-million-dollar deal. The calls home to Dad after every game became a joy. It was the best of times. For about two years.

Then Mullin's father, who was still young, got sick. Cancer. It started in a lung and moved into the liver. For a year, there wasn't anything Mullin could do but pray, and work out to relieve the stress. Drinking was a temptation, but he didn't give in to it. "When my father was very sick," says Mullin, "being in the house was very stressful. So I'd run, and try to sort things out. I'd ride my stationary bike in the garage until two or three in the morning.

"My dad was so tough. He'd say, 'Don't worry about me. I'm going to be all right. Take care of yourself. Take care of your mother.'

"The last five minutes when he was still with us, I was in there crying and sweating. And he wakes up and says, 'What—have you been working out again?' Five minutes later he stopped breathing. He just stopped. Nice and peaceful. Just like that."

Mullin believes that he can still feel his father's presence. "I miss calling him," says Mullin, "but I still talk to him sometimes. I know he's still watching." Once, at a game, "I was about to come into the arena, and I could just feel him—a warmth inside of me. I could feel . . . I knew he was worrying about me.

"I said, 'Don't worry about me. I'll be okay.'"

Tim Hardaway, trapped by reporters, was the last player out of the locker room before a game against Dallas. He hadn't learned yet that one of the perquisites of stardom was to blow off the press before the game. If you did that, you only had to deal with them after the game, and that was much easier—then you could talk about the game for fifteen minutes without saying a single thing.

I asked Hardaway if he was disappointed that he hadn't made the Olympic team. "Oh, no, not at all. I'm not a star."

"Come on, Tim, you were All-Rookie and an All-Star."

He smiled mischievously, as if this were a secret only he and I knew.

"I got 'ninety-six to look forward to," he said. "Me, Pooh Richardson, Kenny Anderson, we got time. Actually, I hope they don't need me—I hope Magic plays."

But thirty minutes later he showed why he was still a strong candidate to take Magic's place. He was rocketing downcourt with two Dallas Maverick defenders waiting for him under the basket. As they converged on him he rifled the ball from his left hand to his right—through his legs—and then back again, through his legs: the famous UTEP-two-step. The defenders literally crashed into each other. Then, from out of nowhere, Mullin appeared, and Hardaway flipped him the ball. Mullin got his shot off. Rimmed out. One of the Mavericks grabbed it and tried to hurl it downcourt. But it hit the large ass of Golden State rookie Victor Alexander, who looked like George Foreman —not a young George Foreman, just George Foreman. The ball skittered toward the sidelines. All the Warriors started jogging downcourt for the in-bounds play. Except Hardaway and Mullin. Mullin flew after the ball and got to it just before it crossed the line. He grabbed it, spun 180 degrees, underhanded it to Hardaway, and crashed into the courtside seats. Hardaway made an easy lay-up. Then Hardaway ran over and untangled Mullin from the spectators.

Hardaway and Mullin walked back downcourt with their arms around each other's shoulders. The crowd screamed.

"Be a fah-thuh to ya chiiild!"

The locker room was all but empty. Trainer Tom Abdenour was ministering to the usual cuts and bruises, and Hardaway and Mullin were just breaking free of the reporters.

One of the Warrior PR people came in with a little boy who would break anyone's heart. He had a flat forehead, a rectangular face, and eyes that were too far apart.

"This is Norman," the PR guy said to Mullin.

"Hey, Norman!" said Mullin, as if the child were an old friend. "You enjoy the game?" Norman gave little sign of comprehending. Norman was a victim of fetal alcohol syndrome. Mullin didn't know that, though. Mullin wasn't very concerned about alcohol anymore. It wasn't even tempting.

"Stormin' Norman!" Mullin enthused. "You need a cap, my man!" He took off his own cap and put it on the boy's head. "Hey, Timmy, come meet my man, Stormin' Norman."

Hardaway came over. He watched Mullin closely and did the same things Mullin did.

Then Mullin pulled himself away. He wanted to go call his mom. He called her after every game now.

7

Mike Jordan
Is a Dork

**Dueling Egos • Isiah's Revenge •
Karl Malone's Night of Fear • Michael's Badass
Friends • Black Gold • "I Am Not a Crook"**

God is a verb.
—R. Buckminster Fuller, 1963

I fear Allah, thunderstorms, and bad airplane rides.
—Muhammad Ali, 1975

If God did not exist, it would be necessary to invent him.
—Voltaire, 1770

Every man is crucified upon the cross of himself.
—Whittaker Chambers, 1952

RREeee! Tires grated against black ice and asphalt.
Grabbed it. The cobalt Testarossa jerked to such a sudden
stop it looked like a special effect. "It's himself!" yelled a
security guard. The gate swung open. Snow poured out of
the black Chicago sky.

The Testarossa eased into the parking lot and crept
through sooty slush to a spot just in front of Chicago
Stadium. A raggedy band of kids ducked under traffic

barricades and engulfed the car, their steamy breaths forming a cloud around it. They looked hyperactive, underfed, and ferocious, like, Lord of the Flies Goes Antarctic. "Hey, MichaelMichaelMichael!" shouted a little black kid pressed against the driver's door. He was wearing a knockoff Bulls jacket thick as one-ply toilet paper and was built along the lines of a chickadee. The door cracked open. "MichaelMichaelMichael-I-rode-the-bus-two-and-a-half-hours-*please*-Michael!" He shoved an Upper Deck trading card and a pen at Jordan.

"Where you bus in from?" said Jordan, taking the pen and card.

"Cicero."

Michael gave him The Look, the same one he gives Porky Pig in the Hare Jordan ad. Cicero was no more than twenty-five minutes away. But he couldn't blow the kid off, especially in front of so many people. That wouldn't be like Mike, and these days he always had to be like Mike. He signed the card.

"Thank you, Michael, thank you." A security guard in a heavy yellow coat closed Jordan's door, and Jordan vanished. The kid hustled over to the older crowd who'd stayed behind the traffic barricades. "This *real!*" he yelled. "You saw it! I got Pippen's too. How much you gimme!" Guys started grabbing for their wallets. The bids topped out at thirteen dollars; Jordan was generous with autographs, and that drove down the market. Pippen's fetched seven dollars.

The security guard sneered at the kid, "Hey, det sucks. Whattaya gonna buy wit twenty bucks?"

The boy looked at him with utter contempt. "Air *Jordans*."

The weather was almost worse in the bowels of the Stadium. It was cold down there too, and a foul liquid that seemed to be urine was raining from old iron pipes. The Jordan era had generated money for a new hundred-million dollar stadium, but The House That Mike Built was still a couple of years off.

Jordan hurried to the training room and hopped onto a table to get his ankles taped. Then Karl Malone's gofer stuck his head in the door. "Karl's ready now," he whispered to one of Jordan's underlings. "So you can tell Michael he can leave."

Jordan's manservant would have none of it. He wanted to make sure *his* boss was the last to show up for a Jordan-Malone Olympic portrait.

So Michael's guy waited a few minutes and then went to the Utah locker room by himself. "Mike'll be there any second," he said. "Send Karl on down."

Karl's guy looked over at Karl. Karl looked away.

Mark Eaton said to Malone, "You hear about that plane that crashed?"

"You bet I did," said Malone. For several minutes they discussed the crash; the more they talked, the grimmer Malone got. Malone's gofer stood and waited.

Finally, Malone had had enough of dueling egos and headed for the door.

As he walked down the hall, he was surrounded by a phalanx of nervous-looking guys in suits. "Karl got a threat," explained a Utah executive as they hurried past.

"Because of what happened with Isiah?" I asked.

"Yeah."

Utah coach Jerry Sloan, with no apparent concern, watched them sweep by. Sloan had once quit a coaching job just before his team's airplane had crashed, killing everyone. There were a lot of physical threats in the NBA, and sniper fire was just one of them. The constant travel was more dangerous, and the action on the floor was even scarier. Both these dangers were infinitely more frightening than the issue that currently had the sportswriters dithering: Magic playing in the All-Star Game and Olympics. Magic had announced he wanted to play in both, and the journalists were freaking out. What if he *bled*? To most of the players, it seemed absurd. Magic's blood wasn't nearly as scary as Karl Malone's elbow.

Malone had balls, though, to even show up in Isiah's old

neighborhood. He'd practically killed Isiah in their last game. It would have been easy to sit this game out in the downtown hotel where he was hiding, away from the rest of the team.

The ugliness had stemmed from Isiah's exclusion from the Olympics. Apparently wanting to prove he was better than Utah's John Stockton, Isiah had burned Stockton for 44 points in Detroit. Then, when Isiah had gone to Utah, a retaliatory Malone had smashed into Isiah as Thomas was streaking in for a shot. Malone's elbow had ripped open Isiah's forehead, and blood had spurted all over the floor. Isiah had needed forty stitches to close the wound, about half of them inside his head. Thomas had been outraged, saying, "It felt like I'd been shot in the head. I was scared. I could have died on that play. Doctors tell me my forehead will be numb for two months."

Malone had been unrepentant. "It's amazing," he'd said, "that the Pistons do the intentional shit they do and get away with it. But we do something *clean*—by accident—and they make a big deal like that."

Isiah had accused Malone of being "too chicken to apologize."

Then, when Isiah had heard that Malone's punishment was only a $10,000 fine and one-game suspension, he'd been almost inconsolable. People close to him said it was the only time they'd ever seen him naked of his legendary drive. He'd said, "I just don't give a fuck about playing anymore."

When Malone had seen that many people considered the brutal act intentional, he'd also become dejected. He'd meant to hurt Isiah, but not to tear his head open. Didn't people know he was a *nice* guy? He, too, started thinking about retirement.

A few days ago Malone had called Isiah to straighten things out. Isiah had done his Sweet Zeke thing. But he'd told Malone to watch out for snipers in Chicago. He had fans there, he said, who just couldn't be controlled. A beautiful move. On the one hand, it was the ultimate in professional courtesy. On the other, a cruel mind-game.

Malone was still thinking about retiring when he trudged out to meet Jordan. An hour from now, it would be his job to assault Jordan, and he knew he would be hated tonight. And—conceivably—killed. He had a two-month-old daughter. He was rich. He didn't need this.

Malone and Jordan each reached out to shake hands as if the other guy's fingers were covered with raw sewage. They both gave the photographer steely stares when he pleaded for them to emote. Who'd this guy think they were—Pat Sajak and Vanna White? The photographer saved the "smile" shot for last. Their smiles consisted of lips pried slightly apart. Jordan evinced absolutely no gratitude toward Malone for the throttling of Isiah. In the off-season, the enemy of your enemy was your friend. During the season, he was just another asshole trying to kill you.

Malone murmured "good game" and abruptly headed off. A Chicago writer tagged along and asked the requisite Isn't-it-thrilling-to-play-Michael question. Malone grumbled, "This is just another team. Doesn't mean shit to me."

When Jordan got back to the Bulls locker room—a dingy little hole with Coke-stained carpet—he dropped the badass demeanor he'd put on for Malone. "You know, that Isiah-Karl thing, that's just a marketing thing, an image thing," he said, tightening his sneakers. "You got the image of Karl Malone being a muscle guy, and he *profits* from that image. You got the image of Isiah being a Bad Boy, and he profits from that. That's just the nature of the business right now."

Jordan suddenly looked sad. "It's *such* a business now, man," he said. "And you gotta wonder sometimes: How did it ever get to be . . . such a *business?*"

He drifted off into his pregame ritual of parceling out his tickets. From outside the door came an ungodly hubbub; there were a flock of hucksters out there who'd gotten past one level of security but couldn't get into the locker room. They all had something to sell. And wanted Jordan to sell it.

Michael Jordan, the ultimate global immortal, had reached the highest level of public life: he received great rewards simply for being, not doing. He had, in fact, alchemized an international mania of people wanting to "be like Mike."

This phenomenon was absolutely extraordinary. No other athlete, entertainer, or political figure in recent history had achieved it so fully.

The essence of Jordan's being—the thing that made others want to be like Mike—was that he, and he alone, could do something mankind had always dreamed of. He could fly. It wasn't a job or a duty; it was simply *what he was:* the flyer.

This essence had been packaged with great skill by agent David Falk, by Nike, by the NBA, and by the TV networks. The high production values of modern broadcasting and advertising—slow motion, stop-action, etc.—had revealed his powers to everyone: the guy really *could* fly. It was a perfect, supernatural, godlike image. It sold like crazy.

Only one problem. People can't fly. And nobody's perfect.

And the media—in its eternal cycle of mythologize-debunk-mythologize-debunk—had begun to point this out. It had started when Jordan's team had won the championship last summer. He'd reached the top of the mountain. He was king. He was God. The mythologizing was complete. So it was time to debunk.

One story after another had ripped him apart. Now Michael Jordan was losing control of his image. And it was killing him. He'd spent twenty-eight years sculpting that image.

God knows, he hadn't been born with it. Once upon a time, Michael Jordan had been just a scared, insecure little kid with jug ears. A dork. A black dork. In the South. That little kid had known early on that he'd better learn how to *do* something and do it well. Because he didn't like what he was.

Then he found out he could do one thing better than anyone. He could jump. Jump so high it was like flying.

So he became the boy who could fly. And the image slowly began to build.

Now they were trying to take it away.

Therefore, Michael Jordan had also been thinking about retiring.

As Jordan finished earmarking his tickets, assistant coach Tex Winter watched Jordan out of the corner of his eye. This was Winter's forty-sixth year of coaching, and he was still trying to figure out how players got psyched up for a game. The one guy he couldn't figure out was Jordan. To Winter, it looked as if Jordan were completely preoccupied. But Winter knew that in a matter of minutes, Michael Jordan would move into a mental state that was almost incomprehensible. But . . . *how?*

The closer the game got, the better Jordan's mood got. The reporters gradually took off. Now he didn't have to be like Mike. And in a few minutes, he could go upstairs and *do* like Mike.

Thank God for that.

• Saint Michael's Church of Da Bulls

The anthem began, and the Stadium fans rose and put their beers over their hearts. Best fans in the league. Bar none. They wore sweaters, ate bratwurst, and didn't have any pretensions about being "knowledgeable"; they were just here to hero-worship, primal-scream, and watch Da Bulls slaughter people. And one thing they most certainly did not give a rat's ass about was Michael Jordan's media backlash.

A quick survey had revealed that the Stadium fans were unimpressed by the evidence against Jordan. Specifically:

—Michael didn't go to the Rose Garden to suck up to George Bush. *(So?)*

—When he should have been in the Rose Garden, Michael was apparently playing grand-a-hole golf, dropping about $165,000. *(So? That's the same as me dropping about a hundred bucks.)*

—But he dropped it to bad guys, one of whom was later

shown to be a coke trafficker, and one of whom was later shown to be murdered. *(Did Mike kill the guy? Did Mike do coke? No! So?)*

—Jordan was depicted in *The Jordan Rules* as tough and vain. He even slapped Will Perdue. *(I'll slap Perdue—get his ass over here.)*

—Michael angered Nike, which sells T-shirts, by doing a Hanes underwear ad. And he alienated the advertising community by switching from Coke to Gatorade without a decent interval. *(Stop—you're breakin' my heart.)*

—Okay, how about *this?* The National Stuttering Project was incensed that Jordan was using the insensitive line "That's all folks" in Hare Jordan. *(Get-the-hell-outta-here.)*

Last month, Magic had come to town and told reporters to get off Jordan's ass—that they were driving him out of the game. The fans were in total agreement. When the lineups were announced, Jordan, as usual, got his standard thunderous ovation.

He waited until the second half, however, to "Jordan." Until then, he'd mostly pumped in jump shots. Michael usually made most of his points from jump shots. But fans didn't realize that. All they saw were the flying dunks, the impossible shots. But the impossible shots were mostly just for purposes of psychology. When you made them, you took control of your opponent's mind.

Second half, close score: Mark Eaton, 7–4 with arms rising to about twelve feet, got an offensive rebound right under the hoop. He hopped upward for a soft dunk. As he went up, Jordan flew in off the wing, both arms up like a fan doing the Wave. He kept rising and rising until he was right behind Eaton. Then he rose a few more inches, grabbed the ball with both hands, and plunked it off Eaton's chest. Eaton looked dumbfounded, like, *this just doesn't* happen *to me.*

Eaton stared down at Jordan, and said, "Jee! Zuss!" Jordan said, "Yo!" and winked.

Tex Winter was again watching Jordan out of the corner of his eye, as Jordan spread his tickets on the locker room's indoor-outdoor carpet. Getting up for Utah last night had been one thing, but how would Jordan get up for Miami tonight? Jordan *hated* midseason games against second-rate teams. No challenge.

Jordan seemed distracted, like last night. Winter knew that if he told Jordan something, it probably wouldn't register.

But to a sports psychologist, this wasn't distraction at all, but an adoption of the "disassociative state." The disassociative state cuts the athlete free from his pain, fatigue, and emotions. It's essentially a hypnotic state. It allows the athlete to shift into a slow brain-wave condition called the alpha-wave state, which is much more calming than the normal beta-wave state. The pinnacle of the disassociative condition is the legendary zone of altered consciousness. When an athlete goes into the zone, his brain waves slow even further, to the rare theta-wave state. The only thing slower than that is delta-wave, which is sleep.

Another advantage of the disassociative state is that it helps the athlete visualize the moves he hopes to make. He can visualize a particular move before the game starts and also just before he makes the move.

Some sports psychologists think that by visualizing a move, the athlete sends minute signals from his brain to his body. These signals constitute a form of rehearsal, giving the body the "muscle memory" it needs for certain situations. Then, when these situations occur, it feels as if they had already happened. The name of this concept is psychoneuromuscular theory. It sounds fairly improbable until you compare it to any other explanation of why certain elite athletes—like Bird, Mullin, or Jordan—can "see the future."

Sports psychologists believe the greatest athletes have a superior ability to use these mental techniques. Tex Winter thinks so too. Winter also thinks that great athletes are great learners. Not necessarily of linear, logical, left-brain material like grammar or literature. Athletes are often notoriously bad at language, contributing to the perception of them as stupid. But they're often brilliant at grasping right-brain matters of spatial integration and organization—which gives them a big advantage in sports.

Furthermore, Winter has, like other educators, discovered that some people are mostly visual learners (who learn by seeing), while others are auditory learners (who learn by hearing), and still others are motor learners (who learn by doing).

Horace Grant, for example, was strictly a motor learner, while John Paxson was mostly a visual learner—an X-and-O guy. But Jordan could do all three—unlike most other players in the NBA. And that gave him a hell of an edge.

I sat down in front of the locker next to Jordan's and talked to him about some of this stuff.

"What do you do to psych yourself up for a game?" I asked.

"Nuthin'. You try *not* to get all psyched up. You try to relax. You try to make it *fun*. I don't treat it as pressure. No matter how much pressure there is."

"Do you visualize situations before a game?"

"Yeah. We go through the scouting report, and I visualize what the guy I'm guarding is going to do, what his tendencies are, and how am I gonna play against that."

"How often do you find yourself doing exactly what you'd visualized?"

"Most of the time."

"No kidding?"

"No kiddin'."

"Jeeze. How often do you go into the zone of altered consciousness?"

"Whenever we need it, really."

"So it's something you can will yourself into?"

"I wouldn't say 'will.' I just play myself into it, then see myself in it, and then try to apply it. But for the most part, I'm fully aware of what's going on, and how I should be implementing my abilities in the system we run. Or try to run."

Jordan wasn't in love with the Bull's offensive system. Tex

Winter had created it—the intricately patterned triple-post offense—about thirty years ago, and Jordan often felt it stifled his intuitive instincts. It hadn't been too thrilling when Jerry Krause had run up to Winter after last year's championship game yelling, "You did it!"

"Do you go into the zone every game?"

"Yeah. I mean, in different ways. One night offensively, another night defensively." Occasionally when he was in the zone, he would feel a "ball of power" surround him—a field of energy that gave him a feeling of total control. Sometimes these forces would come easily, sometimes not. "But I always go by instinct. You can't do it intellectually. You gotta stop thinkin'. You just gotta be aware of all the people on the court and what they like to do, and then go by instinct. Sometimes, though, the defense changes and hits you with something you didn't see in the visualization. Then you gotta create, and that's *all* instinct."

"But I'm guessing that when you go to shoot, you forget about everybody else and think about just the shot."

"No, no—you *don't think* about the shot; you focus on it, but you don't want to *think* about it. But, yeah, you put everything else outta your mind when you shoot. You're not worried about gettin' back on defense, or where the rebounders are, or anything else. Just that shot. That's your whole world."

"This is off the subject, but when you jump, does it feel like you can fly?"

"Sure it does. Once I leave this earth, for as long as I stay in the air, it feels like I'm up there flyin' and bein' creative. But it's like that for everybody. Even Jerry Krause." He smiled broadly; making fun of your fat boss was one of the perks of being Michael Jordan.

"You're wrong about that," I said. "It doesn't feel like flying when I jump. And I don't even wanna *think* how it feels for Jerry. One last thing. What's it feel like to be Michael Jordan and go out there and play basketball?"

"Right now? Right now, with all the stuff that's comin' down on me? It feels like . . . therapy."

• Gambling Is a Sin

One hour later: Jordan yelled "Get out" at tree-tall Bull's center Bill Cartwright and dribbled fitfully on the perimeter. Cartwright leaped out of the paint. Jordan rushed in. He felt the "ball of power" begin to form around him, felt it shoot out at his teammates, even at the writers in the rows under the basket. It was a tremendous feeling. Indescribable. Time stopped—then started clicking forward in slow motion. He looked into the eyes of Miami's Glen Rice, who was standing between him and the basket. Time didn't stop for Glen Rice, or many other players.

Then Michael Jordan saw the future. It was a vision he'd carried in from the locker room.

He saw his head jerking left and saw Rice follow it with his eyes. Rice tilted ever so slightly to the left. Then: explosion. He pushed off with his right foot, smashed down one hard dribble, grabbed the ball, knifed at Rice's unprotected right . . . leaped . . . floated . . . floated . . . waited for Rice to fall . . . saw Rice's arm stretch out as he fell, ducked under it to catch a foul . . . JAM!

Jordan saw the whole thing in hard, bright focus. Caught in the zone of altered consciousness, he felt unemotional and content at the same time.

Horace Grant, laminated with sweat, was suddenly at Rice's left. Jordan snapped his head toward Grant. Rice fell for the fake as Grant hardened his body. *Smack!* Rice bounced off Grant and tried to say "shit," but it came out with an uncontrolled burst of air: *"Cheet!"* Jordan darted forward off his right foot. The ball of power stayed with him. He smashed down one hard dribble, grabbed the ball, leaped toward Rice's unprotected right, and felt time stop. In slow motion, he rose . . . kept rising . . . rising.

But then Rice was somehow in front of him—not like he'd visualized it—and Rice dumped his arms and chest and shoulders into the still-rising Jordan. Another "hard foul." Not as hard as the torture Karl Malone had put him through last night, but still so hard it felt like getting hit with a board. It pissed Jordan off. The league exploited him without protecting him.

Jordan's integrated movements fell all to pieces. His arms and legs flailed every which way as he plummeted to the floor, butt-first. But he held on to the ball. And just before his tailbone hit the Stadium's jagged old floor, he pulled his arms back into the ball of power and flipped up the basketball. It hit the glass and rolled in as he landed on his ass and blurted, *"Hooo!"*

Grant stood over Jordan with his hands out as Jordan sat Indian-style on the floor. Time came back. He could again hear the crowd. His ass hurt. He felt a sense of complete ease and control. He took Grant's hands.

Pippen came over. Pippen knew better than to slap him on the ass; he touched Jordan's hand softly. Scottie understood. Three years ago, he didn't understand. Now he did. Jordan smiled his little one-sided smile. Pippen smiled back.

Then Jordan stepped to the free throw line and began once again to drift into the zone. Therapy was working.

John Paxson was skipping rope at the luxurious health club in Deerfield where the Bulls practice. Chicago forward Cliff Levingston walked in. "Hey, Cliff," said Paxson, "you lose any money at cards last night?"

"No," said Levingston happily. "Just three hundred and fifty dollars."

"'Cause he cheats," said Jordan, hurrying through the weight room to the gym, where no reporters were allowed. As soon as Jordan got a ball in his hands, he started making two-dollar bets with Pippen on trick shots. Jordan, an astonishingly fast healer, showed no ill effects from last night's beating-as-usual against Miami.

Paxson watched Jordan through a glass partition. Paxson supposedly resented Jordan for usurping his role, but that was bullshit. Pax was a perimeter shooter, not a driver or ball handler, and in a backcourt with Jordan, that was the best thing you could be: not like Mike. If you competed, you died. I called Paxson "The Anti-Mike," and he liked the description. The only thing haunting him was the specter of Yugoslav point guard Toni Kukoc. If Krause landed Kukoc, Paxson was history.

Pippen bet Jordan he couldn't make a left-handed three. Jordan lined it up, took a breath, missed. "Damn!"

"You lose."

"Double or nuthin'." Jordan hated to lose. Especially to Pippen. Some people thought Scottie could be greater than Michael, and Jordan didn't like that.

Jordan shot again before Pippen could decline. Missed again. Missed again. Made it.

"You better eat your Wheaties," said Pippen.

Paxson said, "The damnedest Jordan shot I ever saw was in this gym. He drives to the hoop, goes under it, leaps, spins one eighty, shoots over the top of the backboard. It sinks as he hits the wall. Bet him five he couldn't do it again. Lost the five."

Nobody seemed too circumspect about the gambling issue, even though it was the only serious mistake Jordan had made. He'd gotten caught when two of the people he'd lost money to had been investigated. One guy, convicted drug figure Slim Bouler, had had his money seized by federal authorities. A $57,000 check from Jordan was in Bouler's stash. Then another shadowy character, Eddie Dow, had been gunned down, and $108,000 in uncashed checks from Jordan had been found on him.

Jordan had stuck with a story that the money to Bouler was a loan to build a driving range. Weak story. Ranges cost more than that.

Jordan had even less to say about the checks to Dow. Jordan made a couple of I-am-not-a-crook statements and let it ride. He'd said, "I'm no Pete Rose. I wasn't involved in any point-shaving or betting on basketball." David Stern had slapped Jordan's wrists and forgotten about it. The last thing Stern needed during this crucial era of international expansion was to have the league's godhead look like a con. Besides, lots of players gambled. At the All-Star games, players would blow tens of thousands at card and dice games. It was one vice that almost matched the game high but wouldn't get you banned from the league. Anyway, all the Olympians regularly gambled their entire careers diving for balls, and compared to that, risking a hundred thousand bucks on golf was small potatoes.

For weeks after the gambling story broke, Jordan had been hounded by the press. If *The Jordan Rules* hadn't been on the best-seller lists, the media would have probably dropped the Michael's-dark-side angle. But the book was getting great publicity, mostly because it pointed out milquetoast "sins" by a deity. It had shown that Jordan was impatient with less talented players (like Cartwright), frustrated with the Bulls' "equal opportunity offense," that he'd blamed Pippen for having a migraine during a big game, that he'd slapped Perdue, that he was sometimes selfish, and that he manipulated the Bulls management. It had, in short, shown him to be human.

But Jordan had flipped out over the book. He apparently *liked* being a god.

When practice was over, a reporter told him he'd just been named the Associated Press Athlete of the Year. He tried to get excited. But he was also being named *Sports Illustrated*'s Sportsman of the Year, and *Basketball Digest*'s Player of the Year. Not only that, he was on his way to his third Most Valuable Player award, and sixth consecutive scoring title. His "Michael Jordan's Playground" had just been named the top recreational video of the year, he had the highest TV quotient of any athlete in the world, he had just been named the most admired figure of young people, and had the hottest ad (Hare Jordan) on television. Plus, the Bulls, at 29–5, had a good chance for the best record in NBA history. So it was hard to get worked up.

Finished with the media, he ducked into a bathroom. A little blond kid, about ten, had been waiting with his dad for an autograph. The dad said, "I've got the guts if you do." The kid didn't hesitate for a second and barged into the bathroom. The dad too. I figured that if they had the guts to ask, I had the guts to watch, so I followed them in. But inside the little bathroom, there was no Michael Jordan. Just a pair of big tennis shoes in the only stall, with red warm-up pants bunched around them. The kid started to slide his basketball card and pen under the stall. But his dad grabbed him just in time. Hustled him out.

Back outside, the kid's eyes were big. "God, Dad," he whispered, "Michael *poops.*"

• Wilmington, North Carolina

The exaltation of Michael Jordan was a long process, one that took roots before he was even born. His parents, James and Deloris Jordan, were bright and ambitious people who had improved their station in life almost as much as Michael had his.

James Jordan, a sharecropper's son, grew up near the Angola Swamp of North Carolina. He began his career as a forklift operator for General Electric, eventually became a mechanic, then a dispatcher, and retired as a white-collar supervisor of three departments. After rearing their five children, Deloris Jordan began working in a drive-up teller window, advanced to head teller, and retired as the United Carolina Bank's chief of customer service. The Jordans were always struggling and always won their struggles. Michael was born in 1963 during one of James Jordan's self-improvement projects—attendance at a G.E. training school in Brooklyn.

Michael always was, and still is, close to his parents, who help run the Jordan Foundation. "Everything starts with them," he says. His mother, in particular, continually encouraged Michael to reach greater heights. She was, in fact, the prime instigator of the Jordan Foundation, which affords Jordan no small part of his immortality.

"Lots of parents," says Deloris Jordan, "have this feeling that once you reach a certain age that, well, 'I'm done with you.' That's not my outlook. I'm still here."

Michael's image has always been one of her primary concerns. "Everyone," she says, "wants a piece of whoever is successful and has a good image. But it's the ones who keep things in perspective, like Julius Erving and Arthur Ashe, who are the leaders and role models."

Race was an early source of the Jordan family's concern with image. The mid-1960s was a new era for black Americans, in which some could gain respect and success if they made enough sacrifices. One sacrifice was making the effort to maintain a scrupulous image. By the time Michael was born (the fourth child), the Jordans had moved about fifty miles south to the racially tense town of Wilmington. When the Jordans arrived, the schools were not fully integrated, and an important civil rights case divided the town. But the Jordans encouraged their children to be color-blind and supported little Mike's close friendship with a white boy (David Bridges, still one of his closest friends). This encouragement was, in part, an attempt to maintain the image of being upwardly mobile, new-era black Americans. But it was also just because Bridges was a clean-cut, wholesome boy.

Sports, another healthy, character-building outlet, was also encouraged by the Jordans. Eventually, James Jordan would build a basketball court behind his house, a large split-level he built himself. The Jordan boys were good at sports. Especially Mike.

But Mike (it wasn't "Michael" until a college PR guy rechristened him) was not an easy child. He didn't have a very good self-image. He had big Dumbo ears and an older brother who incessantly teased him about them. "He was always testing us," recalls James Jordan. "If we told him the stove was hot, don't touch, he'd touch it. All the kids had chores, and sometimes he would get into one of his moods and purposely mess them up. One time I found out that he was paying other kids to do his chores, and that really got me."

Part of Mike's problem was that he was just lazy. He had abundant energy and aggressiveness (having inherited his vigorous dad's endocrine system), but he refused to channel it into drudgery. His siblings worked as tobacco cutters during the summer, but Mike tried it one day, complained of back strain, and never returned. The Jordan family, fighting upward through the working class, could ill afford that kind of indulgence.

"One summer," Jordan remembers, "my mom said, 'You just got to work,' and she got me a job as a maintenance man in a hotel. I just couldn't do it. I could not keep regular hours. It just wasn't me. From then on, I never, ever had another job."

Another reason he quit the hotel job, though, was because of image. It made him look like . . . a Negro. He complained to his mother, "What if my friends saw me? The boss had me out on the sidewalk, *sweeping!*"

Mike did not excel in school. As a high-school freshman, he was expelled three times, once for leaving to play basketball, once for fighting, and once for smashing a Popsicle onto the head of a little girl who'd called him "nigger."

He wasn't particularly popular with girls. His hair was cropped so closely other kids called him Bald Head, and he had a lot of insecurity about his ears. "I'd look in the mirror and feel I was ugly," says Jordan. "A lot of guys picked on me, and they would do it in front of the girls. They would joke about my haircut and the way I played with my tongue out. The girls would laugh at that, and right then, I was dead. I couldn't get a date with anybody. I'd go to the prom and other parties stag, stand up against the wall with the other stag buddies, and tease the people on the floor."

Jordan took a home economics class because he thought he'd have to live his entire life alone. "I always thought I was going to be a bachelor," he says. "No one would marry me. I would end up doing my cooking, my dishwashing, my clothes washing, my dusting."

There was only one area in which Mike excelled. Sports. At seven, he'd told his mom he'd someday be an Olympian. He became an excellent pitcher and hitter, almost pitching his team into the Little League World Series. He was quarterback of his high school's football team. He was even better at basketball. He could jump like no one else. He practiced hard but didn't consider basketball work—it was just a game. As far as his psyche was concerned, though, it was not just a game. It was the cure. It was the cure for a feeling he had deep in his soul: Mike Jordan is a dork.

But basketball provided one final humiliation. Mike was cut from his high school team as a sophomore, mostly because he was only a little over six feet and another guy was 6–6. Jordan recalls, "I'll never forget how hurt I was when I saw the list posted in the hall. I cried. I was pissed. I couldn't cheer them on. I wanted them to *lose,* to prove they made a mistake. I think, to be successful, you have to be selfish."

The disgrace prompted Jordan to begin 6:00 A.M. practice sessions. He averaged 25 points for the junior varsity, grew to 6–3½, and became a prominent local player. Still, as a senior, he didn't make a list of the top three hundred college prospects and received only moderate interest from recruiters.

Then came Howie Garfinkel's Five Star Camp in Pittsburgh, where good high school players got excellent instruction. Jordan was named MVP two weeks in a row. "It was," he remembers, "as though somebody had tapped me on the shoulder with a magic wand and said, 'You must emerge as somebody—somebody to be admired.'"

When the University of North Carolina recruited him, he showed them incredible athleticism: 360-degree spins, dunks, alley-oops. He was a good shooter too, but it was the flying that caught their attention.

Deloris Jordan liked the family atmosphere at UNC and also its proximity to Wilmington. So that's where he went.

When he arrived, he felt as if "everybody was a superstar and I was the low man." That feeling didn't last long.

"You could see him becoming more sure of himself in everything he did," recalls UNC teammate James Worthy.

In his freshman year, the apotheosis began. It started with The Shot. NCAA Final Four. Championship game. Jordan versus Pat Ewing of Georgetown. Prime-time television. Last seconds. Georgetown up one. Jordan with the ball. The lane was clogged: Tyrannosaurus Pat in the Valley of Death. Jordan dribbled. Shot. Perfect. National championship.

No other achievement in his college career, or even the

1984 Olympics, compared to The Shot. Over the next two years, his growing fame came from his athleticism. He was the boy who could fly.

By the time he was drafted by the Bulls, he'd shed his dork image. He'd grown into his ears, was handsome, a ladies' man. He was . . . Michael. But he still had the ferocious competitiveness, born of insecurity, that he'd used to overcome his low self-image. He desperately wanted to win every contest—cards, pool, Ping-Pong, video games.

His mother encouraged Michael to select powerful agent David Falk as his representative. She liked that Falk had a young black attorney on his staff and seemed concerned about not just Michael's impending contract but also his long-term image.

Falk believed Jordan had enormous commercial possibilities. Not because he was such a great basketball player. Landing James Worthy two years before had been a bigger thrill for Falk; Worthy was the number-one pick in '82, and Jordan was only number three in '84 (after two centers, Olajuwon and Bowie). But James Worthy couldn't fly. The camera didn't mythologize him.

Falk believed he would not have to "package Michael Jordan," but could just "expose who he is and what he is to corporate decision makers." One of the first corporations Falk contacted was Nike.

The Nike executives knew Falk had great things in mind before their first meeting even began. If Falk felt lukewarm about a meeting, he'd start it by extending his hand in a cold-fish fashion. But if he smelled serious money, he'd bound across the room with his hand outstretched, fingers spread. The more excited he was, the wider the fingers would be. As he kicked off the first Nike-Jordan meeting, his fingers were fanned wide as spokes in a wheel. Falk wanted his rookie to have his own shoe. And get a royalty. Because *Michael could fly.*

Problem there. To put it delicately, the only people who had their own shoes had certain . . . demographic advantages. They were golfers or tennis players—guys who appealed to the middle and managerial classes. Arnold

Palmer, for instance. Arnie still made about $10 million a year—more than almost anyone else in sports—and he was thirty years past his prime. But Palmer was—to get right to the point—white.

Falk had heard it before—specifically, from Converse and Adidas, who'd passed on Jordan. Blacks couldn't market to whites. But Falk had a hot marketing concept. Nike, which was looking for a way to hype its new air-sole technology, could call Michael's shoes Air Jordans.

Nike, however, was considering spreading its money among several new players, including Barkley and Ewing. But Barkley was overweight and Ewing had zero charisma. They decided to focus on just Jordan. Nike was floundering financially, and the deal scared hell out of them.

Jordan's only concern was that Nike give him a new car. Toy-level money thrilled him.

When Jordan saw the promo tape Nike put together, he was blown away. It was a high-production-value montage of his highlights, set against the Pointer Sisters' "Jump!" It was the first time he'd seen special effects applied to his jumping. Until that moment, he'd never realized how much it looked like flying. He'd only known it *felt* like flying. But the image was even greater than the act. His childhood friend Fred Whitfield says, "I think that was the first time he was really impressed with himself."

The first Air Jordans, ironically, didn't even have air-soles. They were just an old line repainted black and red.

Then David Stern tried to queer the whole deal. New to his job, flexing his muscle, Stern was trying to shift the balance of power in the league from player-dominated to executive-dominated. With many NBA players reportedly using cocaine, Stern felt there was a real crisis of authority. So he cited a clause against colored shoes and had Air Jordans banned from league play.

The publicity ignited the line. The shoes were rad, bad, and dangerous to wear. And they were expensive. What more could a consumer ask? Air Jordans made $130 million the first year. Then Spike Lee's hip Mars Blackmon commercials hit, and annual sales reached $200 million. Air

Jordans saved Nike. Other companies noticed. Blacks could market to whites. Or at least Michael could.

As Jordan's NBA career unfolded, Falk lined up a group of select sponsors, all willing to mythologize Michael. A prominent ad executive notes that Jordan gradually gained "a level of value as a commercial spokesman that is almost beyond comprehension. It never happened before and may not happen ever again."

Jordan's deification had little to do with the success of his team. When he joined them, the Bulls were a rat pack of high rollers and has-beens. It was reasonable, of course, for the bad teams to get the high draft picks and best rookies, but that didn't make it easy to endure. After his first exhibition game, Jordan walked into a team party and found just about everyone there drunk or coked up. He pivoted and split, and that set the tone for his early years in Chicago. Nor was he particularly interested in all the women who began throwing themselves at him (a favorite trick was to lie in front of his car). "Girls who chase you," he says, "aren't the ones you're interested in."

In his rookie year All-Star Game, he flaunted the Nike logo, even though players had been asked to downplay their endorsements. Some of the NBA veterans were angry and froze him out of the offense. It hurt him. It hurt even more when Bulls management tried to sit him out most of a season after he'd broken his foot. Jordan thought Jerry Krause was trying to lose on purpose to sweeten the Bulls' draft position. Nor was he happy during the years the Pistons would prance in, brutalize him, and win championships.

Nevertheless, he could still fly. As the NBA game evolved from center dominated to guard dominated, he reached a level of success no one could have predicted. He began piling up scoring titles, won two MVP awards, defensive awards, quickly reached immortality-level wealth through his endorsements, fell in love, got married and had two sons, and finally won a championship.

Throughout all of this, he competed with utter ferocity. A true warrior, he risked his career hundreds of times diving for balls in meaningless games. He even had a "love of the game" clause written into his contract, allowing him to play in pickup games during the summer.

No one ever thought of him as a dork anymore. Except maybe, in lonely moments, himself.

And on his long climb up the mountain of deification, no one tried to push him down. Until, of course, he reached the top.

• Being the Bitch

"You look tired, Mike," said Bulls coach Phil Jackson, the league's resident ex-hippie and all-purpose philosopher.

"I was up all afternoon with the kids," said Jordan. Jackson nodded sympathetically. He got along well with Jordan. If he didn't, he'd have never gotten his job. But Jackson also looked worried; big game in a couple of hours—Charles Barkley was in town.

Jordan was crazy about his sons—Jeffrey, three, and Marcus, one. They loved him without knowing about his image. These days, that was rare. Jordan was also deeply in love with his wife, Juanita. She, too, was more attracted to Jordan the person than Jordan the legend. They still had frequent candle-lit dinners, he lavished her with jewels and clothing (which he picked out himself), and they were very much like young lovers in public. "She was always very independent," Jordan says. "She knew how to work and provide for herself, which is what I loved. I never wanted to take away her independence." Juanita—very attractive but not model-gorgeous—was an executive secretary for the American Bar Association when they met. Contrary to legend, she did not throw herself under his car.

Now she helped channel Jordan's torrent of favor seekers. She was good at saying no. "I know it makes me look like a bitch," she says, "but I can't worry about it, because I'm protecting what we have. If that's what I have to be, I'll be a bitch."

One of the things she protected was the sanctity of their

North Shore home. Nice home—but nothing like the place he was building in Highland Park: 26,000 square feet, with a guest house, eight acres, and garage big enough for his dozen cars (Porsche 944S2, BMW 850i, Ferrari Testarossa, Jeep Cherokee, Nissan 300ZX, Corvette, etc.). The new place would also house all of Jordan's toys: an indoor six-hole putting green, a 20,000-watt remote-controlled entertainment complex, multiple gaming tables, and a health spa. There would also be several rooms for Jordan's lavish wardrobe, which was probably his favorite toy. He dressed with exquisite style. At the moment, he had on an olive raw-silk suit with matching accessories. Gold and silver peeked out discreetly. Very discreetly. As a rookie, an ad guy had advised him to "lose the Mr. T. starter set," and he'd taken it to heart.

But now it was time to put away childish things and get ready to kick Charles's big butt. Actually, Jordan felt sorry for Barkley and had called him this afternoon. Barkley had been arrested for a bar fight in Milwaukee and was dying to get away from Philadelphia.

"It's not so hard to lose the fun of the game," Jordan said, peeling off his olive silk socks. "Everything gets so political.

"Sometimes Charles says what a lot of us want to say. Everybody's got a little devil on their left shoulder, and Charles's devil is just a little bit bigger, and the devil's always goin', 'Say something, Charles.' But he's a good guy.

"My advice to him would be, let basketball be your solution to all your problems away from the court. Step onto the court, get a good sweat, play hard, then step off the court ready to deal with the solution.

"That's what I turned to this year when I lost the fun for the game. I went back to the original love that I have for the game, and pushed everything else aside."

But fifty minutes later, Jordan was deviling Barkley. He had hold of Barkley's jersey and wouldn't let go. Barkley pulled away. The jersey strained. It came off one of Barkley's shoulders, revealing a rake-mark of scars—Charles always took a beating. "Damn, Mike!" Charles barked.

But Jordan didn't seem to hear him. He was off in his own world.

Moments later, Jordan got a pass from little whippet B. J. Armstrong on the fast break. Jordan rock-'n'-rolled toward the hoop, leaped, accelerated, glided, and then in midair he seemed to freeze. Like a cartoon character. So quickly it was almost invisible, he whipped a sidearm pass to Will Perdue. Perdue pushed down an easy dunk.

Philadelphia coach Jim Lynam, who was at war with Barkley and fighting for his job, yelped, "Oh, God!"—like he'd seen it all before but didn't want to be seeing it now.

" 'Fuck you, Michael!' King finally said. 'All you're interested in is scoring and taking every shot. Maybe if you passed the ball to somebody else for a change, instead of worrying about winning the scoring title, somebody else on this team could do something.' " Cleveland's "Super Fan" was reading from *The Jordan Rules* at the top of his lungs. He would read passages, then—to the delight of the other fans in Cleveland's stadium—he'd pummel a Wheaties box bearing Jordan's picture. Jordan ignored him.

But he heard him. Jordan hated the book.

In fact, the book was much more complimentary to Jordan than Jordan realized. However, only the most controversial material had been excerpted in newspapers, and that was all Jordan had seen.

The parts of the book that pissed him off most were the passages about his friction with teammates. Jordan, despite his godhood, really was one of the guys and didn't want anyone thinking otherwise. To him, team camaraderie was the most spiritual element of sports. It obliterated divisions of race, money, and appearances—all the things he'd been sensitive about during his dork years. To the guys, he was still just Mike.

This season, he'd made a special effort to rebuild the relationships that had suffered during the Bulls' tense and painful three-year drive toward the championship. Now Pippen was almost like a little brother, and Jordan even got along with Perdue, Cartwright, and Grant.

Jordan, fired up by Super Fan's abuse, took the ball downcourt himself. He head-faked Craig Ehlo, shoulder-faked, stutter-stepped, leaned forward, then was almost magically leaning backward as he shot. *Swish.* Lenny Wilkens shook his head. "Hey," he yelled to Ehlo, "I couldn't have defended that." With the unspoken: And I'm a Hall of Famer. Jordan's shot was reminiscent of The Shot—not *the* The Shot (in college) but the other The Shot (the last-second jumper that killed Cleveland in the 1989 playoffs). Cleveland's The Shot had been pivotal in the rise of the Bulls and the fall of the Cavs. And it had been pure Jordan. In the huddle before the shot, coach Doug Collins had drawn up a surprise shot for journeyman center Dave Corzine. But Jordan had smacked his fist on Collins's clipboard and snarled, "Give me the fuckin' ball!" He'd made an incredible leaning jumper. The Cleveland fans had never forgiven Jordan. They hated him here. Cheered when he got hurt.

The Bulls won tonight's game going away. It had been billed as a contest between the two best teams in basketball. But it was no contest.

On his way off the floor, Jordan winked at Super Fan. Super Fan couldn't help but smile. Even when you hated Jordan, he was still God.

Jordan crashed in a heap, like a crumpled piece of paper. He'd tried to avoid David Robinson under the hoop, so he'd darted left and tripped over the hip of all-meat Terry Cummings. Jordan hit the floor so hard his head bounced twice.

Will Perdue, the player Jordan had slapped, was the first to arrive on the scene and began shouldering Spurs out of the way so that no one could "accidentally" step on Jordan. Perdue looked gray with worry. Paxson, whose role Jordan had usurped, was there next, hovering over Jordan protectively. Jordan grabbed the top of his head and squeezed it so hard it made furrows in his scalp. He began to monitor his body: Does everything move? Is anything ripped? It helped him deal with the pain.

Pippen and Grant, who'd been crosscourt, raced over, their faces drawn. Jordan muttered, "God-damn-God-damn-God-damn."

Grant, the gifted player who was the most resentful of Jordan, reached out and gently touched Jordan's left hand.

Pippen, the Olympian Jordan had always overshadowed, took the right hand. Pippen asked softly, "You okay, Mike?"

Pippen answered himself: "You're okay, M.J."

Pippen and Grant slowly pulled him up. All four players helped Jordan to the bench.

He was the soul of their team. And he was the soul of the game. He was an insecure little kid—a dork—who'd used basketball to become a god. To some extent, they had all done that. They were him, and he was them.

And still: none of them could fly. All were mortals; all would die. None of them were like Mike. Not even Mike.

8

Scottie Sees It Differently

**Isiah Joins the Bobsled Team • Jerry Krause:
The Horror! The Horror! • Being Unlike Mike •
God, With an Attitude • The Pippen-Jordan
Tag Team • Barkley's Unpublicized Knife Fight •
Not Tonight, Mike, I Have a Headache**

The little boy reminded Pippen of himself as a kid: light as a
leaf with big eyes that didn't quite trust. "Who's it to?"
asked Pippen, shuddering as a blast of snow slapped them
both.

"Aw-don't-worry-'bout-that. Just sign it, would be cool."

While Pippen signed the trading card, he drawled, "How
about, 'To whom it may concern'?" He smiled gently, his
eyes wrinkling behind his glasses. Pippen knew the kid was
going to sell the card, and that it would sell better without
being personalized. But he couldn't get pissed off. He'd once
been as poor as this kid looked.

RREeee! Jordan's blue Testarossa screeched to a halt
outside the lot. "It's himself!" yelled a security guard.

The little kid lit up. "Hey, I gotta get Michael!" he said,
grabbing for his pen and the card.

Pippen ignored the slight. "Stay here," he said. "He'll be
drivin' right over here."

The pack of kids by the gate started ducking under traffic
barricades and following the car, but it drove right over to

124

where Pippen and the boy were standing. The kid hopped a couple of steps and was suddenly pressed against the driver's door by the crowd of children. The door cracked open. "MichaelMichaelMichael-I-rode-the-bus-two-and-a-half-hours-*please*-Michael!" the boy shouted.

Pippen did a lightning backpedal toward the players' entrance. "They're all yours," he said to Jordan. But Jordan didn't hear him. Didn't even seem to see him.

No one else did, either.

Pippen smiled a secret smile and was gone.

• Isiah Bites the Dust

When Jordan got back to the locker room after posing for an Olympic portrait with Karl Malone, the room filled with talk of the Isiah-Malone skirmish. It seemed to make Pippen uncomfortable, and he got more involved than was necessary with the lacing of his shoes. Pippen, too, had clashed with Isiah. It had happened during the season's first Piston-Bulls game. Pippen's best friend Horace Grant had collided with Laimbeer, and while Grant was off-balance, Laimbeer had tripped him and kicked him. Pippen had tried to run over to help Grant, but Isiah had shoved Pippen from behind. The push had infuriated Pippen. After the game, he'd said, "Isiah's a cheap-shot artist. I should have expected it, but I wasn't looking for it. If Isiah makes the Olympic team, *I won't play.* I don't want to be involved with him. I don't like him. He's too phony, too fake."

Isiah, at this point in the season, was playing superbly— just the way he needed to play to make the Olympic team—19.4 points and 7.4 assists per game. With Magic questionable for the Olympics, Isiah's chances of making the team should have been excellent. But he was screwed. He was a joke. In the last *Esquire* Mike Lupica had written, "Rebuffed in his attempt to make the Olympic basketball team (and in his subsequent application for citizenship in Latvia), Isiah Thomas joins Willie Gault, Edwin Moses, and Herschel Walker in Albertville, France, where he steers them to a second-place finish in the bobsled competition. Heartbroken by the near miss, he storms off the floor during the medal ceremony, taking his teammates with him."

Isiah was the first casualty in the scramble for the last Olympic positions. He'd drowned in bad blood. Too many people thought he was phony—sweet on the outside, ice inside. And too many players had carried the bruises of his hacks and jabs. He was popular among a broad section of lower-paid players, because—as president of the Players Association—he always came out on the side of the rank and file. But it wasn't the rank and file who ran the league. It was the stars. And they'd had enough of his duplicity. The Selection Committee would be nuts to take him.

Now the viable candidates were Dominique Wilkins (who was pushing Jordan for the scoring title), Dennis Rodman (who was averaging an amazing 17.4 rebounds), Drexler, and Brad Daugherty (who were having their finest seasons), and Tim Hardaway (who was getting more famous with every game). For the college position, Shaquille O'Neal seemed to be a lock.

Joe Dumars and Reggie Miller had gotten off to relatively slow starts, and that hurt their chances. Dumars seemed to be sulking over all the attention Isiah had gotten for not making the team. In Detroit everyone knew he was as good as Isiah. Why didn't they know it anywhere else?

"You still mad at Isiah?" I asked Pippen.

He pulled his head up from his shoes slowly, as if it weighed a hundred pounds. "Naw, not now. I'm a pro. I can get along with anybody."

I gave him a skeptical look, but he didn't respond. He'd been in the league over four years now, long enough to lie without blushing.

"That little kid in the parking lot—did you know he was getting your autograph just to sell it?"

"Well, you see the same faces again and again. You gotta know what they're doin'. But, hey, it's cold out there, right?"

A Bulls' assistant came by and gave Pippen his tickets for tonight's Utah game. He didn't have nearly as many as

Jordan, whose tickets were spread before him like a beach towel.

"Did you know you were one of Daly's first five choices to be on the Olympic team?" I asked Pippen.

Now *he* looked skeptical.

"Really," I said.

He grinned half a grin. "I wasn't aware of that. That surprises me. Over Larry?" I nodded. "I wasn't even sure I was one-a the candidates. All I knew was that, well, my day was comin'. *Some*day, at least."

"What was the Olympics' biggest attraction for you?" It was a warm-up question, something to break the ice. I always got the same stock answer: "Playing for the country." But Pippen didn't automatically burp it up. He was one of the few Olympians who didn't act all misty-eyed about Uncle Sam. As a poor rural black, the system had always been stacked against him and his family. Life in the American working class was tough enough, but life in the starving class was another story entirely. Pippen's wealth was a fluke, and he knew it. He gave his thanks to God, not the trickle-down system he'd grown up in.

"The big attraction? Well, there's twenty-seven teams. Twelve players on a team. *All* these players are great. And I'm *one of the chosen few*. It's took me *long* time to be that." He repeated the phrase, savoring it: *"The chosen few."*

One of the Chicago reporters, who knew Pippen much better than I did, said, "Come on, Scottie—you like the Olympics because it takes you out of Michael's shadow."

Pippen nodded. Slowly at first, then faster. "That, too," he said.

"That *especially*," said the reporter.

"That, *too*," said Pippen. He wasn't going to let a reporter outquote him. He was, after all, a star.

"That thing about Michael keeping Isiah off the Olympic team," I said. "Do you think that really happened?"

"You'd have to ask Mike about that," said Pippen.

So I did. Jordan said, "It wasn't me. After it happened, you saw reports from different people saying they didn't want Isiah on the team—hey, Scottie!" he shouted across the locker room. "Did other people want Isiah on the team?"

"Not everybody," said Pippen.

Jordan gave me a satisfied look, like, See—that proves it.

Pippen didn't add anything to Jordan's observations. He'd learned not to try to top Jordan—not on the floor, and not in the locker room.

• Better Eat Your Wheaties

But sometimes he just couldn't help it.

In the second half of the Utah game, Jordan materialized from the sky to strip 7–4 Mark Eaton of the ball—a mind-twisting play that made the Utah players look weak and stupid. But right afterward, Stockton rocketed down-court, paused in front of little B. J. Armstrong, then shoved his open hand into Armstrong's belly. Armstrong went, *"Uhhh!"* and Stockton slipped past to score, giving Jordan a triumphant look as he trotted back: We're even. But then Pippen came screaming down the lane with the ball, soared, and caught David Benoit in the gut with his knee. Benoit crashed to the floor. Foul on Pippen—but Pippen gave Stockton a look that said: How do you like *this* half of the Tag Team? Then Pippen stole the ball, drove in an arc around the paint, outquicked Stockton, and outmuscled Karl Malone to score. It was a tremendous display of speed, grace, strength, and size. A display not even Jordan could equal.

In fact, assistant coach Tex Winter thought Pippen had even greater potential than Jordan. "Michael wouldn't agree with that," says Winter, "but Pippen has those long arms, and great reaction, and can jump over the moon. So can Michael, but Pippen's a little *bigger*. Pippen's just scratching the surface."

Pippen was one of the most physically gifted players in the world. Like many great athletes, he'd gained his size relatively late, long after he'd learned the finesse skills of smaller players. His combination of attributes (size, speed, agility, and strength) allowed him to play point forward and gave him an almost insurmountable edge over practically everyone he faced. And he had one other unique advantage—every day in practice he played against the best player in the world. Why, then, after four years, was he only scratching the surface?

Because of Jordan. Jordan made him crazy. Jordan made him scared. And it had been going on for four years.

Pippen had come to the Bulls as a notably insecure young man. He had fire in his heart, but also a lot of fear. Bad things happen to the mind when you grow up thinking that the operant phrase in your career will be, "Would you like fries with that?" Pippen had grown up poor, semiliterate, and black in cracker country. On top of that, he wasn't notably good-looking. That kind of early life buries fear deep in your heart.

Then Pippen had been thrown up against Michael Jordan: God. God *with an attitude.*

Small wonder that Pippen had suffered terrible attacks of doubt.

But he'd also had great courage. And—like every other player on the Olympic team—he'd had a family that loved him unconditionally, and that love had placed confidence at the core of his being. The confidence was even deeper than the fear.

Year after year, he'd studied Jordan. Jordan the player, and Jordan the man. And from watching Jordan, he'd learned how to play, how to act, and even how to feel.

The following night, in the Miami game: Jordan leaped up to shoot up, and Glen Rice laid a vicious block on him, knocking Jordan onto his ass. Jordan sat there, stunned. Pippen ran over to Jordan, giving Rice a look that said: This ain't over. He helped Jordan up. Jordan looked pretty foggy, like he was either deep into the zone or deep into his pain. What would Mike want?

What Mike *wouldn't* want was somebody slapping him on his poor bruised ass. So Pippen just touched Jordan's hand gently.

Jordan smiled.

The smile warmed Pippen's heart.

Mike wanted to gamble. He'd just made an amazing shot at practice in Deerfield. He'd run for the hoop, leaped, and tucked the ball behind his back with both hands, cradling it just over his butt. As he'd flown, he'd leaned in and flipped the ball up with both hands. *Swish.*

"Bet you two bucks you can't guard that," he'd said to Pippen.

Jordan tried it again. Pippen waited . . . waited. Blocked it.

These days, Jordan was a joy to practice with. Jordan's shots in games were flashy, but in practice—where he could cut loose with playground moves—he was surreal. And almost as competitive as in games.

Early in Pippen's career, when he'd still felt like nothing compared to Jordan, Pippen had played better in practice than in games. Jordan had thought it was because Pippen didn't care enough. But it had been because Pippen had cared too much. He'd been too uptight to be his best in games.

Now Jordan wanted to bet Pippen he could make a left-handed three. Pippen took the bet, but he wasn't crazy about gambling. Especially with *real* money.

When he'd first signed with the Bulls, as the fifth pick in 1987 (behind David Robinson, Armon Gilliam, Reggie Williams, and Dennis Hopson), Pippen's primary concern had been minimizing financial risk. He'd traded big upfront toy money for a longer guaranteed deal. He'd also been worried about how much he'd get if he were released after his rookie year—a strange concern for a lottery pick. "He wanted security," says his agent, Jimmy Sexton. Pippen had been talking to Sexton about annuities before the subject of a car had even come up.

While Pippen had been in high school, his father had had a stroke, and two of his brothers had suffered disabling illnesses. From that point on, Pippen had been obsessed with rescuing his family from the underclass. After he'd signed his Bulls' deal, he'd bought his family a house, his mother a car, had started sending home checks, and had put himself on an allowance.

But Pippen had locked himself into a long-term, relatively poor deal that would, ironically, later eat away at his self-confidence.

Jordan shot five times before he hit his three.

"You better eat your Wheaties," Pippen told Jordan.

That felt good. Four years ago, he wouldn't have said that. Maybe not even last year. The Olympics had changed things.

• Mind Games with Sir Charles

The Philadelphia game was an hour away. Jordan was sitting on one side of the locker room, telling a crowd of reporters that Barkley should let basketball be his therapy. Pippen was on the other side, almost alone, working up hostility for Barkley. By the time he stepped onto the court, he'd hate Barkley's guts. But after the game, they'd be pals again. It was a mental technique he'd learned from Jordan.

"You gotta be a little angry to play against a player of Charles's caliber," said Pippen. "You gotta anticipate how physical it will be." ("Physical" was player-speak for "brutal.") "You just gotta go out there and get in the first blow."

"Do you try to get inside Barkley's mind?" I asked.

"Definitely. *Lotta* mind games go on out there. It's *all* mind games."

I walked down to the Philly locker room to see Barkley. The iron pipes overhead were still raining piss. The basement of the Stadium had probably been pretty spiffy when F.D.R. had hung out here while they'd nominated him upstairs, but that was long ago.

When I walked into the 76ers' locker room, Armon Gilliam was saying to Barkley, "I read a thing said you had a hard time with women in college."

Barkley looked flustered. "No, man," he said.

I interrupted: "Pardon me, Charles."

But before he could say anything, I heard from somewhere near the ceiling a replay of my own voice, but with the flatness of my Corn Belt twang heightened. It sounded like a redneck chipmunk: "Pardon muh-ee, Cheerles."

Gilliam persisted. "Yeah!" he said. "It said you couldn't get anywhere with women until you were in the NBA."

"NO-NO-No-no," said Barkley, his inflection descending just like in his "Angel Charles" Nike commercial. "It didn't say 'anywhere,' it said '*every*where.'"

"Bullshit. It said you were shy." He pointed at Barkley's half-naked crotch. "I've *seen* it and know *why.*"

"*You* don't know about women," said Barkley, heat rising in his voice. "You're far too ugly to know about such things. You look like Buckwheat."

The best Gilliam could do was: "You just an ugly mother*fucker,* is your problem."

Barkley just went, *"Fuhhh!"* Why pretend this was just kidding among pals? Barkley was doing everything he could to manipulate a trade. But the only real possibilities—to Phoenix for Chambers, or to Portland for Duckworth and Kersey—were petering out.

I sat down between Barkley's locker and the corner of the room. "Hey!" said Barkley. "That's Charles's space!" I got up. "Fuck you want, anyway?"

"It's a bad time," I said.

"Naw," said Barkley, "it ain't a bad time."

"It is for *me.*" I needed to get on Charles's good side, and rudeness was one thing he respected.

But as I was taking off, I heard, "It is for me"—in the same ugly impersonation. I spun around. Manute Bol was grinning. "It izzz fur muh-ee," he repeated.

There was no way I could get pissed at Manute. While a guy like Jordan was definitely a humanitarian—seeing up to two hundred dying children each year—Manute spent his summers working the African famines, *saving* children.

Besides, he was 7–7. I let it slide.

That night, after the game, Barkley—who was still under indictment for a Milwaukee bar fight—was accosted in a lounge. This time, though, the guy had a knife. Barkley's teammate and friend Jayson Williams smashed the attacker with a beer mug. The guy with the knife was arrested, and Charles kept the whole thing out of the papers.

Pippen heard about it the following morning. "I don't *ever* want to be in the kind of position," he said, "where people taunt you and think they own you. I've seen Mike go through that.

"You know," he said, "there's a lot of good things about not being Michael Jordan."

"I'd settle for it," I said.

"That's what I used to think," said Pippen.

● Hamburg, Arkansas

When Scottie Pippen was a child, he had big dreams. He dreamed he might one day be a supervisor in a paper mill and own a double-wide trailer. The dreams, however, were pretty unrealistic.

People from Scottie's level of the rural South's underclass generally didn't rise to supervisory positions or live in double-wides. They did hard labor and lived in shacks—like Pippen's family.

Pippen's longtime agent, Jimmy Sexton, believes that he'd never really seen poverty until he'd seen the house Pippen had grown up in. Sexton's primary thought had been: Twelve kids lived here? Pippen's father worked hard for low pay in a paper mill in Hamburg, Arkansas, a poor little town in the steamy Mississippi River Valley, just north of Louisiana. The primary lesson Pippen learned from his parents, he says, was "how to survive." It was a tough area in a tough time. Away from home, the only protection Pippen had was his big brothers—he was the youngest of twelve kids.

Pippen had no significant outlets to take his mind off the poverty, racism, and toil. He wasn't very good at school, and he wasn't very good at sports. As a high school senior, he was just 5–9 with legs thin as pencils. He wasn't big enough to be on the high school football team and had to be the towel boy. But he didn't consider it humiliating. It was clean, light, indoor work. For a Pippen, that was great. Only one Pippen had ever gone to college, and it didn't look as if Scottie had a chance.

Then things got worse.

When Pippen was a high school sophomore, his father collapsed on the floor of their house after a long shift at the local paper mill. Severe stroke. Preston Pippen was paralyzed and unable to speak. After that, all the kids had to work constantly to keep their world from collapsing. Scottie did housework, baby-sitting, and odd jobs. He did find time to play a little basketball, but because of the stroke, his father didn't get to see him play. But Pippen's father didn't miss much. The athletic director of the University of Central Arkansas saw Pippen play point guard in a high school game and later remembered him as "skin and bones. You would never have thought he would make any kind of player. He had some talent, but he was *so* small and skinny."

The basketball coach at Central Arkansas was also unimpressed. "He was *weak. No* strength. You'd have thought All-Conference was as good as he would ever get." Pippen didn't make the varsity until his senior year.

Pippen's high school coach recalls, "People would ask me all the time, 'Why are you starting *him?*'" Pippen's coach, however, thought Scottie had the potential to be an adequate high school point guard.

No college would give Pippen a scholarship, but Central Arkansas did offer him a grant to be the basketball team's towel boy. Pippen, who'd already been rejected by two local colleges, jumped at it.

But Pippen played in pickup games with the UCA players and held his own. When two of them got injured, he joined the team. But he was no good. "I was a nobody my freshman year," he recalls.

However, he started eating well, lifting weights, and growing. He was determined to make it through college. His family was in desperate need of help, and if he could land a white-collar job—like gym teacher—he could funnel some money home.

Entering his second year, his small-man skills remained,

but he added about eighty pounds and six inches, eventually growing to 6–7 and 220. The extra strength and size made an enormous difference.

"As a sophomore," he says, "I was better than any player on the team."

That was good for Pippen's sense of self-confidence, which didn't amount to much. But in terms of clawing his way out of the sub-working-class, it wasn't very meaningful.

By Pippen's senior year, though—when he averaged 23 points—a few people in the NBA knew about him. One of them was Marty Blake, the legendary scout who worked for the league and sent reports to every team. Blake was high on Pippen but couldn't get anyone else to believe in him. Only about twenty college players stuck in the pros every year, and virtually all of them were from major schools.

But Bulls GM Jerry Krause was intrigued by Blake's reports. Krause sent top assistant Billy McKinney to Arkansas, and McKinney thought Pippen had an NBA body: long arms, fast legs, big hands, strong back. McKinney didn't know if Pippen had an NBA mind, though; Pippen had never been in a high-profile, high-pressure situation. All of Pippen's competition, McKinney reported, was "like amateur night at the Y."

But Krause was interested enough to want to draft Pippen. He hoped to grab Pippen in the second or third round

To Krause's horror, Pippen starred in every predraft camp he attended. Krause tried to get agent Jimmy Sexton to take Pippen to Hawaii—all expenses on the Bulls—which could make other teams think Pippen was irresponsible. Sexton passed.

Interest in Pippen was building. Krause feared that Sacramento would take Pippen with the sixth pick—two spots ahead of Chicago. Krause hit the phones, and by midnight before draft day he had a deal with Seattle. Seattle would take Pippen at number five (provided neither Reggie Williams nor Armon Gilliam were available). Then Seattle would trade Pippen to Chicago for Olden Polynice, whom the Bulls could get at number eight.

Choosing Pippen with such a high pick was a hell of a risk. "If Scottie hadn't been what we thought he could be," says Krause, "he'd have gone down as Krause's Folly. I'd have been ripped from pillar to post."

Pippen was shocked. Something *good* had happened to him. "Honestly, I didn't expect to be drafted that high," he says.

But Pippen wasn't as shocked as Michael Jordan. "I'd never heard of him," says Jordan.

For the first time in the life of anyone in his family, Pippen had a shot at real money. He didn't want to blow this chance, because he thought it might be his last. Most NBA players grow up being told how great they are. Pippen hadn't, and it had profoundly affected him. He was not nearly as arrogant as most NBA players. And not nearly as confident.

Pippen authorized Sexton to settle for a six-year deal at $5.1 million, with several safeguards to protect him if he flopped. It worked out to $765,000 a year—less than he could have gotten from a short-term deal with fewer safety nets. He sent most of the money home and saved what was left. He wanted a Porsche 928S. But wouldn't get it. Too risky.

His first day of practice, he insisted on guarding Jordan. It was an unusual thing for Pippen to do. But he felt pressured to justify his high selection in the draft. He did well.

Then the season started. And he fell on his ass. Nothing he did seemed quite right. The more important the situation, the worse he did. He was indecisive and lacked confidence. He was afraid. And Jordan smelled the fear. He hounded Pippen in practice and chewed him out after games.

To some observers, it seemed as if Jordan was just trying to challenge Pippen to do his best. But to others—including Pippen—it felt like Jordan was just acting out his obsession to win every contest, every time.

Jordan recalls, "It was just a matter of him believing in himself. When he got here, you could see he had the right tools. It took some time for him to get his confidence on this level—because he's competing with some of the best."

Like Mike, for example.

Playing with Jordan, and against him in practice, was a constant strain on Pippen. "It hurt," says Pippen. He knew he would never get the ball much while playing with Jordan, and when that happens, "You may never be able to get to be a top-caliber player. You know you have to take a backseat to him, but you *always* want to be a competitive player. Playing with a guy like Mike, you have to take a lot of pride in what you're doing."

But everything seemed to eat at Pippen's pride. His first year, his back hurt, and one reporter wrote that "Pippen's ability to play with pain—*any* pain—is a question." Chicago trainer Mark Pfeil doubted Pippen's toughness. Pippen had back surgery, though, and it helped immensely.

Then, 1989 Eastern Finals. Chicago was ahead of Detroit 2–1. Laimbeer rammed his elbow into Pippen's head, giving him a concussion. Jordan blamed Pippen for missing the rest of the game. Chicago lost the game and the series.

Eastern Finals again, 1990. Detroit again. Series tied 3–3. Pippen stood by Grant waiting for the game to start. "Do the lights look dim to you?" Pippen asked. Pippen was blinking like crazy. "I'm having trouble focusing," he said. He took two aspirin—and felt as if a bomb had gone off in his head. He had the only migraine headache of his life, so severe he later had a CAT scan to check for tumors. He shot 1–10. Chicago lost. Jordan was livid.

The press hounded Pippen for his two "disappearing acts." His confidence plummeted. The following year, 1991, he didn't make the All-Star Team, as he had in 1990. He tried to negotiate a new deal. But Krause stonewalled. Pippen wanted to escape—he wanted to get away from the Bulls and from Jordan. Jordan was like Big Brother: always watching.

But then, in the last half of the 1991 season, things began to change. Much of it had to do with the Bulls' complete adoption of Tex Winter's "triple-post offense." The offense, which spread the guards and center into a triangle around the paint, gave Jordan fewer shots and Pippen more. It also encouraged Pippen to play point forward, making the most of his extraordinary athleticism.

Also, during this time, Pippen began to see how valuable he could be in areas other than scoring. That seemed to simultaneously take pressure off him and add confidence.

As Pippen blossomed, Jordan backed off. And it became clearer to Pippen that Jordan's criticisms had been constructive, not sadistic. Pippen began to see Jordan not as Big Brother, but as a big brother, even though Jordan was just two years older. And as Jordan's media backlash began to hit, Pippen saw that Jordan's role was as difficult as his own. Pippen stopped envying Jordan. Practices became more fun, less bloodthirsty.

Much of the reason for the turnaround, though, was simply Pippen's courage. After Pippen had made it to the Bulls, his father had finally gotten to see him play, on television. Preston Pippen had been unable to speak, but he'd cried. By 1991 Preston Pippen had died. But the rest of Pippen's large family, still mostly in Arkansas, depended on Scottie.

He came through for himself and for them.

New Jersey assistant coach Brendan Suhr thought Pippen's emergence during the last part of the '91 season "was the most dramatic improvement of a player I've ever seen in this league."

Teammate John Paxson was also impressed: "This whole game is confidence. And Scottie's playing with a great deal of it."

Even Jordan was impressed: "He's playing the way I want him to play. He's got a lot of confidence. He's starting to show he can be a franchise-type player."

Just before the '92 season, Pippen renegotiated his contract. $18 million over five years. More than Jordan. He celebrated with a cheeseburger at Bennigan's—and the Porsche 928S he'd always wanted.

And then came the Olympic team.

* * *

Scottie Sees It Differently

The Bulls' play was as beautiful as a fine ballet. The Spurs, victim of the Bulls' rhythm and flow, looked wooden and old.

Even if this Bulls team didn't set the NBA record of 70 wins—which they had an excellent shot at—they would be remembered as one of the greatest teams ever. Their mix and chemistry were unparalleled.

Horace Grant, who would be a superstar on any other team, pulled a defensive rebound away from David Robinson and hit John Paxson on the wing. But Paxson didn't make the mistake of fast-breaking by himself. He waited, and hit Pippen, who dribbled over the half-court line and rifled a perfect pass to Jordan.

Jordan went up and tried to twist away from David Robinson. But he smashed into the hip of Terry Cummings and crumpled like a wad of paper.

Jordan lay on the floor, moaning, "God-damn-God-damn-God-damn."

Pippen sprinted over. He felt a hot, awful feeling in the pit of his stomach. He wasn't thinking about the 70 wins or another championship. He was thinking about Mike.

He took Jordan's hand. "You okay, Mike?"

Jordan didn't answer. What would Mike want? He'd want somebody to take over. So Pippen answered himself: "You're okay, M.J."

Pippen helped pull Jordan up. Jordan looked a little better. But he needed Pippen now—needed him badly. The knot in Pippen's stomach began to unfold. He could help. Help Mike. Help his family. Help himself. He could start by taking over this game—just like he'd seen Jordan do hundreds of times. He patted Jordan's hand gently. Jordan gave him a look. It said, Thank you. Scottie Pippen loved big brother.

9

Magic's Field Trip to the Real World

Manchild in the Promissory Land •
The Arrested Development of Magic Johnson •
The Persecution of Dominique Wilkins •
The Not-So-Secret Sex Orgy • Jerry West
Gets Bitchy • Michael vs. Isiah, Round Three •
Teasing the Poster Child • The Playboy of
the Western World

Abstain from fleshly lusts, which war against the soul.
—Saint Peter

Life is short; play hard.
—Reebok commercial, 1992

The things you learn in sports, coaches often remind young players, are the things you needed to know in life: teamwork, focus, tenacity, and self-confidence. If you learn to succeed in sports, you can succeed in life.

Too bad it's utter bullshit.

Too bad for Magic.

For Magic, sports was over. Real life had started. And it was *not the same*. In the world of sports, he had been in control: of the ball, of himself, of his opponent. The rules had been clear. The games had been fair. But real life, for him, was . . . out of control. The real world was chaotic. No rules. Not fair.

So Magic was dying to get back onto the court. He was pushing to get into the All-Star Game and into the Olympics. He was talking about playing for the Lakers in the playoffs and maybe playing for them next year. Or maybe he'd play in Europe.

There were stories in the papers saying he was already beginning to suffer from AIDS symptoms. The stories had started when reports surfaced indicating his immune system had already begun to fail. Supposedly, his immune system's T-cells had dropped below a count of 500, which meant he might develop AIDS within a year or two. There was speculation that he'd had HIV for as long as three years before his November AIDS test.

But he felt great. He was running four miles a day, lifting weights, and playing full court at his health club. He was ready for action. Whatever his prognosis, he wanted to *play*.

Some of Magic's friends, however, were trying to keep him out of the All-Star Game. Jerry West was being a real bitch about Magic coming back to the Lakers. And a worrywart in Australia was whining that if Magic showed up in Barcelona, he wouldn't let the Aussie boys play.

On top of everything else, Magic's honeymoon with the media was over. When he'd first announced he had HIV, the press had dutifully cranked out the tearjerker stories, declaring him a saint for facing death like a man. Laced into many of the articles was the half-wit notion that because finally a beloved figure had the AIDS virus, *now* we would all pull together and whip it. Corollary to this idea was: "If *anybody* can beat AIDS, Magic can"—as if he could just outhustle it. After this angle ran its course, the media needed a twist. The obvious one was: "Magic: Hero—or *Hedonist?*" They said Magic's downfall had come from his own horny behavior and warned, Kids-don't-try-this-at-home. They jumped on Magic for saying he'd tried to "accommodate" as many women as possible. They accused him of having an adolescent's attitude toward women. They even gave big play to Martina Navratilova's claim that if she'd gotten AIDS, the public wouldn't have cared, because she was gay. As if that, somehow, was Magic's fault.

The gay political community was in a hell of a fix. They didn't know what to do with Magic. On the one hand, they fanned rumors that he was bisexual—rumors that went back to his college days. But they also wanted to preserve his image as a hetero stud, so that more money would go to AIDS.

George Bush had the same problem. Should he ride Magic's popularity? Or treat him like a whoremonger? Bush appointed Magic to a blue-ribbon AIDS panel but recoiled in horror when Magic announced that he wanted the panel to actually *do* something.

What seemed to hurt Magic most, though, was his friends not wanting him in the All-Star Game. When he'd announced that he had HIV in the Laker locker room, A. C. Green had been the first Laker to hug him. Now A. C. was saying Magic shouldn't play in the game. So were Barkley, McHale, Danny Ainge, Jerome Kersey, and others. Most players thought Magic *should* play—but they weren't the ones getting media.

The media was chasing guys like McHale, who was saying players' hands were always covered with cuts and scrapes—as if Magic had the Hands of Death. Trail Blazer team doctor Robert Cook had just said, "The idea that a blood-borne disease can't be transmitted in a game is totally erroneous." Another NBA team doctor thought that up to sixty NBA players had HIV, and that everybody should get tested. But that position would never get past the Players Association president—Magic's buddy Isiah. Testing was one step away from banning all players with HIV, and Isiah was doing everything he could to support Magic.

The tables had turned in their relationship. Now it was Magic who needed Isiah. Isiah, to his credit, wasn't rubbing Magic's nose in the dirt over the politics of the Olympic selections.

But there was nothing Isiah or anyone in America could do to solve Magic's problem in Australia. The head of the national basketball program there wanted the Olympic Committee to ban Magic from the Games. If that happened, it would be disastrous for Magic. Not just because he wanted one last dance with the boys. But also because of money. Since his HIV announcement, his endorsements had been shaky as hell. He needed the Olympics to buff his image and keep his fiscal house of cards from tumbling. He needed his money men now more than ever—especially because he wasn't getting much support from the old home team.

After a career as a one-team warrior for the Lakers, Magic was getting the cold shoulder. A long-held dream of Magic's was to own the Lakers. He'd believed that would happen around the time he hit middle age. But when he'd been diagnosed with HIV, he'd decided not to defer the dream. Immediately after his retirement from the team, he'd gone to owner Jerry Buss to ask if he could buy the team when Buss retired. After all, Buss had always told Magic that he was like a son to him. But in their meeting, Buss had let Magic know that "son" was just a, well, a figure of speech— and that he was giving the franchise to his *real* children.

At that point, Magic had started hoping he could cut short his field trip to the real world and start playing for the Lakers again. But Jerry West hadn't sounded at all excited. In fact, he'd sounded pissed off. The Lakers had made an offer to point guard Sherman Douglas, which would be nonvalid if Magic returned. West had complained, "I just wish he'd make up his mind what he wants to do. It puts us in a very awkward position."

Magic wasn't the only ex-Laker that West was approaching with an apparent attitude of What-have-you-done-for-me-lately? When Kareem had offered to come out of retirement—and donate his salary to AIDS research—West had been indifferent.

Enter David Stern. He solved Magic's All-Star problem in about two seconds. Stern said: Let Magic play. If he bleeds, take him out. Brilliantly simple. Magic was in awe of Stern. He was short, white, and pudgy—but, man, did he know the real world.

So Magic got his All-Star okay while the other players

were still sweating out the voting. For the Olympic hopefuls, it was a crucial All-Star Game. If they couldn't make the All-Star Team, there was no way in hell they'd make Barcelona.

• Screwed Again

Dominique Wilkins watched tape on a monitor while he took off his clothes, his face as sour as if he'd been sucking lemons. Thousands of his All-Star votes had vanished from the league's computer, and now he was behind Larry Bird in the voting. Wilkins was averaging 28.5 points—second to Jordan, and 10 more than Bird, who was hurting so badly he was considering retirement.

"They said it was the computer's fault," an Atlanta reporter told Wilkins. "The computer was downloading the votes, and *bam!* Up in smoke!"

"Up in smoke," said Wilkins, shaking his head and trying to squeeze out a smile. "Unbelievable."

"Unbelievable?"

"Yeah. As in, I don't believe it. I hope somebody's investigating it."

"The league is. Do you think Bird will even *play?* They say his back injury isn't the same old injury as before."

"Sure that's what they say," said Wilkins. "But it's gotta be connected somehow. It's all in the same back, isn't it?" Wilkins sighed. "Oh, I guess it doesn't matter," he said. "The coaches will put me on." I couldn't tell if he was being sarcastic.

"If you don't make the All-Star Team," I asked him, "do you think that'll ruin your chances for the Olympics?"

"I'll make it."

"Which?"

"Both."

But four days later he ripped apart his Achilles tendon. His season was over. Now Isiah wasn't the only Olympic casualty. The list of hopefuls was getting shorter.

• "It's *practice*, Earvin!"

"Hey, Mike!" Isiah turned on his Sweet Zeke grin, shining it full-force on Michael Jordan at the All-Star Game practice. "Watch!" Isiah threw up a left-handed hook that banged off, then boomed his deep Bela Lugosi laugh. Jordan smiled—sort of. Relations between them were still chilly. Business was in the way.

Jordan had just announced that he didn't want the NBA putting his picture on its T-shirts and trinkets. He'd already cut a deal with Nike that gave them exclusive use of his likeness. Nike, after all, paid Jordan $8 million a year, and the NBA merchandisers paid him . . . zip. The NBA, though, was grossing $1.1 billion a year from product sales, and the majority of it came from Bulls merchandise. So it was an easy choice for Jordan. But Isiah was pissed.

Half a million per year of the NBA's merchandising money went straight to the players' pension fund, which Isiah safeguarded as president of the Players Association. Even though $500,000 was only a small percentage of the NBA's take, Isiah wanted to keep money from the Jordan trinkets coming. Lately, he'd been screaming like a Wobbly about solidarity and the masses. But most of the superstars were siding with Jordan. They wanted Jordan to run for Players Association president.

So it wasn't easy for Isiah to drum up All-Star camaraderie in the humid gym where the East team was faking its way through a practice.

The East coach, Chicago's Phil Jackson, strolled over. "One of the most important things," he said to the small group, "is spacing." He started talking about the "UCLA offense." Dennis Rodman paid scant attention.

"Right," Rodman said to Joe Dumars, "but as soon as the game starts, it'll all break down."

A little later, when the West team took the floor, there was a different feel. It emanated from Magic. He wanted to *win*. Not just because it was probably his last NBA game. Magic *always* wanted to win. He ran the floor of the cramped gym hard, with almost desperate intensity. At one point, Mullin caught an underhand bullet from Magic, dribbled a step, and sank a jumper. "Don't pull up!" Magic yelled. "Drive on in!"

"It's *practice*, Earvin."

"That's *right*," said Magic. He grinned the Magic grin— but Mullin didn't let it happen again.

After practice, Magic looked glossy and happy in a coat of sweat. "Feel good to be playing with NBA guys again?" I asked him.

"That's what it's all about, man. Michael, Isiah, all the guys—bein' out there rubbin' elbows with 'em, shootin' the bull, that's what I miss most."

"What's more important to you tomorrow—to play or to win?"

He had to give that some thought. "I play to win," he said. "You want to have fun at the same time, but fun, to me, is winnin'."

Reporters clustered around him. It was hot and hard to breathe. "You feel a strong sense of anticipation?" somebody asked.

He nodded hard. "You start *sweatin'*. The closer it gets, the more I get goose bumps and chills runnin' through my body."

"This is obviously not how you expected to close your career," said a reporter. "Are you disappointed?"

"It's a *great* close," Magic said. "First the All-Star Game, then the Olympics. I can say good-bye tomorrow, and I can say good-bye in Barcelona. Or I could say, this is the start of a comeback. If I don't come back to the NBA, I could go play in Spain or Italy."

"Charles said they're not gonna cut you any slack out there tomorrow."

"I'm not askin' for no slack. I'm comin' right at them, just like they're comin' at me. That's the *fun*."

"Isiah said he'd hug you, kiss you, then try to beat the shit out of you."

"I'd be disappointed if he did it any other way. I would be like, 'This is *not* Isiah.'"

"Is there any one letter that you got that you maybe cherish more than the others?"

"So many of 'em—we'd be here all week. Haven't even got through all of 'em—two, three hundred thousand. There's one from a little guy in New Jersey—he's ten—and he wrote a poem for me, talkin' about how his situation was like mine. That one was special."

"What's the one message you want to convey by playing?"

"That you can go on and live. That people who have whatever—a disease, a handicap—whatever it might be, that they don't have to feel they any different."

"Who's gonna carry the torch in the NBA after you retire?"

"Well, you got a lot of guys to choose from. Michael. David Robinson. Patrick Ewing. Dominique. Isiah. But I wouldn't pick nobody. Dr. J didn't pick me, and nobody picked Doc. What happens is, somebody emerges and says, 'Hey, I'm the guy.'"

"If you could write a script for the game tomorrow, how would it end?"

"I'm tryin' to come up with an ending now. I just can't. I got every chapter, every situation, covered—except the ending. You know how you type something and just tear it out and throw it in the wastebasket? I've torn up so many pages. But I can't come up with an ending. I still gotta find that dot to put at the end." He'd just signed a $5 million book deal, but he said "dot" instead of "period."

"How's your book going?" I asked.

"Great!" The Magic smile.

When he smiled, I couldn't help but be jealous. His smile burned itself into my brain. But later I found out his deal was for three books, and that the "money book" would be his memoirs—which would probably be published posthumously. I could still see that Magic smile, but I never again saw it in the same way.

Magic was winding down. He seemed somehow less animated, even less sure of himself, than he had when I'd talked to him in the past. He had a different persona. Part of him was the same old Magic: the Natural, the man-child to whom everything came easily. But there was another element to him now. It was more wise and more caring. More mature. But it was not happy. It was: poster child.

• Sex, Lies, and Videotape

A beeper chirped. A guy in a gray suit punched numbers into his cordless phone. "How long?" he said. He pushed the disconnect button, then dialed again. "Hi. They told me about eighty seconds."

In front of him swirled a surreal mix of light and sound, all centered around a fifty-foot-tall orange basketball. The lobby of the Dolphin Hotel, where the NBA was staying in Orlando for All-Star weekend, was the hub of a series of parties, receptions, and meetings. Under the basketball, which hovered over three giant TVs flashing NBA highlights, were loose groups of NBA power brokers and stars: Jerry West, Donnie Walsh, Jack McCloskey, Artis Gilmore, Isiah Thomas, Charles Barkley. Downtown Julie Brown was doing her best to be conspicuous, but no one was paying attention.

Upstairs were high-stakes card games, dangerous liaisons, secret meetings between general managers desperate to make trades, and conquer-the-world conferences between agents and players. The Dolphin didn't usually see this much action. It sat in the heart of Disney World, and the usual clientele wore T-shirts and mouse-ear hats.

The beeper rang again. The guy in the gray suit grabbed his phone. "Okay, go!" Ten seconds later, the elevator beside the guy opened and there stood Magic Johnson. Almost instantly, the whole lobby seemed to rush toward him, like fire getting sucked into a vacuum. The guy in the gray suit walked in front of Magic, bulldozing a path. Magic kept both hands on the guy's shoulders. In Magic's wake was Cookie, who looked tired and fragile.

The beeper buzzed again. The guy spread his arms wide, opening a little space for Magic and Cookie. They slipped past the gift shop and parked in front of another elevator. Cookie looked into the gift shop. Looked away. The elevator opened. David Stern was in it. He held out his hand, as if he were welcoming Magic into his home. Magic and Cookie stepped in, and the doors closed.

"Where's Magic going?" I asked the guy with the beeper.

"Just a quiet dinner with the commissioner."

"In one of the dining rooms?"

"Oh, no. They'd drive Magic crazy in a restaurant."

It was, in a way, a jarring image: Magic spending his last night in the NBA cooped up with a middle-aged money man like David Stern. Since his college days, Magic had stomped the earth like a bull elk, crazy with earthly passions. Exactly how crazy was just now coming out.

The tabloids were full of him these days. Nasty stories. He was trying to make a big joke out of it—the same old Aliens-Find-Elvis joke that *everybody* made when they got creamed by the tabloids. But the joke sounded even weaker than usual. Because the papers had pictures. Magic had *not* been careful. For example, there was one story about a sex orgy at his Bel Air home. Lots of lurid details: group sex, exhibitionism, sex with beer bottles, etc. Ugly. Almost unbelievable. But somebody had been videotaping, and a still photo from the video was in the paper, showing Magic transfixed by the mostly naked body of a young black woman. Right on the front page. With the headline: "Magic's Secret Sex Orgy." The paper had apparently timed the article for All-Star week, while Magic was big news. There were also photos of him posing proudly with porn stars and strippers.

It was a hell of a thing to have staring out at you and your wife from a gift shop news rack. Just the thing to impress the commissioner. A real conversation-starter.

• A Weird Message from Gomorrah

Tom Heinsohn gripped his cigarette Continental-style, between his thumb and forefinger, and raised his voice over the hubbub of the players getting dressed for the Legends' Game. "Okay! Let me ask a half-ass serious question! Okay, guys?" Nobody shut up. "This is half-ass *serious,* okay?" A few heads looked up: Dave Cowens, George Gervin, Rick Barry, Dave Bing, Norm Nixon. "Okay," said Heinsohn, "how many of you have played basketball recently?"

All the heads went back down. Suddenly everybody was interested in their new Converse tennies. "Two years," said Bing.

"Ten months," said Cowens, "but I was 0-for-twelve then."

Heinsohn shook his head. "Okay!" he said, clapping his hands. "We're *ready!*"

They trooped out to play.

It was a little sad. None of them were poor; Bing, in fact, had made himself wealthy in the steel business. Barry was doing great as a broadcaster. But not one of them—these men of incredible talent and spirit—had anywhere near the money of a Jon Koncak (5.5 career average; $1.5 million salary), Danny Ferry (8.6 average, $2.64 million), or Felton Spencer (7.1, $1.07 million). Every one of these guys was an immortal—by playing standards. But in the real world, unprotected by immortality-level money, they were just tall, middle-class men groping toward middle age. They still had to work for a living.

None had hit immortality-level money for one simple reason. They'd all played before Magic had entered the league. Magic had changed everything.

Magic—and to a lesser extent, Larry Bird—had saved the NBA. Magic and Larry had each offered something different. Bird had been great—and white. Magic had been great—and boyishly enthusiastic. At a time when sports had been increasingly perceived as a business, Magic had made it look *fun.* He'd looked like a kid playing a game. He'd played with abandon, risking everything diving for balls. And his indifference to money had made him wealthy.

When Magic and Larry started in 1979, TV broadcast rights (the prime source of players' salaries) sold for less than $20 million. In 1992 the rights went for $218 million. During the same time, cable rights went from $0 to $57 million.

As the NBA's TV profile had risen, so had the marketability of its players. Advertisers realized that an athlete who was on TV several times a week was a more valuable spokesman than a movie star who made one film a year. Advertisers also realized—after watching Michael Jordan save Nike—that blacks could market to whites. At least, Michael and Magic could. They could do this because they were nonthreatening to whites. Michael was safe because of his mythic image: the boy who could fly. Magic was safe because he was so full of the joy of youth.

Once Jordan had proved he could cross-market, Magic jumped into the contest. The first thing he did was find a mentor—Joe Smith, president of Capitol-EMI Records. Smith, a courtside Laker fan, represented Magic for free, enjoying the brush with sports glamour. In 1987 Smith restructured Magic's twenty-five-year, $25 million Laker contract. An astounding deal in 1981, it had turned into a ripoff because of the NBA's increased TV revenue.

Magic began soaking up Smith's savvy. "We'll be having dinner," Smith says, "and I've got to stop myself, because he's just drinking in everything. I say, 'Wait a second, I didn't write the book on this thing.'"

Smith found Magic an apt pupil. "He admires success," says Smith. "He came to my house—I have a real impressive house I bought nineteen years ago in Beverly Hills—and he was just knocked out, looking at everything in the house, even furniture. He's impressed by those kinds of things, in a good way.

"We ran into each other coming off MGM flights, and I told him, 'Hey, you're flying MGM!' And he says, 'Yeah, but you *own* the airplane.' He wants to be an industrialist, a conglomerate."

To further that end, Smith introduced Magic to another Laker courtsider, Michael Ovitz. Ovitz, the most powerful man in Hollywood and a major force in Pacific Rim business circles, was reluctant to involve himself in Magic's affairs. Ovitz ran the Creative Artists Agency and represented many of the world's most prominent entertainers. However, says Magic: "I got the feeling he did not want to take me on. But over four or five meetings, after he asked me questions dating back to my childhood, he finally said, 'Okay, I'll take you on.' Oh, happy day!"

Ovitz wanted to limit the number of Magic's endorsements and to get him intimately involved with the companies he did endorse. He also wanted to pull Magic away from just athletic products. Ovitz was particularly interested in the two largest soft drink companies, Coca-Cola and Pepsi. Both wanted Magic as a spokesperson. Magic and Ovitz held out for an equity position.

Ovitz put Magic through a business training camp, with tutorials, simulations, and a curriculum of heavy reading. Then they approached both companies. Magic was ready. He'd quickly learned many of the finer points of business dynamics. "As soon as I go into an office," Magic says, "I'm reading the situation. Where's he sitting—where's he gonna make me sit? Are his feet on the desk? Is he gonna make me wait?"

Magic soon became an excellent businessman. His boyishness was charming—since it came from a fierce warrior. Magic didn't trumpet his stats to the business types, but sports was the foundation of his charisma. It was the source of his fame, his fortune, and his confidence. Without sports, he'd have been just another pushy young overachiever.

Magic made headway with both Coke and Pepsi, and Pepsi made the best offer. He could buy into the Washington, D.C., distributorship. It cost him about $20 million, but it gave him a piece of the action. Julius Erving, one of Magic's idols, had made a similar deal in 1985 that would keep him at the immortality level forever.

Magic began visiting his Pepsi plant regularly, taking notes and talking to the truck and forklift drivers. He schmoozed with buyers and drummed up new business. "I've been with Pepsi for thirteen years," says the distributorship's vice president, "and Earvin can run with anybody I've worked for. I mean, he's in Hawaii on vacation and I get a call from him about a vending proposal. He's for real."

Magic and his money men gradually set up deals with Nintendo, Nestlé, Spalding, Target Stores, Kentucky Fried Chicken, CBS–Fox Video, Converse, and Campofrio (a Spanish meat company). They also established Magic Johnson Enterprises, Magic Johnson All-Star Camps, and Magic Johnson T's. By 1992 Magic was raking in about $12 million a year in endorsements and millions more from his investments. His net worth ballooned to about $100 million. His leveraging capabilities were extraordinary; a promissory note from him was gold. He was within striking distance of having the money and credit to buy a basketball franchise.

Then he got HIV.

By All-Star time, none of his endorsements had collapsed. But they were all teetering. He no longer had the perfect, boyish image. In fact, he had the modern version of leprosy. He'd screwed his way into it. He'd jeopardized his wife, his baby, and countless other women.

Now he was running all over the country, doing what he called "God's work." He seemed to believe he'd been chosen by God to lead a moral reawakening in America.

But admen liked their heroes simple—not ironic. And the idea of Magic—on a mission from God, telling kids to stop having sex—was just too weird.

Magic needed to get back on the floor. He needed a game. A big game.

Magic sat in front of his locker, pulling on an NBA uniform for presumably the last time. He'd been reminiscing about his family, his college days, the early years with Kareem. A small group of reporters hovered around him.

Somebody asked, "If you could change anything, what would you change?"

Magic looked incredulous. "Change?" he said. "Nuthin' at all. *Nuthin'.*"

It was an extraordinary statement from a man with a fatal disease.

• Lansing, Michigan

Magic Johnson's father did an excellent job of protecting little Earvin Johnson from the most brutal hardships of the real world. He did this by absorbing those hardships himself. Once, he described his life to Magic this way: "I'd like to say it was like death, but I've never seen death. So maybe it was worse."

Earvin Johnson, Senior—the Big E., as his seven kids referred to him—was one of ten million faceless heroes of the lower working class. To survive in the lower working class—especially as an urban black—required great will. But to prevail required heroism. And the Big E. prevailed: all of his children went to college.

The Johnsons lived in a poor section of Lansing, Michigan, among other black families employed by the auto factories. The neighborhood was full of children, but there were virtually no bicycles—no one could afford one. Magic grew up in a small two-story yellow house. Once, when he visited the house as an adult, his first thought had been: "How did we all live here?"

Magic shared one of the three bedrooms with his brothers, Larry and Quincy. His four sisters shared another, and his parents had the other. The family's living conditions were not much better than those Magic's parents had grown up in. Big E. had been raised as a Southern sharecropper. Magic's mother, Christine, had also grown up in the rural South. Their families had been poor but had enjoyed the beauty and friendliness of country life. In Lansing they had a little more money. But Lansing wasn't very beautiful and wasn't very friendly.

Big E. worked two full-time jobs for nineteen years to drag his family out of the lower working class. From 4:00 P.M. until 1:00 A.M., he operated a metal-grinding machine in the Fisher Body plant. The machine was dangerous, throwing off sparks that burned his clothes and skin. After that shift, he cleaned the shops for about two hours, then went home to sleep for about five hours. At 9:00 A.M., he returned to the shop to haul away loads of trash in his pickup. Then he had a couple of hours off before he punched in again. For a while, he didn't have his trash-hauling job but pumped gas seven hours a day. Big E., luckily, was a storehouse of energy—a trait Magic inherited.

But his two incomes weren't enough to cover all the bills. Christine Johnson, besides taking care of the kids and home, worked full-time as a school custodian.

It was an exhausting, dismal existence. But, for the most part, Magic's parents were able to shelter their kids from it. The children were well taken care of and were not asked to do more than help out with chores.

This freed Magic to pursue his interest in sports. Even in grade school, he was an outstanding athlete, and he quickly became obsessed with sports. In contrast to the world around him, sports was dramatic and exciting, with clear heroes and obvious winners. Sports was, of course, a highly contrived, symbolic world—but to little Earvin, who excelled in that world, it was real and alluring.

Basketball soon became the only sport Earvin was seriously interested in. The only time he got to spend with his father was on weekends, and their main activity was watching NBA games on TV. Big E. knew the game well and schooled his son in its intricacies: footwork, head fakes, blocking out, defensive stances. "His passion became my passion," says Magic. After the games, they would go outside to practice. By sixth grade, Magic was six feet tall, an excellent shooter and a good ball handler.

In seventh grade, the help Magic's father had given him paid off. Over two hundred kids showed up to try out for the basketball team. The coach had everyone shoot lay-ups with both hands—something Magic's dad had taught him. The drill eliminated all but twenty-five of the kids. Magic ran home and thanked his dad.

By the end of eighth grade, he was a celebrity. He was 6–5 and regularly had his name in the paper. Players from all over town came to his neighborhood to challenge him. The only player who came close was Jay Vincent, who would later play in college with Magic and play in the NBA. Vincent, says Magic, "was top gun in his neighborhood, and I was top gun in mine."

Even while he was in junior high, strangers would stop Magic on the street and tell him how great he was. He tried hard to keep his feet on the ground, but it wasn't easy.

Then Magic met Dr. Charles Tucker, a streetwise, twenty-seven-year-old black psychologist who worked for the school district. Tucker, who had come close to an NBA career, was among the first to recognize that Magic was good enough to play professionally. Shortly after they met, Tucker challenged Magic to one-on-one. Tucker hooked Magic, grabbed his shorts, and stepped on his toes. Magic was infuriated. But Tucker told him, "You have to learn how to play the pro game." It was the first time any informed person had told Magic he could go pro.

Against his desires, Magic was bused to predominantly white Everett High. He played for a conservative, fundamentals-oriented coach who hated what he called Magic's "fancy stuff." But Magic played the way he wanted to play, and his coach accepted it. By his sophomore year, he was good enough to make the All-State Second Team and to elicit the nickname "Magic" from a local sportswriter. His mother, a devout Adventist, didn't like it—sounded too occult. College recruiters began showing up at the Johnson house.

That same year, Charles Tucker introduced Magic to Kareem Abdul-Jabbar after a Pistons game in Detroit. Magic was thrilled. As they were driving home, Tucker told him, "Someday some kid will shake your hand and brag about it."

"You really think so?" Magic asked.

"Yep. But just keep your head on. That's the hardest part."

Vanity, however, was hard to avoid. One source of it was Magic's obvious sex appeal. Like other young sports stars, Magic was very popular with girls. He would go to parties at the apartment of Michigan State basketball star Terry Furlow, and, as Magic recalls, "The place would be filled with girls, and they'd all be looking over at me and smiling."

By his junior year, Magic was playing one-on-one against NBA superstar George Gervin, who was from Detroit. That year, he was also named to the All-State First Team. By now, he'd already developed his obsession with his team winning. Ever since he'd begun playing, his own glory had been certain—the only success he had to worry about was his team's.

As a senior, he says, "The game came so easily to me that I thoroughly dominated our first four or five games, scoring thirty, forty, or whatever I decided that particular day." His coach asked him to hold down his scoring, to get the other players involved. He did it so effectively that his team won the state championship.

Magic chose to attend Michigan State mostly because he wouldn't have to leave Lansing. He wanted to be close to his parents. And he liked being a local celebrity.

"On campus," Johnson wrote in his book *Magic,* "I literally stopped traffic. People from all walks of life introduced themselves to thank me for choosing Michigan State." Magic roomed in a dorm with Jay Vincent, became a part-time disc jockey at a disco, and made the most of campus nightlife.

Playing at the college level was not a big adjustment. Even as a freshman, he says, "I felt I could play in the NBA. But I just wasn't sure if I wanted to just yet. I was only eighteen years old." His first year, he made several All-American teams and was approached by the NBA's Kansas City Kings, who had the first pick in the draft. They offered him $250,000, but he turned it down.

His sophomore year, he made the cover of *Sports Illustrated* and led Michigan State to a national championship with a win over Larry Bird's Indiana State. Years later, Magic would remember Bird sobbing into a towel as the game ended.

Magic turned pro after his sophomore year. To him, though, it didn't seem like a startling dream-come-true. It was just another inevitability. Not yet twenty, he'd been a star for almost twelve years.

Before Magic played even one game in the NBA, Detroit GM Jack McCloskey offered the Lakers the entire Detroit team for Johnson. The Lakers turned McCloskey down.

After winning his first NBA game, Magic jumped into the arms of a shocked Kareem Abdul-Jabbar. Before the year was over, his enthusiasm profoundly affected the NBA. His boyish exuberance—coupled with his passing skills—was extremely telegenic and lured millions of new fans.

Magic concluded his first season with the most spectacular game of his career. With the championship on the line, and Kareem disabled by a severe migraine, Magic started at center and played all five positions. He finished with 42 points, 15 rebounds, 7 assists, 3 steals—and his first championship. Years later, after Magic found out he had HIV, he often turned to a videotape of that game for solace.

After weathering a minor controversy—his role in the firing of blowhard coach Paul Westhead—Magic and the Lakers began one of the most extraordinary runs in NBA history. Coached by Pat Riley, with Kareem in the middle, James Worthy on the wing, and Magic at the point, the 1980s Lakers became, arguably, the best team in NBA history. They won five championships and were in the Finals nine times in twelve years.

Magic's individual achievements were equally astounding. He won three MVP awards, was on the All-NBA First Team nine times, was on the All-Star Team ten times, and was the All-Star Game MVP once. He led the league in assists four times and in steals twice, and set the NBA career record for assists.

Magic, a legend since puberty, broke new ground with almost every step. He became the first athlete to reach rock star status—and Jordan was the only other one who ever achieved it. But Magic was more hip than Michael. Magic starred in rock videos and basked in celebrity.

His home became a hub in the Hollywood social scene. Among his closest friends were Hollywood "Black Pack" playboys like Eddie Murphy and Arsenio Hall. For years, they partied wildly, following a loose pattern: weekends at Carlos and Charlies, Tuesdays at The World, Thursdays at the Comedy Act or Paradise 24—then to someone's house (usually Murphy's) for long parties with legions of women.

Because of his untamed sexuality, Magic resisted getting married. His sexual encounters numbered in the thousands. He would often go to bed with several women in a day.

What was most shocking about Magic's life-style was that he engaged in it during the era of AIDS. Hollywood was devastated by the epidemic. In Hollywood AIDS was the most high-profile malady of the century. Magic, however, not only engaged in virtual nonstop sex with a high-risk group—promiscuous women—but did so without even using condoms.

It's hard to make sense out of that kind of behavior. Magic Johnson was a very bright young man and almost a genius in street-smarts. But his sexual behavior was idiotic.

It's impossible to understand why Magic engaged in this behavior. Maybe it was a way to confirm his success. Possibly, because his greatness was so natural—seemingly inevitable—it had never seemed as secure to him, or as deeply founded, as it would have if he'd struggled mightily to achieve it. In bedding so many women, perhaps he reassured himself of his success.

There's also another possible explanation, one endorsed by a number of sports psychologists. "Athletes often grow up thinking that they're immortal, not susceptible to the laws of nature," says Dr. Steven Ungerleider, author of *Beyond Strength: Psychological Profiles of Olympic Athletes.*

"Almost every teenager thinks that way," says Dr. Ungerleider, "and athletes often fall prey to arrested development, staying at a teenage level of maturity. They can often avoid the maturing process of enduring consequences, and paying the piper. The people around them—their teachers, parents, girlfriends, buddies, even the local police —put them on a pedestal, and don't hold them accountable. So they don't go through the same socialization as non-athletes.

"It keeps them from growing up. There's a moratorium

on psychological development. Sometimes, they end up living in a dream world."

When Magic found out he had HIV, he began to wake up from his dream.

But it was hard. He wanted to believe that he'd simply reached another new level: playing the point for God.

But the real world kept intruding. It told him: You're not God. You just pushed your luck, and it ran out.

Recently, Magic had been accused of being in denial about his illness. His response: "What's all this 'denial'? I've always been the same when things go wrong. One time, right after I moved into my house, I ripped up a whole side of my Rolls. I called my agent up, and I was laughing at what I did. And he said, 'Magic, what's the matter with you? You just smashed up your Rolls!' And I said, 'Well, what can I do? It's done, and I can't do anything.'"

Then Magic had paused and groped with his hands. "Of course," he'd said, "this time is different.

"This time I can die."

● Into the Night

The locker room was full of tension. Golden State's Don Nelson, coach of the Western Conference team, was hardly speaking at all. Nor were any of the players. They were fixated on winning. It was a very unusual atmosphere for an All-Star Game.

When they came out, the announcer saved the introduction of Magic for last. When his name was called, each member of the team came up and embraced him. It was Isiah's idea—he'd worked it out with the players the day before. Isiah, who didn't want anything to spoil Magic's day, was on his best behavior. At one point, when he and Karl Malone were lining up for a free throw, he faked throwing an elbow at Malone and laughed.

Then, early in the game, what everyone feared: one of the players crashed into Magic. The courtside reporters looked horrified, like they'd get infected just watching. Reggie Lewis, who'd dumped Magic, then walked in front of Johnson as Magic stepped to the free throw line and said something to him. Magic belted out a laugh. And again the reporters looked horrified; they thought Lewis had just made an AIDS joke. They glared at Lewis like, First you endanger *everyone in the front row,* and now you're *teasing the poster child!*

But then Barkley bashed into Magic, and Rodman got him, and everyone calmed down.

Magic began huffing and puffing. On the TV screen, he looked strong, but close up, you could see his chest heaving. Incredibly, though, his play was excellent. He and Drexler led the West to a big lead. Nobody on the East seemed to care. Except Jordan. He was pissed. He wanted to win.

In the stands, Cookie Johnson watched distractedly, unsmiling. Every time Magic got whacked, she seemed to cringe.

Three minutes left. Don Nelson—still feeling Clyde's wrath for bad-mouthing Drexler years ago—left Drexler and Magic in the game. They were the only viable candidates for All-Star MVP, and Nelson didn't want anybody saying he'd tried to influence the outcome.

It looked like Clyde would win. He had 22 points to Magic's 16, and led the West in rebounding. It was a momentous game for Clyde—exactly what he needed to climb over the other Olympic candidates. He wanted that badly; his face still got tight every time somebody mentioned the Olympics.

Then Magic hit a three-pointer. The East came downcourt, and Isiah got the ball on the right side. The other players cleared out, and Isiah, grinning, started dancing through his fanciest playground moves as Magic guarded him. Magic was grinning, too, but holding his ground. Isiah got nowhere. As the clock ran down, he threw up an airball.

Magic downcourt. He pulled up deep. Fired. Another three. The crowd screamed.

Now Jordan went one-on-one against Magic. Settled for an eight-foot jumper. Off.

Clyde got the ball downcourt. Seconds left in the game. All that one-on-one had him crazy with competitive lust. He dribbled on the perimeter. Eyed the hoop. Dribbled. Looked up again. He was *dying* to score. He passed off.

To Magic. Isiah was in front of Magic. Magic started to drive. Stopped outside the three-point line. Leaned back. Tossed up an off-balance, one-handed shot. Isiah, watching Magic's eyes, thought, "No way that's going in."

Isiah turned around. *Swish.* Isiah said to himself: "Magic!"

The horn shrieked.

Long after the locker rooms had cleared and the reporters had sprinted off to file the usual identical stories, Magic summoned his family to a private room. They all posed with him for group pictures. First Mom and Dad and Magic, then Cookie and Magic, then all the brothers and sisters, then his son, Andre—every possible combination. Magic was smiling the Magic smile. But he looked heartbroken. Lost. "I feel like I'm in a dream," he said, "and I don't want to wake up."

The family left. Only a few players remained. Magic spotted Clyde. "You were wonderful," he told Drexler.

"For you, babe," said Clyde.

Magic pulled himself away from the players. The locker room got deathly still.

He began working his way out of the stadium, through corridors filled with electronic equipment. Just before he got to the exit, a beautiful young black woman hurried up to him. "Hey, MVP!" she said.

His sagging face lit up. "You *came,*" he said. He embraced her and whispered into her ear. She smiled and hurried off. I have no idea who she was.

Then he was walking alone again. As the exit got nearer, his steps got slower and slower. The corridor was brightly lit, and the Florida night outside—framed by the jamb of an open door—looked black and empty, like deep space. Magic started taking baby steps toward it. He scanned the small group around him for familiar faces. Couldn't find any. He turned all the way around. Nobody. His steps were heavy, as if he were dragging a weight.

Suddenly, a rustle of energy. From nowhere, Michael Jordan appeared.

"Mike!" Magic's eyes caught fire.

Jordan put his arm around Magic's shoulder. Magic put his arm around Jordan's shoulder.

Jordan said something, and Magic bellowed a laugh.

They faced the exit together. They took three giant steps toward it and disappeared. Into the night.

10

Charles Barkley in Hell

Fighting the Fat Diet King • Dancing on Jimmy Hoffa's Grave • "The Olympics Is About Money" • Foul Language on Valentine's Day • Two Mean Sons of Bitches • Grandma Kicks Some Ass • Bobby Knight's Ugly Shoes • Derrick Coleman Treats Charles Like a Weenie

Cruelty without purpose is barbaric. Cruelty with purpose is not cruelty. It's efficiency.
            —Captain William Bligh, 1799

Show me a good loser, and I'll show you a loser.
            —Jimmy Carter, 1975

Rarely does a boy hold a predominantly negative opinion of his father without holding the same opinion of himself.
            —Dr. Richard A. Warshak, 1992

A TV guy wanted to know why I was in Philadelphia on such a foul, dark February day. "For Charles," I said. "What's Valentine's Day without Charles Barkley?"

Jack Ramsay, still buoyant from his election to the Hall of Fame, floated past. I congratulated him. "How come you're in Philadelphia?" he asked.

"To talk to Charles. What's Valentine's Day without—"

"A massacre," said Ramsay.

"What do you mean?"

"Charles isn't talking to the press. And when he does, it's not very pleasant."

"Great. Damn! Maybe I oughta just bag this and go on up to New York. Ewing's always bugging me to spend more quality time with him."

I went to the locker room to see if it was true. But Barkley wasn't there yet. He was making a big point of showing up late, to avoid his teammates and reporters. Charles, I'd been told, was on his worst behavior. He was still busting his ass to get traded, and the trading deadline was now less than two weeks away. So he was pulling every rotten stunt he could think of to make himself unwanted.

Every day now, Barkley thought about winning a championship—the one achievement that would immortalize him, along with golden boys like Magic and Michael and Larry. And every day—knowing this team could never win one—he got increasingly pissed off. For him, Philadelphia had turned into hell.

But he must have felt his escape plan was working, because he'd been in almost daily contact with Jerry West for several weeks now. West was ready to pull the trigger on a trade of James Worthy and Elden Campbell for Barkley. That was part of the reason West was being bitchy about Magic's coming back; if that happened, West couldn't afford Barkley. But Sixer owner Harold Katz was reluctant to make the deal.

While I was waiting, I asked Manute Bol, one of Barkley's closest friends, what they did for fun. "Oh, we like to go out and beat people up," he said.

Barkley burst into the room. Instant silence. He swaggered by Charles Shackleford, the big forward that Barkley considered lazy. "Don't *even* be thinkin' of fightin' me," Barkley said to Shackleford, apropos of nothing. "'Cause I'm a crazy-ass black motherfucker from Alabama."

Shackleford looked hurt, puzzled. "Don't fight you?"

"Yeah," said Barkley, continuing to his locker. "I'm a crazy-ass . . ." His voice fell to a mumble.

"Pardon me, Charles," I said, "you got a minute?"

He shook his head like a dog shaking off sewage. "I'm on vacation from the media," he said. "I haven't talked to those assholes in six weeks." He was punishing the media for reporting that when he'd gotten arrested for his Milwaukee bar brawl, he'd been with a woman. That kind of sportswriting was hard on a marriage.

He looked up and smiled sweetly. "Ever since I stopped talking," he said, "my life's been *so* good."

I could have reminded him that he wasn't really on vacation from media—that it was still TV that paid his salary. Instead, I tried the pity approach. "Jeeze," I said, "I came a long way to talk to you."

Mistake. He smelled fear. "So what am *I* supposed to *do?* Buy your plane ticket?"

"Oh, to hell with it," I said. "I'll just watch the game."

"Y'ain't gonna see much."

I didn't know what he meant. Until midway through the fourth quarter. By then it was obvious. As nearly as I could tell, Barkley was *sleepwalking through the game:* not trying to lose—but trying to stumble through the game like a wino with a nerve disease. He was *weak.* He was ridiculous. He took only seven shots, and scored 6 points, a season low. And this was against the Nets, a team of airheads and slugs with an eight-game losing streak. It looked like Barkley was showing owner Harold Katz just how bad he could be. It was like, Look, Harold, my trading value just went down another million dollars—wanna *keep* stalling?

With the Sixers down 5, coach Jimmy Lynam pulled Barkley from the game. Charles slumped onto the bench and stared into a cup of green Gatorade. When he finally got back in, it was pitiful. Derrick Coleman pushed him around like he was a little weenie who'd wandered onto the wrong playground.

Funny part was, Charles Barkley was very possibly the best player in the world. Better than Jordan. That's what David Robinson thought. Doc Rivers, too. Barkley had, in fact, won the Schick Award—a statistical index of value—

three times in seven years, compared to Jordan's two. For speed-plus-strength, no one matched him.

But today, he was just a punk.

After the game, Barkley stood in front of his locker with his back to the room, his arms spread on the locker tops in a crucifix position. The reporters steered around him like he was radioactive.

A Sixer official walked by. "Hi, Charles."

"Don't fuck with me, man."

"I'm not fucking with you. I'm just saying hi."

"I *mean* it, man. Don't *fuck* with me." The guy cleared out.

One of Barkley's friends in the Philadelphia press inched over and said very softly, "Can I ask one question, Charlie? Seven shots. Was that a conscious thing?"

"It was conscious."

Jack Ramsay, working the Sixer games as a broadcaster, looked grim. He said to a friend, "Boy, Jimmy usually takes the highs and lows really well. But—did you see him?"

When the locker room started to get jungle humid from hot showers, I plunged through what I thought was an exit. But it led to the coaches' room, which was off-limits. Lynam was in there alone, looking small and sweaty, smoking a cigarette. "Sorry, Coach," I said. He smiled. It was the saddest smile I've ever seen outside a funeral.

• The Asshole Factor

Charles was passing Valentine's Day candy around the locker room, going up to each player's stall and proffering a big red heart filled with little chocolate hearts. The candy was a gift from a fan. Most of the players took a piece. Some, including Shackleford, didn't. Manute Bol said, "Can I have another piece, please?"

After Barkley made the rounds, he handed the box to a ball boy. "Get this candy away from me." Barkley—a former fat-ass—was usually slim as a gymnast. Now, though, he had a puff of blubber on his waist. Maybe it was part of his trade-me strategy.

A New Jersey reporter sat down next to Barkley; the Sixers were in New Jersey to play the Nets again. "Gotta give the Nets some credit, huh?" said the reporter, trying to drum up a warm-and-fuzzy quote about the home team, which was part of a beat writer's job.

But Barkley wouldn't play along. "Give them some credit, my ass. They're a punk motherfuckin' team. We'll even it out tonight."

Brian Oliver, a good friend of Barkley's, nodded enthusiastically, bouncing the caricatures that were printed onto his shirt. It was an expensive-looking shirt, emblazoned with the slogan "Let's Bone," and featuring stick figures in various sexual positions.

Dave Hoppen, the big white center from Nebraska, put his gym bag next to Barkley's and said, "Gettin' nailed pretty bad on *Outrageous,* I see."

"NO-NO-No-no," said Barkley. "My book's sellin' great."

"I was talking about the reviews, not the damn *book.*"

Barkley shrugged. "Well, it's sellin' great. It even sold two copies in Nebraska."

"No, it didn't," said Hoppen. Hoppen liked Barkley. When Barkley had said Hoppen was only on the team because he was white, Barkley had spent a lot of time with Hoppen—all of it unpublicized—convincing Hoppen he'd been trying to make a point about racism, not Hoppen.

"Well, if it didn't sell in Nebraska," said Barkley, "that's because the only thing they wanna buy books about is how to grow corn."

"Charles," I said, "you talked to that New Jersey writer— how about talkin' to me?"

"I'm on vacation," he said.

"Look, if you act like an asshole, I'm gonna say that you acted like an asshole."

"Why would you do *that?*"

"'Cause I'm a Prussian warrior and the meanest son of a bitch in journalism."

He looked at me, like: My brother! "Sit down."

"Thanks." I turned on my recorder. "How come the Olympics are important to you?"

"For the chance to play with the other great players. It's the opportunity of a lifetime. Did you want me to say, rah-rah America?"

"No, I like the truth better. That's why I wanted to talk to you. How come you usually tell the truth, instead of the usual line of bullshit?"

"My mother and my grandmother taught me that. And my grandmother was strict. Real strict. Being honest should be important to everybody. But it's not."

"What do you think the Olympic players have in common?"

"Their intellect. They understand the game and see it in a different way. Like, they see things going slower than other players do. And they see things in advance. I don't react while something's happening. I react before it happens. It's a gift."

"Are there other areas of life where you can apply that gift?"

"No."

"Do you get in the zone of altered consciousness very often?"

"Now and then. It's a great feeling. You feel like you can do anything."

"Does it matter much to you if you start in the Olympics?"

"I wanna start. If I don't, it's not that big of a deal. But I *don't* wanna go in there and get five or ten minutes. I wanna play, like, twenty or twenty-five minutes."

"Are you disappointed the Soviets and Yugoslavs aren't at full strength?"

"Yeah, I am. But it's made that part of the world better, and that's a hell of a lot more important than basketball. It means nobody has even a chance of beating us, though."

"What if you guys get in ego battles?"

"That won't happen. People are always tryin' to put down people who are good at something—you know, sayin' they got big egos. But people are stupid."

"Did it bother you that of the first eight guys they picked, you were the last one, because of what they called the citizenship factor?" I was careful not to say "asshole factor." I may be a Prussian warrior, but I'm not stupid.

His face clouded. "Who told you that?"

"Guys on the Selection Committee."

"Well, they lied. They picked the players with the biggest names, the ones that can make the most money. So get real and gimme a break. They're not concerned with stuff like citizenship. The Olympics is about money."

"You think they're trying to use you for their own gain, then?"

"They're tryin' to make money. But I'm not like these other guys. I'm not an Uncle Tom. I'm legit. I'm a man. And the league don't tell me anything. They don't tell me what to do."

He slipped his shirt over his head, revealing his strange round shoulders. Barkley was one of the strongest men in the NBA, but he didn't lift weights, so instead of having sharply defined rocks and ridges of muscle, he had arms and shoulders so smooth they looked inflated. Running down them were scars that looked like stretch marks, made when men much bigger than him had ripped his skin apart. He saw me looking at the scars.

"They really beat hell out of you out there, don't they?" I said.

"I'm twenty-eight, and my doctor says I've got the body of somebody thirty-eight. My body hurts all the time."

An hour later, out on the floor, it was easy to see why: Derrick Coleman was again working Barkley over, focusing his abuse first on one part of the body, then another, like a prizefighter. After ten minutes of it, the referee finally called a foul. "Yes!" Barkley snapped at ref Eddie Rush. "The whistle fuckin' works!"

A fan in the front row yelled, "Give him a technical—he

used The Word." Rush gave the guy a quick, strange look, like, Is this your first NBA game? Actually, it might have been. New Jersey was one of the few places where you didn't need a season ticket to get a good seat. It had terrible attendance figures. The only cool thing about the Meadowlands Arena was that Jimmy Hoffa was supposedly part of its cement work. By Newark standards, that was a charming legend.

Throughout most of the game, Barkley's torpor continued. Lynam kept shuttling him out of the game, looking increasingly frantic as Barkley moped to the bench.

Late in the game, the Sixers were up by two. Barkley grabbed for the ball but got Coleman's little finger, bending it backward. Rush called a foul. Barkley looked incredulous: You let us tear each other's bodies apart, then call a foul when I twist his *pinkie?* Barkley put the ball on the floor and said, "You fucked up, man." Blast of whistle. Technical on Barkley. Charles looked at the ceiling. Boos rained down. Joy in Newark! This crowd actually contained—of all things—*black people.* They were dancing in the aisles.

Lynam looked suicidal. It was a terrible time for a technical. Or maybe a good time, depending upon your goal.

Barkley went to the bench with his face twisted into disparate compartments, like a cubist portrait: angry eyes, pouting mouth, determined jaw, quizzical eyebrows.

He looked like everything but himself.

• Leeds, Alabama

"Sigmund Freud," says Frank Layden, "would jump out of the grave to examine Charles Barkley."

Charles Barkley was the most complex person on the Olympic basketball team. He was a man full of contradictions, and a man who created conflict in the world around him. Most of the Olympians were notably single-minded; they were oblivious to irony, self-contradiction, and everything else that could make you crazy at the free throw line. But not Charles. He thrived on contradiction.

Dave Coskey, former Sixer PR director, defines Barkley this way: "Charles is the exact opposite of most modern athletes. Most of these guys are jerks who want you to think they're nice guys. But Charles is a genuinely nice guy who wants you to think he's a jerk."

The inner conflicts in Charles Barkley seem to be mostly rooted in his conflicts with his father, who abandoned him. But just as central to Barkley's personality is the rock-strong love he always got from his mother and grandmother. These two opposite influences—abandonment and love—formed Barkley's core. In strong people, these influences are the classic creators of inner-directed, creative behavior. In weak people, they're the classic precursors of insanity.

When Charles Barkley's mother gave birth to him in 1963, she was, she later said, "a baby having a baby." When Charles was born, Charcey and Frank Barkley had just graduated from high school in Leeds, Alabama, a little town just outside Birmingham. Charles was relatively small—six pounds, twelve ounces—and was so anemic that he had to have blood transfusions through his feet for six months just to keep him alive. Neither Charcey nor Frank had much of an education, nor any marketable skills. Furthermore, America's racial tensions—focused on Birmingham and Montgomery—were at their zenith. Life was hard. Too hard for Frank. He split. Charles wouldn't see his father again for eight years. By then, Frank would be remarried, with stepchildren he treated better than his own children.

By the time Charles was old enough to realize what had happened, he hated his father. Not just for leaving him, but also for leaving his mother. Frank sent home no child support and rarely communicated with Charles. In his book *Outrageous,* Barkley writes, "I came to think of him as an evil man, because only an evil man would leave his wife and son."

Charcey got a job as a maid, cleaning white people's homes for $15 a day. She also worked in the high school cafeteria. She went straight from one job to the other.

Charles, his mother, and his maternal grandmother—

Johnnie Mae Gaither—lived in a one-bedroom apartment in a government housing project. Johnnie Mae was feisty and tough. She packed frozen meats in an assembly line and rarely missed a day of work, even when she was sick. She had tremendous energy and aggressiveness, and both traits were inherited by her daughter and by Charles. She was a strong disciplinarian and was strict with the kind of language Charles used—though she often used profanity herself.

"Granny and I are like twins," says Barkley. "We're both determined, stubborn, and very aggressive in whatever we set out to do."

Charles didn't require a lot of discipline, though, because he was an unusually mature little boy. In some ways, he filled his absent father's role. "I could always sit down and talk to Charles like a man," says Charcey. "That's what he always was, a little man. When it came to our financial condition, he was always very understanding." Charles did much of the housework and did an excellent job of it. When Charles did misbehave, though, Grandma stepped in—and she knew how to kick ass.

Charles was also very open emotionally. Every day, he told his mother he loved her, and he was always openly affectionate with his mom and grandmother. He was also gentle and soft-spoken with other kids, in part because he was small for his age. He was shy, especially with girls.

While still in grade school, Charles faced a major decision. He had two primary interests—basketball and petty theft. They were both exciting, both offered camaraderie, and both were an outlet for Charles's anger. Being a mature child, he chose the less destructive avenue and put a great deal of energy into basketball.

At first, he wasn't very good: too short—just 5–7 until his junior year in high school. Often, he was bullied in games. But he had an innate ability to jump, and he worked as hard at that as his mother and grandmother did at their jobs. He began jumping over a three-and-a-half-foot fence in his backyard, hour after hour. His grandmother, afraid he'd rip apart his testicles, would sit and watch him—as if that could prevent catastrophe. He also became obsessed with his jump rope. Charcey recalls, "While every other kid in the neighborhood was going to movies or was out dancing, Charles was either jumping our fences, jumping rope, or doing something to improve himself physically." He spent hours on the court, often at night, when the older, meaner kids were gone. He became a skilled point guard.

When he was a junior, a prominent member of his high school basketball team quit, and Charles got his first significant playing time. He also began growing—reaching 6–1 by the end of the year. But he retained the skills and grace he'd learned playing guard. He also showed a remarkable mental aptitude for rebounding, sensing where the ball would land by gauging its angle and speed. Unlike almost all other great rebounders, he didn't try to box out his opponent but relied on anticipation of the ball's movement.

As a senior, he was a star. He was 6–3 and 250—too big to ever be bullied again. He'd learned that he could successfully channel his anger and aggressiveness into basketball and still keep the approval of his mother and grandmother. He could be "bad" and good at the same time.

He carried too much fat, but he could rebound like hell, averaging 17.9 a game. Basketball, he was beginning to believe, could enable him to fulfill his dream: getting a decent education and a decent, white-collar job. He never considered playing professionally. "I had no hope," he says. "I just wanted to get a job, and live and die in Leeds."

Even though he became popular because of basketball, he was still shy with girls. Girls found him attractive, but he was more interested in basketball.

He was recruited by Auburn University, which was about one hundred miles southeast of Leeds. Not many other schools were interested. "Nobody offered me shit," says Barkley.

At Auburn, Barkley ran head-on into coach Sonny Smith, an old-fashioned, ass-chewing basketball fascist. Smith took the worst possible approach to Barkley, who already hated male authority figures. Barkley was too inner-directed to need Smith's boot-camp harangues and didn't tolerate them.

With the ferocity of a wounded animal, Barkley set out to dominate the team and force Smith to curb his tongue. Charles played with bloodthirsty intensity. But Smith refused to start Barkley and wouldn't stop bitching. Smith called Barkley "fat-ass." Made him run the stadium stairs. Hit him. Supposedly, Smith's cruelty had a purpose—but to Barkley, it just seemed like sadism.

Halfway through his freshman year, Barkley told Smith, "Fuck it. I'm gone." He went home. His grandmother, Barkley says, "didn't say much—she's so much like me that she understood exactly. She would have done the same thing. She might've even punched Coach Smith." But his mother, desperate for her child to escape poverty, wept and begged him to return.

He returned and became a star. His scoring wasn't outstanding, but he rebounded extremely well, especially for a player who never got taller than 6-4½. His weight remained a problem, though, going as high as 270 (about twenty pounds over his pro weight). Tormentors had pizza delivered to him during a game, and sportswriters tagged him with names like Boy Gorge and the Round Mound of Rebound. He hated the teasing.

In his sophomore year, pro sports agents began visiting him and handing him envelopes stuffed with dollars. It was the first sign that he had the potential to play professionally. The loans, which eventually totaled about $20,000, were against NCAA rules and fed Barkley's cynicism. He later repaid them and didn't sign with the agents who'd given him the money.

He considered quitting school after his sophomore year but realized he'd probably sacrifice about a million dollars by being drafted so young. He decided to stay in school, but before he told Sonny Smith, he laid down the law: No more bullshit—treat me like a man. Smith backed down. Over the next year, Barkley became a superstar. "Charles Barkley," Sonny Smith later said, *"was* Auburn basketball." At the same time, Auburn football and baseball were being similarly dominated by another young player who'd grown up not far from Leeds—a former dope-smoking good-old-boy named Bo Jackson.

During his third and final year at Auburn, Barkley established strong national credentials. Strong enough to merit an Olympic tryout. But again he ran into a male authority figure he couldn't stomach—Bobby Knight. He clashed with Knight immediately, then made the mistake of mocking Knight's old-fashioned wingtip shoes. He got cut, in favor of guard Steve Alford, one of Knight's Indiana boys.

In 1984 he entered the best draft of the modern era: Michael Jordan, Akeem Olajuwon, Sam Bowie, Sam Perkins, John Stockton, Kevin Willis, Otis Thorpe, Michael Cage, Tony Campbell, Alvin Robertson, Jay Humphries, Vern Fleming, Jerome Kersey. Barkley was the fifth pick. The Sixers offered him $75,000. He told them to go to hell.

Barkley attended training camp unsigned—an unusual and gutsy move. And a successful one. He had a great camp and signed for $2 million over four years. He sent much of the money home to Mom and Grandma. They weren't ready to quit working, but they needed help, particularly with one of Charles's brothers, who'd suffered a stroke from cocaine abuse.

Then Charles got to know his new coach, Billy Cunningham.

To Barkley, Cunningham was just a replay of Bobby Knight and Sonny Smith—arrogant, loud, unfair. When Sixer star Julius Erving made a mistake, Cunningham wouldn't say anything, but when Barkley screwed up, he caught hell. Erving didn't do anything to protect the rookie, and Barkley found Erving aloof and unlikable. But the other Sixer star, Moses Malone, became a father figure to Barkley, the first he'd ever had. "Without Moses," says Barkley, "I would have never survived that season."

When Malone was traded, Barkley was devastated. It was the first of a series of stupid trades and draft picks that ruined the once-powerful Sixer franchise. Most of the front-office screwups were the fault of owner Harold Katz, who'd made a fortune with his Nutri-Systems diet empire and therefore seemed to consider himself a basketball genius.

Barkley existed uneasily with Erving until Dr. J's retirement. The local press, though, was reluctant to recognize Barkley as the emerging leader of the team, much preferring Erving.

But Barkley's on-court achievements demanded his ascension. In his first seven years in the league, only one player, Olajuwon, totaled more rebounds than Barkley— and Olajuwon was eight inches taller. Barkley never averaged less than 20 points after his rookie year, and he topped out at 28.3. He was on the All-NBA First Team four consecutive years, on the Second Team two years, was on the All-Rookie Team, was an All-Star Game MVP, won three consecutive Schick Pivotal Player Awards, and made six All-Star teams.

Opposing teams found that he could outquick every big man and outmuscle every quick man.

One reason for his greatness was his ability to harness his intense emotions. "A game for Charles is a passionate experience," says one of his former coaches, Matt Guokas. "I've never seen anyone so ferocious in wanting to prove he's better than his opponents."

"With Charles," says Jimmy Lynam, "you've just got to accept the whole package. He's an emotional player, and that emotion is what makes him so great."

Barkley's basketball success was matched by success in his business and personal life. His salary rose to the $3 million range, with a nine-year, $29 million deal. He also signed a $500,000-a-year deal with Nike and became one of their most prominent athletes. Although he lost a small fortune in poor investments arranged by an agent, he became one of the wealthiest athletes in America.

To some degree, he reconciled his relationship with his father. Also, in 1989, he married a former legal-aid secretary and model. Shortly after that, he and Maureen Barkley had a daughter, Christiana. His primary attraction to his wife, he has said, is that "she stands up to me." Maintaining a healthy marriage was not particularly easy for Barkley, though, because, as he says, "I'd never been around a successful marriage in my whole life." The marriage, however, has endured.

But while his personal success grew, his team fell apart. And it made him crazy. In 1986 Katz traded Moses Malone, Terry Catledge, and two first-round picks for Cliff T. Robinson and Jeff Ruland. Katz also gave up two firsts to acquire Manute Bol and Jayson Williams. In addition, he got rid of Rick Mahorn to bring aboard Charles Shackleford and Mitch Wiggins, and gave away the first pick in the 1986 draft (Brad Daugherty) for Roy Hinson and cash. By the end of this nonsense, the Sixers were gutted.

Barkley clashed bitterly with Harold Katz over the front-office idiocy. Katz—one more hated male authority figure —endured Barkley's wrath. At times, Katz seemed to indicate that he would make the changes Barkley wanted. They did, after all, have the same goal: a winning team. But Barkley didn't trust Katz. And Katz never made the changes.

Barkley began misbehaving. He got into a fight outside a bar. At NBA games, he inadvertently spit on a girl and purposely spit into a heckling fan's hand. He accused Katz of pandering to racism (for keeping Hoppen) and of stupidity. He bad-mouthed his teammates in his book and to their faces. He racked up a record number of fines from the league. When he was stopped for speeding, police found a weapon in his car (a semiautomatic pistol). He made a joke about wife-beating.

Finally, by early in the '92 season, Katz had had enough. He began trying to trade Barkley. The current deal he was considering was Barkley to the Clippers for Charles Smith, Loy Vaught, and two first-round picks.

At last, Katz and Barkley wanted the same thing.

At last, Charles Barkley could trust Harold Katz.

• In Charles's Face

"You're persistent," Barkley said when he saw me standing over him as he laced his sneakers.

"I've just got a couple of questions. Do you regret any of the incidents you've been involved in over the last few months?"

"I do," said Barkley. "That thing in Milwaukee. Where I hit the guy? I wish I'd hit the motherfucker *twice.*"

"The bad press doesn't bother you?"

"Any time you're exceptional at something, you're going to take criticism. People are jealous. People in the media are jealous. Some of my teammates are jealous. That goes with the territory of being top dog."

"You're just not into the jock role-model trip, are you?"

"Just 'cuz you can play basketball, that should *not* make you a role model. If I do something stupid, and a kid does it, all's it means is the kid's stupid."

"Dave Coskey says you're a nice guy but want people to think you're a jerk."

"That's not accurate. I don't want people to think I'm a jerk. It's just that, if I do something nice for someone, I don't do it to get on TV and get more endorsements. It's nobody's business. You should do it out of the goodness of your heart."

"I've talked to guys who were here on ten-day contracts, and they say you let them stay at your house and drive one of your cars."

"So what? I just think it's more important to be a good person than a good basketball player. Basketball's not that important to me."

"No offense, but I think now you're lying."

"NO-NO-No-no. I love to play the game. But it's not a game anymore. It's a business."

"What'll you do when you retire?"

"Absolutely nuthin'. Play golf every day. Enjoy life. Take care of my business ventures."

"Is it hard for you to see sick kids?"

"Sure. But you have to do it, because it brightens them up.

That's the best part of all this stuff. Havin' that power. The power to brighten up a little kid who's hurtin'. Now get the fuck outta my face. I gotta go to work."

He stood and brushed past me on his way out the door.

I couldn't help it. I liked Charles. He was an African-American warrior and the meanest son of a bitch in basketball. I *liked* him. So shoot me.

The players huddled around Lynam as he scratched plays onto a clipboard—everybody but Barkley. The huddle broke. "No fouls!" Barkley bellowed as they walked back onto the floor. "No fouls! No fouls!" The crowd at the Spectrum coughed up a feeble little cheer. Pathetic. Close game. Last minute. Against the hated Pistons. National TV. And you could still hear individual voices above the crowd.

But Barkley was charged up. He always was when he had a chance to win. It was in his blood.

Barkley got the ball and drove to the basket hard and straight as a train. Dennis Rodman was waiting. They clashed in midair, a wreck of twisted limbs, and Barkley got his shot off. No good. He ducked past Laimbeer for the rebound, but just before he got to it, Rodman tipped it to Dumars.

Hersey Hawkins plowed into Dumars. "NO-NO-No-no!" Barkley shrieked. "No motherfucking *fouls,* motherfucker." Hawkins ignored him.

Dumars—still a candidate for the last Olympic spot—sank the free throws. It was over.

Twenty minutes later, Barkley sat in front of his locker, radiating hostility. Reporters were talking to practically everyone in the room except the one person they all wanted. If one of them had approached him, they'd have all flocked over. But nobody had the guts. Including me. In this kind of situation, Barkley could eat you like meat.

A Philadelphia reporter—a news anchor—wandered into the room with a little boy in a red cap and blue shirt. He left the boy with Armon Gilliam and walked up to Barkley. "David just lost his father," he said softly. "Could you say hi to him?"

"Of course." Barkley immediately approached the kid. "Hey, David, you enjoy the game?" The boy nodded. "How old are you?"

"Eight."

"How's your family doin'?" Barkley sat down by the boy.

"Okay," he said. He paused. Barkley looked into his face. "Not so good."

"Know what?" said Barkley. His voice was suddenly soft and singsong; he sounded for all the world like Mr. Rogers. "I lost my dad when I was a little boy." The boy nodded. "And know what? Your mama really loves you." He touched the boy's shoulder very gently. "You wanna take a picture? Let's take a picture." He led the boy to his locker, where somebody flashed a snapshot.

As soon as Barkley and the boy were out of range, Charles Shackleford murmured, "I wish *my* dad would die."

Manute Bol giggled. "Don't say that."

A man with a fat gut, a fat cigar, and a booth-tan wandered into the room. It was Harold Katz.

Katz ignored the other players and sat down next to Barkley. "Charlie! How's it goin'?"

Barkley seemed genuinely pleased to see Katz. Finally, they were working for the same thing: Barkley's departure. "Oh, I was depressed for a while," he said, "but I'm gettin' my head together. Me and my wife were havin' problems— you know, all the time apart—but we had a long talk last night. And it's okay now."

"Okay, man," said Katz. "Good deal. But, uh, don't say anything about that to anybody, okay?"

Barkley nodded. The implication seemed to be: your reputation's already shit. How'll I move you if it gets worse?

"You know how it is," Katz said. "You just can't trust *anybody.*"

"NO-NO-No-no," said Barkley.

"Except one person," said Katz. "Me."

Katz gave him a comradely smile.

Barkley returned it. "I *do* trust you," he said.

11

Tyrannosaurus Pat

**Magic & Mike Tyson • Bad Fear in Madison
Square Gulag • Jordan vs. the Lard-Assed
Bureaucrats • Pat Riley's Head Games •
The Insecurity of Height • Quote from
a Whoremonger • War with the Writers**

> Nobody roots for Goliath.
> —Wilt Chamberlain

> If I had my life to live over, I would have
> liked to have ended up as a sportswriter.
> —Richard M. Nixon, 1969

The TV guy was major-market handsome—perfect sandy hair and piano-key teeth—but he looked like he wanted to crawl into a hole and die. His station had sent him to the Knicks' practice to cover a local angle on the Mike Tyson guilty verdict. The best localization they could give him was: What do the Knicks have to say about it? His producers had figured jocks would have the inside scoop, since they were all a bunch of womanizers, misogynists, and whoremongers.

"They especially want Riley," said the TV reporter, "cuz he's close to Magic."

"What's Magic got to do with it?" I asked.

"Well, you know, Tyson and Magic both got into trouble because of women."

"Yeah, but Magic didn't *rape* anybody."

"Right, but Tyson didn't *kill* anybody—and Magic might've killed his own *wife,* plus a buncha other women. *He* didn't give a shit."

"That's cold, man."

"It's a cold town."

But it was obvious from the way he was fidgeting that he didn't relish his chore. When practice ended, he marched straight up to Riley, to get it over with.

"Coach—just a second for a nonbasketball question?"

Riley looked suspicious. "Tyson?"

"Yeah."

"What would I have to say about that?"

"Well, you know, athletes and women—life on the road. You know."

Riley pointed to the door, his face suddenly a mass of wrinkles. "No comment on that, okay? *Okay?*"

The reporter backed off and Riley stomped away. Riley had a big game tomorrow—Bulls. But for Riley, they were all big games.

The reporter pulled himself together and approached Mark Jackson.

"I was hoping I could get a reaction on the Tyson verdict," he said. "You know, athletes alone on the road—that kind of thing?"

Jackson declined politely. But the TV guy was freaked. "I'm just doin' my *job,* man," he said.

Jackson gave him a strange look. "I'm not mad at you."

Patrick Ewing lumbered past on his way to the weight room. The TV reporter looked miserable. But he was a pro. "'Scuse me, Patrick," he said, "but I gotta get a reaction to something."

Ewing held up his hands like someone was trying to punch his face. "I pass," he said. His hands looked small and delicate on his huge body, as if they'd been grafted on.

"Don't-cha wanna hear what it's *about?* It's this Tyson thing—do you think—" But Ewing was gone.

"Don't feel bad," said a beat writer. "I got the same

treatment when I asked him why he was such a good shot blocker."

• Hoya Paranoia

It was quiet in the Knicks' locker room before the Bulls game. Too quiet. Riley didn't like locker room music. The hush made for an ominous feeling. That was probably what Riley wanted. He'd come to the Knicks with a reputation as a master manipulator, and people would've been disappointed if he hadn't tried to play head games.

On the blackboard, Riley had scrawled, "It's a war. But with poise."

Ewing was glaring at a monitor showing Bulls tape. "Pardon me, Patrick," I said, "do you have a second?"

He didn't look at me. "No."

"After the game, maybe?"

"Maybe."

"Okay, thanks. Have a good game." Silence.

Patrick Ewing was the most notorious stone-face in basketball. For years, he'd treated journalists like pock-marked lepers, then had bitched about how they never presented his cuddly side—the "real" Pat Ewing. In fact, though, they'd treated him gently, applying the usual mild clichés: "aloof," "reticent," and "the strong silent type." As far as I was concerned, it would have been more accurate to say: "rude" and "thick." But sportswriting—as it's now perceived—generally demands that all talented players be described in heroic terms. All of them.

Ewing apparently thinks it's savvy to stiff reporters. "You never know what people's intentions are," he's said. "Not everybody is your friend. They might act like they want to be your friend, but they have their own motives. I don't trust nobody right away."

He claims to be indifferent to public opinion—a strange attitude for somebody in the hero business. "People are going to think what they want to think," he says. "There have been enough negative things written about me from high school through college that people already have their own preconceived notion. I have my family and close friends, and those are the people whose perceptions I care about." But his "aloofness" sometimes leaked into his personal life. For some time, he had an answering message that said, "If I wanted to talk, I'd have called *you.*"

The press, he thinks, is racist and powerful. "Whenever a person, especially a black person, stands up for what they believe in, America gets afraid of it, and they're gonna write what they perceive," says Ewing. "Whatever a reporter writes, people believe. That's where they get their beliefs."

It's widely accepted that Ewing learned his antagonism to the press from his Georgetown Hoya coach, the prickly and dictatorial John Thompson, who didn't like his players talking to reporters. But Ewing didn't fault Thompson and the "Hoya paranoia." "When I was there," says Ewing, "I didn't *want* to talk to the press. I just wanted to go about doing things, going to school and hanging out with my friends. I mean, I was getting requests for an interview every day."

But even John Thompson saw that Ewing's press boycott resulted in, as Thompson says, "this idea that Patrick was some dumb black kid, some imbecile or idiot that needed to be pampered or protected."

Ewing himself realized his approach made him look like "one mean, arrogant SOB." But he never changed.

His paranoia, of course, was absolutely ridiculous. As a group, sportswriters are among the nicest, most generous people in the world. Despite constant snotty behavior from jocks, they never stop looking for reasons to like them. Even guys like Ewing.

After I backed away from Ewing, I started jotting down a few notes describing the locker room—something I did in every city. But one of the locker room bouncers eyed me angrily and said, "Wha-chu writin'?"

"What the locker room looks like."

"You writin' down our *plays?* Or what?" He moved between me and a blackboard covered with *X*'s and *O*'s.

"No. Look. It says, 'cheap carpet.' You don't have a cheap-carpet play, do you?"

"You can't write that."

"Jesus, is this like, Madison Square Gulag?"

Michael Jordan was only a few doors away, and I was suddenly missing him very much.

Jordan lit up the whole room—particularly in comparison with Ewing's sour aura. A group of reporters were semicircled around him, laughing and tossing jokes back and forth. The issue of the day was his likeness. He was now at war with not just the NBA but also USA Basketball, the council of elders who governed the U.S. Olympic basketball team.

USA Basketball seemed to be totally flipped out over Jordan's wanting to control his own likeness. They thought *they* deserved the money from it. They were making noises to the effect of, If Michael won't be on our T-shirts, we won't let him play. But Jordan's attitude seemed to be: Right—a bunch of lard-assed old bureaucrats have me *really* afraid, because they have *so* much to offer, and all I can do is fly.

"Nobody wants to be manipulated," said Jordan, as he took off his olive silk suit. "And nobody wants to be taken advantage of. For the last six years, the NBA has profited off my individual usage in their merchandising, and I never got anything for it. They've been making seven hundred and fifty million dollars—a billion this year—and *I'm* greedy because I want those rights back? Hey, come on." Jordan was overstating his case only slightly; the NBA would make a billion dollars on merchandising this year, but only forty percent of that was on Bulls' merchandise (which meant "Jordan merchandise"—unless there's a Bill Cartwright cult I'm unaware of).

"Will other players follow suit?" someone asked.

"They will if they want control. That's their choice. I made my choice. If you want to consider me greedy—great, go ahead."

"Is this a campaign statement for Players Association president?"

"I never asked to be put in that position. Don't nominate me."

"You read *The Jordan Rules* yet?"

"No, and I'm not gonna read it. You read it."

Jordan was loose and relaxed. Across the room, Scottie Pippen—joking with coach Phil Jackson—looked carefree and happy. This game was being billed as the war between the two best teams in the East. It was a big, scary game. But the Bulls didn't seem to know it.

• Ewing Gets Sentimental

Bang-bang-bang-bang: Jordan hit, Jordan hit, Grant hit, Cartwright hit—and the game was over in its first two minutes. The eight-point deficit was about as close as the Knicks would come all night. It was a foul, humiliating loss for the Knicks, almost stark enough to catch the attention of the front row: Michael Douglas, Tom Brokaw, Hammer, William Hurt, Howie Mandel, Spike Lee, and Donald & Marla.

From the beginning, Cartwright was in Ewing's face, forcing Ewing away from his beloved low-post position. Cartwright *always* gave Ewing hell; some people thought it was because Ewing had a soft, sentimental spot for Cartwright. Cartwright had been the Knicks' starting center and Ewing's mentor when Patrick had entered the league. Other people thought Ewing didn't have the hoop-savvy to play Cartwright, who was a serious basketball theoretician.

But then, in the second quarter, Ewing showed why he was the Olympian, and not Cartwright. With Will Perdue in the game, Ewing muscled his way down low—going through about four Bulls, slinging them with his long, muscle-heavy arms. Perdue jumped in after him, but Ewing smashed Perdue in the chest with his open hand. Perdue—7-feet, 240—backpedaled madly to keep from crumpling onto his ass. Then Ewing grabbed the ball, exploded up, and rammed it down as his legs spread wide. When his feet touched down, he balled up his fists and roared an ugly noise that started from deep in his gut. His face got ugly too. It was a rare and transfixing display of brawn, will, and anger. No one else in the NBA—or the world—was quite capable of it. Perdue looked spooked—like a mouse eye-to-eye with a snake.

When Ewing had entered the NBA, this brutal, frightful style was considered the most powerful force in the game. People had assumed that Ewing would lead his team to greatness. But then things changed. As Magic and Bird elevated the art of passing, teams got faster and sharper, and brute strength declined in value. Ewing's era was over before it even began—he was an instant dinosaur: Tyrannosaurus Pat. His first few years were manifestly disappointing.

But Ewing, like all great players, had kept adding dimensions to his game. He improved his rebounding, learned a turnaround jumper and running hook, beefed up his free-throw percentage, and honed his passing skills. Now he had a complete game. *Plus* brute strength.

It made him the most frightening player in the game. And that's apparently what Ewing wanted. Not to be liked. But to be feared.

● **Cambridge, Massachusetts**

Patrick Ewing was born into a world of fear and deprivation—the Kingston, Jamaica, of the 1960s. It was a country dominated by poverty and an illegal marijuana industry. Ewing's family, like the majority of Jamaicans, was trapped in the hardscrabble underclass.

Patrick, the fifth of seven children of Carl and Dorothy Ewing, was always big and strong for his age. He wasn't very good at school, but he had some talent for drawing and even more talent for the country's most popular sports, soccer and cricket.

When Patrick was nine, in 1971, his mother arranged through relatives living in New York to emigrate to America. For two years, she lived alone in Cambridge, Massachusetts, working in the cafeteria of Massachusetts General Hospital. In 1973 her husband joined her and found work in a rubber company. The children came—singly and in pairs—over the next several years.

Patrick was not able to come until 1975, when he was thirteen. He enrolled in Achievement School, a remedial center for junior high students. His reading and speaking skills were below average.

Shortly after his arrival, he was passing a Cambridge basketball court and was invited to play. Ewing, who was already about 6–1, had never touched a basketball. "They said it didn't make a difference," says Ewing. "They just needed an extra body. So I played. I messed up. But I liked it, so I kept on playing, and kept on getting better." He was soon able to dunk. His growth remained constant, always keeping him substantially taller than his peers.

Like most other boys who are tall at an early age, Ewing was awkward. Unlike other Olympians—such as Mullin, Pippen, Barkley, and David Robinson (who was just 5–7 in ninth grade)—Ewing didn't get the chance to develop grace before he reached his full height.

Ewing also suffered from the psychological disadvantages that often go with being very tall. Being exceptionally tall is no easier than being very short—it makes you feel unusual and self-conscious. You're a victim of inflated expectations and often a target of ridicule, especially if you're clumsy.

Being tall robs you of another important (although ironic) advantage: being the underdog. People who are small learn early to compensate for lack of size with extra effort, guile, charm, skill, and cleverness. They learn to be wary rather than arrogant—even if they *act* arrogant. To adopt this underdog attitude, then later grow to a condition of physical power, gives an athlete an extraordinary advantage.

It was an advantage Patrick Ewing never had. He could always rely upon his size and power—even though his height often made him feel self-conscious. "We had to tell him to be tall, walk tall, and be proud of it," says his high school basketball coach, Mike Jarvis.

Jarvis was an important influence on Ewing. Coach of

Cambridge's Rindge and Latin High School, Jarvis believed in the team-oriented, strong-defense style of the 1960s Celtics. He wanted Ewing to be the next Bill Russell. Even in high school, says Jarvis, Ewing "was a hard worker, and if he didn't know something, he'd ask you a thousand times until he got it right." Ewing sometimes worked out in the Boston University gym, under the eye of the young coach there, Rick Pitino.

Ewing, says Jarvis, "became a star, the tall guy, and a great player. But he went through times where he was awkward and clumsy."

By his junior year, Ewing was 6–11, and as a senior he was seven feet. Between his junior and senior years, his weight jumped from 205 to 230—within ten pounds of his pro weight.

Ewing's high school won an amazing three consecutive state championships, losing just one game in those three years. During that time, Ewing spent three summers attending an Upward Bound program at Wellesley College, trying to keep up with his classmates academically. This classwork kept him from attending some basketball camps, but his mother was a strong believer in the importance of education.

There was pain in Ewing's high school years, though. He suffered racial insults while playing—some fans even threw bananas onto the court.

Ewing was allowed to try out for the Olympic basketball team in 1980—the first high school student ever invited to the trials. By his senior year, he was the most intensely recruited high school player in America.

Since Ewing was in a commanding position, Jarvis sent out 150 copies of a letter that detailed Ewing's desires. The letter said that because of his disadvantaged background, Ewing would need daily tutoring, remedial courses, tapes of lectures, untimed testing, and help with writing papers. The letter, though, had an unexpected effect. It fostered a widespread belief that Ewing wasn't very bright. Even so, eighty schools accepted Ewing's terms. Of those, Jarvis and

Ewing's parents selected sixteen finalists that were allowed to make a presentation.

They then narrowed it to six schools—North Carolina, UCLA, Boston College, Boston University, Villanova, and Georgetown. Georgetown was selected mostly because its coach, John Thompson, was also about seven feet tall. Ewing said he preferred a tall coach because someone his height would understand the center position better. That's a pretty naive belief for someone who knew basketball as well as Ewing did. A logical assumption is simply that Ewing just felt self-conscious about his height and preferred being around very tall men. It is, for example, extremely common for the tallest NBA players to choose other seven-footers as their closest friends. As Mike Jarvis says, "Being black and seven feet tall—neither one of those things is easy to be all the time."

Nor was it easy to be Jamaican in America. For years, Ewing had struggled with his communication skills, often in the media spotlight. This—along with his height, his family's lack of money, episodes of racial discrimination, and the traumas of his uprooted childhood—all contributed to his growing aloofness.

When Thompson came to visit the Ewings, he found it an unnerving experience. "Mrs. Ewing was an extremely extraordinary person," Thompson says. "This lady was watching me the whole time, and I swear, I don't think she ever blinked. Not once. I mean, this lady was just *staring* at me. She was *glaring* at me. And not once did she give me so much as one nonverbal clue to what she might be thinking.

"After I was through, she finally asked me what social opportunities our educational environment would provide. I said, 'Mrs. Ewing, it is not a responsibility of mine to get involved with your son's social opportunities. But the city of Washington, D.C., is seventy percent black, if that interests you. And if there are no social opportunities that Patrick can find there as a young black man, he has a problem, ma'am, that I frankly cannot solve.' And she looked at me for a while, like maybe she sort of liked that. But she never smiled, never broke out into a laugh to let me be sure. She just looked at me and said, 'Ha. Funny man. Funny man.' And that was it."

Then, after Ewing selected Georgetown, Thompson went to the Ewing home to sign him, and Mrs. Ewing again put Thompson through the wringer. "After making the usual small talk," says Thompson, "I said, 'Well, ma'am, we're here today to sign the letter of intent, so we might as well get to it.' But she said very firmly, 'Mr. Thompson, you sign for *land*. You do not sign for people.' Well! Right about then I damn near fainted. I thought the whole thing was off. But then Mrs. Ewing broke into a smile and said, 'Carl'—that's her husband—'Carl, sign the papers.' That was her way of saying to me, 'Mister, you had better understand that this is my son, a human being.' You'll never find a mother who loved her child more."

Ewing's success at Georgetown was as spectacular as his success in high school. In his freshman year, he led the team to the national championship game, only to lose in the last seconds when Michael Jordan hit The Shot. At the end of the year, Ewing got several NBA offers, for up to $1 million a year. Mrs. Ewing wouldn't let Patrick consider it, insisting he get his degree.

In his junior year, Ewing led the team to the national championship and was the tournament's MVP. That summer, Ewing won a gold medal at the 1984 Olympics, teaming with Jordan and Mullin.

In his senior year, the Georgetown Hoyas again made it to the championship game but again lost in the last seconds, despite a strong effort by Ewing. But Ewing, the Hoya Destroya, won a number of Player of the Year awards and was a first-team All-American.

Ewing, one of the few superstar basketball players to attend four years of college, got his degree. But shortly before he graduated, his mother died. "Getting that degree meant more to me than an NCAA title, being named All-American, or winning an Olympic gold medal," says Ewing. "I promised my mother before she died that I would graduate on time, and I'm proud to have fulfilled that promise." His mother's death hurt Patrick and seemed to drive him even deeper within himself. She had left him when he was a child—but her leaving had been a measure of her love. It had been at least as hard on her as it had been on Patrick, but it had enabled the family to escape poverty.

In the years before Ewing entered the league, the NBA team with the worst record had automatically gotten the first draft pick. But GMs were so hungry for Ewing that David Stern invented the draft lottery to keep teams from tanking games to get him. Even so, the hysteria about Ewing was so intense that when New York won the lottery, there were some wild accusations that the lottery had been rigged to give Ewing to the league's biggest market. Supposedly, the Knicks' envelope had been placed on dry ice just before the drawing, to differentiate it from the others.

Dave DeBusschere, who was then the Knicks' GM, declared it a "landmark day." DeBusschere proclaimed that Ewing "will become the foundation for a string of very competitive teams for many years to come."

The Knicks had been weak ever since the great Red Holzman's "Golden Era" teams of the early 1970s. And the city had not been patient. As Rick Pitino puts it: "If you're going to be involved with a loser, the last place you want to be is hell. The next to last place is New York." When Ewing came aboard, the city rejoiced.

But the exultation didn't last long. Before he'd even played an NBA game, Ewing got in a fight in an exhibition game and screwed up his elbow. Then he played his first league game and twisted his ankle. Toward the end of the year, he needed arthroscopic surgery on his right knee. Ewing played in only fifty games his first year, and the Knicks finished last. In spite of all that, Ewing won Rookie of the Year and made the All-Star Team.

But his game was far from complete. He shot too many fallaways, was not a great rebounder, was easy to fake off his feet, and couldn't hang on to the ball.

Furthermore, he had a lot of problems with his coach, the bitchy, whiny Hubie Brown.

Ewing's second season got off to a turbulent start. Hubie

got canned almost immediately, and when he left, he accused: "The guy who is not doing his job is Ewing." Then Ewing slipped on the floor and missed nineteen games. When he came back, Cartwright had a firm grip on the center position, and Ewing had to play power forward—not his best position. Another rotten year. The Knicks finished last again.

It was becoming clear that Ewing alone could not save the franchise. In fact, as the 1980s closed out, the style of the league changed. The dominating-center motif was abandoned.

Ewing's cachet in New York plummeted. He was not Saint Patrick and he certainly wasn't Broadway Pat. Fans just couldn't find a reason to embrace him.

Then came Rick Pitino—who'd known Ewing since Patrick had stopped by the Boston University gym as a kid. Right after Pitino was named the new Knicks coach, he met with Ewing and told him, "I'm an easy guy to get along with, especially for you. The only guy I don't get along with is someone who doesn't work hard."

Pitino began orchestrating a wide-open pressing system, similar to the one Georgetown had used. Ewing liked it. The Knicks franchise had a legacy of great defensive teams— particularly under Holzman—and Pitino's team was one of the best. Pitino's emphasis on defense helped Ewing, whose shot blocking made him a strong defensive force. Ewing also liked Pitino's gung-ho attitude. The Knicks began to win.

In '89, they won 52 games and took the Atlantic Division. Ewing's production was solid—22.7 points and 9.2 rebounds. But Pitino burned out quickly. After two seasons, he returned to the college game.

His replacement, Stu Jackson, focused the offense on Ewing, who racked up great stats—28.6 and 10.8. But, again, the Knicks were mediocre, going 45–37. The following year, 1990–1991, Ewing also played well (26.6 and 11.1), but the Knicks were even worse (39–43).

The losing—after so many victories in high school and college—was chewing at Ewing's guts. In 1990 he said, "I still think of myself as a winner. When I finish playing and they put Patrick Ewing's name in the book, next to it I want to see: 'He won.' I don't want to see how many points he scored or how many rebounds he got. I want to see: 'He won.'"

Ewing wanted out.

He wanted to go to a winner. Winning, for him, was the heart of the game. Other than money, it was all he got out of basketball. He didn't get the love and affection that other great players got, because of his image among some sports fans as a nasty and half-bright zombie. He'd never gotten the endorsements the other superstars had, and he never would. He wasn't very popular in New York, and in the rest of America, most people considered him effective, but he was not a guy they'd cross the street to have a beer with.

He wanted *out*.

In '91, GM Al Bianchi got the ax, and legendary winner Pat Riley took over as coach. But Ewing had lost faith.

He wanted out.

• Pat to City: Drop Dead

At the end of the 1990–1991 season, Ewing stormed out of the Knicks locker room, kicking towels as he went. The war had begun.

Within about a month, Ewing's agent, the powerful David Falk, demanded that the Knicks make Ewing a free agent, allowing Falk to shop Ewing on the open market. If that happened, Ewing would demand—and probably get—an astronomical salary. Along with his freedom. Ewing was, after all, one of only three great centers in the NBA (along with Robinson and Olajuwon).

Falk said that there was a clause in Ewing's contract that allowed Ewing to be a free agent. The clause said that if Ewing wasn't one of the four highest-paid players in the league, he could shop his services.

Falk's claim, though, seemed ridiculous. Ewing *was* one of the top four. Only Jordan, Olajuwon, and Hot Rod Williams made more.

But Falk claimed that because Larry Bird was getting a huge $7.1 million bonus in 1991, Bird was making more than Ewing. Ewing's contract, however, clearly stated that bonus money didn't count.

Despite the apparent absurdity of Falk's claim on its face, the Knicks countered by offering Ewing $33 million over six years. It would make Ewing the highest paid team player in the world. It was a hell of a lot more money than the Knicks really owed Ewing. Under the terms of his existing contract, they only owed him $14.2 million over four years.

As they bickered, other teams began salivating over Ewing. Ewing gave Riley a list of teams he wanted to be traded to: Portland, Phoenix, the Lakers, Washington, Boston, and Golden State.

The plot sickened. Golden State suddenly decided it wanted to give Chris Mullin a raise to $3.2 million—which would have bumped Ewing (at $3.1) out of the top four and made him available to other teams. Such as: Golden State.

The Knicks were pissed.

Then it got even weirder. Golden State backed away from the Mullin raise. Somebody had apparently gotten to them. Maybe it was David Stern, telling them to cut out the bullshit. Or maybe it was the Knicks, warning the Warriors not to fire the first shot in what would be a bloody war.

Shortly after that, Ewing's contract dispute went to an arbitrator. Ewing lost. He was stuck in New York. At $14.1 million—not the $33 million he'd already turned down.

The trade talk intensified. Knicks' GM Dave Checketts said that if Ewing wanted out, "I would make every attempt to accommodate him."

It never happened. Checketts wanted more for Ewing than any team would give.

Riley met with Ewing again, schmoozing about how he was going to build a winner. And Checketts came back with his original $33 million offer, which would mean Ewing would get $50 million for his twelve-year stint with the Knicks. Checketts also made some smart moves, sending Jerrod Mustaf and Trent Tucker to Phoenix for rugged

It was the most exotic game of H-O-R-S-E in basketball history. And Magic won it, sinking shots that were crazy and wild and beautiful. Joy seemed to overwhelm him. He wanted to return to the NBA. Even if it would cost him his life.
JIM PATTON

"I want to play in the Olympics because I want to play with the other great players," said Barkley. "Did you want me to say, 'Rah-rah America'? That's bullshit."
CAMERON STAUTH

Ewing didn't get the love that other great players got, because of his image among some sports fans as a nasty, half-bright zombie. But inside Ewing was a wounded child.

JIM PATTON

Magic—during his winter of '92 field trip to the real world—addresses a crowd in his new role: poster child. By now, the inevitable has finally begun to sink in: he's going to die.

CAMERON STAUTH

The Odd Couple: Barkley and Laettner. "Nobody else wants to talk to him," said Barkley, "so I felt sorry for him. He's like the ugly duckling. I took him under my wing." It was a bizarre role reversal for Laettner. At Duke, when he snarled, people cringed.

JIM PATTON

Arrogant. Suspicious. Brilliant. Stockton skipped charm school, but he's the smartest man in basketball.

CAMERON STAUTH

When Jordan's $165,000 in alleged gambling debts were revealed, he faced his toughest media scrutiny ever. Now real reporters—not sportswriters—were hounding him. And they didn't give a damn how high he could jump.

CAMERON STAUTH

"After Stockton got hurt playin' Canada," said Malone, "everybody and their grandma from the Jazz front office called him." The Jazz's message was clear: *If you get hurt in the Olympics, we're going to kill you.*

JIM PATTON

Chuck Daly was the best quick & dirty coach in the NBA. And the best manipulator of egos.

CAMERON STAUTH

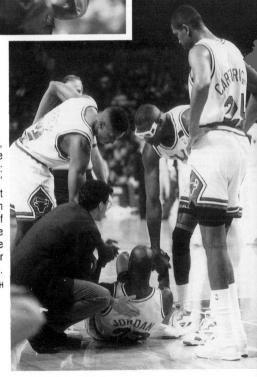

Pippen asked softly, "You okay, Mike?" He answered himself: "You're okay, M.J." Pippen and Grant slowly pulled Jordan up. He was the soul of their team, and the soul of the game. The jealousy and anger were forgotten.

CAMERON STAUTH

Clyde was second best. He sat at the right hand of God. But it wasn't good enough. Clyde wanted to *be* God.

JIM PATTON

Air Mullin in a rare drive to the hoop. He preferred unglamorous perimeter-shooting. But not being a glamor-god had its advantages—like being able to walk down the street unmolested. When asked if he attracted mobs in Barcelona, Mullin said, "It depends on who I'm with."

JOHN McDONOUGH/*SPORTS ILLUSTRATED*

Sometimes Bird would lie in bed, stare at the ceiling, and wonder if it was still worth it. When his back pain finally became unbearable, he made a promise to God: Get me through the Olympics and I'll retire.
JOHN McDONOUGH/*SPORTS ILLUSTRATED*

When Magic wrenched his knee, he thought it might be the end of his Olympics—maybe the end of his career. Even so, minutes later he was laughing and smiling. He'd always been unrelentingly positive. Now, with his illness, he had to be.
MANNY MILLAN/*SPORTS ILLUSTRATED*

As they walked off the medal stand, Magic gathered the Boys in a spontaneous moment of prayer, and of brotherhood.
RICHARD MACKSON/*SPORTS ILLUSTRATED*

In the end, it wasn't the Olympic action that made Magic want to come out of retirement. It was love.
RICHARD MACKSON/*SPORTS ILLUSTRATED*

power forward Xavier McDaniel and picking up John Starks and Anthony Mason.

Ewing—who had no options left—began to think that New York wasn't such a bad place after all. He took the $33 million. Called a press conference. He said, "New York is a great town. I started my career here, and I definitely would like to end it here."

Then he said a remarkable and disturbing thing.

He said, "I've been hearing other people say the New York crowd is going to boo. But even at the end of last season, there were some boos. I've been booed occasionally at the Garden. It's part of life."

Part of life? Being booed at home? When you're one of the best in the world?

That wasn't a "part of life" for any other Olympian.

And whose fault was that?

It must have been the fault of the press. They can be so cynical.

Plap! The meat of Ewing's open hand smacked against Will Perdue's soft white cheek, leaving a patch of red that would gradually turn blue-black over the course of the evening. Perdue, infuriated, scanned wildly for a referee. None in sight. *"Jee-zus!"* he huffed, stomping away.

Ewing looked at him with dead eyes.

The Knicks were in Chicago, looking for revenge for the butt-whipping they'd gotten earlier in the week.

Moments later, Ewing got the ball on the left side, dribbled a couple of steps toward the left corner, then shot with his right hand. It clanged off. Riley knotted his arms over his chest. It was a dumb shot, and Ewing took it constantly. When a player is on the left side, close to the baseline, he's supposed to shoot with his left, because it's closer to the basket and harder to guard. But Ewing couldn't do it—or wouldn't.

Cartwright came into the game, lurched into the paint with his butt pressed against Ewing's groin, then spun and gave Ewing a vicious whack across the ribs with his forearm.

Ewing didn't flinch. Then Ewing caught a pass from Jackson, held the ball with one hand and Cartwright with the other, and flipped it into the hoop. The game was very close. The Chicago fans were screaming, and gnawing on the long-necked beer bottles they'd sneaked in.

But then, with the Bulls up two and a minute left, Jordan stole the ball and scored. Then Ewing got a shot, but it was the same old wrong-handed jumper, and it missed. The Knicks rebounded, but Pippen blocked Ewing's shot, flashed downcourt, scored—and it was over. Riley jackknifed into his own crotch.

For about the millionth time in Ewing's NBA career, he'd been beaten by two "little" guys.

Ewing trudged off the court looking like death. Down in the crummy visitors' locker room, Ewing stayed in the shower as long as he could, then slumped onto a bench with a towel around his waist.

A reporter asked him if this was a moral victory. Ewing glared at him. "It doesn't matter that we played well," he said. "We lost." That was all he had to say.

He stared off into space. Patrick Ewing was unhappy. Very unhappy.

Patrick Ewing would probably always be unhappy. He'd been that way too long to change. He probably told himself that he *could* be happy—if only the Knicks would win the championship. But he'd won three high school state championships, and it hadn't been enough. He'd won a national college championship, and it hadn't been enough.

Patrick *needed* his unhappiness. It was his armor. It was his narcotic. It was him.

12

Getting David's Mind Right

**Zen and the Killer Instinct • Glue-Sniffing
Therapy • The Most Valuable Player in the World •
"David Doesn't Have a Clue" • Could It
Be . . . um? . . . um? . . . Satan? •
Cowboy Boots and Snake Stomping • Win One for
the Gipper or I'll Kill You • Memories of the Motor
City Bad Boys • Karl Malone Evens the Score**

> The unexamined life is not worth living.
> —Socrates, 440 B.C.

> Basketball jones, I gotta basketball jones,
> gotta basketball jones, yeah-a-yeah.
> —"Basketball Jones," 1972

> Victory or death.
> —Captain William Travis, in his last letter
> from the Alamo, 1836

The Spurs' tiny locker room began to clog with bodies and
the heavy musky smell of nervous jocks. Off in a corner,
Vinnie Johnson and I were talking about his famous double-
oh-seven shot.

With 00.7 left in the last game of the '90 Finals, Vinnie hit a jumper to win Detroit's second championship. "Man, I was so deep into the zone, so focused, that there was no way I was lettin' anybody else take that shot," he said. "I *knew* I'd make it. It was just one of those times where I was in my own little world—I'm unstoppable, like I got a big *S* on my chest.

"And then the guys were all *over* me—you know, 'Way to go, Way to go!' But I'm pushin' 'em away, 'cause I wanna *stay in that zone.*" His face glowed with the memory.

A couple of players glanced over, glanced away. It wasn't entirely cool to show emotion before a game. But I pressed it, because I was here for David Robinson, and all I'd been hearing was how Robinson could be the greatest player in history if he could just learn focus and toughness. Vinnie was a master of those qualities, and I suspected that's why he'd been brought here in midseason.

"Can you hear the crowd when you're deep into the zone?"

"Some of it. But you don't wanna lose that focus, so you block it. You just think, 'What am I gonna do next?'"

"So even when you make a big shot like that, you don't feel too much emotionally?"

"No. If you get emotional, you lose control. I like to take all that emotion back to the locker room after the game and sit back and go, Oooh yeah—what a great game."

The guys around us seemed to be getting distinctly uncomfortable. Not only were we talking about the mind, but we'd used that ugly little word "emotion."

"Do you visualize shots before you take them?"

"Sometimes—'specially if I know they're callin' my play next. Then I can see myself doin' the kind of move I'm gonna do."

Rod Strickland muttered, "It's gettin' kinda *deep* in here." He meant deep in bullshit. Strickland was not notably cerebral. The great basketball writer Dwight Jaynes had said that Strickland made decisions about as well as a twelve-year-old in a Baskin-Robbins.

"Is Robinson easy to get along with?" I asked Vinnie.

"Very easy. He's a real nice guy. Sometimes I think he's

too nice. I think he needs to get a little meaner. Sometimes you gotta sack people out there."

"Do you have to be angry to do that?"

"Naw, it's better if you separate out your anger from just plain aggressiveness. 'Cause anger is an emotion and gets in the way. Aggressiveness is more like a natural part of the zone."

Strickland couldn't take any more. "Oh, bullshit, man," he said. Vinnie didn't even glance at him.

David Robinson glided in. He came from the training room, where he'd been spending a lot of time lately, getting patched up and taped back together. One measure of success in the NBA is how badly other teams brutalize you.

Robinson had a different demeanor than any other superstar in the league. Most of them were so self-obsessed that it showed in their faces: eyes that rarely made contact, mouths twisted in self-consciousness. But Robinson's eyes seemed to notice everything, and his mouth always looked half-amused. He seemed older than the other players, even though, at twenty-six, he was younger than many.

"You believe in the zone?" Strickland asked Robinson.

Robinson mulled it over. Canted his head to one side. "As a cognitive process, sure," he said to Strickland. "Don't you?"

"Fuckin'-A!" said Strickland. "That's what I'm *sayin'.*"

For half a second, Robinson looked bewildered, like: What in God's name am I *doing* here? But he just nodded politely and sauntered to his locker.

I had to leave. It was getting too deep.

• Stupid David

Robinson came out for the tip-off with a big thirty-two-teeth smile. Extended his big hand to Hakeem Olajuwon. Olajuwon, scowling, grabbed it, let go.

Moments later, Robinson was scowling. Olajuwon had pushed him out of the paint—if you want to call fists to the kidneys "pushing." Robinson inched back toward the hoop, as if he could still hear ex-coach Larry Brown screaming, "Get back in!" But Olajuwon kept pounding Robinson's kidneys and pulling his love handles—such as they were on a 235-pound guy with a thirty-three-inch waist. Robinson's shoulders and face got glossy with sweat, and a thousand-yard stare settled into his eyes.

Coach Bob Bass cupped his hands and yelled, "Stay with him, Dave!" Meaning: Stay in the game, space cadet. Sometimes Robinson daydreamed—about music, his new wife, anything—and it made his coaches crazy.

But Robinson had another habit that was even worse. One that was a crime for a basketball player. He *thought*.

He couldn't help it. David Robinson had been born with a crippling defect: too much brain. Specifically, too much left brain. The left hemisphere of his brain, which governs logic, was a *monster*. It had given him a 1,320 S.A.T. score and a brilliance at practically everything he'd tried, from music to electronics to mathematics. But on the basketball floor, it was a killer. The worst thing a basketball player could do was analyze the game and his own actions—and Robinson analyzed *everything*.

The players with the great basketball minds were guys like Larry Bird and Chris Mullin. They gave every evidence of being right-brain dominant—better at intuitive, "holistic" thinking than linear thinking. In an interview, which required the logic of articulation, a guy like Bird could sound like Bobo the Simple-Minded. But Bird was brilliant on the floor—seeing spatial relationships and sensing patterns that went way over Robinson's head.

Earlier in the year, Larry Brown had gotten so pissed off at Robinson's inability to grasp basketball subtleties that he'd said, "He doesn't have a clue."

But shortly after that, Brown didn't have a job. The Spurs' owner wasn't satisfied with the team—but it wasn't Robinson he blamed. David Robinson was the most valuable basketball player in the world.

Robinson's value was astronomical. Michael Jordan, who was at his peak, was probably more valuable *this* year. But Robinson had five fewer years of wear and tear than Jordan and was still improving. The Bulls would have traded Jordan for Robinson in five seconds.

Cotton Fitzsimmons had recently called Robinson "the greatest impact player since Kareem." Cotton thought Robinson had already surpassed Jordan, Magic, and Bird. "They're all MVPs," he said. "This guy is more."

Pat Riley thought Robinson was better than Bill Russell, whom many consider the best ever. "David is the spitting image of Russell," said Riley, "only David is a better athlete."

Robinson had, in fact, finished first in the 1990–1991 *Inside Sports* Total Individual Performance Rating, a complex index that ignored theatrics and focused on a player's complete game. Robinson scored 23.2, to Jordan's 22.2, Karl Malone's 19.2, Magic's 17.2, Ewing's 16.9, and Barkley's 15.3.

In short, good player—if only he could *get his mind right.* Maybe sniff some glue, kill some brain cells. But that wouldn't have been David Robinson's style. Because— besides having brains—Robinson (a devout Christian) was the NBA's resident Holy Man, and such a gung-ho good American that he made Douglas MacArthur look like a pinko. Plus, there were finances to consider. Robinson was a true golden boy—a magnet for money, trailing only Michael and Magic.

So David Robinson would have to endure being brilliant and manage his career as best he could.

As Olajuwon continued to pound at him, Robinson seemed to disappear. Bob Bass pulled him out of the game.

Robinson didn't get back in until midway through the second quarter. As soon as he hit the floor, little Avery Johnson zipped down the lane. He was going to outquick Robinson, like he did every other center in the league. He slashed to his left, made the ball disappear, spun, ducked, and exploded upward.

Straight into Robinson's steel-cable right arm. Robinson had *matched* Avery, move for move. Avery put the shot up anyway, and Robinson smashed it down so hard it seemed to go half-flat when it hit the floor.

Bass blew out his breath and shook his head. The crowd stomped their cowboy boots and waved homer-hankies (or "rowdy rags," in the local lexicon). Terry Cummings grabbed both of Robinson's hands and did a head-bump routine. Robinson did the head-bump very reluctantly; he was in the NBA, but he wasn't *of* it.

Spurs' ball. Willie Anderson got it at midcourt and slid it underhand to Robinson near the basket. Robinson looked like he wanted a jumper, but hesitated, put the ball on the floor, and tried to go back up. But by then Olajuwon was there and Robinson had to pass. Anderson looked frustrated —he didn't have half of Robinson's intellect, but he was twice as hoop-smart.

Then, on the other end of the court, Olajuwon hooked Robinson and pulled him to the floor. As Robinson lay there, Olajuwon, off-balance, walked all over him—just stomped him like a snake. Jess Kersey blew his whistle. Foul on Robinson. The crowd howled.

Robinson didn't say a word. Didn't even make a face. He just looked at Kersey with big innocent eyes, like: What did I do, Jess—*writhe?*

He got up slowly. It was only early spring, and his body was already beat to hell. But the stomping got his mind into the game. When the night was over, Olajuwon would have only 6 points. It was the first time anyone had kept Olajuwon out of double figures in two hundred games.

• Lying David

After practice the next day, Robinson sat around the gym at Trinity College. Nice little college. Nice little city. San Antonio was just big enough to finance Robinson's ten-year $26 million contract and small enough to give him time to inscribe every autograph with a Bible quotation.

Robinson was relaxed and happy. Unlike many of the other Olympians, he didn't seem to resent journalists intruding on his private time. And he didn't hand me the usual line of bullshit about how the Olympics were the last thing on his mind.

"How important are the Olympics to you?" I asked him.

"Very important. It's for the *country."*

I didn't follow up with my usual what's-America-mean-to-you question. That question usually brought on a blank stare and brought me closer to the *real* reasons the player wanted to play in the Olympics: money, ego, and the camaraderie of the other great players. But David Robinson was different. He had been willing to go toe-to-toe with the Republican Guard in Iraq, so I took his patriotism at face value.

"You looking forward to playing with the other guys?"

He nodded hard. "Tremendous players! Most intense competitors I've seen in my life. Guys like Charles and Patrick and Karl, you've got to *kill* them to win. To think we'll all be on the same team is unbelievable.

"And I'm looking forward to spending some quality time with them, to find out what makes them tick."

"What do you think all you guys have in common?"

"I don't know. I try to figure that out all the time. If I knew, I'd sell it to people. But I watch a guy like Charles Barkley, and it's his *intensity* that goes beyond the average guy's. He's a warrior. He assumes the responsibility of being a leader."

"You see any problem of there being too many leaders in Barcelona? Too many egos?"

"Those guys are more competitors than they are leaders —they'll put winning first. That's how they'll define their egotism."

"Was losing the Olympics in 'eighty-eight a big disappointment?"

"Definitely. That's a considerable part of the reason I wanted to play again this year. To get that bad taste out of my mouth."

"I heard you were ambivalent about playing, that you didn't decide until late."

"No, I've wanted to play since the last Olympics was over.

Really. When Rod Thorn called, I told him I was definitely, definitely interested. I could spend the whole summer playing basketball. I guess I'm just young and stupid."

I wasn't sure, but I thought he was lying. People close to him had said he *didn't* want to spend all summer playing basketball, and that he'd initially been ambivalent about the Olympics. But his apparent deception made me feel good. At least he wasn't perfect.

I've got to admit, though, that Robinson at least *tried* to be as perfect as he could be. In the summer of '91, he'd gone through a spiritual upheaval, aimed at rooting out some of his imperfections. Primarily: arrogance. Which struck Spurs' beat writer Brad Townsend as pretty funny. "David's about as arrogant as a gerbil," says Townsend.

Nevertheless, Robinson had told Townsend, "I liked myself a lot more five years ago than I liked myself last year. I had to take a strong look at myself and say, 'You know what? This life-style, people saying this and that to me, really made me arrogant. It's really made me think the world revolves around me.'"

The spiritual grappling had a profound effect on Robinson. "This is a powerful, powerful thing," he said, "finding out about your life and finding out how to lift other people up."

When the Spurs' management heard about it, some of them had almost choked. Their attitude seemed to be: "Twenty-six million bucks! For the Flying Nun?"

But Robinson laid that fear to rest. "God doesn't want wimps," he'd said. "He doesn't want people who are laid back. He wants warriors. Because it's a war out there. It's a war between your soul and the devil."

In fact, Robinson was ready to kick a little satanic ass right at home. He didn't name names, but there were some notable bad boys in the locker room. One was Rod Strickland, who missed twenty-one games in 1990–1991 after breaking his hand in a bar brawl, and who was charged with indecent exposure in Seattle. That charge was later dropped, but then Strickland screwed up his rep again by partying until 2:00 A.M. before a crucial playoff game. Another reprobate was David Wingate, who was charged with rape in Maryland and San Antonio.

"We're friends and teammates," said Robinson, "but sometimes friends have to rebuke other friends. I can't sit here and deal with a man's game, because that's not where the problem lies. It lies in his life. And it's not about preaching the Bible to him, it's about straightening him out."

Robinson wasn't just pointing the finger at other people, though. He was also talking about himself. He'd back-burnered his own commitment to basketball. But now, he said, he was ready to commit himself fully, in the name of God, to being the best player possible.

That was exactly what the Spurs' front office wanted to hear. It was what they'd been waiting for. They hoped his commitment to God would give him the quality they had always wanted to see in him: a killer instinct.

● David Kicks Ass

Karl Malone ripped downcourt, pumping his elbows, and as he passed Rod Strickland (who was eighty-one pounds lighter) he swept his elbow into Strickland's chest. Strickland went *"Huhhh!"* and a look of shock and pain flooded his face. He scanned wildly for a ref but none—small coincidence—was in sight. Malone had once again "set the tone"—the NBA euphemism for establishing the game's level of violence. Nobody set the tone better than Karl. Certainly not David Robinson.

But when Robinson got downcourt he leaped into the paint after Malone and caught Malone off-balance with a forearm shove. "Way to go after him, David!" yelled assistant coach Gregg Popovich.

Popovich worked closely with Robinson, teaching him things that came naturally to other players, like developing a killer instinct, mastering the intricacies of the game, and staying focused. A lot of Popovich's lessons boiled down to one thing: learning how to not-think. Robinson's fine mind helped him memorize plays, patterns, and assignments, but it was mostly a hindrance. It was very difficult for someone as analytical as Robinson to not-think. Not-thinking was one of the fundamentals of Zen, and was, of course, heavy with irony: How do you think about not-thinking?

But learning it was crucial. If Robinson could learn to not-think, his right-brain, intuitive faculties would rise to the surface, and many of basketball's complicated spatial patterns would make sense. Also, not-thinking would allow him to play with more emotion, which was the key to the killer instinct. Furthermore, not-thinking would help rid Robinson's mind of its stream of daydreams and allow him to focus on the game.

Popovich thought Robinson was making progress. Robinson already had a killer instinct on defense, Popovich believed, and was learning how to apply the same feeling to offense.

Also, under Bob Bass—who'd replaced Larry Brown a couple of months ago—Robinson had been stationed on the left side of the floor, instead of the right. That allowed Robinson to more frequently use his left hand (his strong hand), and it seemed to make Robinson less hesitant and analytical.

Now that Robinson wasn't overthinking quite so much and was showing more of a killer instinct, he seemed to be doing less daydreaming.

Popovich believed that Robinson's spiritual transformation had helped him iron out some of his basketball problems. The upheaval, Popovich thought, had left Robinson "feeling more comfortable with himself, and more comfortable on the floor. He doesn't feel as much pressure as he used to; he's not trying to please everyone around him all the time. So he just goes out and plays. He's not planning his moves, he's just going out and being aggressive. When people just play, things happen more naturally—and that's important for him. He's never done that before."

Popovich wanted Robinson to have a victory-or-death attitude—and sometimes Robinson did. But it wasn't something you could push Robinson into. Robinson was just too complex for any old-fashioned win-one-for-the-Gipper-or-I'll-kill-you bullshit.

Third quarter: Karl Malone was alone under the Utah basket when Blue Edwards grabbed a rebound at the other end. Edwards heaved the ball toward Malone. All the players started jogging toward Malone, who was certain to score. But Robinson blurred downcourt like a deer dodging gunfire. It was bizarre—he seemed to be *gaining on the pass*. He accelerated. Just before the pass fell into Malone's hands, Robinson went up—Willie Mays–style—with his left hand stretched in front of his body. Grabbed it. One hand. Put it on the floor. U-turned. Raced past the players who were still jogging toward Malone.

He'd outrun a pass. Nobody did that.

Robinson's face exploded with joy. He practically levitated. The cowboy boots thundered. When they really got cranking here, you could hear them at the Alamo, a couple of blocks away.

In the stands, Robinson's mom and dad jumped to their feet.

It was David Robinson at his best. Not thinking, just doing.

Malone looked murderous.

Just before the game ended, Malone got even. Robinson was driving into the paint, but Malone and burly Mike Brown scrunched together and busted into Robinson's midsection, both at once: a 516-pound wrecking ball. Robinson doubled over. He seemed to grab his chest and stomach and testicles all at the same time. His face got brittle with pain. He walked in circles. He made his free throws, then walked in circles again. Bass called time, the sound system ripped into the "Hey" song, and Robinson hobbled to the bench looking as if Malone still had hold of his balls.

After the game, Robinson didn't come out of the training room until most of the other players had gone. Malone had trashed Robinson's body, and Robinson had needed an almost hour-long massage to break up the muscle spasms. He had tendinitis in his knee, and his ankle was hot mush.

He came out with just a towel around his waist and modestly slipped his underpants and pants underneath it. That style of dressing was somewhat unusual in the NBA, even though there were often women in the locker rooms. Many of the guys seemed to enjoy letting it all hang out. They loved to strut their stuff and buff themselves with oil, powder, and perfume before they slipped on their thousand-dollar suits. Robinson, though, had a body that made most of the narcissists look like fat old men. He had wide, thick shoulders that could bench-press two hundred pounds. Huge biceps. His upper body V-ed down to a tiny waist and one of the most compact butts in the NBA. But he never showed off.

"You know," he said to the small San Antonio press contingent, "we're really having *fun* now. We're actually enjoying each other out there, and it's *paying off.*" He seemed shocked that basketball could be fun.

Someone commented on his achieving a triple-double tonight—27 points, 11 assists, and 12 rebounds—while holding Malone to 15 points and 5 rebounds. "This was my first great game in about a week," Robinson said.

Extraordinary statement. The art of being a media star in the NBA was to *never* say you were great—and to *always* make sure everyone else said it.

It was just one more measure of David Robinson's distance from the NBA.

• Virginia Beach, Virginia

David Robinson, in the Trinity College gym, swatted down a shot by his brother Chuck, who was visiting. But Chuck raced after it and barreled toward the hoop. David planted his feet. Chuck gained speed. Bob Bass watched out of the corner of his eye. Chuck was flying. Would David risk his $26 million to whip his little brother? Crash! Bass winced. They both fell to the floor. Got up laughing. "Charge!" said David.

"Foul!"

"Uh-uh. You lie." David usually lost to Chuck. Mostly because David didn't apply himself, partly because Chuck was an excellent player.

"Shooting foul." Chuck went to the foul line, quickly put it up—and got it smashed into his face.

Nothing new. The Robinsons had been going at each other for twenty years. But at least they hadn't knocked out each other's teeth, like they had their father's.

"There's three of us," Chuck said after the game, "and there was never a time we weren't competing. Didn't matter what it was—Ping-Pong, bowling, basketball, academics. *Especially* academics. That was the only area our parents pushed us in. They never pushed us to play sports. They were just supportive of whatever we wanted to do.

"We all did things together, as a family. Dad would go onto the court with us, but we played pretty rough, and he'd get hurt. He lost a couple of teeth. But it was an *accident."*

Their father, Ambrose Robinson, was always competitive himself. Had to be. As a black kid growing up in Little Rock, Arkansas, he'd endured the last days of blatant segregation. In high school, he'd scored higher than most of the white kids on a college entrance exam, so they'd accused him of cheating and made him take the test again in a room full of proctors. He scored higher the second time.

He chose a profession that was relatively free of racism. He became a career Navy man, a sonar operator who was often at sea for up to six months.

When he was home, he was strict. A tense, thin man who chain-smokes and sips beer throughout the day, he once grounded David for six weeks for getting a C. And when he was gone, his wife, Freda, also expected a lot out of David, Kimberly, and Chuck. She worked all day and depended on the kids to do housework, gardening, and cooking. The kids worked hard and stayed out of trouble. "We knew what was wrong," David says. "We had responsibilities, but we had freedom too."

"David would always come to me and ask if I needed

anything," says Freda Robinson. "I used to hold all David's money, and he was thrifty, but he wanted me to know I could use his money."

Freda was very protective of David, partly because he'd almost died as an infant. He'd lodged his head between a bed and a wall. "He was turning blue," Freda says. "I couldn't feel a pulse. I started to give him CPR, and I could hear his little lungs. Then he started to go into convulsions."

At the hospital, they told her it would be years before they would know if he'd suffered brain damage.

"I watched David so closely—to make sure he developed at the pace of other kids."

It became clear he had no brain damage when he began to read at age three. At five, he began to play the piano by ear. From second grade on, he was in programs for the gifted. Soon, he was able to add his mother's grocery bill in his head just by watching the items pass through the checkout counter.

David had a talent for sports but had no interest in focusing on any single sport. "We never did anything too long," says Chuck. "We wouldn't get just the football and go out and play—we'd get the football and basketball and baseball." David's reluctance to focus also showed up in his intellectual pursuits. He was into music, science fiction, engineering, computers, math, composing, video games, electronics—whatever came along. Didn't care much for long books, though. Didn't have the attention span.

He wasn't particularly successful at sports, partly because he was small. He was just 5–7 by ninth grade and didn't reach his full 7–1 until he was twenty. "I was real small in junior high," says Robinson. "I was one of those guys who always sat at the end of the bench. I always felt like a small man. I never felt like a big man."

But he could run, and he could jump. Even at age fifteen, when he was still short, he had a thirty-six-inch vertical leap. Even so, he wasn't good enough to get any playing time on his freshman basketball team. His father asked him if he was afraid he'd be cut. David said, "No—I won't give 'em a chance." He quit.

Because of the sacrifices of Ambrose and Freda, the Robinson children had essentially sheltered childhoods. David's worst racial trauma was when, at age sixteen, he was politely asked to sit out a game of spin-the-bottle because white girls were playing. His high school was ninety percent white, and he assimilated into white social life. "It was hard for me to hang with other blacks," says David. "I felt out of place. I didn't know *how* to be black. I had to work at it."

In his last three years of high school, he began to grow, reaching 6–6. He became his team's starting center but was only second-team All-Metropolitan. His primary excitement as a senior had nothing to do with sports. It was scoring 1,320 on his S.A.T.'s. That score—not his athletic ability—allowed him to achieve a childhood dream, entering the Naval Academy. He wanted to be a Navy man, like his father. "I patterned myself after my dad," he says. "I never had any sports role models. My dad was my role model." He also hoped the academy could teach him discipline, which he felt he lacked.

But at the academy, Robinson smacked face-first into the real world. Unprotected by his parents or anyone else, he was forced to put up with the academy's humiliation and hazing. He hated it. He was on the basketball team, but jocks didn't get special privileges. Chuck, who now plays basketball at the academy, says, "Athletes get treated a little *worse*. It's just the opposite of a normal school. You're as humble as you can be the whole time you're there."

The academy was not only difficult academically but was loaded with special challenges: jumping off a hundred-meter tower, swimming a mile in a limited time, flying a plane, going on a submarine.

In his sophomore year, Robinson experienced another growth spurt, to the delight of his coaches. At Navy, military rules prohibit admission of freshmen over 6–6, so Navy's basketball teams had always been small.

Even on the basketball court, though, Robinson saw more bullying and bitching than he liked. Navy coach Paul Evans was of the old drill sergeant, make-them-eat-shit school. "He was playing mind games to motivate me," says Robinson. "That may work with one-dimensional guys, but not me. I told him, 'You're being a jerk.'" The coach—partly because of Robinson's antipathy—lost his job.

A new coach, Pete Herrmann, "allowed me to be myself," says Robinson, "so I worked harder." By the time he hit seven feet, Robinson was extraordinary. He still had the speed and grace of a small man but now had overpowering strength and size.

He could have quit the academy as a junior and become an instant multimillionaire in the NBA. But: "It was an honor to serve my country."

After making every All-American team as a senior and getting degrees in math and computer science, he began a two-year Navy hitch, which would later be followed by reserve duty. His hitch took him straight to the heart of the real world: a Georgia naval base surrounded by poverty, addicts, and prostitutes. "I was scared to death," says Robinson. "I was a Big Brother to a young boy, but I was afraid to park my car at his house. It was so sad. I realized what a privileged life I had. I got on my knees and asked God to give me a way to give back some of my blessings."

While still in the Navy, Robinson played in the '88 Olympics—for another sports fascist, Georgetown's John Thompson. "Thompson was a dictator," says Robinson. "It was always *his* gym, *his* team. He wants you scared of him. He degrades you. He didn't understand I could be devoted to the game and still have other interests."

Freda Robinson says, "David told us Thompson was trying to destroy him, but that he'd never let him do it."

Robinson had a mediocre Olympics, and NBA people feared the two-year hitch had ruined him.

That perception lasted until his first NBA game: 23 points and 17 rebounds against the Lakers. After the game, Magic said, "Some guys just aren't ever rookies."

He single-handedly saved the San Antonio franchise. "We were in the shitter," says Spurs owner Red McCombs, a local car dealer. When Robinson joined the team, attendance shot from an average of 8,462 to 14,595. If it hadn't been for him, the franchise would have abandoned San

Antonio, which is the league's smallest media market. The worth of the team went from about $40 million to about $100 million.

Robinson's $26 million deal was the best ever for a rookie. Robinson accepted the big money casually, settling into a simple, sparsely decorated condo. "The Bible says it's harder for a rich man to find his way into the kingdom of heaven than it is for a camel to pass through the eye of a needle," Robinson said at the time. "Hey, man—I'm in trouble."

He was Rookie of the Year in 1990, leading the Spurs to the greatest one-year improvement in NBA history (from 21 wins in 1989 to 56 in 1990). Averaging 24.3 points, 12 rebounds, and 3.9 blocks, he became the team's "heart and soul," according to coach Larry Brown. "In one season," Brown said, "this has become David's team."

There was only one problem with that. The year before, it had been Brown's team.

Brown and Robinson began an uneasy coexistence. They were both genuinely decent men, so it didn't degenerate into the standard star war. They played golf together and said nice things about each other in the press.

But Brown was a screamer and was obsessed with basketball. Robinson, however, didn't even remotely have a basketball "jones," (or addiction) and barely tolerated abuse.

"Larry is high-strung," says Robinson. "After a couple of years of listening to him, it gets to be a little too much, and you tune it out."

Their uneasiness softened somewhat when Robinson went through his spiritual transformation in the summer of '91. Brown supported it. "Whatever makes the kid happy and fulfilled in his life is fine by me," he said.

Robinson's spiritual upheaval included a decision to propose to a woman he'd dated but had broken up with. Valerie Hoggatt—an attractive, serious, religious woman— had been Robinson's girlfriend since his Navy days, but she had moved to California in 1990. Robinson realized, though, that "she was the one girl I really enjoyed. She loves God more than she loves me, so if I cross a line, she's got enough respect for herself to say, 'Hey, I'm not going to put up with all that.'" They were married in December of '91 and moved into an elaborate, multistoried $1 million house.

Shortly after the wedding, during a long plane ride to Boston, Brown sat down with Robinson and told him he thought Robinson had been acting hypocritically. Robinson had been talking a lot about compassion and humility, Brown said, but hadn't applied it to their own relationship. Robinson never asked Brown about his family, Brown said, even though Brown often asked Robinson about Robinson's family. It was particularly hurtful, Brown said, since one of his daughters had cancer.

Robinson listened but didn't say much. It was impossible to tell if he was boiling inside—which would have been the typical superstar reaction.

About three days later, Larry Brown left the Spurs. Owner Red McCombs had complained to Brown about the direction of the team, and Brown apparently decided to quit before he got canned.

Some media people thought Robinson was responsible for Brown's departure. They were wrong. He was as surprised as everyone else.

Writers asked him for a comment. He told them, "I just realized recently that Larry and I didn't have the kind of relationship we could have had. I didn't talk to him enough about how his family was and how he was. We weren't as close as we should have been on a personal level. And it was my fault."

Rare statement from a star. David Robinson had shown, once again, that he was in the NBA, but not of it.

Robinson hit from the wing over Charlotte's Kenny Gattison, a 252-pound whopper with ditch-digger's shoulders. Gattison, who had to scratch and claw to stay in the league, looked furious. Before Robinson could even get back on defense, Gattison rammed his arms into Robinson's hands and belly. It was about the only thing Gattison could do to keep from being pulled from the game.

"Be tough, Dave!" yelled Bob Bass. Robinson loved

playing for Bass. Bass was a gentleman—smart and soft-spoken.

Then prime-stud Larry Johnson (6–7, 250) ganged up with Gattison, and they began working over the 235-pound Robinson from chest to thigh. Coming at him together, they looked like your basic dark-alley nightmare. Gattison and Johnson (who'd be this year's Rookie of the Year) had much lower centers of gravity than Robinson, and they squeezed him between them. But they couldn't stop him. Too tall. Too fast. Too talented.

So Charlotte coach Allan Bristow pulled J. R. Reid off the bench to run in and pick up a couple of quick fouls. Reid smacked Robinson hard in the back, but in less than three minutes, Reid was pitted-out and heaving for breath.

Looking like he was on the verge of a seizure, Reid got the ball under the hoop on a fast break and went up for the shot. But Robinson suddenly materialized, sneaked in a hand, and grabbed the ball. It was so quick that Reid continued his shot, as if he still had the ball. "It's *gone*, J.R.!" Bristow screamed. "Get back down!" Time for Mike Gminski.

Gminski (6–11, 260) rushed in, took a quick shot at Robinson with his knee and thigh, then started muscling Robinson every time Robinson moved. With twelve years of NBA experience, Gminski made a difference on Robinson. For about thirty seconds. Then Robinson just went around him and over him.

Robinson didn't try to retaliate for the brutality. He just didn't have a full-fledged killer instinct. He wanted to win. But not to kill.

Allan Bristow looked tired and crazy. He'd thrown his four most lethal guys at Robinson—a combined 1,020 pounds of killer instinct. But nothing stopped him.

At least, that was how it looked.

Nature, however, had laws of its own.

After the game, Robinson hobbled out of the trainer's room into a near-empty locker room.

He eased into his chair, with his back to the room, and began to slowly and clumsily pull his clothes on.

Reporters gathered at his back.

Without turning around, Robinson said, "I sense the hunt."

They began bombarding him with questions. He answered politely, even though Charlotte had just murdered the Spurs.

"I'm looking forward to our next one," Robinson said. "I've got to get this bad taste out of my mouth."

But there wouldn't be a next one. Robinson's season was over. His left hand had been ripped apart inside—so badly that surgeons would have to cut it open to tie it back together.

David Robinson was learning the most basic lesson of the killer instinct: kill or be killed.

He was becoming a part of the NBA.

13

Stockton
& Malone

Attack of the Killer Republicans • The Vanity of
Humility • The Blood of Isiah • Tim Hardaway's
Psyche • The Smartest Man in Basketball •
Johnny Boy, We Hardly Knew Ye • The Little Guy's
Freudian Nightmare • John Stockton's Hate Affair
with Sportswriters • The Baby and the Bully •
Karl the Wimp

Self-denial is indulgence of a propensity to forego.
— Ambrose Bierce, 1899

Vanity of vanities; everything is vanity.
— Ecclesiastes

Sportswriters are a rude and brainless subculture of
fascist drunks whose only real function is to publicize and
sell whatever the sports editor sends them out to cover. The
two keys to success are: (1) a blind willingness to believe
anything you're told by the coaches, flacks, hustlers, and
other "official spokesmen"; and (2) a Roget's thesaurus, to
avoid using the same verbs twice in the same paragraph.
— Hunter S. Thompson,
Fear and Loathing on the Campaign Trail '72, 1972

"A boy's best friend is his mother."
— Norman Bates

"*Kill* 'em, Karl! *Kill* those guys!" A fat lady in a purple "Latter-Day Saints Love" sweatshirt rolled her program into a phallic symbol and thrust it into the ribs of the weaselly little guy next to her. Karl Malone cracked Golden State's Alton Lister in the chest, then feathered in a jumper before Lister could even curse. "Oh! Karl!" she shrieked. Salt Lake's Delta Center trembled with ecstasy. I feared for my life.

I was an infidel, and *they all knew it*. I was sure the Mormons could smell the stench of Coors on my breath. They could see the caffeinated beverage in my hand. And they could see my *beard*—not a God-fearing Brigham Young bush, but a trimmed, big-city media-type beard. For all they knew, I could be a New York Jew. Or worse.

It had been twenty years since I'd been trapped in such a hell of rectitude. Republican National Convention, 1972. Miami Beach. I'd gotten caught sneaking into a Young Republican caucus, and before they were done with me, they had me chanting "Four more years!" and wearing a "Spiro of '76" button. A person will do sick things to survive. Filing my article from that heart of darkness had been an ugly mission, and after that, I'd never wanted another. So I'd started writing about Hollywood and sports, to be around a hipper crowd. Joke was on me.

Before coming here tonight, I'd been in Salt Lake only a couple of times. Once was to cover the execution of Gary Gilmore. Horrible spectacle. I wasn't a fan of Gary's—he was a sick freak who should've been locked in a rock cage like Hannibal the Cannibal. But I knew some of his family and felt bad for them. Besides, I don't like killing.

My other Salt Lake adventure was promoting a diet book. Sold like crazy here. Mormons tend toward blubber, because gluttony is the only fun they tolerate. Except, of course, for watching Karl Malone torture people. That was just their type of good clean violence. Rectitude works in mysterious ways.

That's not to say, though, that Karl Malone didn't *endure* his share of violence. Right now, Alton Lister was ripping and gouging Malone with his elbows and fingernails, con-

centrating on open cuts and soft spots. Malone didn't shrink
from the hits, though. He leaned into them, and it seemed to
bewilder Lister. At tip-off, Lister had stomped onto the floor
like King Kong on steroids, but every time he hit Malone
without killing him, he seemed to grow smaller.

Malone—as he did in every game—was staking claim to
the best part of the floor, the front half of the lane. That was
where about fifty percent of all rebounds came down, and it
was the only place you could get an easy shot. But Lister
wanted the same territory. Lister couldn't shoot and
couldn't dribble, but he knew that if he could keep people
like Malone out of that area, he could keep making his $1.7
million. All the bullies and monsters in the league knew
that. That was why every waking minute of Karl Malone's
life was a war. And it was why Karl Malone needed John
Stockton.

As Malone pushed Lister away, Stockton ripped around
the top of the key with the ball. Malone held up his right
hand. Stockton lurched forward, practically touching the
floor, and suddenly had a clear line to Malone. He
sidearmed a pass. Simple pass. But absolutely perfect. It hit
Malone square in the palm, and Malone dunked it without
using his other hand. Malone had almost 30 points, and it
wasn't even halftime. Most of his points had come from
directly underneath the basket, off Stockton passes.

Stockton's extraordinary passing freed Malone to concentrate on fighting off the monsters. Malone could grapple and
shove interminably, then stretch out a hand and—*whap!*—
the ball would be in it. Stockton was Malone's artillery
support—the gunner who kept the monsters off-balance.

Stockton was also the primary reason that Malone had
become one of basketball's great scorers. And Malone was
the biggest reason Stockton led the league in assists. Theirs
was the most perfect symbiotic relationship in NBA history.

After Malone's basket, he pointed at Stockton. Stockton
pointed back. They didn't do that for themselves. They
hated pointing. It was vain. It was city. They did it for the
fans.

The fans howled with pleasure. They loved Malone, who

was a Baptist and—God forgive him—black. And they adored Stockton, who was a devout Catholic. The boys were fantastic. Heroes. Role models. Of course, they'd never get into *heaven*. But that didn't matter. As long as they got into the playoffs.

After the game, I ran into Tim Hardaway. "I just talked to a Selection Committee guy who said you were a lock for the last pro spot on the Olympic team," I told him.

His eyes brightened. "No kiddin'? That'd be great. But I think Clyde or Isiah will get it. They got the names."

"I know. But you're getting more famous by the minute. You notice a big change this year?"

"Yeah, I've seen that. A lot of media has been checkin' me out—at practice, before practice, before games, after games."

"You think much about the Olympics?" He was supposed to say: No, I just think about the Warriors.

"I think about it all the time."

"If you could vote for Isiah or Clyde or yourself, who'd you vote for?"

He looked at me like I was nuts. "Most definitely, for myself. Most definitely."

I'd been talking to a sports psychologist who'd done some secret testing of players during the '89 draft, when Hardaway had come out, and he'd told me Hardaway had tested through the roof in the category of confidence. I'd asked him how they'd determined that, and he'd said, "Because he totally accepts himself, just the way he is. There's no inner war—no fake modesty, no fake arrogance. Guys like that interpret pressure positively, instead of negatively."

"What was your happiest day this season?" I asked Hardaway.

"That's easy. The All-Star Game. 'Cuz of Magic—seein' him so happy.

"Only one thing could be better than that. Playin' with him in Barcelona."

Stockton & Malone

• You Can't Polish a Turd

The next morning, I wandered into a little college gym where the Jazz practiced. No security guard. None necessary. In Salt Lake, people mind their manners. I'll say one thing for Mormons: they know how to be polite. As far as I'm concerned, they can take over New York anytime they want.

Karl Malone was in a free-throw contest with Tyrone Corbin. Malone, somehow, seemed free of the punishment he'd suffered last night. He was loose, fluid, and happy. He couldn't really have recovered from the beating, because that was a physical process that took time. He'd simply . . . transcended it. Even an open wound over his eye had mysteriously vanished.

Corbin toed the line, paused. "Miss!" said Malone. "Ever-buddy deserve to miss *one*." Corbin ignored him. *"Miss!"* Clanged it off.

Malone's turn. He glared at the hoop. "Everybody can miss one," said Corbin.

"Not me." *Swish.* "Tie game. This for all the marbles." He locked onto the hoop.

"Don't choke."

"I don't." (Not "I won't," but "I don't.") *Swish.*

Coach Jerry Sloan called the team into a huddle. From across the floor, Stockton sprinted over like a scrub trying to make an impression.

"Let's go through a short-clock situation," said Sloan. "Straight-line one, and straight-line two." They practiced an inbounds play for a few minutes, then Sloan clapped his hands. "Okay, that's it." It was the shortest practice I'd seen all year. When you have John Stockton on the team, it's like having a coach on the floor.

Stockton was widely considered to have the best basketball mind in the world. His only rivals were Magic and Larry, but they were now only marginally active in the game. Bird had recently come off the injured list, played spectacularly, then collapsed again. He was about the only person who didn't seem to know his career was over. Magic was still considering coming back for the playoffs, but he didn't seem to be getting much encouragement. His wife, Cookie, was against it.

After Malone shot more free throws, I asked him if he had any fear of being injured in the Olympics.

"Naw," he said in his strange voice, which alternated between a squeak and a rumble. "I think your condition have a lot to do with how healthy you are."

"Do you do aerobics, other than basketball?"

"I don't run anymore like I used to. But I do StairMaster and bike. I got all that in my house now. It beats going to a health spa, standing in line, and either you gawkin' at people or they gawkin' at you. Plus, I lift weights."

"How often do you lift?"

"I can't tell you that. If I tell you that, somebody read it, and they go out and do more."

In fact, Malone lifted twice a week during the season and four times a week in the summer. (If you want to do more and then try to kick Karl's ass—good luck.)

Stockton tried to duck past the few reporters who were at the practice, but I headed him off and asked what aspect of the Olympics he was most looking forward to.

"Playing with the other guys," he said. "I think that'll be tremendous. Especially after playing against them for so many years."

"Do you enjoy playing against other superstar players, like Hardaway last night?" That was usually a safe question. The superstars never got tired of hearing that they were superstars. But Stockton made a face.

"I don't think in terms of superstars," he said. "Period. So you throw out the question."

Caught me off guard. So I made the same mistake again. "What do you think sets the superstar players apart mentally?"

"I don't think like that. I'm sorry. I refuse to answer the question."

"Okay, let me ask you this. What sets Karl Malone apart?"

"I don't know."

"Okay. How about this? What sets *you* apart?"

"I don't know. I don't think about it. I just go out and play, and . . . just play."

"How important is it for you to be on a championship contender?"

"Excuse me?"

"Is that your way of saying it's important?"

"Yeah. I'd have a very tough time on a team that doesn't win. Guess I'll leave it at that."

We talked a little more, but it was about as enlightening as talking to a USA Basketball PR hack.

I spotted Frank Layden, the legendary Jazz president and former coach.

"Sometimes I think Stockton's not too deep," I told Layden.

"That's just his style," said Layden. "He's got a great mind. Remember, he's an Academic All-American. And he's got an amazing memory—instant recall. If he sees Karl Malone on the court, he doesn't have to look again; he knows *exactly* where he is. You're born with that."

Layden was getting wound up. Stockton was one of his favorite subjects. "His decision-making! It's like he has a computer in him that reacts quicker than anybody else. The reason he gets so many steals is because of his anticipation. It's like he can read his opponent's mind."

Jerry Sloan, passing by as he headed out, agreed that Stockton had an extraordinary basketball mind. "He always knows exactly where to go with the ball and how to get it there," said Sloan. "That's why he's such a great passer. He's not flashy—he just knows exactly where the ball should be at every moment. If you need the pass to come in high, or low, or left, or right, that's where it'll come.

"And I'll tell you another reason he's a great passer," said Sloan. "There's an old basketball saying: 'The passer always gets a ride home.' If you take care of the other guys, they're gonna take care of you."

"Why do you think Stockton's so competitive?"

"It's innate. You've either got that, or you don't. I've seen too many guys that I just *can't* motivate. To them, it's just a job. If they don't like to play, it doesn't matter what I say or do. You know, you just can't polish a turd."

"Is that another old basketball saying?"

"No. That applies to life too."

John Stockton's wife, Nada, was courtside before the next game. She's blond and pretty, and everyone knew who she was, but no one hassled her. It wasn't the studious celebrity-ignoring of city people, though, but just a down-home respect for privacy.

"Is it true," I asked Nada, "that John doesn't read anything that's written about him?"

"Yes, that's true. We don't get the newspaper. For a while, we were getting *USA Today* so we could see what's going on in the world. John thinks it's not good to read your own clippings. Either they talk you into a slump or into thinking you're the greatest."

"I would think he'd *like* to see his accomplishments reflected."

"No. If he reads how great he is, it just embarrasses him."

Inside the locker room, Stockton saw me coming and got very interested in his shoes.

"To what extent," I asked him, "do you consider basketball a mental game?"

"It's not too mental. There's no time to think out there. In fact, it's detrimental to stop and dwell on every play."

"How hard is it to not-think, to shut your mind off?"

"Don't know. That's too much thinking for me."

"Have you always been able to shut off your mind?"

"I guess I haven't thought about it."

"Where'd your confidence come from? Have you had it since you were a kid?"

"I don't know. You have to have confidence to get the job done. But it doesn't mean you think you're *better* than anybody else."

"One of my theories is that the most confident players had at least one very nurturing parent. Somebody who accepted them as they were."

"Well, I had great parents. I think the world of my family—but I've never stopped to put a label on them, like nurturing or whatever."

He seemed so uneasy, like he was waiting for me to hit him with the hard stuff: Where were you Tuesday night? Do you own a .357 Magnum? Who's the redhead?

I didn't understand why Stockton felt so uncomfortable. I'd just reviewed practically every word that had ever been written about him, and it was virtually all positive. Besides, compared to all the other types that hovered around the NBA, sportswriters were the least offensive and egomaniacal.

"It strikes me as odd," I said, "that after all these years of guys like me coming up to you, it's still something you don't like."

"You are what you are," he said. "There's going to be certain things about you that change. But you are what you are."

• Spokane, Washington

What in hell did life do to John Stockton to make him so god-awful paranoid and self-conscious?

He grew up safe as Beaver Cleaver: big Irish Catholic family, parochial schools, local college, hometown hero.

But just like in *Twin Peaks* (which was set not far from Spokane) there was a dark underbelly to his shiny all-American story. Stockton grew up vain and competitive in a place where vanity and competition were frowned upon, creating a tension he seems to have never quite outgrown.

Spokane is a middle-of-nowhere town of 175,000, with the looks of Sun Valley and the puritanical, blue-collar guts of Cleveland. It's an agricultural area, white as Wonder bread, very steeped in the stuff flag-waving punks like Dan Quayle call "traditional values." It's just the place for a nice, traditional Freudian nightmare.

Jack and his wife Clementine (yes—Clementine) raised their four kids in an Irish Catholic working-class neighborhood known as the Little Vatican. The place teemed with friendly white priests and bad boys who grew up to be priests. Sound like the movies? Bing Crosby grew up there and stole from his past in *Going My Way* and *The Bells of St. Mary's*.

The Stockton kids went to Catholic schools, swam at the Y, and wrote their names in wet cement. "Johnny Boy," as the third child was known, went to local Gonzaga University (three blocks from home), spent his vacations as a young NBA player in his boyhood room, married his high-school sweetheart, and bought the house next door to his folks'. He says, "I must've gone about five blocks in twenty-two years."

How sweet! Frank Merriwether! Horatio Alger! But there's a ghost prodding John Stockton: the ghost of his grandfather.

John's father, Jack, is the son of Houston Stockton, the star halfback on Gonzaga's undefeated 1924 football team. Houston Stockton spent four years playing pro football and is still big as God in a town that worships its local sports heroes: Ryne Sandberg, Mark Rypien, and Johnny Boy Stockton.

Jack might've followed his dad into sports, but nature screwed him. "My father, he was a *big* man," says Jack Stockton. "But I'm not." In fact, Jack Stockton looks sort of like a cross between his son John and Larry "Bud" Melman.

But Jack Stockton had a competitive fire of his own and crawled out from under his father's shadow. He became high priest of another hallowed institution that's in every Irish Catholic neighborhood: the local pub. Ten days before Johnny Boy was born, Jack Stockton bought a bar.

Jack and Dan's Tavern is strictly a neighborhood joint, the sort of place where everybody knows your name and might beat the shit out of you if they don't. Spending days tending bar and making chili, Jack Stockton honored his father's legend without ever attempting to surpass it. He was safe and secure, and he never complained about his modest lot.

Jack Stockton played the glad-handing barkeep—but he did it with an attitude. There were never pictures of John

Stockton on the walls of Jack and Dan's. Partly because of a Catholic disdain for the sin of pride. And partly because: "My partner and I built this place," Jack says. "If I'm going to hang anybody's picture here, it's going to be mine." It sounds as if Jack—sandwiched between a famous father and famous son, may be holding in some resentment. Nevertheless, John Stockton has never said an unkind word about his father.

Johnny Boy was a familiar sight to the tavern regulars, as a neighborhood brat bumming ice-cream money and as a college student across the street. They liked him. He respected his elders. Stayed out of trouble.

Still, few psychologists recommend saloons for day-care. So Jack and Clementine balanced tavern life with faithful Catholicism. "If I had to identify any specific glue that sealed our family together," Jack recalls, "I would point to the Church." His son echoes the sentiment, even crediting his religious training for his basketball passing skills. "All through school, my faith has taught me that I think of others before I act. Choosing others over yourself makes a person tough."

But putting others first doesn't necessarily make a skinny runt happy. Somewhere along the line—while the priests and nuns were talking about humility and self-sacrifice, while the beer drinkers were talking about Grandpa Houston, and while his older brother Steve was beating the crap out of him at basketball—Johnny Boy got it into his head that he was going to be the best basketball player in the family. In Spokane. In college. In the NBA. In the *world.*

Of course, he didn't advertise this ambition. Pride cometh before getting knocked on your ass. He camouflaged his zeal. Instead of being a shooter (like every other kid in the world), he became a passer.

Coaches loved it. Coaches always love guys who look for the pass—even if they're little guys. And Johnny Boy was little. Not just basketball little. Plain old little. As a freshman with the balls to try out for his high school varsity team, he weighed in at 90. But he was possessed with the game.

He'd play at the grade school, at the Y, at another gym. He'd sneak into pickup games at Gonzaga. He'd stand around courts until the big kids *had* to choose him. One summer his grade school coach announced he'd open the gym at 6:00 A.M. for anyone who wanted to practice, certain that his tiny charges would be nestled at home with Malt o' Meal and cartoons. Johnny Boy took him up. Every morning.

Ed Smith, Stockton's high school coach, remembers Stockton's daily calls for pickup games. The phone would ring and Smith would hear, " 'Open the gym and bring your fat friends.' What were we, twenty-four, twenty-five? It wasn't like we were forty-five. These guys had *played*. John was a five-five ninth grader. He'd play his butt off, and he'd get mad if he got beat by a twenty-five-year-old. Tons of people were as gifted as he was, but he had something other people don't. It's desire, but I'm not sure that word covers it. He won't back down."

Another coach remembers it as vividly: "He'd run face-first into a brick wall at full speed if he had to."

The assessment was literally correct. The Stockton family court was located between a brick wall, a carport, and a picket fence. Johnny Boy, four years younger than Steve and his buddies, was regularly banged off the brick wall. "I used to get the hell beat out of me," Stockton remembers.

Jack wouldn't let Clementine interfere with the backyard warfare, which was so bloody that the Stockton boys were known as Cain and Abel. Once Johnny Boy split Steve's lip when the two went after a loose ball. The older boy, reckoning it an accident, inbounded the ball, then got smacked again by John. Furious, Steve walloped the kid, who wound up on the back porch crying and spewing profanity. Clementine, doing dishes by the kitchen window, heard it all but didn't punish Johnny Boy. "I think she understood the situation," Steve says.

Jack credits the vicious backyard play with Johnny Boy's competitiveness. "He never got beat the same way twice. They'd pop him around pretty good. But the next day, they'd have to find another way to beat him. He really took some horrible thumpings out there, but I think that's what started him thinking, 'There's got to be another way to beat these guys.'"

Some of the things Stockton learned weren't exactly pure. "Everyone always sees this angelic image of the choirboy," says Stockton's college coach Dan Fitzgerald, "but I'll tell you this right now: this kid next door will poke you in the eye to win. He will not cheat, but he will get a piece of you before the game is over."

The angel-who'll-kill aspect wasn't the only kink in Stockton's all-American personality. There was also his vanity about being so humble. Johnny Boy's entire game was based on unpretentious team play: setting picks, moving without the ball, breaking the press, shooting free throws, and of course, passing. It was the ultimate YMCA game, as white as basketball gets: you play hard—play rough—but don't get noticed. You get the thrill of victory but don't have to suffer the spotlight (and the examination that comes with it).

It was a fundamentals-oriented game to match a fundamentalist environment. The nuns and priests liked it. The beer drinkers liked it. And parents liked it. Johnny Boy—who'd found a perfect outlet for the control freak within—became the World's Greatest Y Player.

But he was not classically humble. He was great and knew it. He just didn't *act* like he knew it. He let other guys do the scoring—but he was about as unassuming as Thor.

He was even great enough to get past the liabilities of his scrawny little body. "If you had told me he'd be a chess champion," said his grade school coach Kerry Pickett, "I wouldn't have argued. But I wouldn't have thought he could overcome the physical part of it."

Johnny Boy developed a game that made him valuable to every team he was on. Nothing showy—his passing lacks the theatrics of Bird's or Magic's. But it was endearing as hell to coaches.

Stockton set some Spokane scoring records in high school, but he still looked like a bulimic altar boy. Few recruiters came around. His lucky break came when he was offered a scholarship by Dan Fitzgerald—the coach at Grandpa Houston's school, across the street from Dad's bar. Stockton was grateful but made a joke of it. He called Fitzgerald on Easter Sunday and told him, "Coach, I'm going to Montana."

Playing Gonzaga's flex offense, in which he was strictly a feeder, Stockton had a hard time adjusting his relentless backyard game. Then he found a mentor, conference star Don Baldwin. "The best part of Baldwin's game was the way he thought," Stockton recalls. "And that was always my biggest problem. I was always one hundred miles per hour, no matter what."

So Stockton toned down his game and concentrated on passing. Junior year, he made All-Conference. Senior year, the team was reduced to eight men by injuries, and Stockton was asked to shoot. He led the conference in scoring, field-goal percentage, assists, and steals. He came down with bronchitis, but he still averaged thirty-nine minutes a game. He lost fifteen pounds and went home to Mom's to get ready to play in Europe. He had gaudy stats, but he was still a little white passer from nowhere. Nada Stockton assumed that he'd soon be coaching in high school or junior high. Stockton believed he had the ability to play in the NBA—but he never thought he'd get the chance.

Then a few doors opened, just a crack. Stockton crashed through. He was invited to the 1984 U.S. Olympic trials. Then he was asked to substitute for an injured player at a college All-Star Game. He shone at both events, getting released from the Olympic team in the final cut, along with Karl Malone. Once considered a fifth-rounder in the NBA draft, he was suddenly expected to go in the first.

The Utah Jazz, who needed a point guard to back up erratic Ricky Green, took him sixteenth. His Gonzaga teammates hired a stripper for a party celebrating his draft. But a flustered Stockton, ever the control freak, threw the woman in the family pool before she could finish her act. It was *not* the kind of attention Stockton wanted. He was still Spokane's humblest hero.

Stockton cultivated a public image of oh-shucks-I'm-just-part-of-the team. He never boasted to the press.

But even as his fame for humility expanded, he became increasingly cocksure. While visiting L.A. in college, he'd walked up to Bernadette Peters in an airport lounge and invited her to a game. Then he had come back and told his teammates that he was taking her out that night. Also while he was in college, Gonzaga's sports information department had distributed a weekly newsletter called *The Stock Report*, pushing him (unsuccessfully) for All-American honors. On his first day of NBA rookie camp, he wrote his college coach that, "It's a lot of fun playing with so many great players. They aren't awesome, though. I feel confident playing against them."

In his first season, Stockton did well in assists and steals, but rode the bench. He believed he was more talented than Green, but he was just *spelling* the guy. And John Stockton did not spell guys.

The next season, another door opened. Jazz coach Frank Layden started Green every two games and let Stockton start the third. Stockton grabbed his chance. He held on to the starter's role until February, when, unaccustomed to the NBA schedule, he wilted.

Next year, he was back on the bench. Once again, though, he was near the top of NBA reserves in several categories. But all he could hear was the word *reserve*. "I've never felt lower as a player," he recalls.

So he fought harder. In fact, he never missed a game in his first four seasons. Finally, Green withered. Stockton stepped forward and never let go.

Then came the assists. Phenomenal waves of them. More assists than anyone had ever racked up. Twenty-eight in a single game. An average of 16.4 in a playoff series. Stockton set an NBA record of 1,128 assists in 1988 then broke it twice. Before him, only two men (Isiah Thomas and Kevin Porter) had made more than 1,000 assists in a season, and each did it once. By the end of 1992, Stockton had done it four straight times.

True, Stockton had some great scorers: Karl Malone, Jeff Malone, Adrian Dantley, Kelly Tripucka, Thurl Bailey. But there's a chicken-and-the-egg thing to that.

Stockton became the perennial Jazz MVP, surpassing even Malone. He's been in four All-Star games and has improved his shooting percentage each year.

In '92, Stockton's humility earned him the ultimate honor: selection to the Olympic team. Of course, all he had to do for that was be more humble than Isiah Thomas. And—for John Stockton—that wasn't very hard.

• Blood on the Floor

"You're gonna end up like Isiah!" yelled the fat lady, as Houston's Sleepy Floyd got tangled with Karl Malone. Isiah's name was still a rallying cry in Salt Lake, even though it had been almost six months since Malone had ripped open Isiah's head. In Salt Lake they considered Isiah's forty-stitch wound to be an overpublicized scratch. The whole uproar, according to almost everyone I talked to in the Jazz franchise, was Isiah's fault: because he'd *bled* so much. If there hadn't been rivers of blood on the floor, the refs wouldn't have *overreacted.*

Olajuwon grabbed the ball and came screaming down the sideline like a runaway train. Stockton planted his wiry little body in front of Olajuwon. For a second, it looked like Olajuwon was just going to kill Stockton and be done with it. But at the last second he veered slightly and caught Stockton with just an elbow. The elbow went *"thunk"* in Stockton's chest, like somebody thumping a watermelon. Olajuwon dunked the ball, and Stockton yelled at referee Ed Rush, "What was *that?"*

"Not enough," said Rush.

"How much you *want?"*

Rush refused to respond.

Then the 251-pound Larry Smith sprinted into the game to help Olajuwon pound Malone. Pretty brutal. They caught Malone between them. Olajuwon pinned Malone's arms down, and Smith gave Malone a nasty butt-thrust to the belly and groin. Jerry Sloan yelled at Ed Rush: "Damn, Eddie—how much blood you *want?*" Rush ignored him, just like he had Stockton. But Malone wasn't even blinking. He just shoved back, dug in, shoved, shuffled his feet, and suddenly flung them both off with one explosive breast-stroke. It was an amazing feat of strength. Even in a league of muscle freaks, Malone's physique stood out. His upper arms were like thighs, and his shoulders looked like they'd been inflated with an air compressor.

Houston coach Rudy Tomjanovich pointed at big Tree Rollins, and Rollins jumped off the bench and pulled off his jacket. "Do some damage," said Tomjanovich. Tomjanovich had suffered the worst injury in NBA history—a face-splitting blow that almost killed him—but he'd never lost his taste for a good rumble.

But Malone just started hopping a step backward and shooting over Rollins. The drop step was just one element Malone had added to his game since joining the NBA. Like all the great players, he tried to add something new each year. His first two years, he'd greatly improved his free-throw shooting and his post-up shooting. The two improvements complemented each other; in college, Malone had been reluctant to post up, because he wanted to avoid free throws. But when he learned to make them—mostly by figuring out how to not-think—he became the greatest scorer in the NBA from the line. In '91 he scored 684 points on free throws, almost a hundred more than second-place finisher, David Robinson.

Rollins kept getting his face closer and closer to Malone, and Malone kept bullying him back. Then Blue Edwards banged Houston's Cedric Maxwell, Maxwell flew into Rollins, and Rollins dominoed into Malone. As he hit Malone, Rollins swept his elbow into Malone's solar plexus. Malone, for the first time, looked pissed off. "What you *doin',* man?" he yelled at Rollins.

"What *you* doin'?" Rollins stuck his chest into Malone's chest. Fans leaped to their feet. Refs hustled over. A ball boy ran over to sop up a pool of sweat on the floor and came up with a tinge of blood on his towel. But Malone walked away, and it was finished.

As they lined up for the free throw, Rollins said to Malone, "Didn't mean the elbow."

"It's okay, no problem," said Malone sweetly.

But when the second free throw missed, the war started all over again.

Jazz owner Larry Miller made a point of stopping by the locker room after the game. A reporter had written that Malone felt underpaid, and news like that always got an owner's attention.

Malone negotiated his own deals—which, according to Miller, made Malone even more powerful. "I have to deal straight up with Karl," Miller said, as steam from the showers made the room go light gray. "But with an agent, you can try to *work* them."

"Is Karl pretty savvy financially?" I asked.

"Very. He doesn't want you to *think* he is. Wants you to think he's a good old country boy."

Miller—a car magnate and once one of the best softball pitchers in the country—was quick to admit that if Malone squeezed him, he'd respond. "We've never said to a player, 'You're a bargain, but that's your tough luck.'"

"Why? Because he might come down with a mysterious injury, like Olajuwon did this year?"

"Right. Life's too short. Besides, you've gotta be fair."

I asked him if he was worried about Stockton or Malone getting injured in the Olympics.

"It's a calculated risk," he said. "But this is a once-in-a-lifetime deal."

He told me he hadn't expected Stockton to make the team. Because Salt Lake was such a small market, he said, he didn't think that "the politics involved would allow them both to go."

"Is it hard to keep elite players in a small market?"

"Not Karl and John. We're fair to them. And they *like* it here."

Over in the corner, Malone wasn't grumbling about

money. He was rhapsodizing about his truck. He'd just bought a $200,000 semi and had learned how to drive it.

"It's something I wanted all my life," said Malone.

"So many time, people see a athlete and they say, 'Got a one-track mind.' But there's a lot of guys on this team have things going on. My concept is, in the past truckers sort of had a bad name—bullies of the road and driving unsafe equipment and stuff. I want to look real classy and stuff like that. Even when companies around town have their own truck, my thing is to add a little VIP service, meaning I would drive the truck, make the delivery."

Somebody asked him if he considered himself an intimidator. "I consider myself a player that do what it take within the rules to win a ball game. I have no problem with a hard foul. But the guy you see on the court is not the same guy you see off the court."

"Why did the thing with Isiah bother you so much? To the point where you considered retiring?"

"'Cuz people thought I hurt him on purpose. I foul people, okay? But I don't hurt nobody on purpose."

"Do you think what Stockton does is an art?"

"Yeah, but I don't see it anymore, because I been around it too long. It's just Stockton doing his job. I look at him and he look at me, and that's it—it's not even a verbal thing anymore between us. Sometimes when he throw a pass, we go back downcourt and he say, 'Hell of a catch—I didn't know you could get that one.' But that's all we say."

"You seem like you're playing better lately. Any particular reason for it?"

He nodded, and his face—usually a construction of right angles and sharp edges—seemed to soften. "My little girl," he said. "She's sleepin' through the night now."

His eyes stayed distant. He didn't look intimidating at all.

• Summerfield, Louisiana

Karl Malone is a mama's boy.

If they don't believe that in the NBA, they know it for sure in Summerfield, Louisiana, the wide spot in the road where Karl grew up under the firm hand of Shirley Turner.

Shirley Turner is one of God's strong people. When J. P. Malone walked out on her in 1968, baby Karl (the youngest of eight children) was five; the oldest was thirteen. So Shirley took two jobs—running a forklift in a sawmill and cutting up chickens in a poultry plant—and cooked for another family on the side.

She put cardboard in her shoes so they'd last. When a social worker told her she qualified for welfare, Shirley told her no. "I said it was my responsibility to take care of my children. I believe every tub should sit on its own bottom."

Shirley married Ed Turner, a local plumber, in 1975, and he convinced her to slow down. They invested in Turner's Groceteria and Washateria—a general store, self-service laundry, and restaurant that they still operate.

Two years later, J. P. Malone was dying of cancer. There was only one person he wanted to take care of him. Though he'd left her cold nine years earlier, Shirley drove sixty miles twice a day to nurse him until he died.

The woman was Herculean. She fished and hunted on her own. She chewed Levi Garrett tobacco every day. When the kids didn't have a basketball hoop, she stood on a chair with her arms in a circle.

Shirley found it easy to keep baby Karl in line. "He's nothing but a big old crybaby. I'd just sit him down and look him in the eye. He cried without even getting a whupping."

Soon enough, though, Karl and his older brother Terry went through what Shirley called a "mannish" phase.

"We were the neighborhood busters," Malone recalls. "From when I was twelve 'til I was seventeen, if we went a day and a half without getting a whupping, something was wrong with us."

Once they stole melons from a neighbor's patch and smashed up the ones they didn't cart off. The neighbor came by to talk to Shirley. He didn't want money, just assurance that it wouldn't happen again. Shirley, though, wanted more. For the next six weeks, Karl and Terry chopped wood for the man every day and threw a log on his fire each night.

And Shirley had other methods. One day, she cut off a strip of conveyer belt at the sawmill, named it Mr. Know-It-All, and brought it home for a whip, telling her sons, "I brought you into this world, and I can take you out."

But she never had to go quite that far. Baby Karl found another way to vent his mannish feelings: basketball.

All the Malone kids were big and played lots of basketball. Karl was afraid of standing out. "If I didn't play, I was some kind of freak. That's the only reason I started playing."

But Karl discovered that basketball provided a type of discipline that was lacking even in Shirley's strict house: male discipline. Danny Malone, eight years older than Karl, was the family athlete. When Karl began to sprout at about twelve, Danny put up a makeshift backboard above the red clay behind the house and began challenging Karl. He wanted to toughen up the baby.

"My brother used to be rough with me on purpose," Malone says. "I would shoot the ball, and he would hit me for no reason. I would cry and he would say, 'You little sissy.' I would be fighting mad all the time. I always think back to the times I never beat him, the times I let down and he would always take advantage of it."

Karl became obsessed with beating Danny. Gradually, he learned how to transform his hurt into aggression. By the time he finally beat Danny—after six years of failure—he had also racked up three state high school basketball championships.

At Summerfield High School, where he set scoring records, he was *not* baby Karl. At school, he was mannish Karl. His peers adored him and fed his arrogance.

"I got pretty cocky," he recalls. "I knew I was good and nobody could tell me otherwise. I was a big hero at school. It got so I was beginnin' to think that I was better than other people. That I was special. I was so caught up in myself that I didn't respect other people or care about their feelings."

His arrogance cost him.

When his high school grade-point average fell below 2.0, Malone was told that he'd have to sit out a year of college ball. His scholarship at nearby Louisiana Tech was suspended. Malone had to take out a student loan to cover his freshman tuition.

"Having basketball taken away from me really humbled me," he recalls. "I learned that I wasn't special and that things would not always just come to me. Instead, I was going to have to go out and work hard for what I wanted."

At Tech, Malone got what he wanted. Three league MVP trophies. Two NCAA tourney berths. A top-five national ranking. Malone thought his stock was high, and he left school after his junior year.

Then Karl found out just how obscure he was. He was the ninth big man drafted (behind dogs like Joe Kleine, Benoit Benjamin, and Jon Koncak) and the thirteenth pick overall. The lowest moment came when Dallas, the team closest to Summerfield and Mama, picked Detlef Schrempf. When he finally was selected by the Jazz, and Rick Barry interviewed him on national TV, Karl Malone did just what his mother would have guessed. He cried.

Then he turned prima donna again. Despite the fact that he was so countrified that he thought Utah was a city and that Salt Lake was just five or six times the size of Summerfield (population 400), Malone threatened to play a year in Italy because the Jazz were only offering him $250,000. Simultaneously, he broke off an engagement to a girl from back home.

By the time the squabbling between Malone's agent and the Jazz had ceased, Malone was out of shape and confused. His play was poor.

"There was no intensity," recalls former Jazz coach Frank Layden. "I said, 'Now I know why we got him thirteenth.' He just didn't play hard."

He was pining for Mama. "He was homesick," says Shirley. "That first month he was there, we had a seven hundred dollar phone bill. He wanted to come home. I told him, 'Sugar, that's your *job* now.'" Malone began trying, once again, to channel his hurt into aggression—to go from baby to bully.

Then another daddy stepped in. Adrian Dantley. Dantley watched the nervous rookie in practice and became

Malone's mentor. He gave Malone financial advice. He taught him how to eat properly. And he told him how to play: No diving after lose balls, no playing excessive minutes.

Dantley had long ignored criticism of his own selfish playing style. Layden didn't want his prize rookie taking his cues from a jaded veteran. "Dantley was poison," says Layden. "We had to get him away from Karl."

Malone had a good rookie year; he won a Player of the Week award and made the All-Rookie Team. But Layden thought Malone could do much better. He'd shot only .481 from the line and didn't go inside enough. Also, he was fairly soft—almost pudgy.

The first thing Layden did was trade Dantley to Detroit. Then Layden took Malone aside and told him he could become the leader of the team. Layden said, "Karl, can you do it or not? If not, we'll get somebody who can."

Malone responded—just like he had when his big brother Danny had beaten the hell out of him on the red clay court. He lifted weights. Often. He ran. A lot. His body-fat melted from about fourteen percent to less than five percent. He became a formidable bully—a nice guy off court, but one of the most feared men in the game.

Over the next few years, every aspect of Malone's game improved. He became the quintessential power forward— strong, fast, and nasty. His free-throw shooting neared eighty percent. He averaged over 30 points and 10 rebounds one season. He became a perennial All-Star. And he flaunted it.

The whimpering baby of Shirley Turner became a well-marketed, buffed showoff—in a league filled with showoffs. "When I'm playing," he says, "whatever I do is entertainment. If I give somebody a high-five, that's for the fans. The people who come to the games don't pay one hundred dollars to see some guy running up and down the court looking like a horse's behind."

Malone became the ultimate oxymoron: a swinging black bachelor in white, Mormon, Salt Lake City. He bought expensive toys—monster pickups, a cattle ranch, snakes, and finally a customized eighteen-wheel rig with his picture painted on the side. He acted in a western. He spent a summer working as a highway patrolman. He built a luxurious house in suburban Salt Lake. He learned to fly a private plane.

Malone fired his agents and began to negotiate his own contracts. He publicly balked when lesser talents anywhere in the league got more money than him. His confidence soared. At the 1989 All-Star Game, he visited his mom in her hotel and predicted he'd be the star of the game. He was—winning the MVP.

But the next year, he wasn't even voted onto the starting team. L.A.'s A. C. Green, who trailed Malone in almost every significant category, was the fans' choice—simply because there were so many L.A. fans voting. Green's own coach, Pat Riley, admitted that the fans had goofed. Green himself said, "I would have voted for Karl Malone."

Malone announced, "To me, it's a slap in the face." So he found someone to take it out on: the Milwaukee Bucks. On the night of his All-Star snub, he scored 61 points and got 18 rebounds.

Karl Malone had learned his lesson: When the baby inside is hurt, send out the bully.

Felton Spencer's huge forefinger, long as a paring knife, gouged into Karl Malone's eye.

Malone yelled *"Damn!"* and started blundering toward the Timberwolves' Spencer as a fat tear rolled out of the eye. He found Spencer with his hands. Spencer—about three inches taller and ten pounds heavier than Malone—looked spooked. But Mark Eaton and Blue Edwards pulled Malone off before anybody got hurt.

For a few minutes, the Timberwolves looked tentative, like: for God's sake, don't piss off Karl again. Stockton took advantage of it. His passes were going *everywhere*. Before the game was over, he'd have 23 assists.

That was how Utah killed teams, switching the tone from muscle to speed and then back again: muscle, speed, muscle, speed, speed, muscle—until suddenly the other team was dead. Utah was a superb team, probably the third best in the world, after Chicago and Portland. The playoffs were imminent, and Utah knew it had a good shot at the championship.

Utah didn't have the depth of Chicago or Portland. But Utah had something no other team in the world had: the earth's most complementary pair of players. Nobody matched them. Not Drexler and Porter. Not Bird and McHale. Not Price and Daugherty. Not even Jordan and Pippen.

No one else came close.

Stockton drove under the hoop. It was packed down low: Felton Spencer, Thurl Bailey, Tony Campbell. They all converged on Stockton, boxing him into a prison of tangled arms and legs. He leaped upward. He pivoted in midair. Then, in the thicket of limbs, he found a thin corridor of space. Suddenly the ball zipped through the corridor, as if it were being pulled by a wire.

Karl Malone waited. The ball sailed toward him. No one was near him. He held out his hands. *Smack!* He smiled. Gripped the ball. Licked his lips. Shot.

14

Clyde Is Second Best

The Valley of the Shadow of Mike • Putting Jordan
on Crutches • The Most Boring Man in Basketball •
The Curse of Nellie • The High Price of Sanity •
Shaquille: No Deal • Even If Laettner Is
Gay—So What? • Clyde the Slide

> If you aren't going all the way,
> why go at all?
> —Joe Namath

> A great man is made of qualities
> that meet great occasions.
> —James Russell Lowell, 1860

> I cannot give you the formula for success,
> but I can give you the formula for failure:
> Try to please everybody.
> —Herbert Bayard Swope

If it was ever going to happen, it damn well better happen
now.

Clyde Drexler—in one more look-alike hotel room in yet
another NBA city—was waiting for the phone to ring.

The Selection Committee had met. Two more players had
been chosen to join the ten selected last summer. The two

players they'd chosen would be getting the word right about now. For all Drexler knew, the winning candidates had already been notified—and he wasn't one of them.

Drexler had a crucial late-spring playoff game with Phoenix tonight. Portland was up 2–1 and could put a virtual lock on the series. Clyde had to leave for the stadium in half an hour, but concentrating on the game was a bitch. Would they let him dangle all night?

Hell, yes, they would. They'd let him dangle all year.

● **Remembrance of Things Past**

Like the Selection Committee, I'd been keeping an eye on Clyde all season, because all year he was the front-running Olympic hopeful. Besides that, I'd always followed his NBA career. He was my homeboy; I'd lived in Oregon well before he'd joined the Trail Blazers, and I'd watched him slowly lead the team out of mediocrity. So every time I'd been home this year from my Olympic travels, I'd driven up to Portland to see Clyde.

It was always worth the drive. I swear to God, most of the time, Drexler was as good as Jordan. He was rarely as spectacular, or as aesthetically pleasing, but, very frequently, he was as *good:* He often took control of games and did whatever it took to win them.

Of course, Drexler *is* the star of my home team, so being objective about him is hard. For me, it's like trying to figure out if my wife is really as beautiful as I think she is—I look with my heart, not my eyes.

Nonetheless, objectivity in sports journalism is a *grave* and *sacred* responsibility and not something I would dare shirk. So let's get one ugly little fact on the record. Clyde wins games, but he's never won *the* game—the last game of the Finals. In the most crucial games, when the elite players dominate, Clyde often pales to mediocrity. That's why some call him Clyde the Slide.

At the beginning of the season—especially right after the

first ten Olympians had been chosen—it wasn't always a lot of fun to go see Clyde, because he was feeling pretty damned ouchy about getting left off the Team.

The first time I talked to him about it, he was snappy as a Doberman. Which was unusual for Drexler. Usually, he was as smarmy and coy as a Miss America contestant: "Well, the reason *I'd* like to win is so that I can help *others.*"

Our meeting was in the cramped, sweat-fouled basement of the Oregon State University gymnasium, where Drexler had come for a preseason exhibition game. When I asked him if he felt like talking about the Olympic team, he gave me a look, like: Please, do me one little favor—*die.*

"That's about the last thing I want to talk about," he said. He was particularly pissed off that the committee had chosen the players by position, rather than by overall excellence. Choosing that way had put Drexler head-to-head against Jordan—which was a guaranteed losing proposition. Then, the other positions had gone to people like Stockton, Pippen, and Mullin—guys Clyde could easily whip at one-on-one.

"It shouldn't have been an either/or choice of me or Jordan," Drexler said. "I think we *both* deserve to be on the team. A lot of people would tell you that we're the two most talented players in the league; *I'm* not saying that, but a lot of people do. If that's so, then it makes sense to put us both on. After that, then take all those other guys."

Drexler muttered darkly about "politics" and "control." He'd felt for years that his greatness had been overlooked, and the Olympic snub was the cruelest slight yet.

It was nice to see him admit he was pissed. Usually, he was the ultimate "pleaser," trying never to offend anybody. He tried to be all things to all people—and ended up being nothing at all. Of course, his blandness was a major reason why the media ignored him.

When the game was ready to start, Drexler again adopted his standard gentlemanly demeanor. As a rule, when the Blazers are announced, Drexler runs out last, to climax the intros. But this time, as Terry Porter started to run out next-to-last, Drexler held Porter back and jogged out himself. Then Porter was introduced, and got a stadium-shaking welcome. Two days earlier, Porter had attended his father's funeral, and everyone in the gym knew it. Drexler had just wanted to give his buddy a little lift, and this was the way to do it. There was an empathy in Drexler that was absent in most self-absorbed jocks.

About a week later, the season began. Cleveland was in town, and all the pregame call-in shows were crammed with bitching about why Clyde hadn't been selected as one of the first ten members of the Olympic team. It was Drexler's night to prove he'd been screwed. In the first minute of the game, he grabbed the ball out of the hands of a strong, quick guard, Craig Ehlo—just pulled it away like Ehlo was some punk who'd wandered onto the wrong playground. But ahead of Drexler was cheetah-fast Terrell Brandon. Drexler flew past Brandon, accelerated, and tomahawked the ball down so hard that it bounced up and hit Brandon in the face. Brandon, in his first NBA game, looked stunned and sick. It was a compelling way for Drexler to start the season.

A week after that, while Indiana was in Portland, Magic announced that he had HIV. Before the game started, one of the Portland writers remarked, "You know the first thing that went through Clyde's mind when he heard about Magic? 'I'm on the team! I'm on the team!' " But I talked to Drexler after the game, and I didn't get that sense at all. He looked like someone who'd just driven past a bloody car wreck. Half of what he said wasn't even coherent.

Then came the early-season evening when Michael was in town. The league sent three of its most prominent referees —Mike Mathis, Tommy Nunez, and Jim Capers—as an acknowledgment that this was a big one: the two best teams, the two best players. As the game went to crunch time, Jordan and Drexler took turns killing each other. With time running out, Drexler chest-bumped Pippen, then pivoted and backed in. Backed in. Backed. Whirled. Pump-faked. Began to fall. Almost collapsed. Then shot from a bizarre angle to avoid Pippen's huge looming hand. The ball banked off the glass and dove hard into the hoop. Pippen's eyes fastened on Drexler's face. Pippen saw Jordan play almost every day, but he'd never seen a shot quite like that. The fans howled. A guy almost fell out of the balcony waving a sign that read "I Wanna Be Like Mike. Not."

But Drexler remained absolutely serene. Clyde loved to be cool.

Later that night, Jordan was so whipped and broken that he had to leave the building on crutches.

In midseason, the Pistons came to Portland. Like several other games during the year, this was a *mano-a-mano* match between Clyde and Isiah, who were both fighting for one of the two remaining Olympic positions. Furthermore, this battle would be fought under the nose of Olympic coach Chuck Daly. Early in the game, Drexler made one of his usual astonishing plays, outmuscling Detroit's strongest player and outrunning its fastest. It was an extraordinary display of strength and speed. The only other player in the world with such a singular balance of speed and strength was Charles Barkley. This balance enabled each of them to start—and finish—an amazing number of plays.

As Drexler ran downcourt after the play, he passed in front of Daly. He stared hard at Daly, as if to say: Want to see more in August, Chuck? He stared so hard Daly had to look away.

Just before the All-Star Game, another Olympic candidate came to town—Dominique Wilkins. The image that sticks from that game is of Clyde and Dominique waiting for an inbounds play at the end of the game. They were grappling for position, locked together like two rams. They were in bitter opposition—pushing, clawing, holding—until suddenly they were motionless, in perfect equilibrium. And at that moment, their embrace seemed to be not one of opposition, but of brotherhood.

By the middle of spring, one of the Olympians finally suffered an injury—an event Daly had predicted all along. David Robinson broke his hand. The injury put pressure on Drexler, giving him a perfect opportunity to vault onto the team. Drexler was clearly the leading candidate, having played so remarkably all year that he had a good chance to be named Most Valuable Player.

At Drexler's first game after Robinson's injury, a fan held up a sign that said "Chuck Daly, call Clyde—1-800-MVP." But Drexler had a rotten game that night, missing his last six shots. That was one criticism of him that had never gone away: He choked.

Late in the season, Utah came to Portland for a preview of the playoffs. They were the two best teams in the West, and would probably battle in the Western Finals. With the game on the line, Stockton zipped a no-look pass to Tyrone Corbin. But Corbin butterfingered the pass, went up for his shot too late, and got knocked onto his ass. He screamed "Shit!" and ran back on defense to try to stop Clyde. Drexler darted toward the basket without the ball. Clyde leaped as Terry Porter lobbed a high, lazy pass. Drexler caught it and jammed it without coming down. Drexler grinned at Porter and said, *"Nice!"*

The contrast was startling: "Shit!" and "Nice!" It seemed to portend the outcome of the upcoming Utah-Portland series. And it did.

Clyde would end up falling short of an MVP season. But not by much. He finished a strong second to Jordan, far ahead of third-place finisher David Robinson.

Earlier, former Portland superstar Bill Walton had come up with his own definition of MVP: the best player on the championship team. The moment Clyde heard that definition, he fell in love with it. Because it gave him a *chance*—to be greater than Jordan. And that was his heart's true desire.

Drexler rarely talked about his own personal status in the league. He always claimed that he didn't fixate on personal rivalries, that he just wanted to win, just wanted to help the team, blah-blah-blah. On the face of it, it sounded like just another rancid dose of jock-speak.

But it was *true.* And ultimately revealing, if you waded past the triteness. In fact, Drexler *was* more of a team player than Jordan. He shared the scoring and kept the lid on vain displays of gymnastics. However, his unselfishness and relative lack of pyrotechnics had cemented the consensus that he was inferior to Jordan. You had only to study the statistics and highlight film to believe that Jordan was better.

But did that make Jordan more *valuable?* Not necessarily. If you stripped away the physical theatrics and the ball-hogging, greed-swollen statistics, Jordan was not necessarily better than Drexler.

And, then, if you considered teamwork, Drexler had a clear chance to be superior. Last year, Jordan had almost torn his team apart with his ego. This year, with his gambling, White House snub, and other examples of poor judgment, he'd caused further serious problems. On the floor, he'd undermined his teammates' confidence by hogging the ball.

Drexler, by comparison, had never been anything but upstanding, unselfish, humble—and boring. In a team sport, there was value in those traits. They shifted glory to lesser players and inspired them. Drexler wanted the world to see that he had, by combining excellence with unselfishness, become the most valuable basketball player in the world. He wanted the world to see that he was the best player on the Blazers, and that the Blazers were the best team in the world.

But there was only one way to prove that. By beating the Bulls.

• Too Cool

Phoenix Hyatt Hotel. Twenty-five minutes before the bus left for the game.

The phone rang. Drexler grabbed it.

It was Portland vice president Geoff Petrie. Petrie, a former All-Star himself, was always low-key—almost preternaturally cool. "Clyde," Petrie murmured, "you made the Olympic team. Congratulations. We're really proud of you."

He was in! But Drexler outcooled even Petrie. "Hey, great news," he said quietly. "I'm thrilled. Thanks a lot, Geoff."

"There's just one thing," said Petrie. "You can't tell anyone. We promised not to say anything until they make the announcement tomorrow."

Petrie chatted briefly about that evening's game, then hung up.

He was in! After all the waiting, all the doubt, all the anger—he was one of the golden boys.

Now there was just one goal left.

Beating the Bulls. And Jordan.

Drexler played superbly against Phoenix that night: 33 points, 11 assists, 8 rebounds, 3 blocks. Portland won, and Drexler—*who was in!*—kept his mouth shut about the call.

After the game, a Portland beat writer cornered Drexler and said that he'd just asked Blazer president Harry Glickman if Glickman knew who the committee had chosen. "Harry said he knows who the two players are," said the writer, "but he can't say anything. When I asked if you were one, he just smiled."

Drexler wouldn't take the bait. He simply shrugged. "If it's true," said Drexler, "I'm thrilled. And relieved. I've been asked about it an awful lot over the past few weeks."

The writer got more direct. "Have *you* heard from the Selection Committee?"

Drexler smiled. He didn't even have to lie. No, *he* hadn't.

It was easy for Drexler to stonewall the press. He'd been doing it for years. When he'd first come into the league, nine years ago, he'd been pretty open. But he'd clashed with coach Jack Ramsay, then with coach Mike Schuler, and more often than not, the press had sided with the coaches. Which was . . . absurd! The writers didn't know he was *destined for greatness*. Which showed how much writers knew. So Drexler started smiling a lot and saying very little.

Of course, it cost him to be so lip-locked. The sports magazines and networks steered clear of him, despite his growing stardom. And why not? When guys like Magic and Michael would gladly fill their needs, why screw around with a stiff like Drexler? In fact, it hadn't been until now—the 1992 playoffs—that *Sports Illustrated* had done a profile of him. And even that profile, which should have been a romp through virgin territory, was short, flimsy, and boring. About the most revealing quote in it was "The more I can leave unsaid, the better I feel."

After going through the motions of the postgame interviews in Phoenix, Drexler hopped on the Blazers' private airplane to head home with the rest of the team.

Harry Glickman took Drexler aside on the plane and had him sign the standard contract agreeing to be on the Olympic team. Drexler, typically restrained, told Glickman that all he felt like doing was sleeping for about twenty-four hours. He said he was too tired to even eat.

After Drexler signed the form, Glickman stood up and announced to the team, "You'll be pleased to know that one of your teammates will be playing in Barcelona as a member of the Olympic team." Everybody freaked out. Unlike Jordan, Drexler wasn't resented by his "supporting cast." Drexler gave a humble little speech—"couldn't have done it withoutcha"—and sat back down: the coolest head on the plane.

It was well past midnight when they landed at a small airport outside of town. Still, the place was jammed with fans. The funny thing was, there would have been a crowd even if they'd lost. Portland loved the Blazers—win or lose. It was the team's blessing, and its curse. It was great for business, but it made losing acceptable.

Acceptance of losing, though, was an Oregon hallmark. The state had become a haven for good losers, mostly because of the chronically weak economy—you could survive in Oregon, but it was very difficult to succeed. For decades, Oregon had depended on the timber industry, which was slowly dying. The death of the logging industry was making losers out of thousands of hardworking people.

Nevertheless, people kept flocking to Oregon because of its beauty and graceful life-style. Oregon seemed particularly attractive to young professionals who were sick of the rat race. But once there, they often found themselves mired in diminished careers—even as they grew increasingly addicted to the state's beauty. To cope with the frustration, many of these downwardly mobile professionals—"dumpies"—adopted a studied contempt for the success-at-any-price ethic.

In a sense, Clyde Drexler—easily the most famous person in the state—was its ultimate dumpie. He could have achieved far greater fame and fortune elsewhere, but he'd gotten hooked on Oregon. It was, after all, an organic Disneyland and one of the best places in the world for Drexler to raise his family. Drexler had little in common with the average Oregonian, but he had a rare ability to blend in. About ninety-seven percent of all Oregonians were white, while Drexler was black. The majority of them were lifelong Northerners, while he was from the South. Most Oregonians were middle class or working class, but Drexler had once been relatively poor and was now wealthy. Nevertheless, he was accepted as a true Oregonian.

Drexler, though, sacrificed hitting the immortality level by staying in Oregon. One of his biggest endorsements was selling mattresses for a furniture store. He couldn't even land a Nike deal, even though the company was headquartered in Portland.

But Oregon loved Clyde for his wholesome, nonneurotic priorities. The Blazers *did* blow the championship year after year—but that was okay. In Oregon, it was no shame to finish second. If you thought you had to win every game, it just meant you were . . . insecure . . . and ought to get in touch with your *feelings*.

This attitude seemed to rub off on Clyde. He was, of course, highly motivated: he wanted badly to be the best player on the championship team. He just didn't appear to be as obsessed with winning as people like Michael, Magic, and Larry. To them, winning was a life-or-death issue.

Clyde was sane. Maybe—by NBA standards—*too* sane.

Even so, by the time Clyde got home from the airport, he was wired. He couldn't sleep. He was finally one of the chosen few.

He was in.

The Golden Boys

• Last Gasp of the Selection Committee

Exhausted and beatific, Drexler strode into a packed press conference the next morning, wearing a USA Basketball cap.

He settled into a seat behind a thicket of microphones. He knew there wouldn't be any tough questions, like the ones Jordan had faced last fall during the media unveiling of the first ten Olympians. There just hadn't been much controversy about Drexler's selection or that of the other new Olympian, Christian Laettner. Both had been fairly easy choices for the committee.

When the committee had met—in Springfield, Massachusetts, during the Hall of Fame induction ceremonies—they had come to their decisions relatively quickly, without a great deal of disagreement.

Their discussions had essentially gone along these lines: Clyde was the best player they could take—that was obvious. But, still, the primary question they'd asked last summer remained: Did they really *need* him? They already had Michael at Clyde's position, and Scottie could play shooting guard, too. What they *really* needed was another point guard. They only had Magic and Stockton at point, and Magic's virus made him an uncertainty. Magic had played well at the All-Star Game, but there was no guarantee he could withstand six weeks of practices and games.

If they did take a point guard, a logical choice would be Cleveland's Mark Price. Price had fully recovered from last year's serious knee injury, and he'd had a great year. Price had the support of committee member Wayne Embry (Cleveland's GM) and that of Olympic assistant coach Lenny Wilkens (Cleveland's coach). Unlike some of the other superstars, he didn't think he was God, or even one of the major saints.

Or maybe an even better choice would be Timmy Hardaway. Everybody loved Hardaway; he was probably the best point guard in the game at the moment. He, too, had been excellent all year.

But both Price and Hardaway were scorers more than they

were passers—and that counted against them. The team already had a surplus of great scorers.

Also, neither Price nor Hardaway had the kind of media profile needed to market American basketball globally or to sell T-shirts. They were just players, not institutions.

So the committee, once again, talked about Isiah. Isiah was a scorer *and* a passer. Plus, he was very commercial—he'd sell millions of T-shirts.

But Isiah hadn't played as well this year as Hardaway had. Also, he had never really made peace with Michael. And why piss off Mike? Was it worth the aggravation?

So they came back to Clyde. Okay—they already had Jordan at his position, but so *what?* Both Drexler and Jordan were versatile enough to play three positions. And Drexler had had a tremendous year. Besides, they needed Clyde to help sell tickets to the Tournament of the Americas, in Portland. Ticket sales had been slow, and everybody was worried.

The college-based committee members, though, were still pushing to have both remaining slots filled by college players. With the Soviet Union and Yugoslavia out of the competition, there was no real chance of losing the gold medal—so why not give a couple of college kids some glory?

If they did pick two college players, it would solve one problem—choosing between Shaquille O'Neal and Christian Laettner. At first glance, it seemed like an easy choice. O'Neal was the greater player. But he was strictly a center, and they already had two centers. Laettner, though, could play center and big forward.

Plus, to be fair to Laettner, they had to consider all the work he'd already done for USA Basketball. He'd been on several national teams. Also, Laettner had shown that he was a winner, by leading Duke to back-to-back national championships. Another consideration was his shooting range. He could hit the three-pointer, and that was important in the international game.

The only sensitive area with Laettner was the rumor that he was homosexual—but that wasn't really a factor. Even if it were true, it was nobody's business but his own. Besides, as one observer of the selection process said, "There's already one guy on the team with the AIDS virus. Even if Laettner is gay—so what?"

Laettner was the favorite of the college members—but *how*, they implored, could the committee pass up Shaquille O'Neal? Shaquille would probably dominate basketball into the 21st century. He was huge, fast, talented, and obsessed. About the only thing he'd done wrong was deciding to quit college before graduating and accept the $5 million salary that NBA teams were waving at him. College coaches *hated* to see kids quit early. After all, without an education, how could a youngster hope to *make something of himself*?

By choosing Laettner and O'Neal, they argued, the team would have versatility and strength, as well as two high-profile players who would broaden national interest.

The pro members listened to these arguments, but they weren't swayed. They were worried about the injury and health problems that had already hit the team. Magic, Robinson, and Bird might not be at full strength. Pippen and Jordan would probably be coming to the Olympics straight from the NBA Finals. Choosing more than one college player was just too risky. They needed proven commodities.

So they voted, and neither of the votes was particularly close. Laettner won easily. Clyde did, too.

So Drexler felt totally at ease at his press conference. There were no rumors to dispel or controversies to explain. Unfortunately for the press, however, the more comfortable Drexler felt, the more he recited banalities.

He said that he was "very excited, thrilled, and honored." He said that, "It's a wonderful feeling," and that, "any time you get a chance to play for your country, it's a privilege."

He also said a few other things, none of which were worth repeating. The joy you can get from Clyde Drexler comes from watching him—not listening to him.

If anyone in the assembled media was disappointed with Drexler's bland performance, they didn't let on. Reporters, in fact, generally liked Drexler. Unlike many NBA players, he didn't go out of his way to make them feel stupid, short, and poor.

By the end of the season, the press would name Drexler to its All-Interview Team—without betraying a hint of irony. Obviously, Drexler was a disastrously dull interview. But somehow—without having a single thing in common with most of the media—he fit in with them.

Sometimes, you got the feeling that Drexler could fit in anywhere.

● **Houston, Texas**

Making sense of the rare blend of qualities that constitute a Magic or a Michael or a Larry is extremely difficult. But understanding the qualities that define Clyde Drexler is damn near impossible. Clyde Drexler is the most indefinable personality on the Olympic basketball team. That's because the essential definition of Clyde Drexler lies not in what he is, but in what he *is not*.

He is not a winner. He is not a loser. He is not satisfied with what he has yet achieved. He has not been obsessed enough to achieve more. He is not in possession of a self-confidence equal to Magic's or Michael's. He is not forthcoming about his thoughts.

Most important: He is not a man who owns an NBA championship ring.

The difficulty in defining Drexler has created a mystery around him. But Drexler's mystery—like the qualities that define him—is couched in negatives. The mystery surrounding Michael Jordan—the player most like Drexler—is: How does he do it? The mystery surrounding Drexler is: Why hasn't he done more?

Virtually no person in the world, other than Jordan, can do with his body what Drexler can do. Why then, in a team of Olympians with golden credentials—state championships, college championships, NBA championships—is Clyde Drexler so barren of glory?

Part of it is . . . luck. Luck resides in the soul of sport. Because sport is a contrivance—a short, artificial test of skill—luck is a part of any close win. If victory never depended upon luck, sports wouldn't be fun. It would be too much like . . . real life. There's luck in life, too—but it's usually not a governing factor. In real life, you generally have to manufacture your luck.

But not all Drexler's losses were bad luck. For good or ill, he has been the prime force behind his fate. Most of the failure in Drexler's life has been no one's fault but his own.

In looking at the development of Clyde Drexler, one element stands out. Unlike almost all the other Olympians, Drexler appears never to have had a totally uncritical supporter. Virtually everyone close to him, it seems—even in his own family—reserved their full appreciation for when Clyde would be perfect. And Clyde, like all humans, was never perfect.

This lack of unearned appreciation seems to have undercut in Clyde the one quality common to most of the Olympians: unshakable self-confidence.

It also may have, to some degree, eroded Clyde's resolve to be the best in the world. After all, why try to excel if appreciation comes grudgingly and complete appreciation doesn't come at all? Why obsess over the impossible?

But this aspect of Clyde Drexler is just one piece of him, and Clyde Drexler is a very complex person. He is, among other things, extremely bright—maybe too bright to ever believe that basketball is, in the fullest sense, important.

Furthermore, Drexler may also be too well-grounded emotionally—too sane—to obsess over something like basketball. Sure, he's insecure—*compared to Michael Jordan*—but he's a well-balanced and fully integrated person. He's probably less neurotic than ninety percent of all NBA players.

Nonetheless, his lack of obsession—a trait that Michael and Magic harnessed exquisitely—has become enmeshed in his lack of confidence. It has kept him from performing the drudgery that probably would have perfected his skills (particularly his perimeter shooting). And, once perfected, those skills might have vaulted him past self-doubt.

Thus, instead of pursuing victory with neurotic fervor, Drexler has put tremendous energy into the one thing he does better than any other NBA superstar: fitting in. Drexler blends with his team to an extraordinary degree. This might be exemplary behavior for a backup or role-player. But it's fatal for a superstar. Superstars need to feel they can do anything at any time, and Clyde has never seemed to feel this way. He's just one of the guys.

Thus, in his quest to be accepted, Drexler may be dooming himself to forever finish second.

"Clyde is a likable person," says a journalist who's followed him closely. "But there's something about him that pisses people off. No matter how well he plays, they always think he should be even better."

But journalists are paid to carp. Here's a Western Conference head coach: "He's such a great athlete that he's going to get his numbers. But he's been a failure in every playoff situation he's been in, either because he's bored, or he's frustrated, or the game turns half-court, or who knows what. He's always disappeared. He's always seemed to be one of those guys who thought it was more important to be cool than anything else. What the hell kind of star is that?"

What kind indeed? Drexler has, in fact, been something of an enigma his whole life. He grew up in Houston, the middle child—number four—of Eunice Scott's brood of seven. His mother and stepfather, Manuel Scott, worked in the same supermarket; she was head cashier, he was a butcher. Theirs was a relatively manageable working-class family: all seven kids played sports and attended some college.

Drexler was chubby as a boy. At about twelve, he adopted a regimen of martial arts and weight training. He ran, jumped rope, wore ankle weights—and reinvented himself. He became lean and tough, but retained the humility of the chunky child within.

But while Clyde was remaking himself, one of his brothers

was giving in to the harsh environment around them. The brother was shot and killed a few years ago while trying to rob a store. A younger sister also became, at least for a time, involved in the Houston street scene. "Where I grew up," Drexler says, "there were a lot of bad things around. I think of my brother and sister and wonder why did I turn out the way I did? How did I grow up in the same family, under the same roof, and still turn out so different?"

Drexler tried to reach out to his siblings. "I brought my sister to Portland," he says, "because she was too much for my mother to handle. I thought a change of scenery might help. I had to send her home. I couldn't control her."

Loss of control frightens Drexler. When he was a little boy, he couldn't even bear to watch the Astros lose baseball games on TV, because events were out of his control. "Tears would be coming out of his eyes," his mother remembers, "and he'd be very depressed. I'd say, 'Clyde, what are you crying about?' He'd say, 'They're losing.' I'd say, 'Is that why you're crying? I should fetch me a switch and make you really cry.'" If Drexler had been more confident, he might not have been such a control freak.

Drexler was *always* serious. In high school, he took a year off from basketball because the sport was distracting him from his schoolwork. To Drexler, basketball was just a diversion. The school coach, aghast at losing this 5–8 kid who could dunk, appealed to Eunice. No dice.

Then Drexler sprouted to 6–4. The coach came back, practically begging. "Deep inside I wanted to play, but I didn't have the time," Drexler remembers. "I told him I was more interested in my studies. So he had a conference with my mom and persuaded her. Then he persuaded me."

His family seemed to be the only people who could make Drexler do things he didn't want to. Eunice taught her boys to think for themselves. "I told him never to be persuaded by other people too much," she boasts. "If you think you're right, you don't want to let somebody else come up to you and say, 'Let's do it this way.'"

But it's almost impossible to remain entirely independent

in a big family. Drexler made a hero of his older brother James: "Whatever big brother was doing, I wanted to do. And he was kind enough to take me along and show me the proper way to do certain things."

James was the family basketball player, so Clyde imitated him. "The funny thing," Drexler recalls, "is that James had one of those picture-perfect jump shots—high arc, perfect form, the whole thing. Exactly what my jumper *doesn't* look like." A major reason Drexler played was to win his big brother's approval.

Clyde became an excellent player in high school. But his mother and his brother James didn't let his achievements go to his head. "My mother's pretty much the same way James is," says Drexler. "I can never satisfy them. I could have a triple-double, hold my man below his scoring average, and miss three or four free throws, and the first thing they'll tell me is, 'How did you miss those free throws?'"

Drexler earned All-City and All-State honors, and played impressively in recreation leagues against local pros Moses Malone and Robert Reid. But he didn't interest many college coaches. "He wasn't doing all that flying in high school," recalls former NBA player Rob Williams, who played against Drexler back then. "It started his freshman year of college. He just went crazy."

Drexler was drafted by the University of Houston almost as an afterthought. Houston coach Guy Lewis was more interested in Drexler's friend, Michael Young. "They started recruiting me because they thought it would help them get Michael," Drexler remembers. They got them both, thanks partly to Drexler's desire to stay home.

At Houston, Drexler was part of a phenomenal team. One of the first college teams to employ the break-and-slam strategy that was sweeping the pros, they ripped other teams apart. And they were cool: Known as Phi Slamma Jamma, they featured Akeem Olajuwon, tough-guy forward Larry "Mr. Mean" Micheaux, and Clyde.

Clyde loved his too-cool persona. It allowed him to be cocky without being obnoxious. But it elicited criticism that he didn't try hard enough. Drexler hated that. "It's a slap in the face to credit everything I've done to my God-given abilities," he says. "I never felt I was a very good player. At Houston, when everyone else was partying, I was in the gym with Michael Young at two in the morning. I've always had keys to the gym."

Houston could do everything, it seemed, but win the championship. Twice they made the Final Four, and twice were sent home. They gained a reputation as an unintelligent team. Clyde played well in the Final Four games—but not well enough to win.

After being named All-American, Drexler entered the NBA draft as a junior. He hoped the hometown Houston Rockets would take him with the number three pick. But the Rockets passed, as did a dozen other teams who picked players like Antoine Carr, Sidney Green, Ennis Whatley, and Darrell Walker. Portland took him with the fourteenth pick.

Why had he been rejected? According to current Milwaukee coach Mike Dunleavy, Drexler "had some weaknesses: shooting, ball handling, and decision making." Little things like that.

Drexler, a finance major who worked in a bank during the summers, haggled over his contract and didn't show up until a week before the regular season. Unfortunately, Drexler was on a team coached by legendary Jack Ramsay, and Ramsay was old school. The preseason, Ramsay said, "is the time we set our whole game. If you miss that, you can't recover, because you don't get that practice time the rest of the year." First day of training camp, his team learned to stretch—stretch!—and to throw chest passes and bounce passes. Clyde? Practicing chest passes?

Drexler didn't recover from his slow start. He spent his rookie season backing up Jim Paxson at shooting guard, and Calvin Natt at small forward.

He was pissed. The inactivity chewed at his confidence. "If they're not going to play me, why did they draft me?" he asked. "If I have to ask for playing time, I don't want it. I don't see how Coach Ramsay will know how well I can play if I'm never on the court." But his game showed gaps—a horrendous outside shot, a tendency to lose his cool under pressure, and poor habits on defense (some teammates called him "Rexler": Drexler without any "D"). To Ramsay, though, Drexler often seemed almost self-destructive, refusing to do extra work on his perimeter shots. For years, his outside shooting was weak. It hurt his confidence, because it made him a one-dimensional scorer; still, though, he wouldn't make the sacrifices necessary to improve the shot.

The next year, however, Drexler got a break: Paxson was injured at the outset of the season, and by the time he was back, Natt was hurt. By the time Natt was back, Paxson got hurt again. And by the time Paxson was healed, Drexler had taken his job. Drexler began to get recognition around the league, and he couldn't refrain from indulging in a little arrogance. "He's learned to adjust," Drexler said about Ramsay. "That's why he's such a great coach." Some of the local writers, enamored of Ramsay, portrayed Drexler as a wise guy, and it made him even more reticent.

Drexler was proud of his game, and it gradually improved. But he remained defensive about his shortcomings. He would brook no criticisms, even legitimate ones. Former Blazer Mychal Thompson used to call Drexler "the Shell Answer Man" because he could come up with a reason for any shortcoming. A former Blazer broadcaster recalls that "even if Clyde was clearly beaten by his man on defense, he'd be yelling at somebody, 'Where's my help?'"

Drexler's defensiveness and work habits angered Ramsay, who was a perfectionist. Ramsay was very hard to please, but he did have a genuine concern about his players. At the 1986 All-Star Game—the first of Drexler's six—Ramsay could see that his star was nervous, and he calmed Drexler down. "I was surprised Jack did that," Drexler admits. "He's usually not like that. I'll tell you, it was nice to see a friendly face out there."

But at the end of the season, after the Blazers again screwed up in the playoffs, Ramsay had to resign. Many blamed Drexler. They said his failure to cooperate with Ramsay had made it impossible for Ramsay to stay.

Then things got worse under new coach Mike Schuler.

Schuler was unapologetically obsessive. He was a taskmaster and was often a brittle and humorless dictator. "Schuler was one of those guys who was just consumed by the game," Drexler says. "He actually bragged about not knowing what the Iran-Contra hearings were." Drexler and Schuler were almost always at each other's throats. Schuler thought Drexler was lazy about practice. Drexler thought Schuler played sadistic mind games, particularly with players who were young and vulnerable. Drexler tried to protect some of the kids that Schuler used as whipping boys.

Drexler seemed to shrug off Schuler's criticisms, but the put-downs burned. "I think Clyde's very sensitive to the whole issue of people not appreciating what he does," Blazer VP Geoff Petrie said at that time.

Schuler only lasted about two years, then was fired. As he left, he complained, "We had a lot of bitchers and moaners. The people who I thought could lead the team never stepped forward and did that. There was just something missing. Clyde should've been able to provide that, but he didn't."

When Schuler applied for another job, his colleague, Don Nelson, of Golden State, boosted Schuler by roasting Drexler. He called Drexler the league's most overrated player and said that Drexler "chips away at what an organization is trying to do. He's the worst of all kinds, because he comes off as polite."

The comments infuriated Drexler, who said, "It took every piece of restraint in my body not to go after him when I first saw him." The censure haunted Clyde for years, hurting his reputation around the league.

After Schuler, the Blazers were desperate for a coach who could get along with Drexler. So they chose someone who already had a good relationship with him, assistant coach Rick Adelman. Clyde was so happy that he actually came early to fall camp to practice his jump shooting. That act wasn't entirely his own idea, though; he did it at the urging of his brother James and his mother. His accuracy improved considerably, and he even became a very good three-point shooter.

The Portland franchise grew vibrant. New players began to arrive (Buck Williams, Cliff Robinson, Drazen Petrovic, Danny Ainge), and old ones improved (Jerome Kersey, Terry Porter, Kevin Duckworth). Drexler became an inarguable superstar.

The Blazers began to regularly challenge for the title. But they always froze in the most crucial games. They lost in the Finals in 1990 and the Western Finals in 1991. Clyde played well in both series, but not spectacularly. And in the Finals, only the spectacular prevails.

Drexler became one of the NBA's most visible players, but continued to play it cool. "When things are going good," he says, "you've got to maintain. And when things are going bad, you've got to maintain."

By 1992, things were going *very* well for Drexler. He had married a beautiful and intelligent young woman—an attorney who'd never heard of him before they met. They'd begun a family, and Drexler found that immensely rewarding. He was making over a million dollars a year, with an enormous balloon payment approaching. He'd played in his sixth All-Star Game and had just missed being All-Star MVP in '92. Before 1992 was over, he would be one of five players named to the All-NBA First Team.

Despite his considerable security, though, he remained extremely guarded with the press, ducking every controversial issue.

In the spring of '92, when the L.A. riots broke out— disrupting the Lakers-Blazers playoff series—Drexler had practically nothing to say about it. Even though he'd been active in issues related to the riots, such as inner-city poverty, he didn't express his views.

That wasn't upsetting, though, to many Oregonians. To them, the L.A. riots seemed remote and bizarre.

Drexler was, in fact, beginning to sound more and more like an Oregonian. It was just such a *comfortable* environment. In Oregon—which was proud of its humility—the philosophy was: First place is great, but so is second—as long as you tried rea-l-l-ly hard.

Every year Drexler got more popular. And every year the Blazers lost.

• The Agony of Victory

Portland's Danny Ainge—his hair flopping as he leaped —tried to stick his hand in front of Jordan's eyes as Michael released his shot. Too late. The ball curved in a high, smooth arc and whisked through the net. Another three-pointer for Jordan—his fourth in just the first half of the game.

Jordan bounced rhythmically. He was in the zone of altered consciousness. In a big game like this—the first of the league Finals—he often drifted into the zone. In many of the most important games, the zone would descend on him naturally and without effort—it would just spread over him like warm sunshine.

It didn't happen so easily for Clyde. One of the ironies of Drexler's game was that he made things look easy, but everything came hard.

Terry Porter dribbled downcourt as Chicago Stadium vibrated with a shrill, piercing whine. Porter bullet-passed to Ainge, who flipped it to Clyde. It was time for Clyde to get even with Jordan and break Chicago's momentum.

Jordan blurred past Clyde. And suddenly Jordan had the ball. He streaked downcourt. Ainge grabbed for Jordan, to foul him before he could score. But Ainge couldn't even touch Jordan. He was gone.

To Jordan, this was personal: it was him versus Clyde. Before the Finals had started, the media had focused on the Clyde-Jordan rivalry. Clyde had tried to downplay the whole thing, saying he didn't want to incite Jordan. But Jordan hadn't been so coy. He'd said, sure, he wanted to be number one—what was wrong with that?

Now Jordan was trying to prove his superiority.

Clyde had the ball again. Rushed to shoot. Wild shot. His

eyes flitted around the court and he scowled. Chicago rebounded. Pass to Jordan.

Jordan paused at the top of the three-point line. Drexler, trying to shadow Jordan, stood between Jordan and the hoop, bouncing from foot to foot to avoid inertia. Jordan lunged. Then leaped into the air. Virtually the entire Blazer team collapsed on Jordan. Clyde knifed toward him. Jordan floated—they waited for his shot. Waited more. He passed. The ball sailed in to Chicago's Horace Grant, who was standing patiently under the hoop.

Next time down, Chicago ran a similar play. But this time Grant hurled the ball all the way back to the three-point line, where Jordan was waiting for it. He shot. *Five* three-pointers.

Drexler looked frantic. He'd expected a fierce, body-breaking game. A match of wits and skills. But not . . . this. This was unendurable. The Chicago lead was growing. Drexler called time-out.

In the huddle, Drexler didn't berate anyone, even though that was his prerogative as a star. Drexler wasn't an ass-kicker, and he was proud of that. But by NBA standards, it was just cowardice: Would *Magic* hesitate to hurt a friend's feelings, in order to win?

The Blazers seemed more collected as they took the floor. They worked the ball to Drexler at the three-point line. Drexler drove to his right. He fired a pass crosscourt. But Pippen's long arm swept out and speared it. Pippen blasted toward the Chicago basket and shot a lay-up. Off. But Jordan was trailing. He shoved it down. The fans exploded into their keening wail.

Clyde seemed to seethe. On the Blazers' next possession, he grabbed the ball. He wanted to *take over*. Like he'd been doing all year—in the unimportant games. He wanted to knock the air out of Jordan. Drexler took the ball to the right side. Glared at the basket. Shot a three-pointer. Airball. His face froze.

Drexler ran back on defense, taking his stand near the hoop, waiting for Jordan's drive. But Jordan stayed on the perimeter. He caught a pass. Portland's Cliff Robinson flew toward Jordan with his arm stretched toward the ceiling. Too late. Jordan's shot sailed over Robinson's fingers. It fell into the hoop. It was Jordan's sixth three-pointer of the half. It was also his thirty-fifth point of the half—a Finals record.

Jordan hopped up on his toes. Landed. Hopped again. He shrugged, his palms facing upward. A look of utter bemusement flooded his face. He seemed to say: Even *I* don't know where this is coming from.

Then Jordan shrugged again. Jordan, at that moment, probably wasn't trying to make Drexler look bad. And Clyde *didn't* look bad. He just looked second best.

• A Stake Through the Heart of the Season

Clyde had his hand on Jordan's back, trying to feel which way Jordan would go. He was going . . . *left!* Clyde pivoted. But suddenly Jordan was going *right*. Jordan hooked in front of Clyde as Drexler watched helplessly. Jordan shot; he scored.

The second game was coming to a close, and the series seemed to be over already. It looked as if Chicago would win the first two games, and that lead would be virtually insurmountable.

After a Chicago basket, Portland's Buck Williams grabbed the ball and stepped out-of-bounds for the inbounds play. Drexler was standing in front of Williams, just inside the line. Williams tossed the ball to Drexler—just as Drexler *stepped out-of-bounds*. Blast of whistle. A turnover.

It was an extraordinarily ill-timed mistake. But it was the kind of mistake Portland—and Drexler—often made in crucial situations. Those frequent mistakes had saddled Drexler and his team with the reputation of being stupid. But they weren't stupid. Portland's players were as bright as any in the league, and Drexler was notably smarter than most NBA players. He read books, collected art, was married to a lawyer—he even used *adverbs*.

The mistakes happened for some other reason—perhaps,

lack of obsession. When a team is terrified to lose, it generally doesn't give in to mental lapses. But Portland, and Clyde, had never seemed terrified of losing.

Terry Porter hesitated with the ball at the top of the key, then made eye contact with Drexler. Porter fired the ball toward Drexler. Scottie Pippen lurched for it. Snagged it. Pippen took off for the Chicago basket.

Drexler leaped after Pippen and fell onto his belly, slapping Pippen on the way down. Whistle. Foul on Drexler. His sixth. He was out of the game.

Drexler, his eyes on fire, strode toward the Portland bench, yelling, "Fuck!"

Chicago was up by eight with four and a half minutes left. It was a horrendous time to foul out.

Then a very odd thing happened. Portland made its most stirring comeback of the year. They won.

Clyde sat watching from the bench. He was undoubtedly pleased with the comeback. But part of him had to be in agony.

After the game, he professed to be completely, unequivocally delighted.

As the Finals continued, the national press began to harpoon Drexler. *USA Today* columnist Peter Vecsey hammered Drexler for Clyde's laid-back persona: "Enough of his gentlemanly behavior. Later for his nice-guy image. You can't think about beating Jordan by being permissive or overly respectful."

Philadelphia journalist Bill Lyon described the difference between Jordan and Drexler: "It has not so much to do with talent as it does with temperament. Jordan, by nature, will take a game and mold it in his hands, and he will lash his teammates, goad them, shame them. Drexler, by nature, is more passive. He will make the plays he can and assume the others will fall in dutifully behind."

Clyde may have looked like a gentleman to Oregonians, but to the rest of the country, he looked like a schmuck.

The series moved to Portland, where the Blazers won only one game of three. And even in that game, Drexler did not star. At no point did he confront Jordan directly, grapple with him, test him—and win. Either Drexler wasn't sufficiently impassioned or sufficiently confident—or both.

Back to Chicago. The high drama of the Stadium. The ungodly noise. The spotlights in a darkened house. The music. The beer. Waiting for Jordan to be surreal.

But something went wrong for Chicago. Portland entered the last quarter ahead by fifteen.

Portland appeared to be in complete control of the game. Not Drexler—*Portland*. That was how it was supposed to be. Single players, said the great NBA minds, could no longer win championships by themselves—mostly because there was now such a glut of excellence in the league. Even the greatest player, Jordan, endangered his team when he tried to do too much. The Bulls were considered better this year than last because Jordan was doing less.

This final quarter—this one brief collection of moments —was Drexler's golden chance. It was his opportunity to show that: *Yes,* the Blazers were the best team in the world—precisely *because* Drexler didn't allow his ego to dominate (and castrate) his teammates. It was his chance to show that he was the most valuable basketball player in the world—maybe not the most physically skilled—but the most *valuable.*

Pippen had the ball, edged toward the hoop. Clyde shied away from him. Why risk a foul with a fifteen-point lead? But Pippen scored. Clyde watched the ball fall through the hoop and shook his head.

Jordan was on the bench. Portland needed to build its lead—to twenty or more—to *keep* Jordan on the bench.

Portland's Cliff Robinson had the ball near the three-point line. Drexler was underneath the basket. He was practically begging for the ball. But Robinson pitched up a strange, ugly shot that bounced hard off the backboard. Drexler didn't yell at Robinson, as Michael would have, nor did he do what Magic might have: grab Robinson by the Adam's apple and kill him quickly.

Next time down, though, Drexler made sure he had the ball himself. He dribbled at the three-point line. Pippen swiped at the ball, and Drexler seemed to lose control of it for a moment. Drexler held it for a half-second, then began dribbling again. Whistle! Double dribble! A profound pout settled onto Drexler's face. Jordan pumped his fist from the bench.

It was slipping away. Seven-point game.

Chicago scored, and Drexler again got the ball. He tossed up a long jumper. No good.

Jordan leaped off the bench and ran back into the game.

As soon as he got in, Jordan hit a jump shot over Drexler. Jordan was so quick, and so deceptive, that Drexler didn't even leap.

It was over. Jordan pushed Chicago to a small lead with about a minute left, and then he held on to it.

Afterward, Jordan and Pippen embraced in the locker room. Then the security people cordoned off Jordan's locker with a thick velvet rope. Only Jordan and his wife Juanita were behind it, hugging and holding the golden championship trophy.

It had been an endless, soul-shattering season for Jordan —his hardest ever. There had been so many controversies. The White House fiasco. The gambling investigation. *The Jordan Rules* tumult. The charges that he'd kept Isiah off the Olympic team. The wars with USA Basketball and the NBA over merchandising.

For Jordan, the hard part of life was no longer playing basketball. Playing brought joy and freedom. The difficulty now came from having to . . . be like Mike.

It was immeasurably more difficult than having to be like Clyde.

When the Trail Blazers got home, the crowd was waiting. They chanted Clyde's name.

An older woman yelled, "We love you, Clyde."

Drexler seemed to hear and smiled in her direction. This was no time to start being rude to the fans. After all, the fans supported them—win or lose.

Over the next few days, the *Portland Oregonian* was deluged with letters congratulating the Blazers on having such a great year. The Blazers, they pointed out, were the *second-best team in the world!* What—the letter writers wanted to know—could possibly be better than that? Anyway, with another gorgeous summer here, let's all just enjoy what we've got—and get ready for Clyde to make us all proud again in the Olympic Games!

Clyde, for his part, moped for a couple of days, then started to get ready for his greatest summer ever.

Once again, he was second best. But . . . so what? It was better than being third.

15

The Great Gringo Hope: Larry Bird at the Tournament of the Americas

Larry Talks Trash to Magic • Michael Flirts With Juanita • Magic Flirts With a Comeback • Patrick Flirts with Larry • Karl Gets Pissed • Charles Barkley: Free at Last! • The Great White-Trash Hope • Chuck Daly's Cold Sweat

"Dey's what you call indentured white folks," Kunta's friend explained.

"What dey like?" asked Kunta.

"Dey sticks pretty much to deyselves," said his friend, "but dey awright."

—Alex Haley
Roots, 1976

Guilt is fear of not being loved.
—Dr. Arthur Janov
The Primal Scream

I always feel good. But when I'm fightin', I feel double-good.

—James Earl Jones
in *The Great White Hope*

The Golden Boys

It's a town full of losers, and I'm pullin' outta
here to win.

—Bruce Springsteen
"Thunder Road"

●

● La Jolla, California, June 25, 1992

Ewing thundered toward the hoop, leaped up, and touched
the ball against the glass. But Malone, playing defense,
hurled his body up from behind and smashed down the
ball—and Ewing's right hand. Ewing's thumb crashed into
the rim. The thumb jerked out of its joint and was slit open.

Ewing landed hard—almost coming down on Clyde
Drexler—with what was later described as an odd and
terrible look on his long, sour face.

They hustled him off to a hospital.

Chuck Daly came out to meet the press, looking dark and
tired. He called it a "major crisis."

All the reporters scribbled down his quotes, and many of
them fastened on to the jeopardy angle: Now that the U.S.
team was down to one center, it was *in peril.*

Which was laughable, of course. But that didn't mean it
wasn't newsworthy.

Daly had helped create another good fear-story yesterday,
when the college squad he'd brought to La Jolla for practices
had beaten the pros in a scrimmage.

Supposedly, that had amounted to the dreaded worst-case
scenario: defeat by a team accustomed to zone defense and
the short three-point line. Reporters had collected Daly's
gloomy proclamations and hustled to their modems to
crank out their requisite harbinger-of-disaster stories.

The U.S. pros, the reporters pointed out, had ignored the
perimeter players when the ball had gone inside, only to
have the ball passed back outside for a quick three-pointer.
It was the classic penetrate-and-pitch European strategy
that the Selection Committee's Bob Bass had warned about

last summer. Now it was working! Against the golden boys! Horrors!

Plus, there were other terrifying problems. The players, Daly fretted, were overconfident. "That's the one thing that can beat us," Daly said. "Fortunately, we have the Tournament of the Americas coming up, and maybe a scare or two there will change their perceptions."

And then there were injuries. Not just Ewing's, Daly said, but also "Magic with the virus, Robinson with a thumb injury, and Bird and Mullin with back problems."

Plus: conditioning problems. Drexler, Jordan, and Pippen, fresh from the playoffs, were beat to hell. On the first day of practice, Drexler had been dragging his ass. And Magic was out of shape. The guys he'd been playing against at the health club in L.A. hadn't possessed even a fraction of the speed that all the Olympians had. On the first day of practice, Magic had been shocked. Robinson and Mullin, also, hadn't been able to do full workouts after their seasons had ended with injuries.

On top of all that, there were feuds to heal: Ewing and Jordan, and Drexler and Jordan. A month ago, during the Bulls-Knicks series, Ewing had been smacking the hell out of Jordan every time Michael had come into the paint. And just a few days ago, Drexler and Jordan had been competing fiercely to see who was really the best player in basketball.

Daly had been spending his free time poring over scouting reports. Brazil's Oscar Schmidt! How in God's name could *he* be stopped? Puerto Rico's Jose Ortiz! He was skinny and clumsy—an NBA reject—but what if he *caught fire?* What *then?*

"Coaches worry," Daly lamented.

Goll-ee! How scary!

But then the players trooped out to talk to the press. And to bring them back to reality. Reality being: No team on earth could *possibly* beat the Americans. This was not just the best basketball team in the world. It was the best team *in any sport* that had *ever been assembled*.

Even Ewing—fresh from the hospital, with his thumb in a

splint—showed up for the quote-op. Ewing said he'd be playing again in about a week. "We're still going to get it done," he said. He was very casual—even laughing occasionally.

Then Larry Bird made his appearance.

The moment Bird ambled out, he was swamped by journalists. He endured the commotion stoically, as if this was just another helping of the same old thing—which it was. Bird seemed utterly calm. Bored, actually. There was absolutely *no* sense of jeopardy coming from him—which didn't help the writers who'd already hooked into the jeopardy angle.

But how could Larry Bird be freaked out over a piddly contrived crisis like this? Larry Bird had been to the mountaintop; he'd seen heaven and hell. After a spectacular career, the thing he loved most—basketball—was being ripped away from him. In his own way, he was almost as tragic a figure now as Magic. Unlike Magic, he didn't have a fascinating business-and-public-affairs career to replace basketball. All he could do was struggle to accept his fate.

Bird's back—which had forced him to miss about half the season and five of the Celtics' playoff games—seemed to be holding up. Even so, he was terribly vulnerable to reinjury. If he did tear apart his back again, it would probably mean the end of his career. That would devastate Bird, because his career had long been the center of his life—perhaps the *only* vital part of his life. But even with this hanging over his head, he was supremely serene.

Bird was, in many ways, the most remarkable basketball player in history. He had no outstanding physical gifts; he wasn't huge, he wasn't graceful, he wasn't fast, and he couldn't leap. Nevertheless, he'd manufactured himself into one of the finest players ever. Bird, in his prime, had had the greatest combination of skills of any player. No one—not even Magic or Michael—had performed so well at the game's four primary components: scoring, defense, passing, and rebounding. Bird was a much better shooter than Magic, a much better passer than Michael, and a better rebounder than either.

Most notable of all, he'd accomplished this with essentially just his mind. He had, quite possibly, the strongest will of anyone in the game. Also, he had the most advanced powers of perception of anyone currently playing.

His will was evidenced by his amazing physical skills—which came almost solely from work, focus, and repetition. His perceptual powers were evidenced by his "court vision" —his capacity to see patterns and movements that eluded other excellent players.

Bird could not know what the future held for him. But he was certain of what it held for this team: There was no way on God's earth that it would lose even one game. "We're getting better," Bird told the reporters in his high, Midwestern twang. "We've struggled a little as we've gone along, but it's getting better. The plays are all in. The offense is pretty simple. We just have to get used to each other."

Bird said he was thoroughly enjoying the Olympic experience. "It's a special moment," he said, "because of Magic, and being able to play with these younger guys while I'm the older man on the team."

Still, there was regret and longing. This wasn't more important to him than playing for an NBA championship. "I'd rather be in the NBA finals," he said, "and win a championship for the Celtics."

Then somebody asked him if this would be his last competition. He seemed to go inside himself. "No," he said. The reporters waited for him to elaborate. Silence.

Somebody prompted him, "So, this isn't the end, huh?"

"No." Silence.

Larry Bird was realistic about practically everything. Except himself.

● **Portland, Oregon, June 27**

"Go ahead," said Bird to Magic, "you do it."

So Magic Johnson took the American flag and stood at the head of the U.S. team as it prepared to march onto the floor of Portland's Memorial Coliseum.

America marched out. The crowd screamed. The sound system started blasting the National Anthem. Overhead, images of each American player flashed onto the scoreboard.

It was an astounding collection of men: Magic Johnson, Larry Bird, Michael Jordan, David Robinson, Clyde Drexler, Charles Barkley, Karl Malone, John Stockton, Chris Mullin, Scottie Pippen, Patrick Ewing, Christian Laettner. They had come from every region of the country, from every economic class, from broken families and close families, and from large cities, small towns, and farms. They were all men of wealth and power who had been eager—hungry—to risk their bodies and careers for the chance to play in the 1992 Olympic Games. They were partly driven by the desire to represent America—which meant vastly different things to each of them. Most of all, they were driven by the desire to spend one summer of their lives in each other's company.

They stood on the floor, facing the flag, as the crowd continued to roar. . . . "O say, does that star-spangled banner yet wave . . ."

Magic's skin broke out in goose bumps. Before coming out, he'd steeled himself for an emotional experience. But this was more than he'd thought it would be. His lips were clamped tight, in exaggerated stoicism.

". . . O'er the land of the free . . ."

Tears dropped down the cheeks of Chris Mullin and David Robinson. Each of them had his hands clasped and made no effort to wipe the tears away.

". . . and the home of the brave?"

Larry Bird's face twitched uncontrollably.

That same afternoon, players wandered around the stadium and talked to reporters. The "media availability session," like a similar one the evening before, gave the journalists yet another opportunity to ask Bird what it was like to play with Magic.

"I don't know," Bird said. "He hasn't passed me the ball yet."

Magic looked at Bird and mentioned that in their early NBA years, he and Bird—bitter rivals—had rarely spoken. Bird replied, "I spoke to you one time. I said, 'In your face.'"

"I don't mind you saying that," said Magic, "because we wound up *beating* you most of the time."

"Yeah," said Bird, "but I'm still here. You're retired." Bird was in a good mood and was no longer reluctant to show his playful side to reporters. Early in his career, he'd been surly with writers, but his empathy had expanded as his own physical vulnerability had increased.

Bird said the Olympics were finally starting to seem real to him. "It's getting a lot better, with the opening ceremonies and all," he said. "We've been so isolated—just practice and talking to the press."

On the other side of the room, though, Karl Malone sounded belligerent—as if he needed a fight to settle his nervous system. "I was watching on TV when Russia beat our guys at the last Olympics," he said, "and they lifted the coach up like they had beaten America's best. That *pissed me off.*"

David Robinson was as soft-spoken as ever, but after two months of recovery from surgery and a week of practice with the Olympians, he seemed to have a new appreciation for the kill-or-be-killed ethic. "You can't be soft on this team, or make dumb mistakes," he said, "because they'll *kill* you. Michael's so fast, and Karl's so strong—if you make a mistake, or your head isn't in it, you can end up going down onto the floor—or into the stands."

Robinson said losing the '88 Olympics still hurt. "That was one of the lowest feelings I've had in sports," he said.

Pippen was still revved up from the opening ceremonies. "Playing for the Olympic team gives you a different *feeling* from playing in the NBA," he said. "You're playing for the red, white, and blue—it's a feeling that's hard to describe." Pippen seemed very genuine in his patriotic fervor. Of course, most of his love of country came from being rich. But what was wrong with that? If going from poverty to wealth overnight wasn't part of the American Dream, then what was?

Barkley—making one of his first few public appearances since his trade to Phoenix—looked radiant. He finally had a shot at a championship, and it seemed to intoxicate him. But already ' reporters were starting to whine about "overkill"—blaming the U.S. team for humiliating its opponents before the deed had even occurred. And Barkley did *not* want to hear about it. "If we win by a lot, people will say we're rubbin' it in. If we don't win by a lot, they'll say something's wrong. That's just the mentality."

Barkley looked at an Argentine reporter who didn't seem to be comprehending much of what Barkley said. "You're ugly," Barkley told the reporter sweetly.

One of the reporters asked him if he knew anything about Cuba, the first team America would play.

"Only thing I know about Cuba," Barkley said, "is that they got a scruffy little guy with a beard runnin' the country."

Someone asked him if he was concerned about Brazil's great shooter, Oscar Schmidt.

"*Very* concerned. I worry about him every day now. I'll be right in the middle of my backswing, and I'll be thinkin': 'Oscar! Oscar!' "

He got a good laugh and smiled. Charles *liked* being on the world's stage.

• Flirting with God

The sky turned brilliant: orange, green, bursts of gold, exploding yellow stars, clouds of pink and purple. Nike had about half the Olympic team at a Tournament of the Americas opening-night party, and the sneaker company was putting on the most extravagant fireworks show imaginable. Choreographed with eardrum-puncturing, surrealistic music, the fireworks glinted off the lake that's the center of Nike's immense campus of offices. Ten to fifteen fireworks would explode at once. From horizon to horizon, the sky filled with color and noise.

When things quieted down, the crowd went back to celebrity-gawking and pillaging the vast tables of seafood, prime rib, and strawberry shortcake.

To get away from the heat and press of the crowd, a friend and I ducked inside a lunchroom. It was decorated like a college bar—wooden booths, hanging lamps, framed *Sports Illustrated* covers on the walls, and a big-screen TV in the corner. It was quiet, dark, and empty. We drank ale and ravaged a big pile of crab and shrimp.

Then there was a small rustle. Michael Jordan, his wife Juanita, and a friend of Juanita's strolled in and slipped into one of the booths.

Jordan looked over at us. He waved, smiled, and said, "So long, fellas." It was an inspired greeting—sincerely friendly, but carrying a warning not to intrude.

Jordan, in a green silk suit I'd seen before, sipped a bottle of water and flirted with his wife. For long periods, he'd stare at her and smile. She was relaxed, laughed a lot, and wasn't remotely deferential. Most wives aren't, of course—but her husband was, after all . . . God.

We hit bottom on our platter of seafood and headed out for more. As we walked past Jordan's table I paused to pay my respects.

Jordan, as usual, was friendly.

"I like the beard," I said. "You gonna keep it?"

"I might. Juanita likes it. Maybe I'll let it grow out a little—get it to lookin' like yours." He pointed at my beard.

"Weird," I said, "everybody in the world wants to be like Mike, and you wanna be like Cam."

"Be like Cam, if you can," Jordan said.

"That's good. Is it copyrighted?"

"It is now. I'm too quick for ya."

"I better eat my Wheaties."

Tip-off. David Robinson stood at center court. Checking everyone's position, he glanced at the other starters: Bird,

Barkley, Magic, Michael. But it shocked him. Bird! Barkley! Magic! Michael! . . . Incredible! . . . After all this time, it was finally happening. He felt a jolt of adrenaline and had to tell himself to calm down.

The ball floated up. Robinson slapped it to Magic. Magic loped downcourt in his fast, gawky stride, then fired it to Bird on the right. Bird dribbled hard toward the basket. The Cuban defending him rushed out to cut Bird off. But suddenly Bird was headed in the opposite direction, dribbling with the opposite hand, and the defender looked as shocked as if someone had slapped him in the face. Then Bird changed direction again and backed straight toward the basket, protecting the ball with his butt and elbows. Just as the defender regained his balance, Bird again reversed course, heading away from the basket. He leaped, spun 180 degrees, shot, and started backpedaling downcourt before the ball even ripped the net. It was a quick play (maybe three seconds) and it looked like nothing—until you stopped to break down the mind-killing combination of moves in it.

Bird was back. The crowd howled.

Then it was Magic's turn. After a Cuban miss, he dribbled downcourt with a Cuban on his left, another just behind him to the right, and another directly ahead. Magic started going through a series of head-fakes, so subtle that they were invisible to practically everybody but the courtsiders and players. He jerked his head left and stutter-stepped, and the legs of the guy on his left were suddenly tied in knots. Then he faked right, accelerated, and went into the air at the free throw line. The guy on his right got left behind. The defender in front dug in to take Magic's charge. Magic held out the ball and teased the defender in front. Then he pulled it back and cradled it in both palms. At the last second, he flipped it backward with both hands to David Robinson, who'd somehow sprinted up from behind. Magic pulled his body hard to the left, away from a collision with the defender under the hoop. Robinson leaped—held the ball a half-foot over the rim. Jammed it—so hard it hit his own belly on the way down. The crowd screamed in ecstasy. Robinson pointed at Magic.

Magic shouted, "You the man!" at Robinson.

Magic was back.

Shortly after that, Jordan flashed downcourt and lofted a long pass to Magic in the left corner. Magic cruised down the baseline and leaped up for his shot. But it wasn't a shot; he hooked it with his left hand to David Robinson. But Robinson wasn't ready: a leaping, left-handed *hook pass?* What's *that?* The ball sailed toward the right sideline. But Jordan flew after it! Like it mattered! He outraced it— barely—and grabbed it with his right hand as his legs scissored wide. His body soared out-of-bounds. But before he touched down, he swung the ball *behind his back* toward Bird in the right corner. Bird leaped high, his legs splayed, and hauled it down. He planted his feet. Flexed his knees. Hopped. Shot. Followed through. Rip!

Chuck Daly leaped up. "Good!" he yelled. "Keep up the intensity!"

Barkley stared at Daly. Barkley's jaw fell open. "You got a hundred million dollars' worth of *players* out there, Chuck," he said. "Sit the fuck *down.*"

After the game, Bird sat in a little curtained-off cubicle and answered a few questions. He was low-key and quiet, but there was a hard glint in his eyes. He'd played superbly —17 points on seven out of eight shooting, 6 rebounds, three for three from the three-point line, and 3 steals. He'd looked loose and strong, and had barely broken into a sweat.

"I just wanted to make the first two points," he said, smiling. "In case I didn't score in the rest of the tournament, I could at least say I had two points."

After the crowd around Bird thinned out a little, I said to him, "Jerry West says you're always thinking two steps ahead of everybody else. I was wondering if the mental aspects of your game get rusty when you're out for a long time with an injury."

"Not too much," he said. "Things like your shot can get a little rusty—or your timing—but the way you see things comes right back when you get out on the floor."

"So what they call your court vision isn't affected?"

"No, I always got that. That's just lookin' with your eyes. But as you see stuff, your experience tells you that this or that's probably gonna happen. So then you keep on lookin' at what's goin' on, but you're also lookin' for what's *gonna* go on."

"It must be frustrating to have those mental abilities and not be able to use them."

"Well, it is. Basketball's what I do best. I don't wanna lose that."

But it was already gone. At least for now. Bird had played his last real game in this tournament.

• French Lick, Indiana

Detroit's Dennis Rodman was a tired, frustrated rookie who'd just been whipped senseless in the seventh game of the bitter 1987 Eastern Conference Finals. And Boston's Larry Bird had done the whipping—with his shooting and his fists. So when Rodman was asked about Bird, he got pissed. And said something stupid. He said Bird was "very overrated"—just because he was white. And then Isiah Thomas—equally angry—agreed with the remark. All hell broke loose. Every sports columnist in the country jumped to Bird's defense.

But overlooked in the tempest was the very *premise* of Rodman's statement: *What if Larry Bird were black?* Bird has long borne the pride—and arrogance—of the white race. Bearing the white man's burden has not been all that uncomfortable for Bird, because pride and arrogance are close to the core of his own personality. But Bird's whiteness means something more than the success of a very white man in a very black game.

Bird's whiteness isn't the genteel Rhodes Scholar kind, like Bill Bradley's. It isn't the earnest Boy Scout kind, like Jerry West's, or even the goodfella-gym-rat kind, like Chris Mullin's. Bird's whiteness is the French Lick, Indiana, kind—the alcoholic's-son kind. The white-trash kind. Bird is, in his own phrase, a hick. His success in the NBA is less the triumph of a white man over blacks than it is the triumph of *white trash over itself.*

Make no mistake: Larry Bird has triumphed. He may still be a Beverly Hillbilly, but he is no longer white trash. Far from it. The essence of white trash is inertia: lack of change. For Larry Bird, though, change is constant. He is a man transformed. To understand that transformation is to understand Larry Bird.

Bird's people were among the poorest in the poorest part of Indiana. They were the sort of people who hung their heads in silence around strangers, who drank too much beer and chewed too much tobacco, who roused themselves to violence over tiny slights, who drifted between menial jobs, and lived day-by-day.

When Rodman shot off his mouth, he surely had no idea that Larry Bird was a lot more like Rodman himself than Bird was like Rodman's white teammate Bill Laimbeer (the brat son of an oil company executive). Laimbeer's sort of whiteness exists a million miles from French Lick.

French Lick is a beaten-down hardscrabble town in rural southwest Indiana, nearer to Kentucky than Indianapolis. Before the Depression, French Lick and neighboring West Baden were swank resort spots, blessed with hot springs, legal gambling—and entrepreneurs who knew how to combine the two. Locals served wealthy out-of-towners who drank, gambled, and chased women.

This exposure to big-city debauchery made most residents suspicious and contemptuous of outsiders. When the tourist trade slacked off and the big hotels folded, the locals were even more bitter. The folks who lived in "the valley," as it's known, learned that they could trust no one, that success was fleeting, and that life meant hard work and low pay. "In Orange County you work hard and die young," says one Bird relative. The valley was much like the deep south—poor, uneducated, drunken, and mean.

Young men in French Lick usually had little to look forward to. Joe Bird, Larry's father, was no exception. One of twelve kids, he left school in the eighth grade to help support the family. The Birds were known as the poorest folks in town, and their mother, Helen, was considered the town's meanest woman. But Joe got a couple of chances to expand his horizons: World War II and Korea.

Joe could've made a career of the military, because he was occasionally promoted, but something made him jerk away from discipline and responsibility. He made a habit of turning up AWOL, of getting his rank stripped, and of drinking his way into the brig. It seemed like typical good-old-boyism, but people in French Lick suspected something worse. He was, after all . . . a Bird. Lovable lush Joe came home from the wars jittery and prone to nightmares, and often drank himself into stupors.

Despite this severe posttraumatic stress, Joe seemed like a good marriage prospect to Georgia Kerns. They got married in 1951 and had six kids, five boys. The fourth child, Larry, was born on Pearl Harbor Day in 1956.

They were dirt poor. Joe had trouble holding on to jobs, though he was well liked everywhere he worked. "He had a heart as big as the world, but his drinking problem was bigger," says a relative. The family couldn't depend on him even when he was employed: Joe would blow his whole paycheck on rounds of drinks.

Georgia killed herself to keep the kids fed and clothed. She often waitressed as many as one hundred hours a week, for one hundred dollars. Sometimes there wasn't anything to eat at the end of the week, and relatives would slip into the house and leave bread and milk.

Despite his father's shortcomings, Larry seemed to admire his dad at least as much as he did his mother, ignoring his father's faults. Once his dad hit his mom, and Larry's only reaction was to laugh. In ways, Larry was closer to his grandmother than he was to his mother.

The Birds constantly moved, migrating from one run-down rental to another—often a step ahead of the landlord: seventeen times in eighteen years. There wasn't always money to heat the house, or to replace the furniture the boys broke in their roughhousing. One move was so bare-bones the kids did it themselves with a red wagon.

Needless to say, there were no luxuries: no bikes, few clothes, fewer toys. "A friend of Larry's would say, 'If you can outrun me down to the post office, you can ride my bike for ten minutes,'" Georgia Bird recalls. "Larry used to run his tail end off."

Larry was once given a rubber basketball for Christmas, but the family couldn't afford a pump. He discovered that he could temporarily inflate the ball by leaving it near a coal stove. Once he left it there overnight. It blistered, but he still had to play with the lumpy thing until it wore out.

Joe Bird had been a promising athlete, but his youth had been stolen by the Depression and wars. Larry was more fortunate. Like all boys who grew up in Indiana, he was raised on basketball, an inexpensive game glorified by decades of local tradition. When the tensions of his mother's overwork, his father's binges, and his family's poverty got to Bird, he had a socially acceptable outlet. The basketball court was a controllable space, where menial repetition and discipline counted for something. He got good at it. Poor as he was, what else did he have to do?

When you think of a solitary kid shooting baskets at night to escape a dysfunctional home, you think of a black kid, not a blue-eyed blond one from the Corn Belt. But if there's a child inside Larry Bird, he's alone, shooting baskets in the night. Bird practiced at least eight hours a day and moved in with his grandmother to be closer to the school gym (and also to be closer to her well-stocked refrigerator).

Bird's obsession with practice was typical behavior for the child of an alcoholic. Alcoholics' kids often blame themselves for their parents' failures and try to gain a sense of control over their environments through the repetition of specific tasks. Bird agrees that his work ethic is partly an expression of insecurity: "It's like I get this guilty feeling that I'm not playing enough, that someone is playing more."

Still, while Joe Bird may have inadvertently filled his son with a work ethic, he also passed on his own sense of limited horizons. Larry never thought basketball would expand his life. It was just cheap, and it was the one thing that made him popular with other kids.

Much of Bird's game is, in fact, rooted in his need to belong. His famous passing, for instance, may seem to some the ultimate triumph of the white game, the *team* game. Not to Bird: "When you pass the ball like that, everybody likes you." Of course, you don't become a great passer just because your father's a drunk, but the need to fit in haunted Bird. So did his father's strict law that the family take care of its own. "He told us that if he ever heard we *didn't* stick up for one another, we shouldn't bother coming home," Bird recalls. Bird became a great passer for the same basic reason he learned to fight and talk trash. It was Us against Them. It was the Birds (or the valley or the Celtics) vs. The World.

Bird's sense that his family and his community were looked down upon was reinforced when he became a star at Springs Valley High. Bird played two years on the varsity, setting astonishing records in both years, but he never got much acclaim. He was never named to an All-State Team, and he languished on the end of the bench in a state All-Star Game. Bird was considered too slow and too mechanical, and being from a tiny school didn't help, either.

Being ignored as an elite high-school athlete had to hurt, because in Indiana the best young basketball players were the children of the gods.

Unlike basketball everywhere else, Indiana basketball isn't primarily a poor, urban, black game. The state's best players are often middle-class white farm boys. The state is largely agricultural, and there aren't many things for boys to do in winter except play basketball. Therefore, basketball, in Indiana, is the center of mainstream life.

Another reason that basketball is a religion in Indiana is because of the miracle of Milan High.

In 1954, a high school with a student body of just 162 won the state basketball championship—easily the most popular sporting event in the state. For decades afterward, everybody knew about Milan and knew about Bobby Plump, the kid who made the winning basket. Almost every kid in

Indiana—including Larry Bird—dreamed of being the next Bobby Plump. *Hoosiers*, the movie based on Milan's victory, captured much of the grim, lonely desperation of the young players in outback towns like French Lick. It also revealed how much small towns glorify their high school heroes.

It's called Hoosier Hysteria. And it gets pretty scary. Of the world's twenty largest high school gyms, eighteen are in Indiana. Some high schools with enrollments of less than one thousand have gyms that seat ten thousand. Local school boards are often empowered to fire only two employees—the principal and the basketball coach. Old-timers recall a week when the blizzards were so brutal that people couldn't be buried; that week, 250 high-school basketball games were played, right on schedule.

So, of all places to be overlooked, Indiana was the worst. Bird didn't even get recruited by many colleges, even though colleges typically combed the state. He didn't seem to mind the college snubs, though. Gary Holland, his high-school coach, says, "I don't think Larry thought too much about going to college." College—any college—seemed too far from French Lick. And people from French Lick never went far.

Bob Knight, the eight-hundred-pound-gorilla of Indiana basketball, expressed some interest in Bird late in the recruiting period (after another kid got away from Knight and he had a scholarship to waste). Bird preferred the smaller and less intimidating Indiana State to Knight's Indiana University, but he bowed to the pressure of his coaches, parents, and neighbors, all of whom were in awe of Knight. Photos taken the day Bird signed with Knight show a Larry Bird who looks scared and maybe a bit hoodwinked.

He lasted *almost* a month. Bird was utterly shocked by the vastness of IU—33,000 students, all with apparently more going for them than him. Bird's roommate was kind, lending him money and showing him some social ropes. But it was humiliating for Bird to even share the closet: "I had a few pairs of pants, a few shirts, and not much else. His stuff took over ninety-five percent of the closet, and it's not like he was all that rich. Everywhere I looked, it was like that. I couldn't cope."

The hard-assed Knight did nothing to help his floundering freshman. One night Bird and his fiancée were eating in a restaurant when Knight walked in. Bird worked up the gumption to walk up and say hello. "Larry spoke to Coach Knight, and he just totally ignored him. And it just crushed Larry," the girl says.

Not long afterward, Bird packed his belongings—his jeans, his shirts, his one pair of sneakers—and hitchhiked home. He had visions of a big homecoming.

But all valley people saw was a kid from a nothing family who'd blown his chance. Typical white-trash move; typical *Bird family* move. When valley people saw Bird working on the town street crew—painting fire hydrants and collecting garbage—they saw that Joe Bird's son had found his way to his father's level.

No one really knew, though, how low Joe Bird had sunk. He was miserable. A desperate Georgia asked a hypnotist to put Joe under and ask him about his war experiences. Hypnotized, Joe recalled killing a North Korean soldier up close after the soldier had killed his friend. The memory shocked the family but was harder on Joe. So hard he got violent.

Georgia could take no more. The couple divorced, and Joe went to live with his mother. Georgia still loved him and sometimes allowed him to sleep in the house. She hoped, though, that court-mandated child support would make him take his parenting responsibilities more seriously. Predictably, though, he couldn't make his child-support payments. On February 3, 1975, police showed up at Joe's mother's house to arrest him for failure to comply with a court order. Joe excused himself and went into the next room, where he called Georgia. When he reached her, he announced, "I want you to hear this." He then blasted his head apart with a shotgun.

Bird took all of this with the classic introspective stoicism of the alcoholic's child. He followed the subliminal mantra:

Don't talk, don't trust, don't feel. He dove deeper into basketball. Bird actually enjoyed his city maintenance job, but he realized he would always be considered a failure if he didn't at least try to succeed at basketball. So he enrolled at Indiana State and stumbled into yet another mistake: an undergraduate marriage. The kid who could barely bring himself to sleep away from home was now playing house with a young wife.

The whole thing was too much. "Getting married was the worst mistake I ever made," Bird says. "Everything that ever happened to me, I learned from it, but I'm still scarred by that. That scarred me for life. That and being broke are the two things that influenced me most. Still."

The marriage ended painfully. After they divorced, Bird sometimes returned home. (As his father previously had.) However, Bird's wife was also seeing someone else. She became pregnant, and Bird was afraid the child wasn't his. His ex-wife sued for paternity and won. Even so, Bird had very limited contact with his daughter.

Perhaps to escape this turmoil, Bird completely threw himself into basketball. He began playing—and practicing—like no one in Indiana ever had, averaging more than 30 points and 13 rebounds per game over three years. Senior year, he led his team to the national championship game, where they were whipped by Magic Johnson's Michigan State. Bird won most of the nation's single-player honors—but in a typical French Lick move, he blew off the John Wooden award ceremony to teach a gym class.

Bird had been eligible for the NBA draft the year before, and the Boston Celtics, floundering after years of late draft picks, took a chance on his coming out early. "I never worried about the pros in college," he says. "When the Celtics drafted me, I couldn't have cared less."

But the Celtics, who retained rights to Bird for 365 days, cared. When the Final Four was over, Red Auerbach approached the country bumpkin he hoped would save his team. But he found himself wrangling with a committee of Indiana businessmen who had, with Bird's approval, formed a group to protect their local boy. Bird had surrounded himself with a team of hometown friends to fight the outside world.

The committee and the agent they chose—Bob Woolf—fought the Celtics for the highest contract ever paid a rookie. They got it, but only after a struggle that the Boston papers called the "Hundred Years War."

The Celtics had their savior. Bird led them to the greatest turnaround that had yet been achieved by an NBA team—a 32-game improvement. He was the runaway Rookie of the Year, accepting the award in a short-sleeved bowling shirt. The next year, he led the team to the championship—the first of his three.

Bird and Magic saved the league. When they entered it, the NBA didn't even have a network TV contract for its finals. The games were run on tape-delay opposite Johnny Carson. The bitter and famous Bird-Magic rivalry, begun at the Final Four, continued through four NBA finals. They genuinely disliked each other. One day, though, when they were filming a Converse commercial, they were thrown together for several hours in the back of a limo. They found they had a great deal in common: poor childhoods, loving families, struggle, obsession with basketball, and perceptual abilities of a rare quality. They became friends.

Magic played in a bigger market than Bird, won more rings, and, ultimately, proved a greater and more durable player. But the sad truth is that it was mostly Bird who began filling NBA arenas, merely by virtue of his race. It didn't matter that he was a former white-trash kid who had more in common with (and more respect for) his black teammates than anyone else. He was immediately labeled the NBA's Great White Hope.

Bird's race certainly wasn't lost on fans in Boston. People in that city—which had exploded in the '70s over school busing—loved Bird. They saw in his pale, sweaty face a reflection of their own blue-collar self-image.

Bird was also like Boston in other ways. He was quick to fight and cocky beyond belief, once taunting an aging Julius

Erving so unmercifully that Erving tried to punch him out. Bird kept the Celtics totally insulated from outsiders, discouraging friendships with players from other teams and constantly harping on the "us against the world" theme.

But if someone was in Bird's family of friends, Bird was intensely loyal. One person to whom Bird was loyal—against the wishes of the Celtics—was Nick Harris, a used-car salesman and onetime drug dealer. During the 1985 playoffs, Bird and Harris got into a fight with some other guys in a Boston bar. Harris took a licking from a bouncer, but Bird got the bouncer back, knocking him out. The punch also knocked the Celtics out of the championship. Bird, playing with an injured hand, shot terribly against the Lakers. Bird told everyone he'd hurt his hand in the conference finals. But the fight was typical French Lick. "He's loyal to friends the rest of us don't judge worthy," says a member of the Celtics front office. Bird never spoke about the incident, particularly to the press. "He's suspicious of most people and thinks most people are out to take advantage of him," says a relative.

That suspicion has extended even to his own family. Like many NBA players, Bird built his mother a big house. But he kept an apartment in it and lived there during the summer —so it must have been hard for Georgia to feel that she'd finally gotten a place of her own. Furthermore, he's been known to berate his mother for running up large phone and electric bills when he's not there.

Kid brother Eddie, who also played ball at Indiana State, was given a car by Larry, only to find that there were strict conditions attached. Not only did Eddie have to maintain good grades in school, he had to tend the lawn and have his mother send pictures to Boston to prove he was doing it. Eddie blew it. Bad grades. Tall grass. He lost the car.

Even Bird's new fiancée was not immune to his frugality. When she first moved to Boston, he insisted Dinah Mattingly work to pay for her own clothes and "nonessential" expenses. She got a job as a Kelly Girl and held it for two years.

For many years, Bird was reluctant to marry Dinah. But after about eleven years of living with her, he gave her a ring and said, "You can wear this if you want to."

Bird, who had a recurring dream as a boy that he would one day find a suitcase full of money, was not about to watch his family or his fiancée blow his fortune in classic white-trash fashion.

You can take the boy out of French Lick and give him three MVP trophies and millions of dollars. But you can't take the French Lick—mean, clannish, cheap—out of the boy.

Nevertheless, it is patently clear that not all of Bird's unattractive qualities stayed at the core of his personality. He is now twenty years removed from being white trash. All the people in French Lick who thought that a member of the Bird family could never change were wrong: Larry Bird did change. Basketball was his escape, as surely as it is an escape from the ghetto for many urban blacks.

By the Olympic summer, Bird had a relatively warm relationship with the press. He was a stable husband and an involved and loving father. He seemed at least as comfortable in exclusive hotels as in bowling alleys. And he no longer seemed unnerved by the public prying into his life.

Still, playing basketball was his psychic anchor. It was the only thing that made complete sense to him. It was the only true security he'd ever known. It took care of him, just as it had long ago, when he'd played alone, in the dark.

But playing basketball, for Larry Bird, was becoming an impossibility. And there was nothing to take its place.

• Whipping the Houseboys

Bird was the first player to show up for shooting practice before the U.S. team's second game. That wasn't unusual. In Boston, he was often the first player on the floor.

He stood off to the left side and began raining in jumpers. After a few minutes, Mullin came out and started shooting jump shots from the right. They both had perfect rhythm, perfect form. They never missed. *Swish* from the left. *Swish* from the right. It was as if the two of them were dancing.

Mullin paused for a moment, stretched. "How's the back?" he said.

"I dunno," said Bird. "I never know. It's okay—and then all of a sudden"—he made a face like a guy biting into a 220-volt wire—"Know what I mean?"

"I don't *wanna* know," said Mullin. Mullin stared at Bird as Bird went back to work.

Ewing walked up from behind Bird and grabbed Bird's arm in midshot. Bird jerked his head around, saw it was Ewing, and smiled. They'd become buddies this week. There was something remote and hurt in each of them that had made them reach out to each other.

"Patrick, leave me the hell alone," Bird said.

But Ewing wouldn't.

"Lar-*ree!* Lar-*ree!* Lar-*ree!*" Bird lay in front of the bench, ignoring the crowd. Hot sparks of pain bounced between his spine and his knees. That was a bad sign. The lower the pain traveled, the more debilitating it became. If it got to his toes, he would be incapacitated.

"Lar-*ree!* Lar-*ree!*" Blood dropped off the face of Canadian center Bill Wennington. The Canadians had come out full of bile, stabbing with their elbows and smashing the Americans whenever they could. They were determined not to act like the Cubans had the day before. The Cubans had applauded the Americans during the introductions. Then they'd lined up for a photo with the U.S. stars at halftime and had begged for jerseys and caps. Some of the Americans —Magic, in particular—had been magnanimous about it. But others, like Malone, had gotten pissed off. Malone wanted his opponents to act like warriors, not . . . houseboys.

So the Canadians had vowed to be tough—no matter how badly they were whipped—and before the game Wennington had said that the Americans "bleed just like anyone else."

But Wennington—a 7-0, 245-pound slab of muscle—

had tangled with the wrong combination of U.S. players. Now he had a hole in his face that bandages couldn't close. His coach pulled him from the game.

The Canadians had already kicked the hell out of Stockton, and he'd left the game early, limping off for a hospital. But at least Ewing was back in action.

Pippen, playing point guard, was now ripping downcourt at least as fast as Stockton would have. Pippen, without slowing down, heaved the ball to Mullin. Mullin dribbled a couple of steps, leaped into the air, and—certain he had a trailer—began to flip the ball backward over the top of his head. As he flipped it he swiveled his head to find his target and zeroed in on Clyde, who was a couple of steps behind. Clyde grabbed the ball, took a huge step toward the hoop, then vaulted upward. As he glided to the hoop he windmilled the ball over his head and hook-jammed it.

The stadium thundered. Nike owner Phil Knight, in the front row, almost fell over. Another extraordinary play. The U.S. team—almost impossibly—was better than anyone had imagined they could be. Part of the credit went to Daly; they'd responded to his hyperanxiety by playing as a team. Knowing Daly, that was probably the plan all along.

The U.S. now led Canada by 33 and had beaten Cuba by 44. When the tournament ended, their average winning margin would be more than 50 points.

So this game, like the others, was not a contest, but a spectacle.

And as part of the spectacle, the fans wanted to see Bird.

They began to chant, "We want Larry! We want Larry!" His picture flashed onto the scoreboard, and the building trembled with noise. The chant grew louder: "WE WANT LARRY!"

Bird, sitting on the floor, tugged at his warm-up jacket. Everyone in the stadium seemed to see it. They cheered wildly.

But Bird was just playing with them. He smiled.

To focus attention back onto the game, the PA announcer said, "Ladies and gentlemen, Larry Bird has experienced

some mild discomfort in his back and will not play tonight."
A mass groan.

Bird didn't show up to talk to reporters after the game.
There would be only one real question from the reporters:
Are you finished?
Bird didn't have an answer. And he didn't even want to hear the question. For some time, reporters waited by his interview stall. But he never showed up.

16

Beige Like Me: Christian and the Big Boys in Portland

**Stripped on Television • Barkley's Mascot •
Begging for Magic's Jersey • Lame John Stockton •
Harry and Larry • The Snot-Nosed Preppie •
Sexual Preference • Air Mullin •
Karl Wusses Out • The Getting of Wisdom**

Now ya don't talk so loud,
Now ya don't seem so proud . . .
—Bob Dylan "Like a Rolling Stone"

"All those Ivy League bastards look alike."
Holden Caufield, in *The Catcher in the Rye*, 1945
—J.D. Salinger

●

". . . And *now!* Let's meet the *players!* A six-eleven forward, number four, Chris-*chun Late*-ner!" The PA announcer's voice trailed off. Laettner trotted onto the floor.

And *his pants fell to his knees*. They were plunging further by the millisecond! The horror! The horror!

He grabbed for them. Pulled them back over his big white butt. Looked back at the bench. Jordan was half out of his chair in hysterics, and Barkley had his face buried in a towel, with his shoulders quaking.

Laettner smiled his peculiar crooked half-smile and went about the business of covering his ass.

What did it *mean?* Did this mean he was now one of the guys? Or was it a mean joke—in particular, one aimed at his . . . area of vulnerability?

". . . a seven-one center, number five, *Day*-vud Rob—Rob . . ." Even the PA announcer was breaking up. *"Rob*-inson!" Robinson loped out to Laettner and extended his hand—while he laughed his ass off!

Laettner's face got hard as a brick. This was awful. Just the kind of crap he might've put a freshman through at Duke last year—which right now seemed like a million years ago. At Duke, he'd been Christian the Terrible—the gifted tyrant. He'd been prickly, snotty, loud—and a superhero. He'd pushed and shoved Duke to consecutive national championships. Now, here he was with a chance to be part of history, and his role on the team had basically boiled down to just . . . the Pretty Boy. The comic relief. It pissed him off.

The game started, and America surged to its standard fifty-point lead. Panama—a sad little team that barely had the money to get here—tried a zone defense: *the dreaded zone!* But Jordan and Mullin just stayed on the perimeter and dumped in three-pointers. Good-bye, zone.

Injuries were still the only real problem the U.S. team had. Stockton—who'd hurt his leg in the prior game, against Canada—was out of the tournament and maybe out of the Olympics. When he'd gone to the hospital, they'd x-rayed his leg and discovered a cracked bone.

Despite the injuries, though, even Chuck Daly seemed to be calming down. In this game, he'd virtually stopped coaching. When players would come off the floor, he'd just say something like, "Good job," or "Nice," and leave it at that. During time-outs, he'd stare into space.

It was time to put in Laettner.

Magic walked the ball over the half-court line, and Laettner met him at the top of the key. For as big as Laettner was (6–11, 235) he was relatively agile. He claimed he was the tallest person in the world who could walk on his hands. It had become chic of late to compare him to Danny Ferry, the college star who'd become a bench warmer for Cleveland. But their similarities were on the surface: both were white, both were from Duke, both were College Player of the Year. In fact, Laettner was much more mobile than Ferry, and it was Laettner's agility that made him valuable.

But out there among the Olympians, he looked like . . . Bigfoot. Magic motioned for Laettner to go low and right, but by the time Laettner got there, his defender was in position. Magic bounced the ball to Laettner anyway. The win was locked up, and it was time to feed Pretty Boy some points. It was the least they could do after pantsing him.

Laettner grabbed the ball and backed toward the basket, trying a couple of fakes that didn't fool anybody. He spun to his left and got a little closer. Not close enough. He heaved the ball back to Magic.

Almost as soon as Magic caught it, he bounced it back to Laettner. Again Laettner went into his high dribble, stealing looks over his shoulder at the hoop.

Laettner tried to put on some moves. He looked like he aspired to the "black style" of play. But there was no getting around his whiteness. At his very best, he played "beige."

Barkley yelled, *"Shoot* the damn ball, Christian!" The shot clock was running down: nine seconds.

Laettner tried the same maneuver that hadn't worked before. Eight, seven, six. He looked stuck in mud. He stopped dribbling and held the ball. Five, four, three. Barkley yelled, *"Damn,* Christian!"

Laettner hurled it back to Magic. Magic didn't need to check the shot clock. He heaved up a three-pointer. It clanged off. Daly crossed his arms and scowled.

As they ran back downcourt, Magic yelled over to Laettner, "Just post-up and we'll get you the ball." Magic didn't care if the Panama players heard him. His theory was that if you ran your plays perfectly, it didn't matter *who* knew your plans.

Next time downcourt, Magic made eye contact with Laettner and pointed to the left corner. Laettner started to run over there, but hesitated. "Go!" Magic shouted, pointing again. This time, Laettner did what he was told.

Magic fired the ball to Laettner. Malone ran under the hoop, and stretched his arm out for the ball. But Laettner didn't pass it. He was holding it again. A referee blasted his whistle: three-second violation on Malone. Laettner had left Malone stranded.

Laettner kept his face immobile as he ran back on defense. The game was almost over. He only had one point—no rebounds. Pretty weak. Everybody else had their usual fat stats: Magic had 11 assists; Jordan was 4 for 4 on threes; Mullin was 7 for 8 (4 for 5 on threes); Robinson was 6 for 7 with 8 rebounds. These games were stat-heaven—for everybody but Laettner.

One more chance: Laettner got the ball in the lane with about four seconds left. He took a tentative dribble. Leaned in. Flipped up the ball. It bounced in. The crowd roared.

• Are You Gay, Christian?

Bird seemed surprisingly chipper in his interview cubicle after the game.

"Did you have anything to do with Laettner losing his pants?" someone asked him.

"Naw. They'll *blame* it on me—they blame everything on me. But that's all right. Patrick Ewing probably did it."

Some guy asked him, "Larry, have you *earned* the right to be on the roster in Barcelona?" The other reporters gave him sidelong glances, like: Whoa—that took balls.

But Bird didn't get defensive. At least, not by Bird standards. "Well, I'm here," he said, "so I guess they already answered that."

"Ever consider playing in Europe, cuz of the shorter schedule?"

"Nope. I'm All American."

"How's your back?"

"It feels better than yesterday, but what I have to do is wait until the nerve calms down in my leg. Once that goes away, I'll probably start playin' again. I was feelin' real good until the first game, and I guess I overdid it a little bit."

"You dread the long plane ride to Europe?"

"Yeah, I sure do. That's how I get in trouble. But we're tryin' to make plans now to get over a little bit earlier. If I lie down on the planes instead of sittin' down, I could probably get away with it all right. But when I feel good, I feel good; I like to sit."

"Games gonna be tougher over there?"

"I think when we go to Barcelona, we'll get more focused and quit foolin' around. These guys are playin' thirty-six holes a day. When we get over there, I hope we can cut it down to eighteen."

That got a big laugh. Bird was actually playing to the crowd.

Somebody asked him what it was like playing with the other Olympians. "They're the best. But I don't think this team could beat our eighty-six team in Boston." Big laugh. "That's just because Patrick Ewing isn't a real center." Bigger laugh.

"There's been speculation the last couple of days," said a reporter, "about Magic making a comeback. Do you get a feeling he's thinking about it?"

"I think he's been thinkin' about it since the day he announced he was retirin'. He'll probably get together with his doctors and talk it over. It's amazing. He's really not that old—he's thirty-two, thirty-three years old—but sittin' out a year, it really surprises me that he can come back and play the way he has."

"Are you *saving* yourself, to some degree?"

For the first time, Bird stopped cold. Suddenly, he was the old Larry Bird: the icy hillbilly. *"Saving* myself?" he said incredulously. *"No.* I'm injured. I'm not into *savin'* myself. I'm here to get in shape and play basketball. But if I've got nerve pain, I don't play."

Laettner wandered into his cubicle. There wasn't much action around it—just a reporter from Minneapolis and the reporters who were drifting from one player to the next.

The first question Laettner got was, "Talk about the

pants." By sportswriter standards, "talk about" was a question.

"I don't know who did it," he said in his odd voice, which was a cross between Muhammad Ali and Fonzie. The inflections were simultaneously black, Southern, city, and preppie. "Somebody undid 'em while I was sittin' down— maybe it was Malone, who was next to me, but it was funny. I couldn't stop laughin'. I was laughin' even after the introductions."

That wasn't how I remembered it, but I wasn't going to make an issue of it.

Somebody asked him if he remembered the last time he'd sat on the bench so much.

"There was a time a few summers ago, when I was on a national team. Before that, it was my freshman year of college."

Inadvertently, he'd touched on two of his areas of vulnerability. One was the perception that he was only on this team because he'd volunteered for so many dinky USA Basketball national teams. How else could you explain his getting picked over Shaquille O'Neal? And by mentioning his freshman year, he'd alluded to playing behind Danny Ferry—the specter who now haunted his entry into the NBA.

Still, nobody had mentioned his *main* area of vulnerability. It wasn't an easy thing to bring up.

A writer asked if the pro players were rougher than he'd expected. It was a question he'd been hearing for the last two weeks; big as he was, he looked soft. He wasn't a weight-room freak, so his upper body looked squishy and flaccid— and the pretty face didn't help much, either.

"The physical aspects are *not* overwhelming," he said. "I'm sure it'll get a little more physical durin' the actual NBA season, when there are hard fouls, and when you're gettin' tired and beat up. But that's all part-a the game. I'm used to it. People don't *think* I'm used to it. But I am."

"Is it inspiring to be out there with some of the greats?"

"It is, it is. It's amazing to think about the kids on this team . . ." He quickly corrected himself: ". . . the *men* on this team." That was a mistake he frequently made. "I realize I'm doin' somethin' incredible, but once you step out on the court, it changes. Your instincts are to play, not to think, 'Wow, *Magic*'s throwin' me the ball.'"

Was he unhappy that America's victories had been over-kill?

"It's pathetic that people complain," he said. "Last year, as I was leaving the Pan Am Games, I told everyone that the Olympics would be boring, cuz we were gonna win every game by eighty points. It's just that people question things because . . . they're stupid, I think. You shouldn't *question* this Olympic team—just like a lot of people question me, or they question Duke, when really they don't know *anything.*"

That raised a few eyebrows. Telling reporters it was stupid to ask questions wasn't too hip. So the questions got a little grittier.

"Were you pissed off when people questioned why *you* should be on the team, instead of Shaquille?"

"I wasn't pissed off. I get a little *annoyed* when they question if I can play in the NBA at *all.* Because there's a lotta doubters who say I can't. But even if I wasn't the best player in college this year, I had *done* the most—so I thought that was on my side."

"Done the most?"

"I won two championships." (Not "we won," or "Duke won." "I won.")

"Are you giving anybody grief on this team?" At Duke, he'd been an infamous ass-chewer.

"I'm startin' to loosen up a little and talk back. But that's how they want it. They don't want you to be a wall—and that's not how I am, like at Duke. The word on me is that I nag, don't shut my mouth, talk a lotta junk. That's how I am, and I'm not gonna hide it with these guys."

One of the reporters—I didn't recognize him—seemed to be getting more and more put off. With no preamble, he ventured into an area of major interest to the media—Laettner's sexual preference. It was an issue that had been shadowing Laettner for the last four years.

"How's Brian?" asked the reporter.

"Who?"

"Davis. Brian Davis." He stopped short of saying, "You remember—the guy some people think is your *boyfriend.*"

"Brian got drafted by Phoenix," Laettner said. Then he changed the subject. The guy who'd asked the question walked away, and none of the other reporters followed up on it. After all, it just wasn't the style of sportswriters to blurt out, "Christian, are you *gay?*"

Drafts of cold air swept through the empty stadium. It was so quiet you could hear Bird's shots rip the net from a hundred yards away. He was the only player on the floor, and when he dribbled, echoes ricocheted down from the ceiling. All of his shots were jumpers. That was the only shot his back would allow. But they were almost all perfect. He shot for minutes at a time without missing.

After about twenty minutes, Pippen ambled out and started shooting with Bird. But Pippen didn't have Bird's attention span and started playing with one of the ball boys, a preadolescent kid, maybe 5–4, about the size Pippen had been at that age. Pippen had the kid guard him while he fired up a shot from midrange. As it whipped through the net, Pippen said to the kid, "In yo' face." The boy smiled. What an honor—to have Scottie Pippen's shot in *his* face! Pippen shot it again. *Rip!* "Face!" Again. *Rip!* "Face!"

"You're like me when I first tried to guard Larry," Pippen told the kid.

"When you *still* try to guard me," said Bird, not pausing in his shot.

Rip! "Face!" *Rip!* "Face!" *Rip!* "Face!" *Rip!* "Face!"

Bird stopped and looked at the kid. "How much-a that you gonna *take?*" Bird asked the boy. "Don't you have no *pride?*"

Pippen looked closely at Bird. He couldn't tell if Bird was kidding. All the Olympians studied Bird, as if he were an oracle.

Broadcaster and former Bulls coach Doug Collins wandered across the floor. "How's the back, Larry?" Collins said.

"I dunno, Doug," said Bird. "Wish I did."

Later on, Ewing came out and started horsing around with Bird: the Harry and Larry Show. Bird was having fun. At least he was still one of the boys. He and Magic had been talking and had agreed that being one of the boys was the best thing in basketball. The best thing in the world, actually.

• One of the Boys

Jordan dribbled thoughtfully at the free throw line, then charged toward the hoop—setting off alarms on the Argentine team. They clumped into a tight ring around the basket. Jordan sidearmed a pass to Mullin, who was waiting—all alone—just outside the three-point line. *Rip!* It was classic European-style basketball: penetrate and pitch. It had taken the U.S. about a week to perfect it. The lead began to swell.

Laettner got in the game early, before the lead was even fifty. The U.S. was short of players; Stockton and Bird were out indefinitely, and Drexler was sitting out the game with a sore knee.

As soon as Laettner got in, Magic hit him right under the basket with a bullet-pass, and Laettner banked it in. It seemed to settle his nerves. He began playing less hesitantly than he had in earlier games.

Jordan brought the ball down and paused at the three-point line. Then he attacked the hoop, just like he had before. Laettner stepped behind the three-point line, just like Mullin had a few minutes earlier. Argentina again ganged up on Jordan. Why not? It was *Michael Jordan.* Anyway—could a big guy like Laettner hit a three? Jordan pitched it back to Laettner, and Laettner drilled it. He had excellent range.

The three-pointer seemed to spark Laettner. He began to boogie down the floor in a simple, graceful rhythm. At the Argentine end, he pulled down a rebound and handed it to Pippen. Pippen whipped downcourt, pulled up, and lofted a three-pointer. As the ball arced, Laettner followed its trajectory and walked toward the basket. When he got to the free throw line, he saw something no one else on the floor saw: The shot was long. He leaped high over everyone as the ball hit the back of the rim, and brushed it with his fingertips. It fell softly through the net.

David Robinson, on the bench, stabbed his fist into the air. Stockton applauded. Barkley yelled, "Yo, Chris-*chun!*"

Laettner almost smiled. For a moment, he was one of the boys. The boys didn't give a rat's ass about sexual preference or about race. Their concerns were: scoring, rebounding, defense.

After the game, I went to Laettner's cubicle to talk to him about what it was like to shoot in high-pressure situations. He had, after all, made two of the most famous clutch shots in the history of college basketball. His big shot this year—a turnaround jumper at the buzzer to put Duke in the Final Four—had cemented his reputation as a winner.

"Do you do anything different mentally in those situations?" I asked.

"I don't know. I don't know. It's probably just concentration."

"In crucial moments, do you go into what they call the zone of altered consciousness?"

"I don't know. I don't know. I just play basketball."

That was as much illumination as I could take in one sitting. So I headed over to see Magic.

Magic was saying that the foreign players all wanted mementos from the U.S. team. Some of them were even having their teammates take pictures from the bench. Magic would be guarding somebody, and the next thing he'd know, the player would be grinning at his bench—posing!—while his teammate snapped a picture.

"See, that's one thing that people don't understand when they say America shouldn't be sending pros. We bring something to the players from other countries—and to all the fans in the world—that college guys just can't bring. That excitement. College guys could never do what we're doing for basketball worldwide.

"But it's funny, you know—this guy who was guardin' me tonight, he's like, 'I *gotta* have your jersey, I *gotta* have your jersey.' I kept tryin' to explain to him that we gotta keep 'em, but he didn't understand."

"Do you think Stockton will be okay for Barcelona?"

"If he can walk, he'll be there. But if he can't, you gotta know there's guys lining up for it. They waitin' by their phone, sayin', 'I'm a point guard—call *me!*'"

"Do you think this good feeling between the teams is gonna continue in Barcelona?"

"No. This is as good as it's gonna get. Over there, they *want* us—*lotta* teams there want us—so we'll be ready."

"What do you think of Laettner?"

"Christian is trying to feel his way around. It's tough, because he used to be a star, and now he's a guy amongst stars. He used to dominate, and now he's sittin' here sayin', 'Man!' I don't think he realized how talented these guys are—and he's gettin' a eyeful, believe me."

Barkley, a couple of stalls over, was also talking about Laettner. Barkley had befriended Laettner and had been showing him that there were levels of privilege that not even Pretty Boy knew about. Last night, they'd gone to a Northwest-chic restaurant called Huber's, and Laettner had automatically queued up at the back of the line. Barkley had taken him by the elbow and said, "Come on up front—you haven't learned a thing yet."

One of the reporters asked Barkley what advice he'd given Laettner.

"I told him he gotta stop takin' them little patsy shots inside, and *dunk* the ball when he gets near the basket."

"Have you kinda made him your mascot?"

"Oh, I just felt sorry for him, sittin' by himself all the time. Nobody else wants to talk to him, so I just kind of . . . like the ugly duckling . . . took him out as a last resort. They stuck him next to me in the locker room, too."

"Do you keep him in line because he's a rookie?"

"NO-NO-No-no! He make too much money for me to keep him in line. But I *like* to hang out with people who make more money than me, cuz they won't be freeloadin'."

"I saw girls screamin' at you two guys."

"Well, they scream at him cuz he looks good. They scream at me cuz . . ." Barkley started to laugh, as if he had a secret joke. . . . "I dunno. I dunno. It's just nice to be screamed at."

Across the room, Karl Malone was trying to back away from one of the shrewdest things I'd ever heard him say. He'd said that since the U.S. was winning every game by fifty points, he wasn't going to break his leg—like Stockton had—trying to win. The reporters didn't like that; they thought it violated the warrior ethic. And it did. Shrewdness and heroism are rarely compatible.

"I didn't *petition* to be on this team," said Malone. "I made a sacrifice to be here. Sure, I represent USA Basketball —but my *real* job is with Utah Jazz, and that's more excitin' to me in the long run than gettin' injured in these games. I'm not gonna risk my career for this."

A reporter asked him if teams would still be anxious to send their best players to future Olympics, after watching Stockton, Bird, and Drexler get beaten up. "Everybody and their grandma from the Jazz front office been callin' Stockton," said Malone. "I don't wanna talk to *any* of 'em. I'm scared to know what they might say to me." In other words: Hell, no, teams won't want their stars in the Olympics.

David Stern had, in fact, been saying this week that the next Olympic team would probably be at least half-amateur. That would quell the bitching about overkill and head off a mutiny of franchise owners.

But Stern's assessment had cast a bittersweet light on these games. This amazing team would soon disband. And there would never be another like it.

Magic barged through a crowd of defenders—somehow keeping possession of the ball—as Barkley sprinted downcourt. Magic hurled the ball into a pack of Puerto Ricans that were between him and Barkley, and it sailed right through them. The ball hit the floor hard and bounced into Barkley's hands. Barkley vaulted toward the rim for a reverse lay-up and put the ball on the backboard. But then a

Puerto Rican defender karate-chopped Barkley to the ground.

Barkley's butt made a hard, angry *"thwack"* as it hit the floor. His head jerked backward and crashed into a photographer's camera. His feet suddenly seemed disconnected from his body and flew high into the air. He tried to get up, but the U.S. trainer ran over and held him down. Barkley's chest pumped and he moaned. His head was cut and blood dripped out. He had to leave the game: the Magic Rule.

But it didn't stop the U.S. from building its lead. Once again, the contest was over early in the first half. The fans were restless. They were trying to appreciate the games as spectacles, but they wanted close games—even if that meant the chance of a loss. Because, when it came right down to it, sports fans didn't *really* care if their teams won or lost; in the larger scheme of things, it didn't make much difference. Sports was never a matter of life or death, health or sickness, wealth or poverty. It was a *diversion* from those issues. That was the beauty of sports—a fan could get into a frenzy and forget all about it an hour later. The only reason sports mattered at all was because sports *didn't* matter.

Puerto Rico was trying to penetrate the U.S. defense. They couldn't. The American defense was making all the other teams feel weak and crazy. Magic was behind the dribbler; he let the guy get a few feet in front of him, then darted at him with an explosion of quickness. Magic batted the ball out of the guy's hands. Malone had it. To Laettner. Laettner shovel-passed to Mullin, who was charging toward the hoop. Mullin, alone, jerked across the free throw line. The standard Mullin move would be to hop up and bank the ball in. That would be safe, efficient. And white. Instead, Mullin hurtled up, as best he could: *jammed!* The crowd rocked out. It was *such* an un-Mullin thing to do. It was probably what he did in his dreams. As he came down, a big grin wrinkled his face.

He walked past the U.S. bench. Bird—Mullin's predecessor and alter ego—stood up, smiled, and slapped Mullin's hand. Even Stockton smiled and said something to Mullin.

Seeing the three of them smile like that was a joy.

Beige Like Me

A photo of it would have made the perfect poster for the White Man's Disease telethon.

Laettner also stood and sort of smiled—sort of didn't. He wasn't at all close to Mullin. Laettner was—to some extent —becoming one of the boys. At least Barkley liked him. But he wasn't one of the white boys.

• Angola, New York

Of the original ten Olympians, three were white: Bird, Mullin, and Stockton. These three, for all their differences in personality, achievement, and style, were pretty similar: sallow-faced gym rats who can pass, set picks, move without the ball, shoot a high percentage, and hit dozens of free throws without a miss. They played *white* ball, plain and simple. It wasn't the NBA style that the rest of the world was dying to see.

Still, when it came time to augment the team, yet another white guy was added: Christian Laettner.

In selecting Laettner, however, USA Basketball wasn't getting just another melanin-deprived geek with a devotion to practice. They were getting the Great Beige Hope.

Christian Laettner is the only Olympian to grow up in the Bird-Magic era and to hit puberty in the Jordan era. He was the only Olympian who chose to play basketball not just because of his size but because it was *hip*. Laettner is the whitest kid, with the whitest name, from the whitest school —but he talks, dresses, dances, and acts black. Or, at least, beige. To him, basketball—and the black culture it is so connected to—is cool. And he is cool because he can play it.

Much of Laettner's attitude can be attributed to the NBA's marketing success. David Stern's NBA has given the primarily black sport the hip cachet that no sport has had among whites since the tennis boom of the 1970s. By 1992, Michael Jordan was among the people most admired by high schoolers of all races. Rap music was the official rhythm of the NBA, its advertisers, and their mutual consumers. And by 1992, millions of suburban white kids had decided that the hippest thing in the world was to act black.

So it seems as if Laettner's racial affectations are a race thing, a basketball thing, and—not least of all—an arrogance thing. As if to prove that a white guy from upstate New York can be as wild and tough-ass as any black kid from Harlem, Laettner has assumed a personality characterized by inscrutability, viciousness, and sexual ambivalence. When the Minnesota Timberwolves drafted Laettner, they must've been hoping that they were drafting the '90s model of Twin Cities legend George Mikan. But, instead, they may be acquiring basketball's version of another Minneapolis hero: Prince.

Remember George Carlin's routine about what happens when white guys and black guys hang out together? You don't wind up with black guys nicknamed Skip, but you do get redheaded kids saying, "Wha's happ'nin'?" Laettner attended a southern college and had black roommates, so maybe his spacey black/white twang is just a predictable youthful pretension.

Or, it might be a more deep-seated primal urge. Lou Reed zeroed in on faux-black behavior in a profane and prophetic song called "I Wanna Be Black." In it, Reed says he doesn't want to be a "fucked-up middle-class college student" any longer, but instead wants to run a stable of "foxy little whores." Well, who can blame a skinny, towheaded, suburban giant with a sissified name for acting like a *gangsta*?

"I'm thin and I don't look like a convict," Laettner says, "so they question my toughness." He demonstrates his toughness, though, with obnoxiousness, brutality, and a carefully constructed mask of alienation. Plus: a unique ability to succeed in nerve-shattering situations.

Laettner's childhood doesn't seem to have marked him for such a volatile personality. He was born two weeks after Woodstock, on August 17, 1969. With his brother and two sisters, he grew up in Angola, New York, a town of just a few thousand, some thirty miles southwest of Buffalo. His mother, Bonnie, teaches school there. His father, George,

Beige Like Me

has long been a printer at *The Buffalo News*. Very middle-class, white-America stuff.

The name Christian comes from Bonnie's adoration of Marlon Brando, who played characters with that name in *The Young Lions* and *Mutiny on the Bounty*. Because his older brother was already named Christopher and went by the nickname Chris, Laettner has always gone by his full first name.

Actually, his name might be the glue that first stuck the chip to his shoulder. "It's nerve-racking when you name a baby Christian," Bonnie says, "because from then on, you're always worried that someday he'll wind up behind bars." Her fears of his willfulness were confirmed early. A nursery school report card said: "Too much self-confidence."

Laettner had a plain enough—a *white* enough—childhood: He loved bow ties, always wearing one to church, and would primp endlessly before Mass. He also took piano lessons; like Olympic teammate David Robinson, he can play Beethoven's "Moonlight Sonata." However, he *skipped* down the street until he was about thirteen, causing his parents to worry that he wasn't maturing quickly enough. They decided to hold him back in school for a year.

He attended The Nichols School, an elite prep school in Buffalo that still requires students to wear jackets and ties. In fact, he *loved* Nichols. He had a summer job managing a tennis club. Other than his height, which led to his immersion in basketball, nothing made him stand out from other kids in his secure, small-town world.

Laettner—who has undeniable physical gifts—became an excellent player. He had steely nerves and thrived in high-pressure situations. He was also exceptionally competitive, a trait he adopted early, while competing against his brother.

In high school, Laettner had a tremendous profile, despite the obscurity of Nichols. He was named New York State Player of the Year and led his team to two state championships. He averaged 27.8 points and 17.5 rebounds as a senior, played in McDonald's All-Star games, and was ranked among the nation's best players. Heavily recruited, he was landed by Duke, a perennial Final Four entrant (and loser). Duke is noted for academic excellence and its wealthy and mostly white student body. It's basically just an Ivy League school with a New South accent.

Being white, 6–11, and a good outside shooter, Laettner was heralded upon his arrival in Durham as the next Danny Ferry (while that was still a compliment). But Ferry was a finesse player who seemed to vanish in big games. Laettner, on the contrary, turned out to be a warrior: in an epochal Eastern Regional Final against Georgetown and *its* hot freshman, Alonzo Mourning, Laettner compiled 24 points and 9 rebounds (utterly erasing Mourning, who fouled out).

The Georgetown game set a pattern: The bigger the game and the fiercer the opponent, the better Laettner played. Says Duke coach Mike Krzyzewski, "Since that Georgetown game, he's become as tough a kid as we've ever had here." Laettner thrashed big men Shaquille O'Neal and Larry Johnson in head-to-head play.

His season scoring average, which rose every year, was almost always topped by his tournament average. He became the all-time NCAA tournament leader in points, steals, and free throws.

He won two trips to the Final Four, in '91 and '92, with last-second jump shots. If he never does another thing on the basketball court, Laettner will be immortalized by the 1992 game. Against an excellent Kentucky team, he attempted ten shots from the field, and ten shots from the line—and made all twenty. To top it off, he hit a tough shot at the buzzer for the win.

As a senior, he swept the national Player of the Year awards, had his number retired while he was still playing, and led Duke to the first back-to-back championships since Bill Walton's UCLA days.

At the same time, he made a public spectacle of himself, his temper, and his sexuality. Only some of his behavior seemed related to his desire to be cool. The rest seemed to be just plain cruelty and arrogance.

One side of Laettner wanted the world to know how much he meant to his team: "What they want from me is *life*." The other side abused those very teammates. When he thought they were playing below their highest level, he lashed them with scorn. "If I see satisfied faces in the locker room, I'm jumping all over them," he says. "My problem is being brutally honest. People don't like that. I'm probably a jerk at times."

At *lots* of times, in fact. As a senior, Laettner was, like Ferry, presented with the next *him:* 6–11 Cherokee Parks, a puppy dog of a white kid raised by a single mom on the beaches of Southern California. Laettner shunned Parks socially, beat on him in practices, rode him verbally, and made the kid want to return home. Asked about the 1992 incident in which Laettner stomped the chest of a fallen Kentucky player during Laettner's greatest game, Parks said, "It's *so* Laettner. He's supposed to be like this All-American, this glamour boy, Mr. *GQ*. If you know Laettner, it's such a Laettner move to do something like that."

The Kentucky stomping wasn't Laettner's first such scrap. During the previous year's regional final, Laettner flashed Connecticut's Rod Sellers with an elbow (which the refs didn't see). Sellers, who retaliated by smashing Laettner's head into the floor, was suspended for a game. Laettner was not punished in either incident. He was let off the hook—some writers accused—just because he was white.

But Laettner's meanness was color-blind. During a junior-year loss to archrival North Carolina, Laettner body-slammed the very white Pete Chilcutt to the floor and then verbally assaulted the white ref who gave him a technical.

"You've heard of guys who want to win?" says Krzyzewski. "This guy's got a forest fire inside him."

Complicating his image further were the mind games he played with the press over his sexual preference. With his pretty face and somewhat prissy mien, he'd be under enough scrutiny. But how about walking around the Duke campus as a freshman holding another player's hand? Or running up to his roommate and best friend, Brian Davis, to kiss him on national TV after a dunk? How about telling a reporter that "I spend ninety-five percent of my time with Brian. I don't want anything else; I don't need anything else. . . . All I want to do is be with Brian. . . . That's it: basketball, school, and Brian."

Davis, confronted with questions about this behavior, fueled the fire: "We're so mature we know what being 'friends' is all about. We can tell each other we love each other."

Davis took credit for Laettner's famous narcissism: "Christian used to have a 'Bob' haircut. You know, nothing. Then he went with the skateboarder look. Finally, he got nice. I tell Christian he didn't get smooth until he started living with me. He spends an hour posing in front of the mirror. He knows he's the prettiest man walking."

Only a fool would've been surprised when people talked. When the debate over his alleged homosexuality became public, Laettner acted like a smart-ass preppie and refused to answer yes or no. "It made me seem mysterious," he says, "and I don't mind that. It made people think twice about me, and I don't mind that either." But Bonnie Laettner minded: "I told him, 'Christian, this sounds too bizarre.' He can't live without Brian? My God! Come on!"

The Duke sports information office made much about Laettner's living with a female student for much of his junior year. But Bonnie met her only once. "Christian has always kept his girlfriends private," she says, adding cryptically, "I think she really expanded his horizons."

As the NBA draft approached, general managers around the league tried their ham-fisted best to handle the question of Laettner's sexuality. They all said they doubted he was gay, but admitted they'd check any player for AIDS. They did research, interviewing Laettner's former roommates and others on the Duke campus. They tried to downplay their concern by pointing to other dangerous behaviors: "Who is more at risk—James Worthy inviting two hookers to his room or someone who happens to be gay?" asked one GM. Another executive said he might consider adding a contract clause that would release the team from any financial obligations if a player came down with AIDS.

Beige Like Me

The sexuality question wasn't the only blemish in Laettner's golden-boy veneer as the draft approached. There was also the matter of Krzyewski's threatening to unretire his number if Laettner didn't finish his degree in summer classes. Plus, there was an NCAA probe into a deal Laettner had made with *GQ*. The magazine had agreed to publish his senior-year diary, and people assumed they had offered to actually *pay* him. For a while, it seemed that Duke might have to forfeit its title.

But he got his diploma and cleared up the *GQ* situation. In fact, he was scheduled for the cover of *GQ*, and *People* magazine named him one of the World's Most Beautiful People. Then Minnesota drafted him third overall, behind only Alonzo Mourning and Shaquille O'Neal. Then he was chosen for the Olympic team.

Even after all this, though, there remained one last sobering question about Christian Laettner.

He was playing with the best basketball players in the world. He was ignoring the teenaged girls who squealed for him. He was handling his Olympic garbage-time assignments with a half-smile on his stiff face. But he must have been at least a little bit frightened.

Because the question that deviled him now was this: Was he experiencing the highlight of his life? Before he had played one NBA minute, had Christian Laettner peaked?

• Wise Guys

Barkley strolled into the locker room a couple of hours before the last game, still wearing a Band-Aid over the cut on the back of his immense shaved skull. The polished-head look was big in the NBA; Abdul-Jabbar had started it, and Jordan had elevated it to high style. It was just another expression of the NBA players' fetish for control: If I'm going bald, to hell with hair—I'll beat nature at its own game.

Sitting in front of Barkley's locker was a bowling ball with a bandage on it.

Barkley yelped out his high Eddie Murphy laugh.

Barkley stayed in a good mood as the game began. The U.S. charged off to a 15–0 lead. Barkley ran down the floor with a wild, happy look on his face. "Ya'll *ever* gonna score?" he taunted a skinny little Venezuelan defender.

As the score became meaningless, the game, as usual, turned into a spectacle—a museum piece depicting the art of basketball. The fans witnessed: Magic slipping through the entire Venezuelan team to score a lay-up. Ewing crashing into the Venezuelan "big man" so hard the guy fell flat and spun in a circle, like a break-dancer. Pippen sidearming a pass to Ewing so expertly that you couldn't even see his arms move; the ball just started flying toward Ewing as if pulled by a magnet. Laettner hitting seven of his ten shots and coming within a basket of leading the team in scoring. Barkley staring at Magic while Magic harangued a referee, then shouting, "Fuck, Magic, we're up by forty-five!" Magic pulling off Bird's warm-up pants in the last two minutes and coaxing Bird into the game. Bird making the last basket of the tournament—just like he'd made the first.

After the game, a researcher who was helping me made one final attempt to communicate with Christian Laettner. We'd been wondering what it was like for him to be on the cusp of wealth, at age twenty-two—with the risk of losing everything by playing in the Olympics. After all, if Laettner ripped apart his knee in one of these games—just weeks before he was to sign a contract for $10 or $15 million—he'd be penniless.

"Does that worry you at all—the thought of what an injury right now could mean to your life?"

"The most dangerous thing any of us ever does is drive a car. I'm not doing any of that these days, so I'm safe."

To my researcher, of course, that sounded ridiculous. "Actually," the researcher replied, "as far as getting injured goes, I'm sure it's more dangerous to play against Ewing or Sabonis than it is to drive a car."

No response.

"So you don't feel any sense of superstition about being so close to your pro contract?"

Beige Like Me

"I hadn't been thinking about it. But *thanks* for reminding me." He seemed to smile. But his smile wilted into a sneer. "Thanks a *lot.*"

Charles Barkley, however, was being much more pleasant. He was telling the reporters around him that, "We don't believe the bullshit the media writes about us. The majority of the media is a buncha assholes. Particularly when you live in Philadelphia." Then Barkley got into a friendly conversation with some of his friends from the Philadelphia press.

Bird looked happy. I don't know why. He was in constant pain, and his career seemed to be over. Somebody asked him if he would be watching these games on TV if he wasn't playing in them. "No," he said, "I never watch basketball on TV."

"How come?"

"Because I don't get any enjoyment out of watching it. I get enjoyment out of playing it. That's the way it's always been." The statement sounded very profound when he said it. Looking at it in print, it doesn't seem very profound. That's because the profundity came from the look in his eyes when he said it.

Magic, as usual, had the biggest crowd of reporters. He was telling them how the week had breathed new life into him and made him long to return to basketball. He told them that every night he'd been calling Cookie, who was home with the baby, telling her in great detail about every event of the day. They were discussing his retirement, he said, and would decide together—as man and wife—if he should return.

"What I wanna say now," he said softly, "is *thank* you.

"Stay with us in spirit," he said earnestly. "Say your *prayers* for us. And everything should be all-l-l right." The Magic smile.

In a real sense, Magic didn't talk much about basketball anymore. For him, basketball was often just a metaphor. When he talked these days, it was usually about life, death, love, and happiness. It was about the relationship of those four things—and about their inextricability.

Over the last week, he'd tasted joy again and groped for a

way to hold on to it, knowing that if he did, it might shorten his life. In just the course of a week, he'd seemed to grow in stature, and in wisdom.

Magic Johnson was no longer a case of arrested development.

Magic had grown up.

17

Bad Fear in Paradise

Paranoia in Monte Carlo • Focusing Past Topless Babes • Charles Joins the Swim Team • Grace Kelly Slept With This Guy? • Larry Lays Back • Michael Closes the Casinos • The Demons in Chuck Daly's Mind • Groupies and Wives • The Greatest Pickup Game in History • The Fear of Assassination • The Fear of Cops

There is no one on this earth who
is not twisted by fear and insecurity.
———Doris Lessing,
A Small Personal Voice, 1974

Professionalism is only a husk. The real
person must remain an amateur, a lover of the work.
———May Sarton,
Plant Dreaming Deep, 1968

There is no wealth but life.
———John Ruskin, 1880

"This just in from Hell. Spanish dictator
Francisco Franco is still dead."
———Anchorwoman Jane Curtin,
Saturday Night Live, 1975

The breeze swept in sweet and warm as a lover's caress.

Drifts of foam piled onto the cream-colored sand. Women in half-ounce bikinis—and less—stretched languidly on the shore, anxious for the sun to rise higher and brown their bodies. Roses perfumed the air. And *Daly wanted an early practice.* Jesus!

Forget about the fact that they had dragged into Monte Carlo this morning at 1:00 A.M. Forget that they were already *nine hours* ahead of West Coast time. Forget it was Sunday. Forget that there were gorgeous, ravenous groupies stalking the halls. Forget that their first "challenge" was Angola—a country that had three indoor basketball gyms. Daly was afraid they'd "lost their focus." He wanted to "get them back handling the ball."

Jee-*zus!* Daly had made a religion out of fear—and now they were all monks in his Order of Anxiety. Maybe it was Isiah—with all his manipulating and power trips—who'd made Daly so crazy. Maybe this was Isiah's Revenge.

Daly realized, of course, that Monte Carlo was paradisiacal. He knew it had been chosen as the pre-Olympic training site just to lure the elite players into participating. But now that they were actually here? Early practice!

They closed virtually all of the practice to the press. Had to. What if Angola *got wind of their plans?* It was a boring practice, though; the players were unmoved by Daly's paranoia. A couple of times, Magic had to yell at the guys to stop screwing around.

Bird and Stockton didn't even practice but did their own light workouts. Bird's back, though, was definitely better than it had been in Portland. He'd done the wise thing by limiting his action there. Last week, he'd even felt good enough to attend several days of a Celtics' rookie camp. But he'd been excruciatingly careful there, too. The plane ride to France, which he'd been dreading, hadn't been as bad as he'd feared. He'd gotten a full-reclining seat and had lain back in it with his legs propped on his two-foot-tall Mr. Back Relief cushion. His wife and his one-year-old son, Connor, had come along, so it had been a relaxed trip. Actually, it had been easier than a vacation flight on a commercial airliner, because he'd been able to stretch out whenever he'd wanted. He'd fed Connor his bottle and had let the baby loll around on his flat, hard stomach, which hadn't gained an ounce during his long layoff. At the end of the flight, Bird had gotten off the plane with a minimum of stiffness.

In a short media session after the practice, Bird said, "I did some running and shooting, but I didn't scrimmage with the team. I'm just trying to get to Barcelona healthy." Earlier in the year, Bird had told one of my researchers, "Sometimes, when the pain gets really bad, I just lay in bed and look up at the ceiling, and wonder if it's all worth it." But those misgivings seemed remote now. Bird was acting loose and casual and confident.

Stockton, as usual, seemed edgy and restrained, and mostly just talked about his broken leg. "I could probably run," he said, "but I don't want to do anything that backs up my recovery. I've been walking up steps, running in the pool, swimming and biking. I'm not ready to play forty minutes. But I'm not *needed* for that long."

For Stockton's workout today, he'd ridden a stationary bike. He was still walking with a limp. It seemed absurd, of course, for a man with a broken leg to be preparing to play in the Olympics. But Stockton was gutsy enough to do it. He was probably the toughest guy on the team.

Despite his injury, Stockton was enjoying himself. He'd brought his wife, Nada, and all three of their little boys. Most of the guys had packed their kids and wives onto the charter flight. Mullin and his wife, Liz, had brought their newborn, Sean. Jordan and Juanita had brought both their preschool boys, and Patrick and Rita Ewing were traveling with their one-year-old daughter, Randi.

Bringing the families had changed things a little; now it was no longer a boys-night-out atmosphere. But that was appropriate. Because The Boys were no longer boys.

Jordan hurried by. He was off to play golf. Then to a tennis lesson. Then to a casino. Juanita was watching the kids. Jordan was no longer a boy—but he still knew how to play.

• The American Beatles

"I'm goin' to the *pool,*" said Barkley, right after Monday's two-hour practice. "So long as there's *babes*—with no *tops.* I'm *quittin'* this team. Gonna join the *swim* team. Y'all think I'm Mark Spitz, 'fore the week's over."

Barkley was buoyant. Monte Carlo was having the desired effect on him and the rest of the team. It was impossible not to be happy here. Monte Carlo had been built for happiness.

"This place is a trip," said Barkley. "Damn! People well-*dressed* here. But you can't stay, cuz things *cost* too much. Beer cost you forty dollars. If you're a drunk, this is a damn good place, cuz you can't *afford* to be a drunk. Some people buy that stuff like Boone's Farm and Thunderbird— that stuff's probably six hundred, seven hundred dollars over here."

But Barkley was pissed at Monaco's Prince Ranier. The prince was supposed to have been at practice, but he'd blown it off. "I don't *appreciate* that," said Barkley. "They told us you can't *touch* him, and you have to call him 'your majesty.' I haven't called anyone 'your majesty' since Harold Katz." Barkley was still thrilled to be free of Sixer owner Katz, as well as the team of slugs and misfits Katz had thrown together.

Barkley was not looking forward to dinner that evening with the prince. "We gotta problem," he said. "We're supposed to stop eatin' when *he* stops—but what if we're still *hungry.* What if he has a snack before he comes over, and we're *starvin'?* Whatta you do, like, eat *fast?*" Barkley made a face, and got a laugh. But he wasn't being completely facetious; there was usually a serious kernel in Barkley's jokes. The moral of this joke was: I didn't come eight thousand miles to step back into the Dark Ages of kings and peasants. American capitalism had taken Barkley from peasant to king in about five years. And that, by God, was enough to make *anybody* misty-eyed about Uncle Sam.

Barkley absolutely demanded respect. He had sacrificed too much—and succeeded too well—to accept anything less. The same was true of everyone on the team. They were stars—and culture gods—and expected to be treated accordingly.

Within a week, though, these expectations would attract a flood of criticism—even hatred.

Jordan, who'd helped close the casinos this morning at 4:00, was also talking with reporters about respect. He was recalling the last time he'd been in the Olympics—under dictatorial coach Bobby Knight. In 1984 he'd had no choice but to endure Knight's drill-sergeant approach. When they'd contacted him last summer about the Olympics, Jordan said, "I reminisced about my participation in 1984. It was grueling, two-a-day practices, sometimes three, plus film. If that was going to be the case this year, there's no way I would have been here. Coach Daly assured me there was going to be a lot of relaxation, a lot of fun."

David Robinson was on the same theme, remembering how his 1988 Olympic coach, Georgetown's John Thompson, had dominated the team—trying to infuse it with rigidity and paranoia. "Access to us was difficult," said Robinson. "It was just an air—either you were an insider or an outsider, and outsiders didn't come in. I wasn't used to that, coming from the Naval Academy, where everything was so open. I had never been *anywhere* where the press was the enemy."

Robinson much preferred this year's atmosphere, in which the athletes had most of the power. Robinson was sick of hearing that the pros shouldn't be in the Olympics.

"When you think about college guys playing in the Olympics, with so much money available in the pros—what if you got injured or your value goes down?" Robinson said. "It's dumb."

After practice, a few of the guys, including Pippen and Mullin, went to the beach across the street from their hotel. Barkley went back up to the hotel's rooftop pool, which was cantilevered toward the beach and almost felt like part of the Mediterranean. Barkley, rumored to be estranged from his wife, was here alone. But Jordan wouldn't go anywhere near the water. Couldn't swim. Scared the hell out of him. He was off to the golf course, although it was disappointing:

no carts, no caddies. Nonetheless, he'd get in his eighteen holes.

Pippen wandered around the beach in a black U.S. Team T-shirt—in case somebody didn't recognize him—and checked out the beautiful women, many of whom were topless. The Mediterranean, clear and green, lapped at his bare feet. Around him waddled bloat-bellied Europeans; fitness was still largely an American fascination. Mullin, far too gym-bleached to risk sun, lay in the shade and squinted. "Oh, man, it's a rough life," Mullin said. "Watchin' people swim. Gettin' ready to have dinner with the prince." He shook his head.

But dinner with the prince turned out to be largely a bore. What excitement there was didn't come from the assembled royalty, but from The Boys themselves: Women squealed and men angled for handshakes. It was as if they were the American Beatles. The dining hall was packed with a bunch of tuxedoed Old World types, each of whom was the duke of this or the viscount of that—which was supposed to be cool. But wasn't. Not to the players. The players had all become princes through merit—not birth—and they had eminently more respect for one another than they did for any of the titled gentry. As much as they could, they clumped together. They let the prince come to them.

Prince Ranier was the perfect example of modern royalty: ordinary, foppish, and superfluous. It was hard to imagine that Grace Kelly had abandoned her regal position in the Hollywood meritocracy to marry this guy. It was harder still—seeing him now—to imagine that once upon a time she'd actually *slept* with him.

The prince gave Magic and Michael—sitting at a table together—special attention. But he didn't hang around long. Michael and Magic had to stand in the Prince's presence, and when they towered over you, it was hard not to feel short and dumpy. Even for a prince.

Magic—ever the diplomat—gave a quick speech. In it he said, "The closest I've been to royalty before was Michael Jordan." It was ingratiating—delivered with the Magic smile—but it was a nice little tweak, too. It reminded everyone: You may be kings, but we've got *God*.

Dinner broke up early. The casinos were waiting. So were the topless beaches, balmy and beautiful under the stars.

Besides, there was another minor annoyance on the schedule. They had a game tomorrow.

• American Beauty

A long jumper hit the back of the rim and bounced high into the air. All five members of the French national team—playing the Americans in an exhibition—crouched low, preparing to spring. The ball was still floating in the air when Barkley went after it. He kept rising and rising—as the French players waited for the ball to descend to their range. Rising, rising. The French players jumped. Barkley—now *feet* above everyone—grabbed the ball with one hand and hurled it through the net. Barkley landed softly and sprinted downcourt. The French team, still clotted under the basket, looked dumbstruck. They'd never seen such a combination of strength and leaping ability.

The crowd seemed to hold its breath, then roared. In the small stadium—3,500 seats—some of the fans were close enough to see the Olympians' subtle facial expressions and hear them talking to each other, and that always changed everything for a spectator. From the cheap seats or on television, the play of the Olympians often looked effortless and dispassionate—almost mechanical. But, up close— where you could hear them struggle for breath, and where you could look into their eyes—you could practically see the players' souls, so involved were they with the game. And then you saw that everything they did came from a deep well of passion.

After you saw that—even one time—you never felt the same about them. You knew that they were often still arrogant, and greedy, and hostile. But you also knew that they had, to a degree most people couldn't comprehend, abandoned their lives to love. Their love for this simple game—and for the others who played it well—was complete and profound.

In America, it was becoming the vogue—as the first Olympics allowing NBA players quickly approached—to bitch about the death of the amateur spirit. This amateur spirit: love of the game, not its rewards—was the purest thing in sports. Supposedly, this spirit was terribly threatened by the participation of pros.

Bemoaning this situation made good copy in the sports pages. Sounded lofty.

But it was absolute bullshit.

Because no amateur in the Olympics had a greater love for his or her sport than did each member of the U.S. basketball team. Every one of these elite basketball players would have played virtually all of their lives for free. They had, in fact, all played for free, for about the first fifteen years of their careers. And then, after becoming wealthy, they had made ungodly sacrifices to continue to play. Now, Magic Johnson —who was worth about $100 million—wanted to begin playing again, even though it might kill him.

On the sidelines, Prince Albert—heir to the Monaco throne—was doing the Arsenio fist-churn and going "woof-woof-woof!" Over here, Prince Albert was supposed to be hot stuff. In fact, all the members of the royal family were treated with quivering obsequiousness. Before the game, one of Prince Ranier's minions had approached a USA Basketball peasant and had told him the Prince wanted to watch the game with an expert. Specifically, Chuck Daly. "I don't think you understand," said the American. "Chuck is the coach."

"No," said the prince's aide, "I don't think *you* understand. Monsignor has asked for Chuck Daly." It took a serious negotiation to get the Prince to settle for Dave Gavitt, the president of USA Basketball.

The Prince was wearing a luxurious black suit, but he didn't look particularly overdressed in the one-hundred-dollar-seat crowd. Most of the men were wearing thousand-dollar jackets over Bulls or Lakers T-shirts, and most of the women were sutured into flashy, skimpy spandex outfits that weighed less than their jewelry.

As the game ended, the crowd began to chant, "Ma-jeek! Ma-jeek! Ma-jeek!" It was the fourth time in the game they'd cried his name. He stood by the sidelines and waved. Even Prince Ranier was chanting.

Magic was visibly moved. Maybe he was remembering how they'd chanted "Ma-jeek, Ma-jeek" in Paris last fall—which was now so long ago, another lifetime.

After the game, Magic told the reporters, mostly from the French media, "I'm here to help teach the rest of the world our game, and to inspire the kids." These days, he was downplaying his "mission from God" routine. It hadn't gone over too well; he just wasn't a believable spokesperson for chastity. He was also frustrated with the political work he'd done to fight AIDS. George Bush had just been trying to exploit his celebrity, and Magic was thinking of quitting Bush's AIDS panel. Bush didn't seem to be serious about solving the problem. But quitting would take courage. When Magic had first gotten HIV, he'd said he thought he could beat the disease. Many people had believed him, in part because they knew he'd be fighting it with a great deal of money and political power. To quit the panel would be to admit that he couldn't power-politick his way past AIDS. It would mean facing the fact that he was as vulnerable as people with no political connections.

One of the French reporters asked him if he thought the American victories in Barcelona would be slaughters, like they'd been at the Tournament of the Americas. "It's one thing," Magic said, "to be a bully—but it's another to be beautiful, and play beautiful basketball. These people in Europe want to see us live, just one time. They want to be close to us. The kids want you to touch them. The more we come over here, the better it will be for basketball—and that's what the Olympics is all about."

The French reporters nodded, almost in unison. The world still loved Magic Johnson.

Daly, though, seemed jittery after the game. "We showed the effects of two weeks off," he said. "We were *not* sharp.

The whole team was rusty. We needed this work to get back to the way we *need* to play."

He wanted to have an intra-squad scrimmage tomorrow. Give the guys some *real* competition.

• The Greatest Pickup Ever Played

"I'm bustin' you, M.J.!" Magic taunted Michael. He told Jordan that Jordan better "get into the show"—because if he didn't, Magic's team was going to whip his ass.

But as soon as Magic had said it, he knew he'd made a mistake.

"I'm gonna bring us back," said Jordan, cool and confident.

The scrimmage had started off as usual, with Daly loading Jordan's side with the players Magic considered the better unit. On Jordan's team were Pippen—with whom Jordan always played well—and Bird, Ewing, and Malone. Magic had Barkley, Mullin, Robinson, and Laettner. Daly had stacked the odds against him, Magic believed, as a way to challenge him. Daly was constantly manipulating.

And it had worked. Magic's team had jumped to a 14–2 lead. They'd done it mostly with classic, European-style basketball—penetrate and pitch.

So Magic hadn't been able to resist talking trash to Michael.

But the second Magic mocked him, Jordan got serious. Magic wasn't the only one who was obsessed with winning. Jordan took the ball down himself, hesitated, exploded, and dunked. *"I'm* bustin' *you,* M.J.," Jordan sneered, staring at Magic. Then Jordan dunked again, hit some jumpers, made an assist—and the game was almost tied.

It got personal. Barkley powered down a terrifying dunk over Malone. Jordan scowled at Malone and said, "You gonna let him get away with that?" Jordan dribbled downcourt and fired a pass to Malone. Malone lunged toward the hoop, crashed into Barkley, and smashed the ball through the net.

Stockton sat on the bench, wide-eyed. He'd never seen such great basketball—not at any All-Star Game, and sure as hell not at the Tournament of the Americas. He felt like a fan.

Robinson got the ball and leaped toward the basket. A whistle shrilled. Robinson had been fouled. But the referee, who couldn't speak English, indicated it was a nonshooting foul.

Barkley's eyes got huge. As the rest of the team ran downcourt, he stood, stiff-legged. "What's goin' on!" he yelled at the ref. "You guys got *money* on the game? How can you say that ain't a shooting foul?"

"Charles!" Daly boomed. "Get your ass back in the game!"

Barkley jogged downcourt, shaking his head.

Jordan hit a three-pointer over Magic. Magic looked pissed. He felt like every time he tried to stop Jordan, he just ended up looking at the bottom of Jordan's sneakers.

Magic dribbled downcourt, kept the ball, and shot over Jordan's head. *Rip!*

The fouls started getting brutal. Daly began to look nervous. Foul on Magic. "Just like Chicago Stadium!" Magic bitched. "They picked up Chicago Stadium and moved it to Monte Carlo!"

"It is," Jordan replied, "the nineties!" Ohhh—cold: Michael was telling Magic his era had passed. Magic didn't laugh. This scrimmage, which far surpassed any other contest they'd had since becoming a team, was the greatest playground game in history. And Magic did *not* want to lose it.

Despite its intensity, the scrimmage was a relief for Magic. It had been a tough day. Today he'd announced that after twelve years, he was torching his deal with Converse. He was fed up with them and blamed them for costing him millions in lost opportunities. If they hadn't screwed up, he might have hit the immortality level a decade ago, and would now have enough money to finance his dream of owning a franchise.

"Converse is still living in the 1960s and seventies,"

Magic had said. "They haven't arrived in the eighties and nineties, where advertising and marketing are the keys. When I came on, we had Larry, me, Julius Erving, Kevin McHale, and later Isiah Thomas. I kept telling them they weren't taking advantage of that situation.

"At that time, everybody on the playground was calling Converse shoes 'Docs,' because of Dr. J. I said they should just call the shoes 'Docs.' But they told me a player will *never* sell shoes. Then Michael Jordan came along and proved them wrong. But they're *still* sayin' it."

After dealing with that issue, Magic had addressed the possibility of returning to the NBA—but not as a Laker. The Lakers had apparently pissed him off once too often since he'd retired last November.

First, owner Jerry Buss had refused to sell him the team, then GM Jerry West had sounded ambivalent about his return. After that, when there'd been speculation about Magic's coaching the Lakers, West had been nonreceptive.

So Magic had said that he thought the Lakers might be entering a "rebuilding phase," which he did not want to be part of. He wanted to be with a championship contender. "I'm looking for wherever would put me in the thick of it," he said.

One of the teams he was considering was the Knicks. But that would mean a reunion with intense coach Pat Riley, who loved endless, body-killing practices. Earlier in the year, I'd heard that Magic had long been sick of Riley. Sources on the Lakers had told me that Magic had played a major role in Riley's "resignation" from L.A. in 1990. On the other hand, though, Riley had been steadfast in his support for Magic after Magic had contracted HIV. Also, Riley was a winner—and Magic was fixated on winning.

All of these things had been on Magic's mind before the scrimmage. But now that he was playing, all he had to think about was winning.

But he lost. With a second and a half left, Jordan hit two free throws to ice it. Jordan strutted off the court. Magic still looked pissed.

Jordan stopped to talk to the press. He seemed to be

floating. "I'm not sure people will ever see the true greatness of this team," he said. "But a little of it came out today. And it was a *beautiful thing*. A *really* beautiful thing."

Daly looked relieved. He'd gotten them motivated. And they hadn't maimed each other.

They were ready—at last—for the 1992 Olympic Games.

• Fascist Pigs

The cops weren't sweating. *Everybody* was sweating. You could practically see a gray cloud vaporizing overhead from the sweat of the crowd. But the cops were ice dry.

And half of them were in heavy riot gear—khakis with quilted shins and canvas jackets. It was not the coolest outfit for a tropical Barcelona night.

But the *policia* didn't seem to care about the heat. They could *will* the heat away. You could tell they had that power just by looking hard into their eyes. If you had the *guts* to. I didn't. They scared the hell out of me.

The only apparent concern of the *policia* was keeping this crowd in line—no matter what it took. The U.S. basketball team was on its way, and it was clear that the *policia*'s inviolable mandate was: no assassinations. Not even a *minor* assassination—of a lesser figure, like Stockton.

It had been obvious from the moment I'd arrived in Barcelona that the first order of business in the 1992 Olympic Games was to run a blood-free show. Which was not as easy as it sounded. The Serbs and Croats and Bosnians were murdering each other. So were the people of several African nations. Half the Middle East was looking for someone to kill. There were even separatists in this part of Spain—Catalonia—who would've been happy to blow the U.S. team to Hell just to make the evening news.

But, even without these threats, the *policia* would have probably kept a tight rein on a crowd like this. They seemed to be the kind of cops who *liked* to fracture heads. They were the kind of cops Rodney King has nightmares about.

Supposedly, the Spanish national police force had been

reformed in 1975, after dictator Francisco Franco had died and gone to hell. Now there was no more systematic torture or imprisonment without charge. Well—maybe just a *little*. But not enough for most Spanish people to get worked up about. After thirty-six years of Franco, they were relatively tolerant of . . . aggressive conservatism. In fact, a number of them professed to *miss* Franco. Things had actually *worked* when he'd had his bloody claws in the state. Things weren't so efficient anymore. The reigning attitude now was basically: *"tranquilo"*—which translates roughly to "chill out." Supposedly, the Catalonians were the most efficient and industrious people in Spain. They felt superior to people from southern Spain, whom they called "Africans." But a Catalonian wouldn't last a second in New York City. That, as Charles Barkley might say, is not cultural bias—it's a *fact*.

Most of the people in this crowd outside the hotel, though, were not Catalonians. They were Americans. You could tell. Bermuda shorts. Cameras. Bart Simpson shirts. They wanted to see the *home team*. So did I.

I'd been standing outside the Hotel Ambassador for about an hour, and my nerves were shot. I wanted to get into the air-conditioned lobby. Fat chance. A cop with an automatic rifle slung over his shoulder was standing in front of the door, and the only way to get past him was to be registered —which was impossible, since the basketball team had rented virtually every one of the ninety rooms. The rooms went for nine hundred dollars a day (representing about eighty thousand dollars a day in hotel costs for the team and its staff). That kind of expense was part of the reason USA Basketball had been so frantic when Jordan had challenged their monopoly on merchandising: They *needed* to sell all those T-shirts. Luckily for them, they *had*.

The hotel was very nice, but not exactly what you'd expect for nine hundred bucks. It offered suites, an elegant restaurant, and a well-furnished game room: pool table, Ping-Pong, four Nintendo screens, and about 150 cartridges. There were VCRs in every suite, and you could get in-house manicures and pedicures. Not bad. But nine *hundred*?

Bad Fear in Paradise

I thought *I* was being extravagant to pop three hundred dollars a night for a fifth-floor walk-up. Compared to the USA Basketball crowd, though, I was a miser. But why not cut your own fingernails and pocket the six hundred dollars.

At last! A scream of sirens. A cop in a green tank stuck his head out the top hatch and scanned madly for snipers. A bus with an all-glass front pulled up and out straggled the players' wives and kids. The bus crept through the crowd, and another bus dumped off a herd of USA Basketball executives—all of whom, needless to say, had important and indispensable functions here. They were bitching about the bus ride—two and a half hours from the airport, almost twice the length of their flight from Monte Carlo.

A Spanish boy next to me said, "When Mah-cheek comes, get a signing for me, okay?" The Spanish people, I'd found, were generally more open and helpful than most Americans were and expected the trait in others. How could I tell the kid that when "Mah-cheek" got here, it would be every man for himself? He was too young to know about the American Way. He'd find out soon enough—America owned about a third of the companies in town.

When the players' bus pulled up, Daly was the first to pile out and was followed by the assistant coaches. Then Bird stepped off and got a huge cheer. Jordan hopped off, and an even bigger cheer echoed down the narrow street. Then Magic. The crowd bleated *"Maaaa-jik!"* Magic played to the crowd as best he could, but he got swept into the lobby and disappeared. He was wearing shorts and a short-sleeved shirt, and the front of the shirt looked wet with sweat. Magic seemed tired and distracted. For the first time since his appearances at the McDonald's Open in Paris last fall, he seemed haggard.

Sometimes I wondered why he missed this life so much.

• The Power of the Press

The American Beatles! On tour! It was amazing: the Team had come to a media pavilion for a standard-issue press conference, with no big announcements—on a day when dozens of events were unfolding—and the pavilion was jammed with *fifteen hundred* journalists. Instead of using the usual format, in which each player is installed in his own little area to allow more personal contact, they'd lined up all the players in a row—like the Beatles had done when they'd given press conferences.

I'd gotten too close to this story. I'd been thinking it was mostly my own obsession—but it was clear that the whole world had fixated upon this team.

And that was dangerous—for the Team. Because what the media creates, the media destroys. The media had done this, individually, to Michael and Magic this year—building them as gods, then exposing their human frailty. And the media was almost certain to do it to the Team as a whole. They practically *had* to. That would be the only fresh angle they could wring out of these games. There would be no real jeopardy in the games themselves, because America was certain to win. The jeopardy would revolve around image: Are the U.S. players *good guys* . . . or *bad guys?*

The Boys seemed to know what was coming and played right into it, donning black hats without much coaxing. Somebody asked Barkley about the first team they would play, Angola, and he said, "I don't know anything about Angola—except that they're in trouble." But he said he didn't feel sorry for the other teams. "Why don't they just take their ass-whipping like people and go home?"

Barkley said, "A lot of those foreign guys don't like us because we're the glamour boys. But some of these teams—Lithuania, Croatia, Germany, Spain—they'll give us a good game." He paused. "For a half."

Stockton, who usually took pains to be uncontroversial, got defensive about the fancy hotel they were staying at—which was a topic of great interest to the journalists. "It really isn't a rich and poor question," he said. Instead, he said, it was simply that they were the . . . American Beatles: "The visibility of this team obviously is quite a bit different than that of the other teams in the Olympic Village."

But a reporter followed up by asking Stockton if the Team

wasn't violating the Olympic spirit. "The Olympic spirit, to me, is to go out and beat the other athletes from the rest of the world," said Stockton, "not to live with them. We have a saying in Utah: 'The Indians didn't have dinner with Custer.' So we're not intending to go out and make a lot of friends."

Daly, arguing that there weren't any beds long enough in the Village, asked Ewing and Robinson to stand—as if none of the journalists realized they were tall.

Somebody asked Jordan what it was like "to be called a god." He didn't issue a blanket disclaimer—which would have been wise in a devoutly Catholic country. Instead, he said, if someone called him a god, "I'll take it and run with it."

Even Drexler, of all people, indulged in a public ego trip, saying that the *real* challenge to this team would be taking on the rest of the world. "I'd love to play an all-star team from the whole world," he said. "We'd welcome the challenge." Of course, he had a good idea—it would be inordinately more interesting than the massacres that were approaching. Nonetheless, it raised eyebrows.

The reporters, scribbling madly into their notebooks, looked content. They had a serviceable angle: the Ugly American. It had worked for decades, and it would work now. It would have been better to find out that the whole team was on steroids or that one of the players had gotten arrested for beating his wife. But that was hoping for too much.

Magic looked a little concerned. His forehead was wrinkled. In his calmest diplomat's voice, he said, "We've all put our spirit into this. We gave up our summer. We're here free. A lot of people are putting their livelihoods at stake, but we're having the time of our lives. If we get press, that's fine. If we don't get press, that's fine. We'll only help bring more media here and get everybody more attention."

It was an effectively conciliatory speech, and it took some of the air out of the Ugly American angle.

But then, that evening, Jordan and Mullin blew off the Opening Ceremonies, and the buzz started again.

The Ugly American angle even showed up in the American press. But why not? They had to sell papers, too.

And once the press got rolling with that angle, they had to stick with it. Otherwise, how could they maintain their credibility?

Of course, it wasn't all media artifice. The players were, for the most part, almost comically arrogant. And some of them often acted like complete assholes.

That's what made the angle so easy to sell.

• Fearless

Thunk! Barkley's elbow sank into the chest of a skinny little kid from Angola. The elbow seemed to keep sinking into the chest, deeper and deeper, as if it were plunging into bread dough. Then *sssuck!*—Barkley pulled it back out. The little Angolan, Herlander Coimbra, got a sick look on his face, and he seemed to choke a little. Barkley kept running downcourt. The referee blasted his whistle. The mostly-Spanish crowd, which had been cheering for America, began to whistle derisively. The whole stadium seemed to tremble with the shriek.

Barkley got a technical, and Coimbra made a free throw. It broke the U.S. momentum. Until then, the U.S. had been on a 31–0 run. But over the next few minutes, with Coimbra's foul shot, the U.S. was held to a 46–1 run. But it was enough.

Before the game, Daly had fired up the team by telling them that the Angolan coach had said they didn't play defense. Daly never quit! He was *still afraid.*

After the carnage, though, the U.S. guys were unhappy. They were pissed off at Barkley. Jordan had taken him aside and chewed him out, and then Michael bad-mouthed Barkley to the press. "If he keeps doing things like that," Jordan said, "they could kick him out of the Olympics. There's no *place* for it. We were dominating the game. It *could* cause negative feelings about the U.S."

Well . . . yes . . . it could.

In fact, by the next day, the elbow incident would be replayed on virtually every television station in the world and described in most of the world's newspapers. The Ugly American angle was now accepted as God's truth everywhere on earth.

But Charles didn't care. "He hit me," Barkley said, "so I hit him. It's a ghetto thing—an eye for an eye, you know."

Actually, though, people who'd reviewed the game's tape hadn't seen Coimbra hit Barkley at all. But maybe Coimbra had been really *rude* to Barkley—and maybe that was a ghetto thing, too.

Barkley offered absolutely no apology. He'd met Coimbra after the game, and Coimbra—a hell of a nice guy, a big fan of Charles—had asked that their picture be taken together. Charles had happily obliged. So what was all this *whining* about?

Charles had a recommendation. "If people don't like it," he said, "then turn the fucking TV off."

Charles wasn't worried about it. Charles had no fear.

18

The
Ugly American

Scottie's Revenge • Magic's Mind •
The World's Ugliest Whores • Picasso on Acid •
Outlaw Trinket Punks • Charles to
America: "Eat My Shorts" • Dirty Talk in a
Foreign Tongue • Jordan's Ego •
Gothic-Quarter Hashish

Losing is the great American sin.
—John R. Tunis, 1977

Instead of leading the world, America
wants to buy it.
—Thomas Mann, 1947

The business of America is business.
—Calvin Coolidge, 1925

All Americans are rich.
—*The Ugly American,*
William J. Lederer and Eugene Burdick

"Cobi *sucks,* is the problem," said green-haired Rick, sneering at the pin of the goofy-looking, faux-Picasso Olympic mascot. "I won't trade for him, and I sure as hell won't buy him."

"Okay, Cobi *does* suck, I admit that—he's an overworked pin," said the boy in the blue Michigan State sweatshirt. "But this is *more* than Cobi. A *lot more.* This is Cobi *dunking over Magic.*"

"This is a *bootleg* Cobi dunking over Magic," said Rick, checking the back of the pin for the official Olympic logo. Rick—who'd dyed his hair green today to throw off the *policia*—was a *professional.* Rick *knew* pins. He said he had $8,500 worth of them "back at my crib," and he had $2,000 worth of them right here, pinned to a broad swatch of brown velvet. Rick had financed his trip here selling pins—dime-sized caricatures of various Olympic figures. He'd sold pins at the Winter Olympics in Albertville, and he'd worked two World Series and one Super Bowl. Rick was a "trinket punk," and proud of it. Only problem was: *policia.* He'd gotten run off from here yesterday, he said, for selling pins without a license, and had returned today only under the guise of green hair.

"They busted this buddy of mine—okay?—and they're gonna take him down to the cop shop," Rick said. "And he's holdin', like, *two pins.* They take him down for two—I shit you not—pins. One of 'em's a USA Basketball and the other's that lame yellow torch."

"That's *all?"*said the guy from Michigan State. He knew those pins; some pins were worth $300 or $400, but those pins were tourist trash.

"That's *all,"* said Rick. "It was just that he didn't have the license. He'd *tried* to get the license, but the Olympic guys told him the same thing they told me: "No way, pal—this is *our* monopoly." Cuz you *know* what the Olympic guys are about."

The kid from Michigan State rubbed together his thumb and forefinger: the universal sign for money.

"You got it," said Rick, and they did a soft high-five. "So they throw my buddy in back of one-a those big green vans—with all these pickpockets and perverts—and drag him downtown and toss him into a holding cell. And he's like, shittin' doughnuts, cuz all's he can hear is guys moanin' and screamin', and he doesn't know—is that just the drunk tank, or are they gettin' *confessions* outta people?" Rick squinted over my shoulder. "Put your tape recorder back in your bag real slow," he said.

In a few moments, a cold-eyed national policeman appeared from behind me and motioned at us with the butt of his rifle to get away from the basketball stadium's bus entrance.

After he'd left, I said, "What's wrong with a tape recorder?"

"I dunno. They just don't like 'em. *Hate* cameras. Especially Handycams. Don't even *think* about trying to take a picture of one of 'em. Jeeze," he said, "that was kinda scary. That was the same cop that hassled me yesterday. Do you think he saw my stuff?"

"I don't think so," said the Michigan State kid. "Your buddy. Did he get out?"

"Yeah, he had enough pesetas to pay his fine. *Cash,* man—don't leave home without it."

"It's *everywhere* you wanna be," said the boy from Michigan State. They high-fived again. "Look," he said to Rick, getting back to business, "I'll keep my Cobi, and I'll sell you six—*six*—U.S. basketball players of *your choice* for two hundred bucks. But no Magics. I can sell Magics back in Lansing for *whatever I want.* And I gotta keep some Magics for myself, cuz he's my man."

"Throw in your ticket to the game."

"Noooo. This is *Croatia,* man. *Kukoc.* He's the Magic of Europe."

"Not tonight, he's not. Not against Scottie."

Suddenly, a tank on rubber tires rumbled up behind us, and a policeman popped out of the top and crouched behind a machine gun on a turret. Overhead, two helicopters dove low and hovered, hitting us with their spotlights. The wind from their blades scattered papers and yellow dust. A dozen police cars charged toward us, from different directions, making that eerie *ee-uh-ee-uh-ee-uh* sound that makes you feel like you're Anne Frank. Their flashing blue lights strobed the entire area.

The Ugly American

Rick fumbled around with his pins, trying to stuff them into his shirt. He looked scared to death.

Jesus! Was this *it?* Imprisonment in a foreign country—for consorting with outlaw trinket punks?

A huge bus wheeled around the corner, following a row of cop cars. It headed straight for us. Was it a paddy wagon for arrogant foreign hoodlums?

A crowd that had been lined up for beer broke ranks and engulfed the bus, slowing its progress.

The bus was almost on top of us. "Ho! Lee! Shit!" said the kid from Michigan. "It's . . . America!" Rick fished out his camera and started shooting.

There they were, looking out the windows and waving: Jordan, Bird, Pippen, Mullin, Malone, Robinson, Barkley. Pippen seemed to see me and waved. Then Magic rolled by. Somehow, his eye caught the logo of Michigan State, his alma mater. He pointed at the kid from Michigan State and then gave him the thumbs-up sign. The bus rumbled on past and disappeared down an inclined driveway leading to the basement of the stadium.

The kid from Michigan State was practically catatonic. "That . . . was . . . just . . . fucking . . . excellent! Did you . . . *see* that?"

"I got a *picture* of it," said Rick. "A *couple* of pictures. You and him together. I got him givin' you the thumbs-up, and you peein' your pants."

"Oh-my-God! You gotta give me a print."

"I will. Let's have lunch. We'll talk about it."

"You son of a bitch. This is, like, a sacred thing, man."

"Sports is a business." Rick shrugged.

"But he's my *man.*"

"Have your people call my people," said Rick. "We'll work out the details." He smiled. The police lights were still bouncing off his green hair. I looked for irony in his smile but couldn't find any. "You still have that ticket?"

I don't think he cared about watching the game. He probably just wanted to walk over to the entrance gate and unload it for $200 or $300. He was, after all, a professional. And this was the professionals' Olympics.

The Golden Boys

• The Magic Johnson of Europe

Croatia's Toni Kukoc, a sweet-faced child of twenty-three, made an old-fashioned, two-handed chest pass to inbound the ball. It was hard to understand how Kukoc could look so innocent. He made $3 million a year in salary and about the same in endorsements. His country was in the most vile war Europe had seen since the days of Hitler. But he looked like he'd never seen a moment of suffering, nor one of sin. He was a 6–10 cherub.

But before Kukoc's chest pass had traveled five feet, Michael Jordan had somehow materialized—as if from hyperspace—and grabbed it. Kukoc's face changed. He'd been waiting for this game all of his life, and already—almost before it had begun—it was altering his view of the world. It was making him less innocent. For years, basketball experts had been telling Kukoc that he was one of the greatest players in the world. The standard line was that he was "the Magic Johnson of Europe." Chicago GM Jerry Krause, who'd drafted Kukoc in 1990, had offered him $2 million a year back then, even though Krause was paying Pippen only about $700,000. It had infuriated Pippen but had been terribly flattering to Kukoc. Kukoc had turned Krause down repeatedly, however. Kukoc was making a fortune in Europe and was a god there.

Recently—even though Krause had sweetened the offer to $3 million—Kukoc had again refused it. The Yugoslavian Civil War was raging, Kukoc's family was in peril, and he wanted to stay close.

But Kukoc was dying to know how he would do in the NBA. Was he really as great as everyone said? He'd been looking forward to this game for the answer.

But the game was a sickening shock. Jordan was *so* fast. After Jordan grabbed Kukoc's chest pass, he began to streak straight toward Croatia's Drazen Petrovic, who was blocking his path downcourt. Petrovic, who'd become a star for New Jersey, was quick—even quicker than Kukoc. But Jordan blurred past Petrovic before Petro could even start moving. Jordan took three long dribbles as he sailed toward the U.S. basket, then launched himself. He galloped two steps in midair, then threw the ball down through the hoop with both hands. Kukoc stood and stared.

Petrovic floundered after Jordan and retrieved the ball. Jordan said something to Petrovic; it seemed to be hard-edged, judging by Jordan's expression. I was sitting close to them, but the crowd was cheering too loud for me to hear Jordan. The crowd loved the American team. The Americans were so good they were a fantasy—like a Hollywood movie. Plus, they were rich, and that gave them as much cachet as their skills. Nobody in the crowd could aspire to an NBA career, but *everybody* in the crowd wanted to be rich. Many of the Europeans had grown up in semifeudal societies or communist dictatorships, and to them, the capitalist meritocracy was as intoxicating as wine.

The only thing that pissed off the mixed Spanish and international crowd was demonstrations of American arrogance. To be a rich American was one thing, but to be an Ugly American was quite another.

Jordan was fired up. All the Americans were. The mood in the U.S. locker room had been tense and nasty before the game. Croatia was their toughest competition in the Olympics, and Daly had the guys thinking that with bad luck Croatia could win. That was ridiculous, of course, but when Daly really wanted to, he could twist anyone's head. Daly was a sophisticated man, but one of his favorite writers was sports novelist John R. Tunis, who'd written a number of emotional, simpleminded paeans to the purity of athletic competition. Daly really believed all that old-fashioned, win-one-for-the-Gipper stuff, and he could get players to believe it, too.

But to Pippen and Jordan, the game was more than just another opportunity to give it the old college try. It was personal: It was them against Kukoc. Pippen, in particular, was looking for a fight. For many, many months, Krause had delayed giving Pippen a raise, hoping that Kukoc would join the team. If Kukoc had, Krause would have given Kukoc money that would otherwise have gone to Pippen. That had gnawed at Pippen's confidence, amplifying the insecurity he already felt from competing against Jordan.

Jordan had the same basic grudge against Kukoc. Krause was paying Jordan $2.5 million but offering Kukoc $3 million. That hit Jordan square in the ego.

Kukoc—now dribbling near the three-point line—looked at Pippen in front of him and Magic underneath the hoop, and seemed to gather his nerves. He was, after all, supposed to have some *moves*—he was the *Magic of Europe!* So he lurched toward the basket. The defense converged on him as he went up in the air. He looked left and swung the ball to the right, passing to a teammate with exquisite grace; then the ball went back to Petrovic at the three-point line. Nice ball movement—but they were *back where they started*. The idea was to score.

The same thing happened all the time to teams that played the U.S. They moved the ball well, even spectacularly, but when it came to the moment of truth—*making the basket*—they fell to pieces. It was mostly a failure of the mind. Maintaining focus on the hoop while you battled aggressively was probably the hardest thing in basketball. It was achieved consistently only by people with extraordinary mental abilities—like Jordan, Mullin, Bird, Magic, Barkley, and Stockton. No other players in the world seemed to combine aggression and intellect so effectively as the Americans did.

Barkley got the ball and was muscling down low, right in front of where I was sitting. As a precaution against getting stuck in Press Siberia—up behind the cheap seats, where most of the journalists were crammed—I'd bought a choice, courtside seat for the Games. It hadn't been easy, and it hadn't been cheap, but it was worth it. The people around me were serious basketball fanatics—mostly Catalonians—who came to this stadium all winter long to support the home team, Badalona. Badalona was an industrial suburb of Barcelona and had one of the finest teams in Europe. It was a tough town; Barcelona was like San Francisco, and Badalona was like Oakland. The fans here really knew how to mouth off.

The guy beside me—Carlos—hated Barkley, and kept yelling, *"Bark-a-lee! Come mierde!"* Which meant, he told me, "Eat shit!" Another favorite of his, and of others sitting nearby, was, *"Me cago en tu leche!"*—"I shit in your milk!" When Carlos *really* wanted to hurt a player—and he often did—he'd yell, *"Me cago en la leche de tu puta madre!"* That meant, "I shit in the milk of your mother the whore." Fighting words. But he knew Barkley couldn't understand him, so he did his best to harass Barkley in English. Carlos worked for a condescending American manager at a U.S.-owned factory, and he was sick of American arrogance. He was still pissed off at Barkley for hitting the Angolan.

As Barkley dribbled, with his butt right in front of us, Carlos yelled, "Bark-a-lee! *Fock* you!"

Barkley got fouled. Went to the line. His free throw came off the rim hard, and Barkley leaped after it. But one of the Croatians also went for it, and the ball caromed out of bounds. When Barkley ambled by us, Carlos yelled, "Bark-a-lee! Fock you! And momma!" Some of the other fans were screaming at Charles, too. Barkley took out his mouthpiece and growled, "You shut the fuck up."

Carlos stood and shouted, *"Me cago en la leche de tu puta madre!"* Barkley stalked off. A referee blasted his whistle. Technical on Barkley, for cursing at the crowd.

"I got *Bark-a-lee.*" Carlos grinned.

"That's good," I said, "but don't say anything about his grandmother. That would be the wrong milk to shit in."

Carlos nodded and didn't ask why. He understood family values.

Daly paced the sidelines, confused and hyper. "What happened?" he said. Someone told him, and he scowled.

Barkley seemed to be in his own remote world. Jordan had to tell him they'd called a technical on him.

"What for?" said Barkley.

Jordan said it was for talking to the crowd, and Barkley laughed. When the crowd saw that, they began whistling derisively. The U.S. was losing support. Magic shot a dark glance at Barkley. He was here to stroke the European market, not alienate it.

A few minutes later, Petrovic missed a free throw, and Magic grabbed the rebound. He jerked downcourt with his strange, high dribble, stringing together the constant series of fakes that made defenders crazy. He did a crossover dribble to his left hand, bumped past one defender, pulled the ball back toward his chest, then flipped up a shot. But as he shot, his body seemed to implode upon itself, collapsing toward its center. As he came down he grabbed the back of his knee and walked flat-footed. He limped downcourt, and within seconds Pippen and Mullin were helping him struggle off the court.

There was no way for Magic or anyone else to know how badly he was injured. But it was obviously a knee injury, and that was always ominous. It seemed quite likely, since the Games would be over in a week, that Magic had just played his last minute in the Olympics, and maybe the last minute of his career. But there it was: the Magic smile. He sat on the bench, grinning and high-fiving and yelling instructions to the guys as if there were no possible way anything bad could happen to him.

Just watching him—seeing his joy, his involvement with a game he was no longer part of—became as absorbing as the game itself. He was so unrelentingly positive. It was almost impossible to think of anyone quite like him.

Every time he hoisted himself off the bench, the fans cheered.

And it again became evident, watching him deal so well with this, why his illness, and his resistance to it, meant so much to so many. He was the ultimate warrior, fighting the ultimate war. He was—like everyone alive—doomed. He would die. Maybe soon, maybe not so soon. But he was facing death the way we all should. Laughing. Forgetting about it.

Before the game ended, Pippen stuck one more knife in poor Toni Kukoc—who had virtually no points, no rebounds, no nuthin'. After a blocked shot, Pippen tore downcourt, running so fast he hardly touched the ball to the floor. Petrovic was waiting under the basket. Pippen sprang into the air and looked at Mullin on his left. Mullin reached out for a pass. Pippen passed the ball with his right hand toward Mullin, and Petrovic laid off Pippen. But then Pippen *caught his own pass* with his left hand, transferred the ball back to his right hand, and lofted a perfect underhand lay-up.

Kukoc, watching the whole thing, recoiled. The punishment was complete.

After the game—another complete blowout—The Boys were cocky and relaxed. All the endless talk about potential vulnerabilities now seemed absurd. They'd faced the second-best national team in the world—with the best non-NBA player on earth—and it had been no more difficult than whipping teams like Venezuela or Panama.

Jordan was all smiles. "I'm pretty sure Scottie wants to take the film and send it back to Jerry Krause real quickly," he said.

But Pippen—the adrenaline still coursing through his veins—remained edgy. "Toni Kukoc *could* be a good player," he said, "but he's in the right league. He's not ready for NBA competition. He didn't play as well as I heard he could play. He didn't put up good numbers—but that was *my* job."

The reporters got Pippen to admit it was really Krause he was pissed off at, not Kukoc. "But I can't put Krause on the court," said Pippen.

"Maybe Kukoc was trying too hard," said Jordan. "It was his first game against us, and he was nervous. I know he's better than that."

Someone asked Jordan if he or Pippen would be reaching out to Kukoc—their potential teammate—to make him feel better.

"I don't think Scottie, Pippen, or I are in the counseling business," Jordan said coldly. Jordan was, above all, a warrior, and—easy as the Olympics were turning out to be—this was still a war. Tonight he'd proved a point that was very important to him: The best non-NBA player in the world was . . . nothing.

Barkley looked content. "Scottie had Kukoc *totally* afraid," he said. "He was afraid to put the ball down."

Barkley was still being criticized all over the world—including in America—for elbowing the Angolan player. But Barkley didn't care about the bad press, even in his own country. It was just another example, he'd said yesterday, of "typical American bullshit."

Barkley had a peculiarly American sense of individuality. This New World sensibility—one of defiant independence—was hard to accurately characterize. I believe it was Bart Simpson who captured the attitude best in his signature retort to all critics: "Eat my shorts."

The Croatian interview area was much quieter. Especially around Kukoc. Kukoc seemed shocked that Pippen and Jordan had reacted so violently to him. "There's no reason to hate me, or something like that," Kukoc said. He said he still wanted to play in the NBA, maybe in 1993, but added, "I have to work a hundred percent more if I want to be a real player in the NBA. I never *saw* that kind of defense before."

Magic limped out on his way to a hospital. He seemed unconcerned about his injury. He said he was on his way to see the doctors and get tests. He was, by now, used to doctors and tests.

The injury, he believed—judging by how it felt—was not serious. Anyway—it was just a knee.

• Night Life

After the game, a friend and I went for a walk in the Dark Ages. That's what the Gothic Quarter felt like. Construction of it had begun about two thousand years ago—when Barcelona was just a Roman outpost—and in all this time, the Quarter had never been modernized, yuppified, or reclaimed. It was a historic jewel, authentic in the extreme:

in short—a slum. But after a day of nothing but the Olympics—with its unremittingly homogenized, over-marketed, slick facade—the Gothic Quarter was like fresh air. Its streets were only about five feet wide, just enough for two horses to pass, and tall gray tenements rose on either side. Poor people lived here. For five hundred years, poor people had lived here. Blame Columbus.

Columbus screwed up the local economy by discovering America, and that had turned the Quarter into a permanent ghetto. Before Columbus's discovery, Barcelona—which is on the eastern, or Mediterranean, side of Spain—was a hub of shipping. But after the discovery of America, trade shifted to the western side of Spain, which is on the Atlantic. The city never really recovered. It fashioned itself as sort of the hip, artsy-craftsy center of the Mediterranean and put great energy into boosting its local artists, including Picasso, Miro, and the architect Antoni Gaudi.

Gaudi pioneered a type of architecture that makes Barcelona one of the best places in the world for walking and gawking. His style—*modernisme*—has a theme of come-as-you-are, life's-short-play-hard. It features strange spires, wavy lines, gargoyles, inlaid murals, domes, and arches. Basically, it's Picasso on acid.

The emphasis on art in Barcelona spawned a large and raucous community of artists and intellectuals, who in turn inspired a sense of fun and celebration that's taken over the city. Almost the whole town of 2.2 million is like New Orleans' French Quarter: party central. The mainstream schedule is dinner at 10 P.M., drink until you drop, then take a three-hour lunch the next day.

This vibrant mix of art, history, intellect, and general craziness has made Barcelona beloved by almost everybody who's ever spent much time here. Barcelona is the favorite city of Olympic taipan Juan Samaranch, who's a local boy. And that's why we were here tonight.

The rumor that surrounded Samaranch was that years ago he cut a deal with all of the world's sports moguls and corporate sponsors. The alleged deal was simple. Olympic president Samaranch would kill the centuries-old tradition of amateurism in the Olympics, allowing participation of professionals—who are much more lucrative to promote and exploit. In exchange, the 1992 Olympics would be held in Barcelona. Simple as that.

"Chock-o-la-tay? Chock-o-la-tay?" A cinnamon-skinned African-Arab boy with dreadlocks leaned out of the doorway of what seemed to be a gay bar. The bar was very dark, and everyone in it was male and well-barbered.

"No, *gracias,*" I said. We walked on. "What was that?" I asked my buddy. "Gothic-Quarter Girl Scout cookies?"

"No, man," said my friend—a reporter for one of the major dailies, who was helping me do research. "That's what they call hashish here."

"You should buy some," I said. "You could do a color sidebar on life inside a Barcelona prison. Do you know how to say, 'Please, not again,' in Spanish?"

"Let's get the hell outta here," he said. He wanted to go to Barcelona's most famous street, Las Ramblas, a pedestrian hangout that was always packed all night long. "I hear Barkley's been taking walks there," he said. "Let's try to catch him."

We did. It took another hour and a half of waiting, but there was excellent, dirt-cheap red wine to ease the strain.

But not much came of it. A crowd of kids, mostly Americans, clumped around Barkley as he navigated Las Ramblas, swaggering past an endless stream of sidewalk cafés, news kiosks, boutiques, and bars. With a head full of wine and no tape recorder, I wasn't at my professional apex. What I do remember is passing a small, sad collection of hookers—old, overweight women whose only possible distinction was that they might have been the world's ugliest prostitutes.

"Hey," Barkley said when he saw them. "Looks like the wives of the Olympic Committee."

I didn't know why he was so angry at the committee. But I'd find out why on the following day—when Charles Barkley became the world's ugliest American.

The Ugly American

• Barkley Sound-Bites Off

Charles Barkley strode to the podium and sized up the crowd. He'd been bullied. He was pissed. And now, he was back—with his big brother: Nike. Charles was going to kick some ass. And Nike was going to get some free publicity from it.

The U.S. Olympic Committee had just jumped on Barkley for writing a column for *USA Today*. Athletes weren't supposed to act as journalists, except for their hometown newspapers. Didn't even matter that Barkley had only "talked" the column—spewing out his views to a writer who packaged it as logic. He'd *broken the rules,* and the committee was very touchy about rules.

Mike Moran, head of PR for the U.S. Olympic Committee, had charged, "The attitude that Charles Barkley and the NBA have—that the International Olympic Committee doesn't have authority—is *very* dangerous." Moran said that the U.S. basketball team "is out of touch with the rest of the Olympic team. They *must* abide by the rules, like any other U.S. athlete."

Barkley, though, seemed to feel that Moran's scolding was just so much gas from a windbag who'd been out of the private sector too long. Who did this bureaucrat think he *was?* Charles was ready to bite back, and he had a strong forum to do it in. Nike had rented an entire theater and had drawn a horde of angle-hungry media. To add to the draw, Nike trotted out several other members of Team Nike, including Robinson and Stockton, with Ahmad Rashad as MC.

After an elaborate info-mercial was flashed on the screen, Rashad started reading fat-pitch, set-up "questions" to Barkley and the others. The press was free to sit back and soak up all the wit and wisdom they could handle. Rashad was supposed to keep things "lite" and was casually attired in a baseball jersey—which said "Nike," just in case anyone forgot who was paying for the soft drinks and air-conditioning (a luxury in swamp-hot Barcelona).

The first subject Barkley tackled was his payment for the column. "The committee was concerned I was getting paid for the column," he said. "No! I'm *not* getting paid." Then he dropped his head into his hands and acted as if he were stifling laughter. Getting *paid* for my work? Oh, goodness, no!

The committee, Barkley said, was just "a little jealous about how much attention we're getting. It's an *ego* thing. We don't think we're above the committee, but they shouldn't pick on every little thing we do. We should be given our due for being a great basketball team."

About Moran, he said, "Is that a white guy? That's what happens when you give a white guy power. They try to run everything like a dictator. Tell him we're from *America*. We're a *democracy*."

Next subject: the Angolan he'd smacked. Any regrets? "Yeah," said Barkley. "I wish he was a little bigger. But he might be like Manute Bol. He might have had a *spear*—you don't *know*."

His views on the media: "I'm not going to take basketball that serious. That's one of the problems I have with the American media. Their whole life is built around their jobs. Mine isn't.

"The media," he said, "never let the truth stand in the way of a good story. They're just a bunch of people who are jealous of us because we make so much money."

Ouch! Poor diplomacy. Chilly reception. Once again, everybody jotted down the quotes and got their videotape and audiotape sound bites. And once again, the news sailed around the world that Charles Barkley was the ugliest American.

But none of the reporters seemed to be unhappy. At least Charles was dramatic. And that was more than you could say about the U.S. basketball games. NBC wasn't even showing the games in their entirety—which was pretty funny, considering the amount of hype they'd lavished on the Team.

But it wasn't very funny to the journalists, because they needed the games to be *important*. There was no *news* in these games, and that was killing the reporters, because almost all of them were stuck in the pattern of covering sports as news, in the standard who-what-when-where format. For whatever reason, they didn't seem to realize that sports wasn't news. Sports was a contrived, live-action melodrama, scripted by the characters as the play unfolded. The interesting element was the characters—not the "event."

Luckily for the reporters, though, another off-court controversy was brewing, even as Barkley spoke. And this one would engulf not just Barkley but virtually the entire team.

19

Fresh Meat

**The Once and Future Larry • Mo' Money •
An Ego Thing • New, Improved Whip-Ass •
The Joy of Sax • Jordan's Line in the Sand •
Girl-Watching • Next Victim**

> Alas, regardless of their doom,
> The little victims play!
> No sense have they of ills to come,
> Nor care beyond today.
> —Thomas Gray, 1760

> Professional sports should be reported
> on the entertainment pages, along with circuses
> and vaudeville.
> —Avery Brundage, former Olympic Czar

The stadium in Badalona was drafty and full of echoes—the way it often was when the Americans weren't playing. Even though the other games were frequently close and exciting, there was only a moderate amount of interest in them. It was a couple of hours before The Boys would play, and the atmosphere in the gym was one of unrelieved tedium. But out came Charles, who changed all that.

Barkley sauntered out of the locker room to take some practice shots prior to the Wednesday-night game against Germany, but he seemed more interested in talking to the media than shooting. There was a new problem. A big one.

The U.S. Olympic Committee's Mike Moran had just

dropped another bombshell: Anyone not wearing a uniform that Reebok had made for the medal ceremony wouldn't be allowed to take the stand. Reebok had paid the committee $4 million for the right to suit up every American gold-medal winner—transforming each athlete's moment of pride into an ad for Reebok—and Reebok sure as *hell* wanted the basketball team to be part of the promo.

But that was impossible. Practically all the players had existing contracts that wouldn't allow them to wear another company's outfit.

The committee had tried, some time ago, to get the players to break their existing deals, even though these deals paid millions. But the athletes—most notably Jordan, who made about $8 million annually from Nike—had refused. Now that the committee had the players in Barcelona, though, they were laying down ultimatums.

The players thought it was outrageous. The Boys had been *begged* to play in the Olympics. Some of them—Stockton and Bird, in particular—had suffered great pain to play. Magic had risked his health. All of them had gambled against the ever-present chance of serious injury. They had made *millions* of dollars for the Olympic program. And now they were being treated like . . . punks. Like cheap whores.

When, in fact, they were not cheap. They were very, very expensive.

Barkley, who made $2 million a year from Nike, was telling the reporters gathered around him that he would *never* wear a Reebok suit. "I've got about two million reasons not to," he said. Barkley wondered exactly how they were going to keep him *off* the medal stand. "They'd better bring some *big* guys," he said. But even if they did: "They're going to get their butts waxed."

The Angolan elbowing incident was still rattling around the globe, and Barkley was fed up with it. "The press is so *asinine* that all they can come up with is my elbow," he said. "Here we are at the Olympics, and they're making the biggest story *my elbow.*" His voice shrilled to an angry falsetto.

"It will *never* be like this again. This team has *everything*: speed, power—and me. But I'll just be the answer to a trivia question—Who had the most technicals in the Olympics?"

Outside the stadium, Barkley had noticed, there had been people waving German flags. "I *liked* that," he said. "Of course, you could see they weren't doing it with much confidence."

Barkley, though, was slightly nervous. Croatia's Kukoc had been the best non-NBA player they would face, but tonight they'd go against the best non-U.S. player in the Olympics, Germany's Detlef Schrempf. Schrempf had been the eighth pick of the 1985 draft and had been an NBA star for several years, most recently for Indiana. All The Boys had faced Schrempf many times in the NBA, and it had never been easy.

Of more concern to Barkley, though, was the fact that he was now the Team's number-three point-guard, behind Michael and Scottie. Magic's injury wasn't serious, but he'd miss at least a couple of games, and Stockton was still out.

Running the offense in front of two or three billion television viewers was a little daunting. "It's a scary thought," said Barkley.

He was restless. "See ya, fellas," he said. "We've got to go open that can of Whip-Ass that we bought."

• **The Resurrection of Larry**

When the Team came out for their warm-ups, Bird was with them. It surprised some of the press.

Bird was through. Forever. Everybody had been saying it for the last couple of days. He'd already scheduled his charter flight. He'd already shipped his Mr. Back Relief to the airport—a friend of a friend had *seen* the contraption leaving the hotel.

And why shouldn't he leave? He'd looked stiff as a week-old corpse day before yesterday against Croatia. He'd given the Olympics a courageous try. But he was washed up. He was The Great White Has-Been.

Nonetheless . . . as the buzzer blew to start the game, there he was—reclining, as usual, in front of the bench. His face was as inscrutable as ever.

But Daly put him in the game. Early. What did *that* mean?

Almost as soon as Bird got in, he and Mullin were streaking downcourt—Bird! Running!—with Mullin dribbling the ball. When they got to the free throw line, Mullin bounced the ball to Bird. There was one big German defender stationed under the basket, glowering down at Bird. Bird kept coming. Then Bird did something with his eyes and something with his head: fakes that were so subtle you could barely see them from ten yards away. And suddenly the German defender didn't know what to do. So he did nothing. He stood rooted to the floor. Bird flew right past him, laying the ball in softly as the defender just gaped. Bird U-turned and ran back on defense—nonchalantly, as if *anyone* could paralyze a defender with his eyes and head.

Then came the play of the game. A long German pass slipped free, and Bird and one of the German players grappled for it. The ball fell to the floor and Bird *dived after it.* He had a back fragile as crystal—and $3 million waiting if he could just make it to fall camp—and he was diving for the ball. The German player stayed upright and reached down for it. It skittered away from Bird and rolled toward the hands of the German, who was now straddling Bird. It was at the German's fingertips. But Bird swung his leg back—so that his heel almost touched his butt—and knocked the ball free. He didn't knock it free with his foot, which would have been a "kicked ball" (and a lost possession), but hit it with his lower calf. The ball sprang free of the other player's hands, hit him on the leg, and shot out-of-bounds. America's ball.

It was an amazing play, full of passion, risk, and brains.

Mullin ran over to help Bird to his feet. Mullin grabbed Bird's hand and pulled him upright. Mullin was grinning. He said, "Heyyy!" That was all. But Mullin's appreciation for Bird was deep and full of understanding. Mullin had spent half his life learning Bird's special game—with its mix of precision and intelligence—and Mullin would carry that game into the future. They ran downcourt together: the once and future Larry Bird.

The brilliant forced turnover seemed to inspire Bird. But, in reality, Bird didn't need much inspiration. He just needed a spinal column that wasn't made out of soda crackers. He began hitting three-pointers, perimeter shots, and lay-ups.

Then Ewing blocked a shot, and Bird grabbed the ball. Without a second's hesitation, he hurled it almost the length of the court, nailing Mullin at the other end. Mullin, all alone, was certain to score, but saw Barkley tearing down the court—as if it mattered!—with two Germans huffing along behind him. Mullin tossed the ball behind him, it hit the floor, and bounced into Barkley's hands. Barkley went into a full crouch. Sprang up. Crashed the ball through the hoop.

Barkley's fingers lingered on the rim for a fraction of a second, then he dropped to the floor, his legs spread wide, a look of triumph and power on his face. As soon as he hit, he pointed at Mullin.

As Barkley began to run downcourt, a referee hit his whistle and pointed at Barkley. Technical—for hanging on the rim (which was illegal in international rules). Barkley's eyes flew wide. "God! *Damn!*" he cried.

But it was too late for Barkley to be indignant. He was the Ugly American, and no one was going to let him be anything else.

A few minutes later: Jordan dribbled at the free throw line, and four German players swarmed him. Bird crept in under the hoop, unnoticed. Jordan flashed half-a-foot forward and suddenly had a narrow line to Bird; he thrust the ball through the pack of Germans and hit Bird right in the hands. Bird vaulted up, and so did the defender who'd rushed in to stop him. But Bird's feet never left the ground. The defender's did. Bird jumped—caught the defender's legs for the foul—spun around, shot, and ripped the net.

Magic, in a wild USA Basketball T-shirt, leaped off the bench and swirled a towel. "My man!" he yelled to Bird.

Fresh Meat

Bird looked like . . . Bird. Before the night was over, he would have nineteen points, to lead the team. On an evening like this, it suddenly became clear why he was fighting so hard to stay in the game. Like Magic, he still had almost unimaginable skills. He still loved the game intensely. He loved the life that surrounded it. He loved how it had changed him—from hillbilly to wealthy celebrity.

How could he let go?

Magic couldn't. People close to Magic were saying he was coming back. Definitely. No matter what it cost.

After the game—another standard forty-point massacre —the players from the two teams embraced and posed for a few more photos. As in Portland, the opposing teams here were uniformly starstruck and considered it a great honor to have their asses publicly flayed by the greatest team on earth.

Once again, a "threat"—the Detlef Schrempf menace— had dematerialized. Schrempf had played well—but so what? He was just one excellent player—and the Team had twelve. It was now obvious that every opposing team in the Olympics would just be a sacrificial offering to the gods: fresh meat. But the opposing players—men of considerable pride and passion—seemed to *like* being meat for the Americans. The men from the other teams loved posing in photos with The Boys and even just shaking their hands after the game. It was the greatest possible tribute to the Team.

In the interview area after the game, the talk was of Bird—and Reebok.

Bird's face shone from within. "I'm virtually pain free," he marveled. "I feel *great* right now, no doubt about it. This is the best I've felt in a long time. I just hope I don't do something stupid to mess it up again." He was sitting in a chair—which was unusual for him. He wasn't even squirming.

But Bird wouldn't draw a connection between his performance here and the possibility of playing another year in the NBA. "The way I play here won't have no bearing on what I do next fall," he said. "What I do here, it's about winnin' a gold medal. And that's *it.*"

Somebody asked him if he was going home.

"I am," he said with a tight smile. "A week from Saturday."

Then the obligatory: Are you going to retire? "I've been retired for four years—but nobody noticed."

The talk about Reebok, though, was darker. Jordan drew a line in the sand and dared the U.S. Olympic Committee to cross it. "I definitely will not wear a Reebok uniform," Jordan said. "I don't believe in endorsing my competitors. I've got too much loyalty. That's like asking me to give up my dad." The only difference was, Jordan's dad didn't give him eight million bucks a year.

"I'll do what Michael does," Barkley said. A reporter asked him why. "Cuz he's the richest."

Somebody asked Barkley if he felt he was missing anything by not living in the Olympic Village. "I don't feel like I'm missing anything," Barkley said.

"Besides, I'm a black millionaire. I can live anywhere I want."

Suzie McConnell, a 5–4 point guard for the U.S. women's team, ripped down the floor, arrived at the hoop, and flipped a behind-the-back pass to teammate Teresa Edwards, who banked it up and in. Five rows behind the U.S. women's bench, Magic Johnson jumped up and pumped his fist into the air. "Yes!" he screamed.

Magic, Barkley, Pippen, Stockton, Drexler, Malone, and Robinson were spending their off-day—Saturday, August 1st—supporting the women's team.

Barkley was loving it. The women were *tough.* He kept yelling, "Good pick! Good pick! Hit her again!"

The U.S. women were thrilled. They had the greatest cheerleaders in history. Inspired, they won.

After it was over, Barkley said, "I was very impressed. *They* should play us."

The Boys had been going to a number of different events, supporting various U.S. athletes. Magic, in particular, loved the other sports. Bird had spent last evening at the U.S. baseball game.

But their support for the relatively unknown U.S. athletes was getting virtually no press coverage. It was contrary to the angle everybody was using: The Boys were just Ugly Americans. It didn't make sense for the journalists to contradict conventional wisdom. Who'd believe them?

• Revenge Is Mine

The Team was warming up for the Sunday game against Brazil. The usual stuff: lay-ups, jump shots, free throws. But while they loosened up, some of them shot hot looks at Brazil's great Oscar Schmidt. Schmidt was in trouble. He was playing as well as he always did in the Olympics, but at thirty-five, this was his fourth, and probably last, moment on the international stage. But The Boys were going to show no mercy. They were going to *pull down his pants and whip his ass.* Because of *what he'd said.*

Well, actually, it had been his teammate who'd bad-mouthed them in Portland—saying the U.S. team ought to get serious and forget about golf and suntans. But for several days, they'd all thought it had been Schmidt who'd crossed them. And *that was reason enough to get him:* Schmidt was dead meat.

David Robinson wasn't giving anyone dirty looks, though. Robinson left vengeance to the Lord. In fact, David was yawning. Robinson *always* seemed to be yawning before these games. Over the course of the year, he'd seemed to develop at least a little long-lacking killer instinct. But it took more than . . . poor old Oscar . . . to stir it up.

When the game started, though, it didn't look as if Oscar had much heart for the fight, either. Early on, the ball squirted free near Schmidt, and he just looked down at it. Didn't even dive after it. What was Oscar waiting for—a big game?

The Americans did what they always did: They tore Brazil's offense apart and indulged in their usual spectacular playground moves. Except for Karl Malone. In typical Malone fashion, he piled up his points with methodical, unexciting, hard work. For example: Ewing inbounded to Pippen, who raced three steps, leaped into the air, caught his own dribble with his right hand, and passed it in the same motion crosscourt to Clyde. Clyde, without a moment's hesitation, changed the trajectory of the ball 180 degrees, firing it straight down to Malone, who was standing under the basket. There were two defenders right on top of Malone. But what were they going to do? *Fight* him for it? And die young? No. So Malone just hopped up and banked it in off the glass.

Malone rarely put on the kind of pyrotechnic displays that most of the other U.S. players did, but he *always delivered.* That was how he'd earned his famous nickname: The Postal Carrier.

But heavyweight champion Evander Holyfield, who was sitting a couple of rows behind me, appreciated Malone's brute force. Every time Malone would score or grab a rebound, Holyfield would frown, clap hard once, and boom, "Karl!"

Bird watched most of the game from his belly. His back was burning again. He played about twenty minutes, but his shot was off.

Magic, however, didn't play at all. Even so, he remained the soul of the team, leaping off the bench in his psychedelic USA Basketball T-shirt every time any U.S. player did something out of the ordinary. He illuminated the entire court with his Magic smile.

Even when he wasn't playing, Magic was like an assistant coach to Daly, offering his ideas, and helping enforce Daly's edicts. He was the perfect balance for Daly. Daly was pessimistic; Magic was positive. Daly was always preoccupied with the future; Magic was always into the moment.

In the second half, Laettner—the forgotten man— actually squeezed into the game. Daly was giving Laettner markedly fewer minutes than the other players. Part of the reason was that Laettner was becoming a disappointment.

He was not extremely tough, and he wasn't tremendously skilled (at least, compared to his teammates). Maybe he *was* the next Danny Ferry. Another probable reason for his lack of playing time was that he was being used as an example. By keeping Laettner on the bench until his ass went numb, Daly was telling the NBA superstars: I'm giving you all the minutes I can; look at Laettner—it could be worse!

Just before the game ended, Laettner was trying to establish position under the hoop. But one of the big Brazilian guys shoved him hard, and—*whang!*—Laettner did the most horrifying case of splits I've ever seen. His legs scissored wide, and he fell crotch-first into the floor. For a moment, I was afraid he'd torn himself all the way up to the belly button. But he managed to get to his feet and even stayed in the game.

After the game, the solution to the Reebok controversy was announced. NBA Commissioner David Stern, who'd been keeping a low profile in Barcelona, had worked out a deal. The Boys would wear the Reebok suits, but cover the logo. That was just like Stern: He stayed invisible, but when things got messy, he stepped in with the perfect common-sense solution—one that kept everybody not just happy, but rich.

Stern did, however, get in a dig at the alliance of the U.S. Olympic Committee and USA Basketball. He said commit-tee PR chief Mike Moran was just a "low-level public relations official" who'd "issued an ultimatum that our guys didn't like. So they decided to have some fun with it."

Of course, The Boys hadn't just been "having fun." They'd felt pissed off, insulted, and threatened.

But why shouldn't Stern make Moran out to be a fool tripping over his own ego? The relationship between the NBA and the amateurs was already sour. The pro-amateur connection was shakier now than it had been a year ago, when the Selection Committee had squabbled about the Team's pro-amateur mix.

Charles got in the last word on the subject. He said he'd be *happy* to wear the suit and cover the logo—but *not* because anybody was *making* him. Charles had no obligations to *anybody*. "As a black man," he said, "all I have to do is remain black. Pay taxes. And die."

● Up on the Roof

The long day waned. The slow moon climbed. The lights began to twinkle down below.

David Robinson and musician Branford Marsalis sat on the roof of a building, five stories up, playing saxophones.

Robinson, who'd only been playing sax for a couple of years, was playing tenor sax. Marsalis was on soprano sax. They were playing a duet. The notes dissolved into the starlit night.

There were no lights. But there was a cathedral on one side and a stadium on the other, and both reflected enough light for the two sax players to see.

Robinson felt ecstatic. At peace. For him, this was a dream. It was like . . . being at the Olympics.

20

Team Nike

**Broken Hearts and Twisted Minds • Madness
on Las Ramblas • Magic and the Mob •
Michael Drinks Alcohol • Daly's Prophecy of Doom •
. "Kill 'Em All—and Let God Sort 'Em Out" •
Good-bye Columbus • Gold!**

> You cannot conquer America.
> —William Pitt, 1777

> Power is not pretty.
> —Lyndon Baines Johnson, 1966

> Even victors are by victory undone.
> —John Dryden, 1680

The Boys were going berserk. Just absolutely nuts. At nine
hundred dollars a night, the Ambassador hotel was . . . the
world's plushest prison. When the USA Basketball and NBA
executives had first arranged for the Team to stay there, the
executives had been attracted to the luxury. But what the
execs had forgotten to factor in was: Mardi Gras. Two feet
outside the hotel's door was the damnedest party anybody
on the Team had ever seen. Day and night, an immense
collection of sweating flesh rolled up and down the pedestrian thoroughfare Las Ramblas—like The Blob, engulfing
everything in its path. Once it swept over you, *you became
part of it,* whether you wanted to or not. It was, like: Party or
die! You'd order water and the waiter would bring wine—
and leave the bottle—and before you could polish it off and

drag yourself to bed, two or three red-eyed, howling buddies (or *new* buddies) would roll down the street and suck you into The Blob, and the next thing you knew, you were in the Gothic Quarter with the sun stabbing you in the eyes.

Of course, this life-style wasn't at all conducive to beating every other basketball team on earth by fifty points, so the guys on the Team tended to lock themselves in their lavish cells with their video games and kids and wives . . . and go slowly mad. For them, stepping onto the Ramblas was a mind-twisting ordeal. It was hard to overstate the degree of celebrity that had zeroed in on these guys. The millions of dollars spent by NBC, Nike, Gatorade, Coca-Cola, and the rest of corporate America had motivated almost *half the earth* to watch these games on television. There were more viewers watching than had ever watched *anything*. And all of that energy and curiosity was converging on this *one little medieval side street*. The worldwide attention was like sunlight focusing through a magnifying glass, until it became a tiny, white-hot dot.

In the evenings, when the Team would break out of prison to drive to the suburban basketball stadium, they needed a massive paramilitary escort of tanks, helicopters, police cars, and SWAT teams. Somebody had asked assistant coach P. J. Carlesimo if that didn't make him nervous, and Carlesimo had said, no, it would have made him nervous *not* to have it.

At one point, Magic and Cookie tried to take their baby for a walk. They wanted to just wheel him around in the stroller for a few minutes. And they were damn near trampled! Devoured! By The Blob! The Mardi Gras atmosphere seemed to make people think they had a license to intrude: "Magic—you *gotta* have *one glass* with me, cuz I'm your Number One Fan." But all that was no joke when you had a tiny little infant down there in the stroller.

Early in the Games, when the Team had gone to the Village to get their credentials (like they needed ID?), they'd been mobbed by the athletes—who, of all people, should've been cool about it. Worse still, part of the mob had been security guards.

Mullin, though, still managed to get out onto the Ramblas with Liz and their baby, without being unduly molested. That was one of the secondary benefits of having White Man's Disease—there wasn't a ten-story mural depicting you flying through the air, like there was of Jordan on Barcelona's main drag. Mullin's skin color was also a good disguise; at the moment, to be black in Barcelona was to be an athlete. Mullin had been asked if he had much trouble walking around on the streets, and he'd said, "It depends on who I'm with." The entire Olympic experience hadn't changed Mullin a bit. He hadn't developed rock-star vanity and never would. Mullin was enjoying Barcelona.

So was Magic—despite the craziness. He didn't want the Games ever to end.

There were still four games left. But they were beginning to blur together. It was becoming increasingly hard for the Team to take its opponents seriously. Nevertheless, for each game, Daly tried to get them to be afraid. He had a bottomless bag of motivational tricks, and he was digging out every one of them.

For example: next game—Spain. We know who *that* is, don't we? The *home team*. So, be afraid! Be very afraid!

• Magic Pisses Off the Guys

Oh, my God! The unthinkable! It was happening! Daly was right!

Spain had come out hot in the second half, with a 22–9 run. And midway through the first half, Spain had only been down five. Jordan was sick from exotic Spanish food, and both Magic and Stockton were playing like exactly what they were: still crippled. Even most of the healthy guys were stumbling around like winos in an alley.

But not Barkley. His fire came from within; he didn't need Daly's mind games. He was crashing after every rebound and bulling to the hoop every chance he got. Daly was becoming increasingly impressed with Barkley. Barkley was an incredible pain in the ass, and Daly had no desire whatsoever to coach him beyond the Olympics. But what a warrior! Daly had previously considered Barkley one of the five best players in the world, but Barkley was moving up on Daly's list.

A tough-looking Spanish kid named Andreu fouled Barkley but got knocked onto his butt while he did it. Barkley walked over to Andreu, as if he were going to help him up. But as he stood over Andreu, he just dropped the ball down by him, then walked off. The largely Spanish crowd—who'd been very gracious to the visiting American team—started whistling with rage. My neighbor in the next seat, Carlos, called Barkley something that even *I* don't want to print. Barkley's snotty move pissed me off, too. I couldn't help but feel that when he looked bad, I looked bad. So I yelled, "Bark-a-lee! *Me cago en tu leche!*" Carlos gave me a high-five.

Nonetheless, Barkley led them back into control. The game ended with the standard forty-point margin.

After the game, Barkley found Andreu and gave him a big hug and a U.S. jersey. When games ended, Barkley's competitive anger subsided. He tried to approach Andreu privately, but reporters in the "mixed zone"—where athletes and journalists mingled—spotted it.

As they crowded around him, Barkley told the reporters, "I've been whistled at and booed in *better places.*" He said he just wanted to "get it done, and get the hell out of here. We've been traveling for a long time. It's high time to get this over with."

At least Barkley had straightened out the problem of his *USA Today* column. The committee had said he could *not* be interviewed and then have his interview run as a column. That was *wrong.* They said that he *could* be interviewed, though, and have his interview run as an interview. That was *moral,* and *just,* and preserved the purity of the Olympics.

Jordan looked shaky and discolored after the game. He said that what he'd eaten had "changed my whole body."

Stockton was just happy he'd played. He said he'd wanted

to look jock-tough out there, but that it had been hard for him to keep from grinning. "I'm still in pain," he said, "but I *expected* that. I'll stop limping when we get to the medal games."

But Magic wasn't happy. He wanted Daly to call a practice for tomorrow. He knew that would piss the guys off—but so what?

So Daly called a practice. After all, the next game was against Puerto Rico—featuring the incredible Jose Ortiz, who'd been in the NBA for about fifteen minutes. With experience like that, Ortiz was capable of *anything*.

The next day, after practice, Barkley's eyes looked yellow as cheese, as if they were still caught in the dreamworld. "I'd rather be sleeping," he grumbled. "Everybody got out of bed wanting to get this over with as quickly as possible."

Barkley slumped down next to Pippen. They were buddies now. Barkley was close to virtually everyone on the team; he and Magic were its most outgoing members.

A reporter brought up the tired subject of "overkill"—mentioning the Team's enormous margins of victory over everyone they'd played.

But Barkley didn't want to hear about it. "I'm here to *kill* 'em," Barkley growled. "Kill 'em all—and let God sort 'em out."

Suddenly, he looked much happier. "Hey!" he said. "That's a pretty good *line.*" It was also a pretty old line, but Barkley didn't seem to realize it.

"What line?" Pippen said.

"Kill 'em all—and let God sort 'em out."

"Yeah," said Pippen. "Kill 'em all. Kill 'em all."

The practice made Daly feel much better. "I thought we needed it," he said. "There are just three games left, and we've *got to be careful.* The U.S. *always* wins big in preliminary rounds, and then they get caught in the semis or finals. You get lulled to sleep—and then *anything can happen.* Being an overwhelming favorite doesn't really mean that much if the other team is hot."

Daly had a point. Right now, the U.S. had an average margin of victory of forty-five points. The other teams had the U.S. team *right where they wanted it:* overconfident.

Daly started ticking off memorable sports upsets. "Duke and Villanova last year. Georgetown in eighty-five. The Russian hockey team in eighty."

God, yes. Who could ever forget those?

• One More Lard-Assed Bureaucrat

How long, oh, Lord, how long? How long would this bullshit go on?

No sooner had practice ended than another bureaucrat launched still one more bitter screed against the Team. Where did the committee *find* these guys?

Leroy Walker, a seventy-six-year-old who'd been nominated as the next U.S. Olympic Committee president, was apoplectic about The Boys' accommodations.

Walker had been hanging around the Village and had sat down with a crowd of U.S. athletes around a TV, watching the American basketball game, and—horrors!—some of them had been *jealous.* They were actually rooting against The Boys.

"I may be from the old school," said Walker, "but when I find Americans pulling against Americans, it *bothers* me."

So Walker had decided that he had to *bring the entire Olympic team together* again. The only way to do that, he said, was to make everybody live in the Village. In 1996, when he would be running America's Olympic team in Atlanta, that's what he wanted to see.

He didn't think that the basketball players should have been "put on a pedestal." In fact, said Walker, "I am not convinced yet we had to *have* NBA players on our team. With all the college players we have in the country, if we choose the right ones, we can *still* win."

If pros did compete in the Olympics, he said, "They should follow the same rules as everyone else. If they don't want to, and aren't here next time—I wouldn't care."

NBA Commissioner David Stern didn't waste any time on this one. He went head-to-head with Walker that same day.

"We tried to get the best accommodations for the players," Stern said. "These guys are on the road without their families hundreds of nights a year. What we tried to do was establish a situation where they could bring their families and kids."

But before the day ended, Walker announced that he'd gotten a good response to his initial statements. "Athletes are *looking* for leadership," he said. "If you tell them they have to do something, they *do* it."

But Charles Barkley didn't seem to be "looking for leadership." When Barkley heard about Walker's remarks, he said, *"You* wanna stay in the Village when it's a *hundred degrees,* with no air-conditioning? Sure! Hey, we've got assholes in the U.S., too. *He's* not paying for our room and board, so it's none of his business."

Magic was, as usual, a little more diplomatic. "The USOC hasn't been working *with* us," he said. "It's been more of a power struggle.

"Walker needs to come and understand what it's *like* for us. He needs to see the *crowds.* My wife and I went to walk my son, and there were a *hundred people* following us.

"We're not trying to be arrogant. We're not trying to be different. We've been in the Village. We've supported the other athletes. But we're the bad guys."

In short—Boys to committee: Drop dead.

The whole ugly mess brought into crystalline focus one fact: The NBA superstars would never again be so eager to play in the Olympics. Nor, in all probability, so welcome.

A team like this would never happen again.

● **Fear and Glory**

Daly rambled back and forth in front of the bench, clapping his hands and yelling, "Let's go! Let's go! Let's go!" as the Team sleepwalked through its warm-ups. How in hell could he get The Boys psyched up to play Puerto Rico? And the dreaded Ortiz? Maybe one more "Let's go" would do the trick.

"Let's *go!*" Daly shouted. No response.

By the sidelines, Boris Stankovic was talking to *The New York Times*'s great basketball writer Harvey Araton. Stankovic, who ran the International Basketball Association (which governed world competition), was pissed. He'd been infuriated by Leroy Walker's trashing of the U.S. team. Stankovic seemed appalled that Walker was so anxious to restrict NBA players, after all the politicking it had taken to get them in. "I *hope* Mr. Walker will not decide *alone,*" Stankovic said scornfully. "I hope it will be the U.S. Olympic Committee *and* the basketball association."

Stankovic's sentiments were similar to those of Olympic czar Juan Samaranch, who'd reportedly put in a quiet phone call to David Stern this week, thanking him for the NBA's participation. The U.S. basketball team had been the centerpiece of the Olympics and had justified NBC's payment of about half a billion dollars to Samaranch's International Olympic Committee. Of course, the NBA had benefited, too. Stern had wanted to advertise the NBA globally. And he'd succeeded beyond anyone's dreams.

On the surface, it was weird that two foreign executives were supporting Stern and The Boys, while the U.S. official was roasting them. But it wasn't *that* weird. Stern, Samaranch, and Stankovic were all businessmen. In the emerging new world, business ties were often stronger than national ties.

When the game started, it was obvious that Daly's psyche-up attempts hadn't been necessary. Even though the Team looked bored, it scored the game's first seventeen points. When Puerto Rico finally scored, the stadium shook with cheers. Pity cheers.

The game wasn't close. It wasn't even interesting. It was, in fact, so uninteresting that Christian Laettner played a major role in it, leading the team in rebounding.

All night long, the U.S. seemed to be just waiting for its last two games. Puerto Rico seemed to be waiting for . . .

Dr. Kervorkian, the euthanasia specialist. Every so often, some poor American fan—who'd paid God knows how much to be here—would try to start a chant of "U-S-A, U-S-A!" But even the cheers got lost in the tedium.

There just wasn't any personal feeling attached to this game. It was one friendly nation against another. It meant nothing.

Everybody always talked about trying to divorce nationalism from the Olympics, but nationalism had always been the *heart* of the Olympics. The whole point of the Games— their entire legacy—was to offer a form of bloodless warfare between nations.

If there was anything wrong with the 1992 Games, it was that there were no villains. There was no menacing Soviet empire. No fascist East Germany. No defiantly, unrepentantly racist South Africa.

In the new world disorder, nationalism was slowly being replaced by corporate loyalty. The emerging powers weren't nations; they were multinational corporations. This week, it had begun to seem as if the U.S. basketball team wasn't really Team USA. It was Team Nike.

But there was one great nationalistic battle left. Croatia versus what was left of the Soviet Union.

Exported Soviet communism had helped enslave Croatia for fifty years. And now little Croatia had a chance to fight back.

Croatia's Drazen Petrovic stood at the free throw line with nine seconds left and his team trailing the Russian Unified Team by one point. He could tie it, win it—or lose it. The winning team would advance to the Gold Medal game.

It had been a year of bitterness, fear, and glory for Petrovic. His former country, Yugoslavia, had disintegrated in a gruesome civil war. Friends and family had been in danger. But his homeland—Croatia—had emerged as an independent nation. And he had emerged as an NBA star.

His eyes lasered in on the hoop. He swirled his tongue around in his mouth. He shot. Good! His fist stabbed the air. Tie game. He got the ball back. Gripped it. Swirled his tongue. Glared at the hoop. Lofted it softly up. *Rip!*

Croatia was ahead by one. The Unified Team got the ball. Brought it down fast. Put up a shot—no good. Five seconds left. Four. Three. They shot again. Off. The horn blasted.

Petrovic leaped into the stands and seized a Croatian flag. Waving it, he floated out to center court, where his teammates were embracing and screaming. In the stands, Croatians swept their flag back and forth. Some wept openly. They held up a sign: "America Next."

It was one of the first international achievements by the new nation of Croatia. It was a victory for people who had fought this year with great courage and who had endured unspeakable suffering. The stadium vibrated with emotion. It was an old-fashioned Olympic moment.

The Croatians had achieved their dream: winning the right to be slaughtered by Team Nike.

• Pride and Humiliation

"Sah-bone-*ees!* Sah-bone-*ees!*" Lithuania's Arvidas Sabonis stared at David Robinson, who was under the hoop. Robinson stared back. Sabonis wanted to drive on Robinson. But *should* he? Did he have the guts?

Sabonis, by the conventions of the new corporate world, was a local boy—he'd been playing professionally for the Badalona team. So the fans here accepted him as one of their own.

"Sah-bone-*ees!*" Sabonis went straight into Robinson's face. The burly, blubbery Lithuanian put up a shot and watched helplessly as Robinson smacked it back down.

Several years ago, Sabonis—who was then playing for the Soviet Union rather than Lithuania—had been considered by some to be the best basketball player in the world. He'd been drafted by Portland, and they'd tried every possible diplomatic maneuver to get him out of the Soviet Union. But nothing had worked.

Stifled by the lack of competition and freedom, Sabonis had turned into a party boy. One night he'd slipped down some stairs—according to rumors because he was drunk—and ripped apart his leg. He probably could have fully rehabilitated it, but without the motivation of free enterprise, what was the point? By the time he'd finally gotten free of Soviet repression, he'd been fat and slow.

He was still a hero in the Spanish league, but that was probably as far as he'd ever get. For Sabonis, the world order had changed about five years too late.

Robinson grabbed the shot he'd blocked and made a fast-as-light pass to Jordan. Robinson was everything Sabonis might have been: fast, slim, motivated—and rich beyond belief.

Jordan hauled down the pass at center court, darted toward the basket, hesitated, pulled up, and shot from the perimeter. The shot clanged off and bounced into the hands of Sabonis, who'd shuffled downcourt to stand beneath the hoop. Sabonis looked for someone to pass it to, raised the ball . . . but it was gone! Jordan had rushed in after his shot and had grabbed the ball before Sabonis had even known Jordan was in the area. Jordan banked the ball off the glass and in.

The U.S. was blazing! Once again, Daly had found a way to motivate them. He'd convinced them that Lithuania was the best team in the tournament—even better than Croatia. Also, the heavily favored U.S. women had lost last night. If *they* could lose, Daly had said, *we* could lose. That wasn't exactly logic, but it was close enough. The Boys had come out ready to kick ass.

But Daly was right about one thing—Lithuania *did* have talent. Their Sarunas Marciulionis, who was a star for Golden State, was deft and pit-bull tough. At the moment, as Jordan tried to back in toward the hoop with the ball, Sarunas had his hands all over Jordan's ass and thighs and groin. Sarunas—always aggressive—was all but sexually harassing Jordan, to the point where some guys would have turned around and slapped his face. But Jordan remained unperturbed. After all, what did this hurt, when all winter long he'd probably had visions of tough foreign thugs pulling out his tongue?

Bird, who'd been spending more and more time on his belly in front of the bench, got into the game and started backing in on Lithuanian star Rimas Kurtinaitas, who, like Bird, was a superb three-point shooter. Bird didn't have full mobility, but he really knew how to use his butt to push his defender away. Kurtinaitas had probably grown up thinking he was going to be the next Larry Bird—and now, here he was, in front of three billion viewers, with Larry Bird's butt in his face. In the Olympics, dreams came true.

Even though Bird's movement was limited, he was tossing around tremendous passes: no-look, over-the-shoulder, behind-the-back, drive-you-crazy passes. If this was to be one of the last two games in his career, he wanted to leave basketball the same way he'd come in: passing.

Sabonis, who passed better than most NBA centers, tried some fancy passes of his own. But, often as not, they didn't work. Magic and the other Americans always seemed to know exactly what Sabonis was thinking and would knock Sabonis's passes to the floor.

The Team was playing better than they had in some time—probably better than they'd ever played. In fact, they were probably playing better than *any* team had ever played. After a while, the score got ridiculous. They ended up winning by fifty-one. But even as the score grew, The Boys' excellence seemed to inspire further brilliance—even though the only motivations for it were pride and the simple joy of doing it.

Everyone on the team was learning about joy. They were learning about it from Magic.

All year long, as I'd traveled from city to city, I'd seen these Olympic players reach remarkable heights of excellence. Often, though, they'd seemed detached from the *experience* of their excellence, focusing instead on the results it brought. Emotions were considered a distraction, and most coaches—fixated on winning—frowned on them. One of the mantras of the NBA was: Never get too high;

never get too low. But Magic *never* stayed anchored in the safe harbor of detached feeling.

Magic's feelings *always* rose to the surface. And his feelings were usually ones of glee, satisfaction, and excitement.

Magic was the only player on the team with a serious problem, but he was easily the happiest.

In every one of these games—whether he was on the bench or on the floor—he would be bubbling with joy. Laughing. Grinning. Putting his arm around someone. Shouting encouragement. Teasing. Showing his love.

And his attitude seemed to be rubbing off on the others. Uptight guys like Stockton, Ewing, and Drexler seemed to be a little looser. Barkley, despite his bitching and barking, seemed to be a little less angry. It was almost as if the spirit of Barkley's father—who seemed to be the original source of Barkley's anger—had been reborn in Magic: Charles was getting a second chance at life. Bird—so afraid to let go of basketball—appeared to be less one-dimensional when Magic was around. Robinson, who was always thinking, always analyzing, was getting lessons every day from Magic on how to just . . . react—how to not-think, and just do it.

And Jordan. Jordan was probably closest in temperament to Magic. They both lived on a special plane of perception, seeing things that most people are blind to. And they felt a level of self-confidence that most people can't comprehend. But even Jordan was learning from Magic. He was learning that a person could suffer horrifying disgrace—endure unimaginable public humiliation—and still be loved and still be proud. Jordan was learning that you could lose control of your destiny without losing control of yourself.

Magic's attitude toward life had inspired every team he had ever been on. And those teams had been phenomenally successful. He had brought joy to the warrior's journey. And joy *works*. It wins.

Magic had shown every one of his teammates—in high school, college, the pros, and the Olympics—that each game they played was just another opportunity for joy.

* * *

After the Lithuanian game, Jordan talked quietly. "You know what I'm going to miss?" he said. "I'm going to miss the camaraderie—you know, the trash-talkin' and all that. I'll even miss the practices.

"We should *cherish* this time we've spent together," he said. His mouth curved into a smile, wrinkling the little goatee he'd kept. "Ten years from now," he said, "there'll be *a whole lotta lies* bein' told."

Magic, not far away, was talking about the same thing. "I'll miss this a *lot,*" he said. "Not just leavin' the Olympics, though. It's leavin' *each other.*

"We're gonna miss each other—*so much.*"

A shrill voice pierced the area. "Hey! Hey!" It was Barkley, yelling at a group of Spanish security guards. "You *foreigners!* Keep quiet! I'm *serious!* I'm going to start whipping some foreign *ass* if you don't quiet down soon."

Nice move, Charles. It was as bad as earlier tonight. During the game, when the stadium had been quiet, Barkley had gotten pissed off at something and screamed, *"Mother*fuck!" It had made me want to go sit with the Lithuanians.

The security guards stormed off, and Barkley calmed down. Barkley said he was glad there was only one more game, because he was dying to get home. "One—and done," he said. "Back to America!"

Somebody asked him what he missed about America.

"I miss the crime and murder," he said thoughtfully. "I haven't heard about any brutal shootings or stabbings."

Barkley got in one last dig at the city he'd finally gotten free of. "I *miss* Philadelphia," he said.

• The Golden Boys

I was on my way to the Gold Medal game—chugging down the street in my horrid little rented Ford, sweating through my shirt, using a huge statue of Columbus as a landmark. When—*smack!*—somebody whacked the side of my car with what sounded like an open palm or a book.

I spun around and found myself looking into the hard eyes of one of the Nacional de Policia. He motioned for me to double-park.

I don't know what the hell he said, but he let me know with sign language—and that universal cop charm—that I was about to get a speeding ticket. He wrote "30" on a scrap of paper, and then pointed at me and wrote "35." Apparently, I'd been going five kilometers per hour over the limit, or about three miles per hour too fast.

"We're quite the little nitpicker, aren't we?" I said. I'd learned you could be a smart-ass with most of these policemen—who were *everywhere*—thanks to the language barrier.

"Six-teen thou-zand pesetas, *por favor.*" I must have looked dumbstruck, because he wrote that down, too. It was a hundred sixty bucks. "Cash monies, *por favor.*"

I peeled the bills off; he stuffed them in his shirt and swatted the car again. "Go *slow,*" he said.

I snarled, "You jackbooted menace," and took off—slowly. I *missed* Oregon.

It was thirty minutes before the Gold Medal game. The locker room was quiet. Daly inserted a tape in the locker room's VCR. Images flashed onto the screen. It was the 1972 U.S. loss to the Soviet Union.

It was Daly's last gimmick. But it worked.

It worked because these twelve players *wanted* it to work. They were *always* looking for some reason to convince themselves that *this* was the most important game *ever*. They'd been doing it all their lives. It was part of the reason they were so great.

The U.S. had already massacred Croatia once this week. So there was no reason for The Boys to fear Croatia in this one, final game. But when the guys left the locker room, their eyes were locked into thousand-yard stares.

The game began as many of the games had, with Magic hitting Michael on the perimeter, and Jordan swishing a jumper. That always broke the opponents' hearts. The other teams would prepare themselves mentally for Jordan's drives—but then Jordan would just lay back and pop in jumpers. It reminded teams of how hopeless it was to try to stop him.

Daly had believed, when he'd begun coaching the Team, that Jordan was its best player. But the *margin* of Jordan's superiority had shocked Daly. Jordan was *so* much better than anyone else. It didn't show up in his Olympic statistics, which were quite ordinary. But Daly had never evaluated players by stats. What Daly saw was that Jordan could do virtually whatever he wanted, whenever he wanted.

But Daly loved coaching Magic, too. Magic didn't have Jordan's physical skills. But he had incredible court vision. At the moment, Magic's eyes were bouncing all around the court. His eyes were never still—not for a fraction of a second. Then he saw what he needed: a tiny break in the defense. He hopped upward and pushed the ball toward the basket. Pulled it back. Brought it to his side. Jerked it back in front of him. *Then* shot. By that time his defender had leaped twice and was out of the way. But Magic's shot bounced back. Ewing forced his way into the free throw lane. The ball was at least five feet behind Ewing, but he swung his long arm in a violent arc, grabbed the ball as it began to fall, and hook-jammed it through the hoop.

The Croatians looked startled. The U.S. had so *many* points of power: the passing of Magic and Bird, the inhuman speed of Jordan and Drexler, the brutal force of Ewing, Malone, and Barkley, and the perimeter shooting of Mullin.

And there were no weaknesses.

Still, the Croatians managed to stay close. They were playing with great courage and emotion.

Again Magic had the ball—Magic *always* seemed to have the ball. He dribbled at the perimeter. Hesitated. Then the ball disappeared behind his back. A pass? The defenders scanned wildly. No! He was running! Three defenders charged toward him. Too late. He banked it in.

Drazen Petrovic brought the ball down. He passed to Toni Kukoc. Kukoc had a wild, hard look in his face—he was the *Magic Johnson of Europe*—and they had *humiliated* him in the last game; methodically, and on purpose. But now he was playing superbly. Kukoc had tremendous control over his emotions and possessed the rare quality of being able to transform failure into knowledge.

Kukoc passed back to Petrovic, who leaped to shoot. But Clyde—who'd somehow sensed Petro's move—had leaped first, and swatted the ball away. Barkley seized it. Three Croatians ganged around Barkley—grabbed for the ball. But Barkley—already running—pulled it away from them, put it behind his back, and transferred it to his left hand while he kept running. He flipped it back to his right hand, then smashed it ahead and down. The ball hit the floor and bounced into the hands of Drexler, who was flying toward the U.S. basket. But one of the largest Croatians was already there, waiting. Drexler lifted into the air. Went into his extraordinary power-glide. A huge hand loomed in front of him. He shifted control of the ball from one hand to the other: right, left, right, left, right. The defender froze. Which *hand?*

Both. Drexler protected the ball with his body and shoveled it upward with both hands. It plinked against the glass and fell through the net.

So *many* points of power. When the Games ended, each of the twelve players would have distinguished himself. Barkley would lead the team in scoring, with an average of eighteen points, on seventy percent shooting. Bird would play in all eight games—despite his agony—and he scored nineteen points in the only game in which he felt healthy. Drexler would be fifth in scoring, fourth in steals, and fourth in assists. Malone and Ewing would tie as the Team's leading rebounders. Mullin would be fourth in scoring and fourth in assists. Jordan would show great unselfishness by being one of the lowest scorers, but lead the Team in steals. Stockton would play creditably—with a broken leg. Even Laettner—when he got the chance—scored and rebounded well. And Magic was the Team's leader—offering a contribution that statistics cannot quantify.

Gradually, The Boys began to pull away from Croatia.

The game—and the Team—would end, not with a crucial run of scoring, nor with a last-second winning basket. It would conclude, rather, with a series of images:

- Bird, lying on his stomach. Bird, trying desperately to score when he got into the game, but failing. Bird, immersing himself in the role of cheerleader as his career ended. Bird, cheering passionately—the same way he had played.

- Barkley, outmuscling huge men. Barkley, outrunning small men.

- Robinson, grabbing the ball and dunking it so quickly that defenders stood with their arms at their sides.

- Mullin, standing at the three-point line. Waiting. Shooting.

- Pippen, stretching as he flies through the air—as though he's made of rubber.

- Laettner, sitting on the bench, trying to smile.

- Daly, looking terrified as the lead shrinks to less than thirty.

- Drexler, passing when he has the chance to score.

- Stockton, looking for Malone. Malone, looking for Stockton.

- Ewing, creating fear.

- Jordan, flying.

- Magic, passing. Magic, pointing. Magic, laughing. Magic, smiling.

"Olympic champions . . ." boomed the public address announcer, "and gold medalists!"

Jordan, with a flag draped around him to hide the Reebok logo on his awards ceremony uniform, started to step onto the medal platform by himself. Stopped. He looked up and down the row of American Olympians and motioned them with both hands to step onto the platform. They all stepped up together. They raised their arms over their heads and waved.

The stadium exploded into cheers.

They stood in a long line as the crowd continued to roar. Pippen stood next to Jordan. Ewing stood next to Bird. Stockton was next to Malone. Magic was at the end.

"The medals will be presented by Mr. Juan Antonio Samaranch, president of the International Olympic Committee."

Laettner got his first, bowing his head as it was slipped around his neck. Then Robinson, then Ewing.

"Lar-*ee Bird!*" shouted the announcer. A tremendous ovation vibrated the stadium.

Pippen got his medal. Then Jordan—and again the stadium thundered. Clyde, Karl, Stockton, Mullin, Barkley.

"And Ma-*jeek John*-son!"

Magic, his face full of light and joy, bent over, and the medal was placed around his neck. He flung the American flag he was holding toward the sky, then raised both his arms in triumph and happiness. Barkley buried his head in Magic's chest, and Magic threw his arm around Barkley's shoulder and pulled Barkley closer.

Young women came and presented each of the Olympians with a bouquet of flowers.

The Croatian and Lithuanian players also held bouquets. They looked very happy, and at peace. They hadn't won this symbolic war. But their countries were finally free.

Bird felt strangely unemotional. Partly because none of the games had been close. That had detracted from the drama. Even so, it seemed odd to him that he felt so emotionally flat. Often, when he would watch athletic award ceremonies on television—particularly Olympic ceremonies—he would get tears in his eyes. Bird did not display his emotions. But he felt them.

Bird, though, was close to making a monumental decision. It was clear to Bird—after the pain he'd felt this week—that his body had finally betrayed him. Barring a miraculous recovery, he would have to retire.

This had been his last game.

Bird stood on the medal stand, holding his bouquet. He paused, and smelled the flowers.

As they played the National Anthem, Magic closed his eyes. He thanked God for being able to play in the Olympics. He felt ecstatic.

Then the ceremony was over. The Boys began to wander back to the locker room in a loose group.

"Guys! Guys!" said Magic. "Let's say a prayer." They clumped into a circle at center court and put their hands together, their heads touching one another's. Magic said, "Thank you, God, for lettin' us be here. Thank you for lettin' us stay healthy. We did it. Thank you."

They squeezed each other's hands, and let go.

The interview area was subdued. It was not at all like the locker room of an NBA championship team.

That was not because The Boys didn't feel a sense of accomplishment. They did. They had not been challenged in any of the Olympic games, but they'd faced other challenges, all year long. Some of the challenges had been terrible and frightening. These men—virtually all of whom had transcended basketball—had grappled with the most basic issues: respect, money, friendship, health, loyalty, power, and love.

In most of their struggles, they had been victorious. They had emerged as heroes. And—more important—they had emerged as human.

But the *most* important thing for them had been to learn, over the past two months, that—however isolated they might feel in their unique battles—they were not alone. There were eleven others who shared their level of excellence and who knew exactly how they felt. And who would help.

That was why the mood was so somber. The Team was no longer a team. They were leaving each other.

"This has been one of the greatest experiences for everybody," Barkley was saying quietly. "It's been like hanging out with your *brothers.*" Barkley, who'd been so lonely in

Philadelphia—where there had been virtually no sense of team—said softly, "Everybody here was cheering for everybody *else.*"

Jordan, close by, was saying that Magic had been the inspiration for the Team's togetherness. "Earvin can deal with anyone who walks on earth," he said. "He was able to maintain the chemistry of the Team. He was able to blend the egos. He said things to everybody, the way only he can."

Jordan had changed. He was not the same Jordan I'd spent time with last winter, shortly after *The Jordan Rules* had been published. At that time, he'd been hypersensitive to any attacks—or perceived attacks—upon him, or his image.

But earlier he'd been talking to *Chicago Tribune* writer Skip Myslenski, who'd come to Barcelona to follow Jordan for the hometown paper, and Jordan had said he no longer felt the need to be perfect. "My wife and I," Jordan had said, "we have to have a life of our *own,* and we have to be *relaxed* while we're doing it." Jordan, who'd always avoided alcohol, now allowed himself that small indulgence. Even in public. "If I want to go into a bar and have a beer, I do it.

"I've learned being perfect is something you *can't do.* I'm glad the bubble burst."

Bird, who'd looked exceptionally fragile tonight, was fighting off questions about his retirement. "This is my last game," he said. He smiled. "For tonight. Tomorrow, we don't know." He didn't seem troubled. He didn't even seem terribly concerned.

Whatever wars Larry Bird had fought within himself were now over. And, somehow, he seemed to have won. At least, that's how he felt today. Tomorrow, when playing basketball would no longer be a part of his life, a new type of pain would begin. And he would have to begin looking for new ways to overcome it.

A loud burst of cursing electrified the air and broke the sober mood. "God *damn!*" It was Charles—yelling at a group of photographers with cameras around their necks. "Get those Japanese tourists the hell outta here!"

Barkley was sitting in front of a huge cardboard cutout of

the inane-looking Olympic mascot, Cobi. "Hey, Charles!" said Pippen. "Who's that behind you?"

"It's Scottie Pippen," said Barkley.

Barkley reached into a plastic bag and started pulling out souvenirs. "I stole this," he said. "This is Michael Jordan's jersey. They leave stuff like this around, a black person's bound to pick it up."

Stockton walked by. "Hey, Stock!" said Barkley.

"Shut up, Charles," said Stockton, "you billiard ball." Stockton kept going.

Charles Barkley looked happy. He was going home. He grabbed a reporter's microphone and sang, "*I love you all*—but I got to go *back to America . . .*"

Michael Jordan spotted Magic Johnson.

Jordan approached Johnson and held out his arms. Johnson embraced him. Held him tight.

"It's funny, you know," Jordan murmured.

"It's funny," he repeated. "You're thinkin', 'Man, I just wanna get outta here.'

"And then it's time to go . . ." Magic pulled back and looked at Jordan's face.

"And then," said Jordan, "you wanna stay."

Around the room, in pairs, sometimes in groups, The Boys—The Men—began to embrace.

Epilogue: The 1993 Season

The Magic Smile

**Dead Meat • The Fifth Beatle • Patrick the Teddy
Bear • Hangin' with the Boys • Exhaustion
Bloat • Christian's Mom • Death Threats and
Uzis • Isiah's Revenge • The Rumor • Fathers and
Sons • Girls! Girls! Girls! • Lawyers! Lawyers!
Lawyers! • Little Charles, Happy at Last • Michael
Returns to Earth • The Golden Moment**

> "This is all a dream we dreamed,
> one afternoon long ago . . ."
> —*The Grateful Dead*
> "American Beauty," 1970

> "To see a world in a grain of sand,
> And a heaven in a wildflower,
> Hold infinity in your hand,
> And eternity in an hour."
> —William Blake
> *Auguries of Innocence,* 1798

The Games were over. The Team was gone. My body felt
like a hunk of boiled meat.

I sat slumped in a coffee shop, trying to replace the fluids
that had ballooned my hands and feet as exhaustion bloat
had set in.

"Cameron! *Stauth!*"

I jumped. Who was it? The *policia?* Wanting more money?

"Cameron! Over here!" It was a friend from home, Dr.
Steven Ungerleider, a sports psychologist and author who'd
come to Barcelona to promote his latest book, *Beyond*

Strength. "I've been trying to *call* you," he said, pulling up a chair.

"My phone didn't work. Anyway, I had no time. I've been killing myself trying to stay within a hundred feet of the players."

"The housing's *crazy* here, isn't it? You should've seen the *hole* they stuck us in. *Horrendous* heat. *No* air-conditioning. But here's why I was trying to call you. I spent a day on the phone with my publisher and agent, screaming at them to put us somewhere else. Finally they said, go meet somebody downtown, 'cause there's been a cancellation. So I go to this address they gave me. But it's a strange scene. It's behind barricades, and there's a line of soldiers with Uzis. Finally we get up to the desk clerk, and there's this hush, then— BOOM!—Magic Johnson and Michael Jordan burst into the lobby, followed by Patrick Ewing, Scottie Pippen, and Larry Bird. I turned to somebody and said, "Oh, my God, it's the Dream Te—" "

"Stop!" I blurted. "I might use this in my book, and I don't use that 'Dream' phrase."

"Why not?"

"I'm obsessive-compulsive. But go on."

"So the whole team comes in, and I spent the next week hanging out with them. That's why I was trying to get in touch. I thought you'd wanna *join* us."

"Let me get this straight. While I'm running my ass off chasing after these guys, you're, like, *the Fifth Beatle? Damn!* Oh, well." I flipped on my tape recorder. "Tell me all about it."

"You know, to be honest, if my kids hadn't been there, the players probably would have treated me like just another media person or agent. But kids aren't aware of the status thing, and they pull you across those barriers. Patrick Ewing's little boy, who's absolutely adorable, had sort of a crush on one of my daughters, so Patrick, Jr., spent a lot of time with my kids, and he's just delightful."

"Unlike his dad."

"What? You didn't get along with *Patrick?*"

"He's *grim* as *death*, Steven."

"Noooo. Patrick's a teddy bear. He's a *sweetheart.*"

"Don't play games with me, man."

"I mean it. To reporters—yeah, I've heard he can be standoffish. But if you get to *know* him, he's totally different. Very childlike. Matter of fact, I asked one of my daughters, of everybody she'd met in Spain, who'd she most like to come visit us at home? I thought she'd say Magic, 'cause she adored him. Or maybe Stockton."

"*Stockton?* My *other* candidate for Mr. Warmth?"

"Oh, yeah—John's a great guy. But she said Patrick Ewing. I asked her why, and she said, 'Well, when you see him from a distance, he seems like a big, scary guy. But when he gets up close, he gets littler.'"

"Did you see any of the games?"

"*Most* of 'em. But the first game I went to was almost my last. It was where Barkley elbowed that little Angolan kid. I was sitting with a bunch of Americans, and we were all very embarrassed. I thought about leaving, and not going to any more basketball."

"But not checking out of your air-conditioned room, right?"

"God forbid. Anyway, the next day, David Robinson spoke out against Barkley's sportsmanship—he was the only one on the team to do it. I saw David playing pool in the hotel that night, and I told him how much I appreciated him speaking up. And he said, in his shy way, 'I'm not gonna stand by and let Charles act like a jerk in front of the whole world. We're here representing our *country.* We're role models.'"

"Did he actually make eye contact with you?"

"Yeah."

"Jeez, you really *were* tight with them. Did any of the other players get down on Barkley?"

"I think so. He was alone most of the time. We'd be sitting around the lounge with a group of players, and Barkley would be at the bar by himself, nursing a beer and staring into space. But Bird was pretty much the same way, and nobody was ostracizing him. He just seemed like a shy, quiet guy. I'll tell you somebody else who wasn't one of the boys—Jordan. He was fairly aloof and just wasn't part of the network. The only guy I saw him spend much time with was Spike Lee, who was visiting for a while.

"Every morning, though, Jordan was the first player I'd see. A group of us got up around 6:00 to go jogging, and down in the coffee shop, there'd be Michael in his golf clothes, waiting for a ride to the course. And this was in spite of the fact that the players would have a pizza party every night until about 3:00. Michael seems calm, but actually he's pretty wound up. All the players are. They live in a strange world. I'll give you an example. About halfway through the Games, there must have been a death threat. I'm not sure what happened, because it got absolutely no media coverage. Total cover-up. But one morning, the whole security situation changed completely. Up on the roof, where we often hung out, there were suddenly a *bunch* of police with Uzis and high-powered rifles. And downstairs, the three layers of security became *five* layers. The players are in situations like that all the time. It makes you crazy."

"So when did it strike you that this was an NBA fan's dream vacation—like something you'd win from the Publisher's Clearing House?"

"It never did feel like that. Here's what it felt like. At one point, my wife and I were sitting around having a beer, and Malone and his wife came over and joined us, and Magic came over and high-fived everybody, and said, 'What's the *activity* today, guys?' And I turned to my wife and said, 'You know what this feels like? *Summer camp.* I'm ten years old, and Magic's the camp counselor, wanting to know why we're not outside *playing.*' Which is maybe how these players *always* feel."

"Were any of the players' parents around?"

"The only ones we spent much time with were Laettner's parents. But it was kind of weird because Christian's mother, Bonnie, was writing an article about the Olympics for her local paper, and every time we got together, she'd pull out her notebook and write everything down. She was *very* official. I'd try to tell her, 'Bonnie, could you please put the damn *notebook* away?' But she'd say, 'No, I have to chronicle *everything I do.'* I kidded her about it, but she didn't kid well."

"So that's where Christian got his sense of humor."

"Yeah. Not a charming guy. I saw him all the time, and he'd never crack a smile, even after I got to know his parents. Just he and I were in the elevator once, and, believe me, it was a *long* ride. I remember one thing his mom said. She said, 'Well, Christian's been hanging out with Charles, and the media's been talking about it.' I said, 'Think Charles will rub off on Christian?' And she said, 'Well, Christian *could* stand to toughen *up* a little.'"

"Did you spend much time with Magic?"

"Yeah—Magic was everywhere. Very easy to talk to. Personally, I think he's a great man, and I don't use that term lightly. Sure, he horses around with the kids a lot, but if you had something serious to say, he'd just *rivet* his attention on you."

"Did you get a sense of tragedy from him?"

"Yeah—in spite of the fact that he goes around in this absolutely blissful state. I got the feeling that, deep down, he's beginning to reflect on his own mortality. But he's just not the kind of guy to react to mortality by withdrawing. There's been a lot of talk that he's in massive denial, and it's true that one way people go into denial is to try to save the world. But after being around him, I'd say that, if anything, he's in what's called 'healthy denial,' which is basically just looking at tragedy in the most positive way possible. But you know something else? He really thinks he can *beat* this thing. And who knows? Maybe he can."

"He played with the kids a lot?"

"You couldn't pull him away. He almost missed the team bus playing with them. When his wife flew in, he was *everywhere* with his baby, showing off his son like he had the prize possession of the universe. But he definitely has a serious side. He set up a secret meeting with Juan Samaranch, the head of the Olympics. He got Samaranch to agree to organize a worldwide AIDS prevention program."

"Magic's an astute politician."

"He's a *master* politician—mostly because he can see things from other people's perspectives. One night we went to gymnastics, and everybody in the stadium started cheering. But it disrupted the gymnasts, and he felt terrible about it. He said, 'This is awful, because those athletes really *busted their butts* to get here.' He realized that, as athletes, some of them were his equal. I don't think a lot of multimillionaire jocks realize that about amateur athletes."

"So how did it end?"

"It ended the same way it began. Very comfortably. Very naturally. There was never any sense of: Oh, I've gotta get a picture, gotta get an autograph. It was more like: Well, we all came here to celebrate this experience called the Olympics —and now we've done it. It was like leaving a family reunion. You just had this feeling that you'd see everyone again. But that feeling didn't last. Right after everyone left, I remember telling my daughters, 'You'd better burn this into your memories, because it's not going to happen again. Not to us. Not even to the players. This was meant to happen once. Only once. That's the sad thing about it. But that's the beautiful thing, too. And that's why you'll remember it. Always.'"

When I got home from Spain, the house was dark. My wife was asleep. So was my son, Gabriel. But I had to go look at him.

He was sleeping in his crib. I picked him up and held him. I didn't want to let go. I'd let go too often this year. He'd said his first word while I'd been in Spain. It was "uh-ho!" (as in, "oh-no!"). He'd said it while he was watching my mom monitor some videotapes of Chuck Daly.

I carried him, asleep, into the TV room. Magic was on *Arsenio*.

Sitting in my own home, with Gabriel in my arms, the Olympics felt very remote, unreal. It began to flood over me in chains of flashing images: Magic and Michael walking into the darkness after the All-Star Game; Jordan writhing in pain as Pippen touched him gently; Barkley passing out candy and curses on Valentine's Day; Isiah lying in a pool of his own blood; Magic shooting a blind three-pointer during the world's greatest game of H-O-R-S-E; green-haired Rick in Barcelona; the boy who sold Scottie's autograph; Mullin sitting in his hot tub, listening to "Be a Father to Your Child."

It all seemed dreamlike. Had it really happened? What did it mean?

I'd started the year thinking that I'd learn something about basketball. Instead, I'd learned something about people.

I'd learned that the most successful people are not those to whom things come easily, but those who learn to find joy in struggle.

I'd learned that excellence comes from love, not drudgery.

I'd learned that the greatest people in any profession are artists, motivated less by ambition than by an ethereal vision of perfection.

I'd learned that all greatness requires a little craziness.

I'd learned that every victory brings temptation—and that no victory is complete until that temptation is resisted.

I'd learned that complete absorption in any task—even shooting a basket—can bring inner peace.

I'd learned that if a man really loves what he's doing, he can be happy under any circumstances—even the threat of death.

Maybe most important, I'd learned something about being a parent. I'd found that all the Olympians had at least one parent who'd given them unconditional approval—and that this approval became the foundation of these Olympians' supernatural confidence. It's not very hard, I'd discovered, to give your child unconditional love. Giving unconditional approval, though, is much harder. But it's a parent's greatest gift.

Arsenio flashed onto the screen, and hustled out Magic. Magic swaggered out ultra-cool in a sleek sand-colored suit, did a jivey handshake, and basked in the ovation.

The Golden Boys

When things quieted down, Arsenio asked Magic if his baby had been in Barcelona.

The Magic smile. Sure, the baby had been there. "He was cool," said Magic. "He *slept* through daddy playin'. But I enjoyed him bein' there."

I remembered seeing Cookie, and Magic's mother, holding the infant up and pointing him in the direction of the basketball floor.

Seeing them hold up the baby had reminded me of the time at the Tournament of the Americas when the big, whiskery guy had held up his baby in front of Magic, right after the great game of H-O-R-S-E. The whiskery guy had told Magic, "I just wanted him to see you." And Magic had replied, "Oh, he'll be seein' me." Then, after Magic had walked on past, the father had said to his baby, "That was Magic. I hope some day you can *really* see him."

Arsenio, trying to keep the segment hot, started hammering away at all the controversial stuff: the criticism for not living in the Village, Barkley's elbowing incident, and the rest of the Ugly American charges.

Magic just grinned it all away.

The Team had been the best ever. That was the only memory that would remain.

The segment was winding down. But Arsenio looked restless. He wanted to confront Magic about his comeback. Avoiding Magic's eyes, Arsenio said, "I'll be honest with you, man—I don't think you *should* come back. You've *done* everything. I am *totally fulfilled* as a fan."

Magic's eyes narrowed. Arsenio looked at the audience and pointed at Magic. "I watch him *walk* with his son, and *talk* with Andre, and it's time to do *that* now. But you do what you *wanna* do."

"O-*kaay,*" said Magic. He tried to smile, but his mouth ended in an oval. "Well, I *know* you gonna support me either way."

Arsenio backed down. "Either way, I'm witch-you."

To the audience, Arsenio bellowed, "Either way, we wit' 'im!"

Epilogue: The 1993 Season

They cheered wildly, and churned their fists.

I grabbed the remote control and grazed. Fifty-seven channels and nothin' on. I was exhausted but agitated. I didn't know what time zone my body was in and I didn't want to know.

But I was home.

I hit Play and one of the Olympic videotapes my mom had made clicked on. Gabriel stirred in my lap. I looked into his sweet sleeping face. "I'll bet someday, a long time from now, you'll watch these tapes," I said. "There'll never be another team like this." I should have kept my mouth shut. His eyes fluttered open. He saw me and smiled.

He seemed happy to lie in my arms and gaze at the screen. We watched as Magic swirled the American flag. Magic grinned, and it lit the room. I put Magic's face on freeze-frame. The Magic smile.

Gabriel stared at it. From his first days, he'd responded to a smile. Now he smiled back. He seemed hypnotized by it, and happy.

I left it on as his eyes fluttered shut.

"That's Magic," I said to him. "I hope some day you can *really* see him."

He didn't hear me. He was back in his dream.

I hoped it was a dream of the Magic smile.

The Magic smile. It was bouncing around the room like a strobe light.

It was late September, almost two months after the Olympics, and Magic was in L.A. at the Forum, announcing his comeback.

"God put me here to play basketball," Magic told the hastily assembled crowd of reporters. "I'm not saying there's no risk. But life *itself* is a risk."

Then Magic's doctor, Michael Melman, said something fascinating: Magic "also assumed a risk by *not* playing." It was a heart-rending double-bind: Playing basketball—or *not* playing basketball—could literally kill Magic Johnson.

Magic's pay for the 1993 season would be $14.6 million.

It would permanently secure him at the immortality level of wealth. But Magic no longer seemed enamored of symbolic immortality.

Money appeared to be the last thing on his mind. He just wanted to play. He wanted to be a kid again.

Magic's joy carried into the preseason. Just before his first game at the Forum, he sat in front of his locker, radiating a strange mix of contentment and anxiousness. "I'm very excited," he said. "To walk down that runway again, turn left, see the Forum floor, lead the troops out once again— I've been *waiting* for this."

When he emerged from the runway, he got an ovation that made the stadium tremble.

He played superbly, making fourteen assists in twenty minutes.

After the game, he drank in the rowdiness of the locker room as if it were an elixir. To the writers grouped in a semicircle around him, he said, "I've been lost—and I found my way home. I followed the yellow brick road."

His eyes darted around the room, as if the moment were so perfect he wanted to freeze it.

But the moment, of course, did not last.

What I heard from my sources was that Cookie started to get calls. From other NBA wives. Some were angry, some were kind, but all were afraid. They feared that their husbands might contract AIDS from Magic.

The calls, I heard, freaked Magic out. He hadn't thought Cookie would be drawn into the battle. The calls cast a pall over the preseason.

Then: The Rumor.

The Rumor started slowly, but as the preseason neared its end, The Rumor gained momentum. The Rumor was that Magic was bisexual.

The Rumor was based in supposition: It's uncommon for men to contract HIV through heterosexual contact. Of course, Magic's heterosexual contact had been unusually diverse and frequent, but that was conveniently overlooked. Players in the NBA *wanted* to believe that Magic hadn't contracted the disease through heterosexual sex—because they wanted to continue their own promiscuity.

Another element supporting The Rumor was the fact that it had existed, in one form or another, for a number of years.

And there was another seductive aspect to it: its source. *New York Newsday* alleged that the source was Isiah Thomas.

This presumed source bolstered the rumor greatly. Who was in a better position to know than Isiah?

There was even a motive attributable to Isiah: Maybe he was still pissed off that Magic hadn't gotten him onto the Olympic Team. Isiah denied everything, but it was still big news.

Magic fought The Rumor, but in mid-October, Dave Kindred of *The Sporting News* published a very damaging column. Kindred called on Magic to tell the "whole truth about how he acquired the AIDS virus. He said unprotected heterosexual sex did it. Numbers say that's unlikely. One study says the odds are one in five hundred, even if a man uses no condom and his partner already has the virus. Using a condom with a partner who has no high-risk experience makes the odds one in five billion. A man is hundreds of times more likely to acquire HIV by homosexual contact or by using dirty hypodermic needles."

Magic was outraged by the column, and threatened to sue.

Then things got even worse. A Lansing, Michigan, woman filed a $2 million lawsuit against Magic. She believed he had given her HIV.

Magic admitted he'd had sex with her, but denied giving her HIV.

But she claimed she had tested negative for HIV three times before her encounter with Magic, and had had no other sexual partners eight months prior to sleeping with him.

Furthermore, she said she'd informed him that she was HIV-positive—because of sex with him—prior to his marriage. According to her, she'd sent him a long, emotional letter two weeks before his wedding. The letter, at times angry, ended with: "Read Deuteronomy 5:17"—which says, "Thou shalt not kill."

Magic claimed he'd never received the letter. In any case, he never responded to it.

The woman also claimed that when Magic came to Lansing to get married, she confronted him at a Michigan State field house. She said Magic told her, "But look at me. I can't be sick."

Magic's attorney, Howard Weitzman, suggested that the woman was promiscuous, and could have gotten the virus "from any number of men."

As he'd always done when real life had begun to close in on him, Magic reached for basketball to redeem him.

But, for once, basketball failed to rescue him: Because Magic was no longer just a basketball player. He was now an immortal—a political force, an emblem of power, a figurehead. He was, above all, a symbol: The Athlete with HIV.

And some players didn't want to play against The Athlete with HIV. Nothing personal. Strictly business.

"Look at this," Karl Malone told a journalist, "scabs and cuts all over me. I get these every night, every game. They can't tell you that you're not at risk." Having Magic in the Olympics, Malone said, "was a concept everybody loved. But now we're back to reality."

Other players agreed.

Then, in an exhibition game, Magic cut his arm.

He felt as if everyone in the building was staring at him. Players were watching him out of the corners of their eyes. Reporters were stealing glances. He felt like a leper.

He tried to focus on the game, but kept thinking about the cut.

The next evening, he sat down with Cookie. "I'm not going to have *fun* this year," he lamented.

Two days later, he issued a retirement statement. There was no press conference. Magic Johnson—the most gregarious player in NBA history—did not want to see anyone.

How different it had been when Bird had retired!

Bird had passed up millions in endorsements, just to guard his privacy. He didn't have the money or power that

Magic and Michael had—but he had remained a basketball player, and not become a figurehead.

At his announcement, two weeks after the Olympics, he'd been composed and stoic: vintage Bird. He'd said, "The past couple of years have been very tough on me, on my back, and on my body. So, today, I'm retiring. Whatever you hear, from now, to next year, to the next year, I will *not* be coming back to play basketball."

Someone had popped open a bottle of champagne. Bird said he'd have preferred a cold beer.

He stuck a makeshift sign on his locker—"Gone Fish'n." Then he loped off. With dignity and grace.

It was ironic. It was Bird—not Magic—who'd been virtually *programmed* for self-destruction. He'd been saddled with the alcoholism and suicide of his father, the rustic miasma of French Lick, failure at Indiana University, and years of distrust and isolation in the NBA. All these forces had forged a trap that had been virtually inescapable.

But Bird—mostly through sheer will—had escaped. And triumphed.

He had become a survivor. Now he could survive anything. Even the loss of basketball. He was free.

So, too, in his own way, was Michael Jordan. Jordan had freed himself of godhood. The week before the 1993 season began, Jordan admitted in federal court that his $57,000 check to golfing pal and convicted drug figure Slim Bouler had really been a gambling debt. Then he waited for the public outcry.

There wasn't any.

Because everyone knew that nobody was perfect. Not even "God."

Then, when the season began, Jordan's play was a little flat—by *his* standards. "I'm conserving my energy," he said. "My game is less spectacular now."

Then Jordan began to talk about retirement. Even this talk—which should have struck fans as heretical—created nary a ripple. Michael Jordan getting old and slow? Well . . . why not? *Everybody* gets old and slow.

Nor did anyone bitch when *Forbes* ranked Jordan as the highest-paid athlete in the world, with an annual income of $35.9 million. The consensus seemed to be: What the hell—he'll earn it.

In fact, however, for much of the season Jordan and the Bulls were less than spectacular. The reason: Jordan's and Pippen's Olympic participation. The longstanding paranoia that the Olympians would be broken down was turning out to be valid. Pippen had tendinitis in his ankle because of not resting it in the summer, Clyde had a hard time recovering from knee surgery, and Ewing had lingering ankle problems.

Despite the stress of the Games, however, every one of the Olympians played superbly in '93. All of them, except Laettner, made the All-Star Team. Stockton was leading the league in assists. Barkley seemed headed for an MVP award. Ewing was rebounding better than ever. Mullin was scoring better than ever. Even Laettner was playing well, and seemed probable to make the All-Rookie Team. He was not, as some had predicted, "the new Danny Ferry."

Despite their extraordinary play, the lives of the Olympians were not free of threat. To some extent, the Games had "immortalized" all of them; they were all now held to Olympian standards.

Pippen, whose reputation had been tremendously expanded by the Games, was, more than ever, measured against Jordan. And Jordan was a brutally high standard. Besides, much of Pippen's greatness was siphoned off by Jordan, who still hogged the ball. In one mid-season game, when Jordan took 49 shots and had just one assist, Pippen looked disgustedly at the postgame statistics sheet and then refused to talk to the press.

But Pippen's comparison to Jordan was less painful than that of Ewing and Robinson to the league's extraordinary new center, Shaquille O'Neal. When Shaquille entered the NBA, Ewing and Robinson were immediately eclipsed. Even Karl Malone, the NBA's resident stud, was overpowered. The Olympians were gracious about O'Neal's dominance. But it hurt.

Epilogue: The 1993 Season

Mullin endured a particularly frustrating fate in the post-Olympic year. For the first half of the season, he stayed on Jordan's heels for the scoring title. But just before the All-Star break, he ripped apart his hand. The chase was over.

For sheer perverse irony, though, no one's fate eclipsed that of Clyde Drexler's. Drexler, long personified by gentlemanly behavior and a reluctance to address controversy, was caught up in the ugliest NBA scandal of the year. Several members of the Trail Blazers were, for a time, suspected of the possible rape of a sixteen-year-old girl in Salt Lake, and participation in a sex orgy with two other teenage girls. No charges were ever pressed, and Clyde was nowhere *near* the incident.

But, while the scandal percolated and the names of the suspects were withheld, all of the Blazers twisted in the wind. Including Clyde.

One Olympian, however, was unquestionably happier during the post-Olympic year—Charles Barkley. Free at last, he was leading a supercharged Phoenix team.

I went to visit Charles in Phoenix. I'd heard he was happy down there—almost . . . domesticated. The notion made me very uncomfortable, because it challenged my whole world view. Charles Barkley—*content?* What I discovered was appalling. Charles was in a shockingly good mood almost all the time.

At the end of my stay, I confronted him. "It's all true!" I snarled. "Everything I've heard. You're *happy* here. You're getting *mellow. Mellll*-ow!"

"No, I'm not!" he cried.

But then, almost immediately, he contradicted himself. "I've *always* been happy," he said.

I breathed a sigh of relief. Charles Barkley was still full of contradiction. All was right with the world.

When Magic went to his first game after his re-retirement, he was absolutely miserable. As the national anthem played, he told reporters, "I'm sweating already. I know I should be in my uniform, and I'm here talking to *you* guys. I hate this. I'm driving my wife crazy. She says, 'Go and work out and get outta my hair.'"

Magic was not at peace. "Karl hurt me," he said. "The lawsuit hurt me. Today I hurt a lot by not being out there."

He said he regretted retiring, and was trying to stay away from the game to ease his pain. "Now I work out by myself instead of with the guys. I'm running on the treadmill thinking about what they're doing. Instead of lifting weights with Byron and Vlade, I'm lifting by myself. I definitely want to come back. But I won't. I won't make you guys crazy. Or myself."

After that evening, Magic became more reclusive than he'd ever been. He admitted that his main goal was "to stop being the news."

The only thing I heard about Magic was when a friend of mine ran into him in Las Vegas. His Vegas adventure—covered in the tabloids—sounded like classic Magic. According to reports, he was never far from showgirls, exotic dancers, and a "mystery blonde." Of course, the tabloids are usually heavy with innuendo, but in this case, they had a number of photos that seemed to support much of what they were alleging.

Shortly after that, rumors surfaced that Magic and Cookie were planning to separate. But the rumors were denied by both of them. Cookie said that, "We're getting along better than we ever have."

Magic was in uniform. He was shooting long jumpers in the empty, echo-bouncing Forum. His shot was perfect. Plant . . . release . . . rip! He looked ecstatic.

It was the first time he'd played in months. Until this moment, he hadn't trusted himself to play. He was afraid that if he played, his lust for the game would pull him back into it.

But Laker backup Jack Haley had been bugging him to come over to the Forum to shoot, and so, on this quiet Sunday morning, Magic had driven over to take a few shots.

Epilogue: The 1993 Season

He was shocked at how sharp his skills were.

When he stopped, a small group of reporters hustled over. The writers were hungry for an update.

He told them that he'd been busy with business, and with planning a world tour with other former NBA players.

Someone asked, in passing, if he ever thought about making another comeback. "I'm not returning—right now," he said. "I'm not making a comeback right now."

The reporters were puzzled. Did that mean he *might* come back?

"If I ever was going to make a return," he said, "I would first call the commissioner."

He continued talking about it. "If I came back now, I could handle things better. Everybody could. There would still be concern, but with all the things that have been written and said, I think people are learning a little more about it."

Some of the reporters seemed disturbed. *Another* comeback? Was Magic living in a dreamworld?

Why couldn't he *let go?*

Before he left the stadium on that quiet Sunday morning, Magic picked up a ball and took one last shot. He always wanted one last shot.

From deep in the court, he measured the shot, locked in on the rim, and sailed the ball upward.

It sailed perfectly. It was just one more shot, but it was strangely beautiful.

Sometimes I think that immortality is not to be found in any sort of afterlife, but exists, instead, in the moment. If so, its existence in that moment must be terribly elusive. I believe that if eternity is to be discovered, it can be found only if that moment is realized fully and absolutely.

For that one moment, as the ball sailed toward the hoop, Magic seemed so fully alive, so caught in the moment, so distant from pain and filled with peace, that it seemed possible—not likely, but *possible*—that in this one golden moment, or maybe in a moment still to come, that Magic Johnson might yet find immortality.

Surely he must sometimes feel that if he could just jump higher, stretch farther, take just one more shot, that one day . . .

The ball sailed toward the hoop.

His eyes followed it, but seemed not to see.

. . . it sailed . . .

. . . it sailed . . .

It glanced off the rim. And the moment was gone.

Magic Johnson smiled, and left the gym.

Bibliography

The author would like to acknowledge the following books as resources used in writing *The Golden Boys*. In addition, the author would like to acknowledge his debt to the hundreds of people who were interviewed for this book.

Books: *The Sports Encyclopedia*, David Neft and Richard Cohen, St. Martin's Press; *The Sporting News Official NBA Register* (several editions), Alex Sachare and Dave Sloan, The Sporting News; *Cousy on the Celtic Mystique*, Bob Cousy and Bob Ryan, McGraw-Hill; *The Official NBA Basketball Encyclopedia*, Zander Hollander and Alex Sachare, Villard Books; *Taking to the Air*, Jim Naughton, Warner Books; *The Jordan Rules*, Sam Smith, Simon & Schuster; *Magic's Touch*, Earvin Johnson and Roy Johnson, Addison-Wesley Publishing Company; *The Complete Handbook of Pro Basketball* (several editions), Zander Hollander, New American Library; *The Force*, Jim Savage, Dell; *Magic*, Earvin Johnson and Richard Levin, Viking; *Rick Barry's Pro Basketball Scouting Report* (several editions), Rick Barry and Jordan E. Cohn, Bonus Books; *Red on Red*, Red Holzman and Harvey Frommer, Bantam Books; *Wilt*, Wilt Chamberlain and David Shaw, Warner Books; *The Coach's Art*, Jack Ramsay with John Strawn, Timber Press; *Basketball Abstract*, Dave Heeren, Prentice Hall; *Basketball Heaven*, Martin Manley, Doubleday; *Beyond Strength—Psychological Profiles of Olympic Athletes*, Steven Ungerleider, Ph.D., and Jacqueline M. Golding, Ph.D., Wm. C. Brown Publishers; *1991 Fantasy Basketball Digest*, Alex Ferrari, Jim Ulrich, and Troy Boeldt, Lerner Publications;

Man, Sport and Existence, Howard Slusher, Lea & Febiger; *Heaven Is a Playground,* Rick Telander, Simon & Schuster; *Bad Boys,* Isiah Thomas, Masters Press; *Promoter Ain't a Dirty Word,* Harry Glickman, Timber Press; *24 Seconds to Shoot,* Leonard Koppett, Macmillan Co.; *Giant Steps,* Kareem Abdul-Jabbar and Peter Knobler, Bantam Books; *Life on the Run,* Bill Bradley, Bantam Books; *Raw Recruits,* Alexander Wolff and Armen Keteyian, Pocket Books; *A Season on the Brink,* John Feinstein, Fireside; *Showtime,* Pat Riley, Warner Books; *The Lenny Wilkens Story,* Lenny Wilkens, Paul S. Eriksson Inc.; *Outrageous,* Charles Barkley and Roy Johnson, Simon & Schuster; *Barcelona,* Robert Hughes, Alfred A. Knopf; and *Bird,* Lee Daniel Levine, Berkley Books.

Articles: Hundreds of articles from magazines and newspapers were used for this book. Of particular value were articles appearing in *Sports Illustrated* (many by Jack McCallum), *Sport, Basketball Digest, The Sporting News, Inside Sports, The Sporting News Pro Basketball Yearbook, Basketball Forecast, Petersen's Preview of Pro Basketball, Street & Smith's Pro Basketball, hoop, Dick Vitale's Basketball, Newsweek, Esquire, American Sports* (of Holland), *Maxi-Basket* (of France), *Agent & Manager, FIBA Basketball Monthly, The New York Times, Chicago Tribune, The Boston Globe,* and *The Philadelphia Inquirer.*

Three Months on the *New York Times* Bestseller List!

THE JORDAN RULES

The Inside Story

of a Turbulent Season

with Michael Jordan

and the Chicago Bulls

SAM SMITH

*Including a new chapter on the Bulls' triumphant
1992 drive to repeat as the NBA champions*

Available from Pocket Star Books

913

NOTRE DAME's

GREATEST COACHES

KNUTE ROCKNE, FRANK LEAHY, ARA PARSEGHIAN, and LOU HOLTZ.

The names of these coaches have become synonymous with one of the few teams in college football that can truly be called a "dynasty" —the Fighting Irish of Notre Dame.

Now these four legendary men are seen through the eyes of the inimitable Edward "Moose" Krause. This fascinating memoir combines Moose's own words with those of nearly one hundred former Notre Dame coaches, players, and administrators to paint an unforgettable portrait of four of the sport's greatest teachers and motivators.

MOOSE KRAUSE

AND NEW YORK TIMES BESTSELLING AUTHOR

STEPHEN SINGULAR

POCKET
BOOKS **Available from Pocket Books** 844

THE NEW YORK TIMES BESTSELLER!

RAW RECRUITS

"The most important sports book in years" —*The Village Voice*

The High Stakes Game Colleges Play To Get Their Basketball Stars—
And What It Costs To Win

Alexander Wolff and Armen Keteyian

POCKET
B O O K S **Available from Pocket Books** 742

DITKA

MONSTER OF THE MIDWAY

Armen Keteyian

**THE HARD-HITTING
NATIONAL BESTSELLER**

"A masterful job, the definitive profile of a man most
sports journalists haven't begun to figure out...."
— Jay Mariotti, *Chicago Sun-Times*

*With a new chapter on the controversial 1992
season and the story behind Ditka's firing*

POCKET
BOOKS

Available from
Pocket Books

620-01